AF849228

B
U
P

Marco Buti

THE MAN INSIDE

A European Journey through Two Crises

Foreword by
Adam Tooze

Postscript by
Martin Sandbu

Cover: Cristina Bernasconi, Milan
Typesetting: Laura Panigara, Cesano Boscone (MI)

Copyright © 2021 Bocconi University Press
EGEA S.p.A.

EGEA S.p.A.
Via Salasco, 5 - 20136 Milano
Tel. 02/5836.5751 – Fax 02/5836.5753
egea.edizioni@unibocconi.it – www.egeaeditore.it

All rights reserved, including but not limited to translation, total or partial adaptation, reproduction, and communication to the public by any means on any media (including microfilms, films, photocopies, electronic or digital media), as well as electronic information storage and retrieval systems. For more information or permission to use material from this text, see the website www.egeaeditore.it

Given the characteristics of Internet, the publisher is not responsible for any changes of address and contents of the websites mentioned.

First edition: October 2021

ISBN Domestic Edition	978-88-99902-83-4
ISBN Digital Domestic Edition	978-88-238-8301-7
ISBN International Edition	978-88-31322-35-5
ISBN Digital International Edition	978-88-31322-36-2

"An insider of the European Commission since the late 1980s, Marco Buti is a unique guide through the two crises of the 21st century. The Union has been much more the solution than the problem – as he persuasively demonstrates in this book – and the Commission has played an essential role. There have been limits and mistakes, but the building blocks of integration built in these years have avoided the disruption of the Eurozone and contained the pandemic. We owe it to Buti and the other builders if the citizens' trust has been regained – a necessary condition for further steps in integration."
Giuliano Amato, former Prime Minister of Italy

"Marco Buti and I have not always agreed on issues of economic policy. But I cannot think of somebody more qualified to tell us about the travails of Europe since the Great Financial Crisis. He was there all along. He had a deep understanding of the complex macro and micro economic issues at stake. And he was intellectually honest. An exceptional combination, reflected in this book giving his reflections in real time (something few policy makers would dare to do, preferring to rewrite history and their role in a more convenient way)."
Olivier Blanchard, Senior Fellow at Peterson Institute for International Economics

"This collection of VoXEU contributions shows how history is made. Marco Buti, a man inside the vortex of the making of European monetary history, produced and published a steady stream of reflections, analysis and reform proposals on VoxEU. The collection reminds us of how far the European Monetary Union has come in the wake of two deep crises. The man inside can certainly take a share of the credit and his writings over the last decade are worth rereading, not only for historical purposes."
Beatrice Weder Di Mauro, President of the Centre for Economic Policy Research

Ai miei genitori, Cesarina e Parisio, che mi hanno lasciato scegliere.

To Aurelie, Gregory and Lorenzo who became young adults during the years covered by this book. They're shaping the new Europe.

With endless love.

Table of Contents

Part D.
Real Economy and Convergence During the "Great Recession"

Acknowledgements

This book is an occasion for me to thank all the colleagues with whom I have worked over the years, several of whom are the co-authors of individual chapters in this book. Benefiting from the intellectual prowess and enthusiasm of my colleagues and, later, having the opportunity to guide their work has been an incredible honour as well as a constantly renewed pleasure. I can only hope that my action as senior official first and then Director General and Head of Cabinet at the Commission does justice to the tremendous respect and admiration that I have for their work.

Specifically, for their help on the preparation of this book, I would like to thank Oscar Polli, for excellent research assistance, and Antonella Pirami, for editorial support.

I am grateful to Adam Tooze and Martin Sandbu who not only accepted to write, respectively, the foreword and the postscript, but provided also very helpful suggestions on earlier drafts of the introduction and on the overall presentation of the material.

Most of all, I thank Alyce for her patience, advice and love during long evenings, weekends and holidays while drafting and revising this book. Only love back, a very unequal exchange.

***

The articles collected in this volume are reproduced as published at the time with only limited editorial changes to make them self-contained for today's readers.

The views expressed in this book are personal and should not be attributed to the European Commission or its services.

Foreword

by *Adam Tooze*

"Europe will be forged through crises and will be the sum of the solutions to these crises."

These lines by Jean Monnet are often cited as consolation. They remind us that time and again Europe is counted out, only to rise again, reconfigured and more tightly integrated. Europe came through the empty chair crisis of the early 1960s, the shock of German unification and the end of the Cold War, the exchange rate crisis of the 1980s and 1990s and the setback to the constitutional proposal of 2005. As Monnet predicted, Europe was defined by the solutions to each of those crises.

Those were above all political crises, of immediate concern primarily to the political class of Europe. With the onset of the global financial crisis in 2007 and the ensuing crises of Eurozone sovereign debt, Europe's crisis-driven development continued, but it became an attritional struggle that was far broader in its range. In the 2010s, millions of Europeans, above all young Europeans, suffered prolonged unemployment. Austerity took its toll on European society and its welfare state and European politics bears the scars as well. As Marco Buti puts it, Europe lived under the "curse of permanent existential threats and ultima ratio decisions." The Europe that has emerged in the last decade is more resilient and commands majority support, but it also tougher and, for many, profoundly disenchanted.

In this collection of essays from Marco Buti's time as Director General of Directorate General for Economic and Financial Affairs (DG ECFIN) and more recently as Chief of Staff of the Commissioner for the economy, Paolo Gentiloni, we can follow one of Europe's leading public servants as he struggled to think his way out of the treadmill of government-by-crisis. Europe needs more, Buti consistently argues, than just an accumulation of crisis-fighting measures. As he puts it in chapter 41, co-authored with George Papacostantinou, the crisis response needs to be: "economically coherent, marshalling the policy tools and mechanisms that provide for an effective crisis response, addressing root causes … [.] In the complex EU institutional framework, it also needs to have institutional coherence, leveraging common governance mechanisms while respecting both subsidiarity and the EU Treaties. Finally, it needs to be politically coherent, maintaining citizens' support in what tend to be traumatic and divisive periods." Unfortunately, meeting what Buti and Papacostantinou call the Monnet Compatibility Test, is a very difficult task. It requires bold decisions and permanent institutional advances. Caught in the "middle of the river," as Buti described it in July 2017, Europe remains at risk of being swept away by the current.

Making Europe through crisis is not just costly and nerve-wracking. It also means that our historical vantage point is subject to kaleidoscopic rearrangement. That comes with a certain fascination. Reading this compilation of Buti's essays we can retrace blow by blow his reactions to each new challenge. But it is not just the writer's perspective that shifts. So too does the perspective of the reader.

Today we come to this collection against the backdrop of COVID-19. As far as the EU's economic governance was concerned, 2020 was a "good" crisis. The virus came from outside. It has by 2021 wrought havoc across all of Europe, North and South, East and West. That brutal fact opened the door to collective action. The banking and Eurozone crises of 2008-2015 were different. Unlike the virus, those crises were widely seen as endogenous – driven by too much debt piled up over preceding years. For that reason, the crises were also contentious. Arguments between creditors and debtors split Europe into blocs. And to make matters worse, it was the "wrong" debts that were most to the fore.

It was, as Buti has remarked, an unfortunate accident of history that the crisis exploded first in Greece. That focused attention on public debt and fiscal indiscipline rather than private debts and banks. The politics of the crisis would have been very different if the paradigmatic problem had been the real estate bubbles of Spain and Ireland and the entanglement of Europe's banks in them, rather than the government debts of Greece.

The early essays in this volume are marked by the battles of that moment. Promoted to Director General of DG ECFIN in November 2008, Buti was in the thick of the fight. As befits his role, he mounted a stout defence of Europe's new fiscal framework. If we follow Buti, the rules were neither as inflexible nor as inappropriate as their critics – including this author - alleged.

By the summer of 2012 it seemed that Europe was truly taking a step forward. The path for Draghi's "whatever it takes" had been cleared by an agreement on the banking union. But more was needed. Europe needed a fully integrated capital market. It needed a safe asset. Ultimately, as had always been envisioned, it needed a federal fiscal policy. To promote this development, the EU institutions, with the Commission taking a leading role, drafted a series of proposals - the Four Presidents Report of 2012, the Five Presidents Report of 2015 and the 2018 proposal for a European Investment Function. But, now, the corollary of Monnet's maxim kicked in. With the crisis in abeyance there was no progress. Worse than that, a new distribution of roles was becoming entrenched. As Buti argues, the Rawlsian veil of ignorance was pierced. Since the Northern creditors knew, or at least thought that they knew, the strength of their position, their focus was squarely on risk reduction as a precondition for any significant steps towards risk sharing.

If the line between crisis and normality had been clearly drawn, if all had been well between 2012 and 2020, the ensuing impasse might not have mattered. But, though the acute crisis had passed, there was a pervasive sense that something had broken. After 2013 talk of "secular stagnation" stalked the halls of power. The ECB was struggling to prevent the Eurozone sliding into a Japan-style deflationary trap. As wages and growth stagnated, in many countries anti-European sentiment was on the rise. Divergence took on ever more worrying dimensions. Italy, Europe's third largest economy, was being left behind. Rather than promoting productivity and progress, the Euro came to be seen by many as a form of slow strangulation.

As the seriousness of this situation became evident, we see Buti's assessments not only of the immediate situation, but of the crisis itself, becoming more critical. Whereas he had once expected a rapid recovery from the shock of 2008-2012, the extent of the damage was now obvious. His final reckoning with his time as Director General of DG ECFIN – chapter 38, "Economic Policy in the Rough" - makes sobering reading. At critical moments in the crisis, intergovernmentalism had failed to deliver timely policy responses. Weaknesses of democratic accountability had been exposed. As Mario Draghi made clear in his parting speech at

Sintra in 2019, Europe's policy regime remained lopsided – far too heavily reliant on the central bank.

This assessment too was shaped by its moment - the second half of 2019. At that time the taps of fiscal policy seemed stuck shut. This was a surprise. Public choice theory had assumed that the problem was to discipline politicians from spending too much. If it was true, as Buti argued in one original paper, that politicians were not always punished for taking painful reform measures, it also seemed true that they could become addicted to counterproductive fiscal discipline. If, in the 1980s, the fiscal dominance to be feared was too much spending, fiscal dominance could also be exerted by inaction. Fiscal passivity in the face of the risk of deflation, forced a central bank's hand.

Faced with Europe's impasse, it was up to economists to speak up. The increasing urgency of Buti's calls for action is nicely encapsulated by the piece he co-authored in 2019 with Laurence Boone, chief economist of the OECD (chapter 37). "Right here, right now" is their title. Growth and trade were decelerating to a dangerous degree. And then, like a deus ex machina, COVID arrived.

To say that Europe's public health response to the global pandemic has left much to be desired, would be an understatement. Added to which, in March and April 2020, a ruinous repetition of the Eurozone crisis logic of 2010 seemed on the cards. But then, the game turned. With Paris and Brussels urgently pushing, Berlin decided to declare COVID-19 an exceptional emergency and to greenlight a major step towards a large collective fiscal capacity – a shift from intergovernmentalism to the Community method.

Next Generation EU is not a life support program or a fiscal stimulus of the type that member states have been pushing. It is above all a growth policy. As Buti and his colleagues have been highlighting, for Europe's future, reviving public investment is key. In 2018 they had called for a common investment facility. Now, in the midst of crisis, it had arrived.

Not every aspect of the EU's "community" response to the 2020 crisis has been equally successful. To avoid ruinous competition, Brussels took charge of vaccine policy. As a vaccine producer, Europe has been second to none. Unlike the USA, Europe along with China and India is one of three great vaccine suppliers to world. But slow delivery to Europe's own population caused huge uproar. All the more so because it coincided with another devastating pandemic wave over the winter of 2020-2021. The least that can be said, however, is that Europe has learned. Unlike during the Eurozone crisis, the social shock has been held in check, and fiscal and monetary policy have worked together well. The question in 2021 is whether Europe has done enough to accelerate the pace of recovery, once the health crisis has been contained.

Too often it is missed that what defined Europe for Monnet were not crises as such, but the solution-finding. As the political scientist Hugh Heclo remarked: "...Governments not only 'power' ... they also puzzle. Policy-making is a form of collective puzzlement on society's behalf." (Heclo 1974: 305)

The European Commission is not a government like others. It has less room for the exercise of power. What makes Buti's essays so interesting is that they show us the process of puzzling in action.

The papers collected here are not concerned with technical economics. The Commission's QUEST model remains in the background. The necessary references are to be found in the bibliography. What we see in these papers is the policy-maker's mind at work. The art lies in slicing problems, probing which constraints are binding and which are not. It lies in defining the interaction between constraints. Buti is an adept of the trilemma, a formulation which forces us to recognize the interdependence between choices. Escaping the constraints that they impose often involves thinking laterally. If fiscal integration is politically impossible, can the same effect be achieved through the development of more integrated financial markets? If convergence requires reform, how do you persuade politicians that that is something other than political suicide? If households can smooth consumption or even borrow to take advantage of the new opportunities opened up by reforms, could reform even be a vote-winner?

The confidential official papers of the Commission between 2010 and 2020, will remain behind wall of confidentiality for decades to come. The papers collected in this volume were written for the public. They are part of a debate. Many of these pieces are written as replies. That in itself has value.

It is too often said that Europe lacks a common political public sphere. The years of crisis have begun to change that. National elections matter to the entire EU. A major driver of the common 2020 crisis response was the desire to avoid strengthening a nationalist backlash against Europe. Political publics are multi-centred and multi-layered. In the sphere of economic expertise, recent decades have seen the emergence of a true European public sphere. In the wake of the Eurozone crisis, coalitions of economists – most notably French and German – have sought to construct a new common ground. This kind of search for the middle-ground matters politically. It also influences the Overton window of policy. In the crucial moves towards a common fiscal response to the 2020 crisis between March and May 2020, cross-border agreement amongst experts, was a significant factor shaping opinion, notably in Berlin. The essays in this volume are testimony to the energy with which the economists of the Commission have engaged in these debates, with Marco Buti in the lead. It is not by accident that many of the pieces are drawn from Voxeu, the common platform for European economic policy debate.

If Europe emerges from the solutions found to collective crises, European political community emerges from the collective puzzling that this entails – whether within the Brussels machine, in coalition of national governments, or in the broader public. This collection is living proof of Marco Buti's dedication to that collective undertaking. We are in his debt.

1 European Economic Policymaking under Duress: My Own Account

1 Florence, Oxford, Brussels

This book is not my memoir. I hope to have time to write that once the dust has settled. This book is more and less at the same time. It is less because it does not have the anecdotes that spice up one's personal account. It is more because it shows economic policy formation and thinking in real time, under the heat of the moment. And, in these past twelve years the temperature has often been white-hot.

I come from a very modest background, from a small village in Tuscany. My father was a mason and my mother was a housewife and a seamstress who worked from home. After graduating from the University of Florence with Alessandro Petretto, I received a scholarship and did my postgraduate studies at the University of Oxford. This was during a period – the mid 1980s – when Oxford was blessed with the presence of an outstanding generation of economists: Amartya Sen, James Mirrlees, who were subsequently awarded the Nobel Prize in economic sciences, but also David Hendry, Stephen Nickell, John Muellbauer, David Begg, to name just a few. Christopher Bliss and Tony Courakis were my supervisors. I was at Linacre College, where there was a regular flow of Italian economics students as the college had received financing over the years from Banca d'Italia. There one could join conversations in the common room with Lady Ursula Hicks, a fellow of Linacre, and her husband, Sir John Hicks, a towering economic theorist who had won the Nobel Prize in 1972. I remember them well.

My MPhil thesis was on currency substitution. I would have never imagined that, a few years later, I would be involved in the biggest "currency substitution" ever, the replacement of national currencies with the euro.

After a year working as an economist at the research department of FIAT in Turin, in October 1987 I joined the economics department of the European Commission, the Directorate General for Economic and Financial Affairs (DG ECFIN), in Brussels. At that time, the Commission was a fervour of activity. Under President Delors, the "1992 project" to complete the Single Market and the plan to create a single currency were reviving the European dream after the long period of "Eurosclerosis." As a junior official, I was involved in the tail end of the preparation of the *Cecchini Report* on the cost of non-Europe (Cecchini et al. 1988) and subsequently in the Commission report, *One Market-One Money* (European Commission 1990). In 1998, I coordinated with André Sapir a Commission report on the functioning of the Eurozone, the last comprehensive study prior to the launch of the single currency (Buti and Sapir 1998).

After a period serving in the cabinets of Vice President Pandolfi and Commissioner Vanni d'Archirafi in the 1990s, and a spell back in DG ECFIN, I joined the Group of Policy Advisors of President Prodi where I contributed to the *Sapir Report* on reviving growth in Europe (Sapir 2003). I returned to DG ECFIN in 2003 and was eventually appointed Director General in November 2008. I was at the helm of DG ECFIN under Commissioners Almunia, Rehn and Moscovici. In December 2019, I became Chief of Staff of the Commissioner for Economy, Paolo Gentiloni.

The purpose of this introduction is threefold. Firstly, it intends to set the accelerated changes in the economic approach of the Commission and the EU over the last decade against the external shocks that have impacted the European economy and society. Secondly, it seeks to lay down the main orientations that have been guiding my own work first as Director General for economic and financial affairs and then as Chief of Staff of the Commissioner for the Economy. Thirdly, it attempts to peer into the future by drawing some general principles that could guide the EU's economic policymaking in the aftermath of the dual crisis that has plagued the European economy during the past twelve years.

2 The Pioneers, the Architects and the Builders

The last twelve years have been deeply transformative for the Commission and for the European Union (EU). Some of these changes were imposed on us by circumstances. The global financial crisis which started right at the beginning of my tenure as Director General – and whose ripple effects continued to be felt up until the end of my mandate – was a particularly testing episode for the EU. Even more testing has been the impact of the pandemic crisis that erupted in March 2020. The Commission has itself been an actor of change and, during all these years, I witnessed and participated in a deep transformation of its role and its contribution to European integration and global governance.

From a personal point of view, becoming Director General was naturally the culmination of my career as an economist and as a Commission official. This was even more the case for me since, contrary to a number of my predecessors, my career had been spent entirely at the Commission and, with the exception of only a few gap years, in DG ECFIN. Spending one's full career in the Commission puts me in what could be loosely labelled as the third generation of European civil servants.

The first generation of EU civil servants was that of *The Pioneers*. These were people who still bore the trauma of World War II. They were deeply convinced that unrestrained competition between European nation-states could lead to potential catastrophe. For them, the European project was one of peace and of hope in a continent that was still recovering from the massive destructions incurred in the first half of the 20th century.

Tommaso Padoa-Schioppa, who was Director General of DG ECFIN – then called DGII – from 1979 to 1983, initiated the second period, that of *The Architects*. In the economic sphere, this generation concluded the Single European Act, and the Maastricht Treaty and then negotiated the launch of the euro. These senior officials transformed the ideals of the pioneers into a concrete institutional architecture allowing an ever-greater integration of European Member States. I came to know and admire Tommaso in later years when he served as member of the board of the European Central Bank (ECB) and subsequently as Italy's finance minister. His passing in 2010 was a big loss for Europe. Although during the time of the financial crisis Tommaso no longer had a formal role, I believe that we could have better managed the crisis with his advice.

Amongst *The Architects*, a special place is occupied by Giovanni Ravasio, Director General of DGII between 1990 and 2001. Giovanni was someone I worked very closely with as head of unit and he was someone who believed in me. Whilst Tommaso Padoa-Schioppa is the intellectual father of the euro, Giovanni Ravasio can be legitimately considered its practical father, the one who delivered.

The creation of the Economic and Monetary Union (EMU) and its day-to-day running marks the beginning of a third generation of officials, *The Builders*, the first representative of whom is my immediate predecessor, Klaus Regling, who during its first decade both helped guide the Eurozone and strengthen its foundations. This third generation managed the Eastern enlargement of the EU and the enlargement of the Eurozone to the current 19 members.

We had then to steer towards a "hard" maturity of the EU, tempered by the financial crisis that broke out in 2008, shaken by Brexit and tested to the limit by the economic shock caused by the COVID-19 crisis. The priority, hence, moved from integrating the various economies of the Member States to maintaining the consistency of the various pillars of EMU and ensuring it would evolve from a fragile construction to a viable currency union able to withstand future crises. The stress test of the crisis transformed our work into that of firefighting and repairing. In this respect, it is telling that Klaus Regling, following his time at the Commission, became the head of the European Financial Stability Facility (EFSF), the temporary fiscal backstop of the Eurozone Member States, and then the first Managing Director of the European Stability Mechanism (ESM), in October 2012.

The progress in European integration throughout these crises owes as much to the ideals and qualities of the leaders of Europe, as to the shared conviction that this was the only way forward to preserve the existence of the EU. The United Kingdom's decision to withdraw from the EU, following its June 2016 referendum, proved that the potential danger of European disintegration was all too real. However, it has become increasingly evident that the prophecy of the EU's founding father Jean Monnet, that "Europe will be forged through crises and will be the sum of the solutions to these crises," should lead to bold decisions and lasting advances in European integration and not into a curse of permanent existential threats and *ultima ratio* decisions.

Eventually, the crisis response by the EU has to pass what I dub in chapter 41 the "Monnet Compatibility Test" entailing economic coherence (adequacy of the policy reaction), institutional coherence (action taken at the right level of government), and political coherence (the public's support). I contend that the EU failed, at least partly, such a test when managing the 2008 financial crisis whilst it has a chance to succeed in dealing with the pandemic.

The Commission has taken a proactive stance in renewing its role and taking a forward-looking view on economic and monetary integration. In doing so, it has undergone an enormous transformation. Compared to twelve years ago, the Commission has moved from a committee-based, macro-fiscal role to a more confident actor engaged in global governance, present in economic and policy debates, and more connected to political and social realities. Its action has broadened considerably, through a larger scope of its economic surveillance, the work on financial assistance programmes and its new role in investment support. The steering of the EU's economic response to the pandemic, Next Generation EU, potentially represents a quantum leap in European integration.

The papers collected in this book in the form of chapters retrace my personal intellectual journey over the past twelve years. Many of them are written together with Commission colleagues, but also with fellow economists at the IMF and the OECD. Most of the papers were published in Vox CEPR.

I have selected these papers having in mind the different roles of the Commission in policy coordination. In particular, as I explain below, the Commission acts as referee, consensus builder and promoter of integration. Accordingly, some chapters try to explain the logic of the Commission's thinking in applying the common surveillance framework, most notably the EU fiscal rules. Other chapters attempt to bring together the national and European policy makers on projects to reform the architecture of the Eurozone or on shaping global governance. Several of these papers were published in the run up to important meetings of EU finance ministers (Eurogroup, Ecofin) or meetings of the G20 to prompt a debate on key policy issues. Finally, a number of chapters aim at pushing forward the intellectual frontier of economic and political integration. Here, my aim was to "think out of the institutional box," going beyond the short term debate. Given the complex nature of the European coordination game, the latter chapters often encompass a multidisciplinary approach.

As the reader will quickly realise, these papers are not the expression of a consistent overarching story, they do not all sing from the same script. This is due to the evolving circumstances, the varying institutional constraints and the evolution of my own views. In short, what is presented here is economic policy conception and implementation in real time, not a (convenient) *ex post* rationalisation.

The emphasis in the chapters written until and including the Eurozone sovereign debt crisis is on structural reforms and fiscal prudence. These were signalling devices to markets about the commitment to safeguard the integrity of the euro. They were also used as a means to create the political conditions for equipping the Eurozone with the missing crisis management tools and for making progress in completing its architecture. These analyses essentially reflect the "Brussels-Frankfurt consensus" prevailing at the time. In the relations amongst the fiscal authorities and between the latter and the ECB, strategic positioning and political economy considerations prevailed over purely economic reasons. In some cases, these strategic interactions led to positive decisions (for instance, the decision of creating the Banking Union by the European Council in June 2012 underpinned the "whatever it takes" of Mario Draghi the following weeks). In other cases, it has entailed an inadequate fiscal stance and incongruent policy mix (a case in point is the tightening of the fiscal rules in 2012, in the middle of the slump, as a condition to agree on the permanent firewall for the Eurozone, the ESM).

In more recent years, the need emerged to achieve a more symmetric adjustment within the currency area, lessen the dependency on external demand, and factor fairness considerations into policy actions. In line with the evolving macroeconomic theory, this new approach led to more emphasis on the role of active fiscal policy for propping up demand and rebalancing the policy mix, and on "structural reforms 2.0" to boost potential growth while ensuring equality of opportunities. Ensuring an adequate fiscal stance and a coherent policy mix, thereby moving away from a strategic behaviour, is increasingly recognised. My focus on reconnecting EMU's domestic and external agenda has been also behind the call for completing the architecture of the Eurozone and promoting the creation of a safe asset. In 2020 and 2021, with the critical reassessment of the EU's policy response to the financial crisis, this evolution has come to full completion. This reassessment has underpinned the proposals by the Commission to tackle the economic fallout of the pandemic.

The reader will notice that, with the coming of age of EMU (and myself), the articles are characterised by a more assertive tone, a clearer analytical framework, and bolder policy prescriptions. The same features I hope you will find in this introduction.

3 The circumstances: the global financial crisis, the rise of populism and the pandemic

The last twelve years have been all but business as usual for the European project and the world at large. Globally, major shifts have taken place both in parallel to and as a consequence of the financial crisis. These shifts have accelerated following the COVID-19 crisis. Technological advances and globalisation have changed how production and capital are distributed across the world, with the economic gains being strongly tilted towards multinational firms, international finance and capital. The sense that the economy is not working for everyone has become widespread. The centre of gravity of the world economy, which was clearly balanced between the United States, Japan and Europe – mostly the G7 countries – has become more elusive. The rise of China, first as part of the so-called BRICs, then alone, coupled with the disengagement of the US during the Trump presidency, has deeply affected the world economic order. The economic fall-out of the COVID-19 crisis has given a further boost to this global shift. In the developed world, the realignment has been accompanied by a fragmentation of the old order and a rise in populism.

During this period, the economic paradigm of European integration has evolved significantly, leading to a fundamental rethinking of the bases of policy coordination. Whilst such reconsideration is still ongoing, Next Generation EU has the potential to bring European coordination to a new high. At EU level, significant progress in economic and financial integration has taken place since the financial crisis, but we have also witnessed an erosion of trust within the Union that only reverted following the decisions to cross "deep red lines" in the response to the pandemics. Across the Member States, the political landscape forged in the aftermath of the financial crisis has become more diverse, hence presenting greater difficulties in finding common ground and forming a political consensus. On the positive side, the response to the economic fallout of the COVID-19 crisis is helping to overcome both the crystallisation of the North/South divide and the perception of the EU as an agent of globalisation – rather than as our best response to it.

The global financial crisis

The fall of Lehman Brothers in autumn 2008 and the ensuing wave of macro-financial shocks that impacted the world economy became an existential threat for the European Union, and notably the Eurozone, which was hit by the crisis with still an incomplete architecture. The unprecedented nature of the crisis meant that, at first, little was understood about the exact nature of the phenomena at play: for a while, policy makers at national, European and global level were literally without a conceptual compass.

The way in which the crisis unfolded tainted the narrative on its nature. Because of Greece's fiscal crisis, many also tended to view the other vulnerable countries through "fiscal lenses," which I believe was a mistake. For instance, if Ireland had come to fall before Greece, events could have unfolded quite differently, and we would probably be telling an altogether different story today. With the main focus on fiscal retrenchment, financial sector reform and the recapitalization of banks did not receive adequate priority at first. The proposal of creating a Banking Union had to wait for the sovereign debt crisis and was only put forward following the Euro Summit of June 2012. The result was wrong sequencing: we spent the years 2010-2012 reforming the Stability and Growth Pact (SGP) to tighten fiscal rules instead of launching the Banking Union and recapitalizing the banks. The overwhelming emphasis on fiscal sustainability, coupled with an overoptimistic view of the chances of cyclical recovery, led also to a premature withdrawal of fiscal stimulus, a mistake that is not going to be repeated in the aftermath of the pandemic (see chapters 38, 39 and 41).

The focus of EU coordination remained on fiscal policy whilst we lacked a proper framework to deal with financial inter-linkages and spillovers. For instance, when Greece needed assistance, no EU instrument existed. The hastily arranged "Greek Loan Facility" (GLF), based on bilateral national loans, was an emergency stopgap, which quickly proved to be an unsatisfactory arrangement. More generally, we did not sufficiently encompass the interdependencies amongst Eurozone members (either via banks' portfolios or via current and capital accounts) and vulnerabilities were treated in a country-by-country fashion.

During the course of the financial crisis, new instruments were added and a number of fundamental improvements in the design of EMU and in policy surveillance were put in place: the creation of the ESM and the first pillar of Banking Union (the Single Supervisory Mechanism) are the most important examples. However, given the acute market pressure and the need to act swiftly, the actions taken sometimes focussed on addressing symptoms rather than the underlying problems.

As the threat faced by the EU became existential, with the very purpose and objectives of the Union put into question, it was ultimately necessary for national leaders to step in. Accordingly, when common solutions were most needed, the so-called Community method gave way to more intergovernmental decision-making. To recall, the Community method is characterised by the sole right of the European Commission to initiate legislation, the co-decision power between the Council and the European Parliament, and the use of qualified majority voting in the Council. By contrast, in the intergovernmental method, the Commission's right of initiative is shared with the Member States, which generally act unanimously, and the European Parliament has a purely consultative role. The European Council (and the Eurogroup as its implementing arm) ended up playing the leading role. This development was spelled out in the speech by Chancellor Merkel at the College of Europe in Bruges in 2010 which coined the "Union method," as opposed to the Community method (Merkel 2010). The Union method *de facto* codified the intergovernmental approach and added to it the leadership of the European Council not only in terms of political guidance on tackling the financial and the sovereign debt crisis, but also in its daily management: dealing with the crisis became *Chefsache*.

As I explain below, throughout that period – which culminated in a narrowly averted Grexit in summer 2015 – the Commission had to play second fiddle. It tried to act in the common interest despite the division between creditor and debtor countries, with the former having the upper hand. As a result, the Commission was forced to take positions that often turned out to be unpopular with governments and citizens in both vulnerable countries (where it was identified as the enforcer of austerity) and core countries (where it was seen as promoting bailouts without adequately addressing risks of moral hazard).

While the institutional mechanisms developed during the crisis led to deeper integration of the EU, they were mostly not supranational in nature. The increased reliance on intergovernmental methods was probably inevitable at the time, but operating within that framework in "peacetime" would imply unwelcome consequences (see chapter 10). In short: (i) by requiring unanimity, intergovernmental decision-making can delay or impede progress; (ii) it does not always ensure democratic accountability at the appropriate level; and (iii) the transparency standard for intergovernmental institutions and bodies is generally lower than for EU institutions.

As a result, in economists' jargon, the intergovernmental method *de facto* implies the optimisation of the sum of separate national interests rather than that of the common interest. During his spell as Italy's finance minister, Tommaso Padoa-Schioppa used to say that finance ministers needed to come to Brussels with two hats, that of their country and that of the European Union or the Eurozone as a whole. Throughout the crisis, most often Ministers had in mind only national considerations, until the markets put their backs against the wall, forcing bold but belated and often half-hearted decisions. The change of priorities proved transient: as market pressure subsided, national priorities re-emerged, leading to delays and backtracking.

The prevalence of the sum of national interests rather than the pursuit of the common interest resulted in a permanent division between "creditors" and "debtors." Several fundamental reforms and instruments of the EMU architecture aimed at protecting vulnerable countries. However, in their design, they clearly bore the hallmarks of the strongest countries. The adoption of those reforms under duress implied a lack of full ownership, which came back to haunt EU economic governance in the post-crisis period.

The inconsistency between European responsibilities and domestic accountability resulted in decisions being taken too late, as *ultima ratio* (see chapter 38). To overcome that, the EU decision-making process would need to operate under what Rawls calls "a veil of ignorance" (Rawls 1999): when taking important decisions in the EU, countries should not reverse-engineer the short-term national implications of such decisions. This proved impossible during the crisis when the division of countries between creditors and debtors crystallised their conflicts of interest. The debate between risk-reduction-first and risk-sharing-first brewed mistrust and led to a stalemate that has so far prevented the finalisation of the Banking Union.

Progress will require abandoning narrow and myopic national self-interest. This should not only be out of concern for the countries most affected by the crisis. It should also recognise that, as European economic history teaches us, today's creditors may very well end up being tomorrow's debtors. Adopting a truly "political insurance" approach to solidarity (Habermas 2018), as embodied in Next Generation EU, may well be the main lesson learned from the tortured response to the financial crisis.

The rise of populism

The financial crisis created the breeding ground for Eurosceptic political movements, which questioned the very bases on which the European project is built. Globally, there has been a growing backlash against the multilateral world order and its institutions, with populism and protectionism on the rise. In Europe, this trend culminated with Brexit. The economic hardships the crisis triggered in many countries, in combination with a skewed perception of Europe's actions to tackle it, alienated parts of the population from the European project: 48% of Europeans have stated they "tend to not trust" the EU versus 43% who have stated that they "tend to trust" the EU (European Commission 2020c).

While the nationalist, populist parties did not claim an outright victory in the 2019 election, their increasing presence certainly is a cause for concern. A quarter of the seats in the European Parliament were taken by anti-EU parties, up from a fifth in 2014. The origins of this development are clearly multi-faceted, difficult to comprehensively address and not unique to the EU. Trust in national governments is actually lower than trust in the EU.

The perception that European processes and institutions are detached from the reality of ordinary European citizens is widespread. This reflects an increasing divide between centre and periphery, notably between rural and urban areas: whereas metropolitan areas are often thriving, capturing agglomeration effects and benefitting from economies of scale, many provincial areas are left behind – economically, but also culturally and politically.

For all its tragic consequences, the response to the pandemic provides an opportunity to re-energise Europe and reconnect it with ordinary citizens. Eurobarometer surveys reveal that overall support for Europe is increasing (63% in December 2020 considered that their country's EU membership is "a good thing"). There is strong and rising support for the euro: in summer 2020, three quarters of Europeans said that the euro is good for the EU, which is the highest approval rate since the single currency was introduced in 1999.

The Commission has stepped up its actions to address economic and social fragmentation. Many new EU initiatives and instruments are designed precisely to achieve more internal cohesion and ensure that nobody is left behind. Next Generation EU is the most prominent example of a strategy ultimately aimed at preserving economic, social and territorial cohesion in the aftermath of the pandemic. These efforts can only succeed if national policy makers play their part, which is often not the case. Populists should not get away with misrepresenting facts and spinning the narrative of "the people" against an opaque force they depict as "Brussels."

Traditionally, the European Commission is used as a useful scapegoat for national governments, when these governments pass politically difficult reforms. In the past, the EU's prevailing view was that this was a small price to pay; the European project was not under threat due to its large popularity. This view, however, is no longer sustainable. Blaming Europe is often inconsistent with the high level of subsidiarity in many national policies. Blaming Europe also nurtures a sentiment of expropriation of national politics and contributes to the feeling of political disenfranchisement that in turn breeds discontent against national decision-makers (see chapter 22). Lack of political ownership of the EU is costly. For example, relentless criticism of decisions made in common and scant knowledge about how the EU operates made it easier for opponents of the EU to distort facts in the United Kingdom's referendum on its withdrawal from the EU.

Whilst the COVID-19 crisis led to a refocussing of political priorities away from the populists' favourite issues (most notably migration), the threat of populism remains a substantial danger for the EU. In Europe, there is a need for recoupling growth and social cohesion. In particular, the political and economic risk of what one may call the "1% economy" (characterised by very low real growth and inflation, and an increasing share of income and wealth accruing to the very rich) has to be acknowledged and addressed. Next Generation EU represents the opportunity to shake off, at least for a period, the "fourth 1%": the one referring to the limited size of the EU budget.

Correctly identifying these risks and offering concrete solutions is the name of the game going forward. The commitment to integrate the UN Sustainable Development Goals into the European Semester offers a chance to make the longer term aspirations of citizens come to fruition and suggest avenues for the renewal of the common project. The growing awareness and concerns of citizens for climate change and environmental damage must be the foundation for renewing the European project. As these are issues that transcend national borders and circumstances, the European Union is best placed to tackle them. The priority given by the Commission presided by Ursula von der Leyen to the environmental transition gives us the opportunity to reshape Europe's growth model and "build back better" after the pandemic crisis.

The impact of COVID-19 and the policy response: why this time it may well be different

As the European economies were still recovering from the financial crisis which followed the bankruptcy of Lehman Brothers in 2008, they were hit by an even bigger shock. The COVID-19 crisis has led to a downturn of historic proportions, much deeper than that witnessed during the Great Recession. For several EU countries, the COVID-19 recession is twice the size of the one that followed the financial crash. For the EU as a whole, GDP is set to return to pre-crisis levels only in 2022. Over and above macroeconomic indicators, the crisis has created huge social distress, very large financing needs, and a sizeable investment gap (see chapter 39).

A major worry has been the potentially uneven impact of the crisis on different countries. Both the severity of the recession in 2020 and the following bounce back differ markedly among Member States. Of all stylised patterns used by economists to characterise the COVID-19 economic impact, the most appropriate one may turn out to be a "K-shape" recovery capturing the divergences between countries, regions and sectors. Amongst the large EU countries, Germany suffered a much smaller downturn than France, Italy and Spain and is bound to come back to pre-crisis GDP levels earlier. Even more worrying are the long-term dynamics: comparing the GDP level in 2021 with that in 2008, the last year before the financial crisis, the German and French economies are 12% and almost 8% larger, respectively. Spain's GDP in 2021 is at the same level of 2008, while Italy still sees a reduction of almost 8% since 2008.

If not tackled effectively, these centrifugal forces may undermine the integrity of the single market and the economic and political viability of the EU project. Taming such risks is what underpins Next Generation EU, the recovery instrument that will provide €750 billion (in 2018 prices) of which €390 billion in grants and €360 billion in loans, to be financed via issuing common debt to support investment and reforms, with an emphasis on favouring the green and digital transition. This package complements the measures agreed by the Eurogroup in 2020 for a total of €540 billion in support of healthcare spending, the unemployed and short time work, and credit to the private sector.

As recalled in chapter 41, the EU response comes on top of national fiscal measures (€500 billion for the EU as a whole in 2020) and liquidity measures (€2500 billion) which were allowed by the triggering of the General Escape Clause of the SGP and the temporary loosening of the state aid framework. National measures complemented the planned ECB purchases of €1850 billion under the Pandemic Emergency Purchase Programme (PEPP).

The policy response to the COVID-19 crisis has been much faster and more ambitious than during the financial crisis. As I argue in chapter 39 a key role was played by the different nature of the crisis (an exogenous, rather than a policy-induced shock), which *de facto* put aside moral hazard concerns. During the financial crisis, the policy mix was unbalanced: for most of the years, monetary policy was the only game in town. With insight, the fiscal stimulus of 2009 was withdrawn too soon, at the first signs of growth. As a result, too much of the onus of supporting the economy fell on the shoulders of the ECB. Consequently, and paradoxically, "fiscal dominance" was achieved via excessive fiscal prudence: in the presence of self-imposed fiscal constraints, the externalities arising from a negative demand shock largely outweighed those related to the risk monetisation of public debt. This turned on its head the conclusions by Sargent and Wallace's "unpleasant monetarist arithmetic" (Sargent and Wallace 1981, see chapter 38).

The experience during the financial crisis showed that achieving an appropriate Eurozone fiscal stance only via horizontal, bottom-up coordination of national policies is exceedingly difficult. During the COVID-19 crisis, to help offset the asymmetric outturn of the crisis, a complementary central fiscal intervention proved paramount. The strong role for the EU budget via Next Generation EU will complement horizontal surveillance with vertical coordination, as originally proposed by the Sapir Report (Sapir et al. 2003, Buti and Nava 2003).

Stronger reliance on domestic sources of growth has implications also for the geopolitical role of Europe. Policy makers have become increasingly aware that, in a more fragmented world where rules-based multilateralism has been until recently called into question, an export-led growth model and a large external surplus are a source of vulnerability. This has paved the way to a stronger reliance on the EU single market as "indigenous" growth engine and domestic policy action to sustain economic activity.

In sum, this time it may well be different. The domestic political conditions appear to be there for an effective response to the crisis, with a decisive role for the EU level and a renewed boost to horizontal and vertical policy coordination.

4 The role of the European Commission in policy design and coordination

Within the economic sphere, the overarching goal of the European Commission is to foster economic stability and resilience based on inclusive and sustainable growth. Sustainable growth – which takes into account the fiscal, social and environmental dimensions – is the only way to increase well-being. It is especially vital for those people and regions that are lagging behind: without growth, redistribution is more difficult and the public resources needed to invest in climate change mitigation, people and skills become scarcer. Stability is important because it provides businesses and people with the confidence to adapt to rapid changes and seize new opportunities.

While the ultimate economic goal of the Commission has remained virtually the same over time, the macroeconomic developments of the past twelve years have resulted in a significant evolution of its role.

The Commission plays multiple roles in ensuring that Member States treat their economic policies as a matter of common interest. First, as directly derived from the EU Treaty, the Commission acts as a *referee*, a well-respected body in charge of the common surveillance rules. It also has a role in reconciling different national sensitivities and interests by acting as a *consensus builder*. In parallel, the Commission acts as *integration promoter* by contributing to push forward the frontier of EU policy coordination, including through independent economic analysis.

While those three roles are traditional ones, two additional roles have emerged over the past years. First, during the Eurozone sovereign debt crisis, the Commission, in cooperation with the ESM and the International Monetary Fund (IMF), was instrumental in the implementation of rescue programmes of Greece, Ireland, Portugal, Cyprus and, limited to the banking sector, Spain. Acting as *enforcer of rescue programmes* proved to be both politically and institutionally very delicate. Second, the implementation of the so-called Juncker investment plan heralded a role for the Commission, as *enabler of policy plans*. The latter role will be brought to a wholly new level by the implementation of Next Generation EU with the Recovery and Resilience Facility at its heart.

The delineation between the various roles is not always clear-cut and their relative weight has been shifting over past years. The financial crisis and subsequently the pandemic crisis have challenged the Commission in undertaking all of these functions and in reconciling them with each other. For example, at times, due to the increasingly political nature of economic coordination, building consensus has come into conflict with its role as a referee.

Referee

The Commission is formally responsible for the application of the Treaty's provisions on economic policy. While the focus was in the past on fiscal surveillance, the financial crisis widened and deepened the role of the Commission on economic coordination. With the so-called "six-pack" and "two-pack" legislation adopted in 2011 and 2013, the coordination of fiscal policy was considerably reinforced and the Macroeconomic Imbalances Procedure (MIP) was added, within the broader surveillance under the so-called European Semester. With the outbreak of the COVID-19 crisis, the Commission faced the challenge of applying a rules-based framework not adapted to the situation at hand. Hence, in March 2020, it decided to invoke the so-called General Escape Clause (GEC) that suspended the adjustment requirements of the SGP. This provided the Member States with the opportunity to adopt very expansionary fiscal policies to support the economy.

The concrete implementation of the strengthened roles provided to the Commission by the revamped regulatory framework has not been straightforward. As regards the SGP, three main issues have arisen. First, the appropriateness of the fiscal rules has been increasingly questioned in an environment of persistently low growth and inflation. Second, there has been an attempt by Member States to limit the discretion of the

Commission by codifying all the possible fiscal and economic situations. Third, the difficulty of imposing sanctions on sovereign states has come to the fore, in particular during periods of economic stress. Regarding the surveillance of macroeconomic imbalances, the full potential of the MIP has admittedly not been fully exploited. First, the corrective arm of the procedure, which involves the adoption of a corrective action plan, has never been launched. Second, the procedure has been applied in a largely asymmetrical way, focussing on current account deficits and domestic imbalances, acknowledging only partly the negative Eurozone-wide spillovers of persistent external surpluses.

Consensus builder

During the financial crisis, Member States often disagreed on the economic diagnosis and, even more, on the appropriate policy response. Hence, finding common solutions proved challenging. This led the Commission to complement its role as a guardian of the Treaty with that of consensus builder. This has raised questions of institutional balance between the Commission and the Council, the institution where Member States attempt to forge a consensus. Whilst, as discussed above, the Union method gave a prominence to the European Council in the management of the financial crisis, the relative role of the European Council and the Commission changed in the post-crisis period, with the Commission re-emerging as a key player. Such a role has been further enhanced by the economic response to the COVID-19 crisis which, as argued above, put the Community method back at the centre of European policymaking.

Whilst consensus building requires trade-offs domestically, it has served the EU well in international fora. A welcome outcome of the financial crisis has been the strengthened role of the EU in global governance, in particular through its participation in the G20 and the G7. In the longer term, such a role will be safeguarded and enhanced only by aligning the domestic and the external agendas of the EU. Most importantly, it will be necessary to complete EMU's architecture to enable it to count more in global affairs and to boost the international role of the Euro. The goal of "open strategic autonomy," which emerged during the pandemic crisis, represents a new frontier in Europe's role in global governance. A single voice in international fora – even if just at the Eurozone level – would hence be the natural outcome of deeper EU integration.

Integration promoter

The Commission has been at the forefront of shaping the analytical case for European integration, in particular in designing the architecture of EMU. This role of promoter of new ideas and policies – incorporating the latest developments in economic theory and practice – will become even more important in the post-pandemic economy. A world of interconnected and complex challenges where the social and economic fabric has been undermined, calls for the ability to take a holistic view informed by theoretical and empirical knowledge. The ongoing fundamental reconsideration of macroeconomic policies and structural reforms in a "low for long" environment and much higher levels of public and private debt, must feature high in the analytical agenda of the Commission, the Eurogroup and the Council (see chapter 41).

By promoting evidence-based policy-making, the Commission can boost its relevance and acceptability. The Commission's analyses over the past several years exemplify the importance of continuing to push the frontier of economic knowledge. Notable examples are: the effectiveness of fiscal policy when monetary policy is at the "effective lower bound"; the international role of the euro; and a possible design of a safe asset for the Eurozone. A number of these studies are presented in this book. A mature and self-confident institution such as the Commission can only benefit from embracing path-breaking analytical experiments.

Enforcer of rescue programmes

The evolution of EU surveillance during the crisis from purely committee-based to more hands-on involvement in vulnerable countries' economic policies marked the emergence of a new role for the Commission: that of enforcer of rescue programmes. The Commission played a crucial role, together with the IMF and the ESM, in redressing the economies of programme countries. In particular, its action was crucial in safeguarding the integrity of the Eurozone during the Grexit crisis.

However, the Commission paid a hefty political price for undertaking such an endeavour. This became most evident during the Greek crisis. On the one hand, the Commission was perceived as an agent of the creditors and the enforcer of austerity, a view that was widespread not only with the Greek public, but also in other vulnerable countries. Negative economic situations were too often blamed solely on the reform packages and fiscal retrenchment enacted under the Troika. On the other hand, the Commission was also unpopular among governments and the public in countries such as Germany and the Netherlands, since it was perceived as being too lenient with Greece. The lessons learned collectively during the financial crisis will hopefully prevent the resurgence of situations requiring the Commission to play a role that was perceived at times as that of agent of the creditors (see chapter 38).

Enabler of policy plans

Under President Juncker, the European Commission started to play a more active role in restoring growth and investment in the EU. The increasing importance of the role of enabler of plans aiming at promoting growth and investment helped move away from a purely "disciplinarian" perception of the Commission. The implementation of Next Generation EU and most notably the Recovery and Resilience Facility, will bring such a role to a new quantitative and qualitative high. With its scale and innovations in both spending (direct transfers to Member States under the Recovery and Resilience Plans or RRPs) and revenue (issuance of euro denominated debt), the Commission will, *de facto*, gradually become the EU and the Eurozone Treasury.

The implementation of RRPs will herald a new phase of relations between the Commission and Member States. In monitoring the execution of national plans, it will be necessary to overcome the "asymmetric information" between the Commission and the Member States. The effective implementation of the RRPs – especially by the largest beneficiaries – will be crucial not only in helping European economies to recover after the pandemic, but also in rebuilding trust and in overcoming the divide between North and South within the EU. Whether Next Generation EU will remain a "large one off" or represent a shift in the paradigm of European integration will largely depend on the success of the RRPs.

The Commission has reorganised internally to fulfil these new duties in an effective manner. Such adaptation will have to continue in the years to come.

5 Some lessons for the future

In the last decade, the European Union and its institutions have undergone a structural transformation to adapt to an increasingly challenging economic and political environment. The need to respond to two unprecedented crises in rapid succession tested the European Commission's resolve and imagination to the limit. The challenges related to managing the pandemic crisis when the scars of the Great Recession were still healing and "building back better" put the bar of policy and institutional ambition even higher.

Based on my personal involvement in crisis management and response, I would draw six key lessons in approaching EU policymaking in the years to come:

1. *Avoid "inverted pyramids."* Often, there is a disproportionate focus in EU policy surveillance on matters that are objectively less important. Although not always fair, a criticism has often been levied in the past at the EU for getting bogged down in the "decimals." Policy surveillance should be recast to address what the EU Treaty dubs "gross errors." The internalisation of spillovers (not only economic, but institutional and political) should be the guiding principle. Crucially, the implementation of RRPs will provide the opportunity to emphasise "gross advantages" as well.
2. *Do not fall victim to the "partial equilibrium" syndrome.* The financial crisis demonstrated that tensions in one corner of the Eurozone could have powerful consequences elsewhere and, under certain circumstances, become systemic. The stronger toolbox put in place during the financial crisis will help on that front, but it is unlikely to be sufficient. As the response to the COVID-19 crisis has shown, taking into account interdependences between countries (in the application of fiscal and macroeconomic surveillance) and between policies (notably fiscal and monetary policies), will be important to capture the Eurozone "general equilibrium" dynamic.
3. *Fight against "complete contracts."* During the financial crisis, the lack of trust amongst Member States and between the latter and European Institutions created suspicion in some countries about the use of any discretion in the implementation of the fiscal rules. This led to the attempt to codify all possible states of the world in complex

algorithms so to avoid discretionary decisions as much as possible. The over-engineering of the SGP is the quintessential example of this *dérive*. However, as economic analysis and experience show, complete contracts do not exist. Moreover, the increasingly sophisticated algorithms, often based on unobservable variables, add to complexity which itself undermines the effectiveness and transparency of surveillance. If the rules of macroeconomic and fiscal surveillance are to be simplified, Member States have to accept that the Commission applies them using the appropriate degree of economic judgement.

4. *Remember that going from A to B is not a straight line in Europe.* The different sensitivities and complex political realities in the EU mean that proposals must usually appeal to different audiences and be accepted by countries with different social and political preferences. Therefore, achieving a consensus is often cumbersome and requires complex negotiations and "lateral progress." Actually, aiming at drawing a straight line between A and B may be detrimental to the eventual success of the initiative. For instance, the call to boost public investment resonates better in certain countries if it is presented as demand policy whilst in others if emphasis is put on its supply side effects. Another example is the work on a safe Eurozone asset: emphasizing its role in market deepening and strengthening the international role of the euro gives it a better chance of success than casting it as part of fiscal union.
5. *Red lines are there to be crossed.* As part of discussion in the Council or in the various Committees and *fora* of the EU, national authorities often arrive, as is natural, with a number of red lines dictated by domestic political considerations. Most of these red lines become less compelling if the common interest is brought into the picture and the time horizon over which certain policies or reforms are assessed is lengthened. An essential role for the Commission is to provide the intellectual arguments to help identify the lines that need to be crossed and hence help lower the "discount rate" of national policy makers. The Commission did so in its proposals to tackle the economic fallout of the pandemic.
6. *Do not become a "Japanese holdout."* The example of soldiers such as Teruo Nakamura, a private in the Imperial Japanese Army who was posted on his own on an isolated island and surrendered only in 1974,

> almost thirty years after the end of World War II, should inspire a lesson. Policy projects or approaches can at times be pursued long after their political relevance has passed or their economic rationale has proven obsolete. In that respect, "the difficulty is not so much to develop new ideas as to escape old ones," as John Maynard Keynes famously remarked. Avoiding such a trap is particularly crucial today as the traditional economic paradigm is severely questioned.

Shaping tomorrow's European economy is tantamount to building-back-better after the pandemic. It will require courageous political decisions. Within the EU, only the European Commission and its economists have the analytical capacity, the institutional competence, and the *esprit de finesse*, to accomplish such a task.

Europe 2008-2021: A Chronology

2008

Eurozone macroeconomic indicators	
Real GDP growth rate	0.7%
Inflation rate (annual average)	3.4%
Unemployment (% of active population)	7.5%
Budget balance (% of GDP)	–2.2%
General government debt (% of GDP)	69.7%
Current account balance (% of GDP)	–1.8%

1 January: Malta and Cyprus join the Eurozone

15 September: Bankruptcy of Lehman Brothers accelerates the global financial crisis (see chapter 38)

14-15 November: G20 Leaders summit in Washington reacts to the global economic and financial crisis (see chapter 35 and 38)

26 November: Commission proposes a European stimulus plan of 1.5% of GDP (€200 billion) (see chapter 38)

December: Marco Buti appointed Director-General for Economic and Financial Affairs after Klaus Regling (see chapter 1)

December: EU balance of payments assistance programme to Latvia (see chapter 38)

2009

Eurozone macroeconomic indicators	
Real GDP growth rate	−4.5%
Inflation rate (annual average)	0.3%
Unemployment (% of active population)	9.6%
Budget balance (% of GDP)	−6.2%
General government debt (% of GDP)	80.3%
Current account balance (% of GDP)	−0.3%

1 January: Slovakia joins the Eurozone

2 April: G20 Summit in London decides to triple the resources of the IMF, resist protectionism and ensure the emergence of a sustainable global trade (see chapter 38)

16 October: Greece announces public deficit would top 10% of GDP. Eventually the budget balance would become 12.7% two weeks later

1 December: Herman Van Rompuy appointed as European Council President, his economics background helped the crisis management of the Eurozone

2010

Eurozone macroeconomic indicators	
Real GDP growth rate	2.1%
Inflation rate (annual average)	1.6%
Unemployment (% of active population)	10.1%
Budget balance (% of GDP)	−6.3%
General government debt (% of GDP)	85.8%
Current account balance (% of GDP)	−0.3%

10 February: Beginning of the second Barroso Commission; Olli Rehn appointed as Commissioner for Economic and Monetary Affairs

2 May: First three-year adjustment programme for Greece; assistance provided by Commission pooling of national loans, the so-called Greek Loans Facility (see chapter 38). In total, Eurozone countries pledge €80 billion and IMF €30 billion

10 May: ECB announces Security Market Programme, the purchase of a limited amount of government securities

10-11 May: European Financial Stabilisation Mechanism (EFSM) is established. Based on the EU budget, at €60 billion, it is much smaller than the proposal of the Commission (see chapter 38)

7-9 June: European Financial Stability Facility (EFSF) established as a temporary intergovernmental arrangement, with a total volume of up to €500 billion. Klaus Regling becomes CEO (see chapter 10, 22, 38, 39)

26-27 June: G20 Summit in Toronto states that the recovery is underway and commits to at least halving their deficit by 2013 and to stabilising public debt-to-GDP ratios (see chapter 38)

29 September: Commission proposes to reform EU economic governance, the so-called Six-pack, which strengthens fiscal surveillance and extends it to macroeconomic imbalances (see chapter 3 and 4)

18 October: At their meeting in Deauville, Chancellor Merkel and President Sarkozy agree on a EU Treaty change to create a permanent crisis resolution mechanism that will also foresees the possibility of sovereign debt restructuring (see chapter 38)

21-29 October: European Leaders agree to create an intergovernmental permanent fiscal backstop, the European Stability Mechanism (ESM), to replace the EFSF (see chapter 10, 22, 38, 39, 41)

2 November: Chancellor Merkel, in a speech at the College of Europe in Bruges, spells out the "Union method" that provides for a leading role of the European Council in the Eurozone crisis management (see chapter 1 and 10)

28 November: EU and IMF grant assistance to Ireland, following the country's request on 22 November

2011

Eurozone macroeconomic indicators	
Real GDP growth rate	1.7%
Inflation rate (annual average)	2.7%
Unemployment (% of active population)	10.2%
Budget balance (% of GDP)	–4.2%
General government debt (% of GDP)	87.7%
Current account balance (% of GDP)	–0.4%

1 January: Estonia joins the Eurozone

17 May: European Council agrees on a financial assistance package to Portugal, following the country's request on 7 April
11 July: ESM Treaty signed by Eurozone Leaders
7 September: German Constitutional Court rules that the rescue packages agreed are not against the German constitution. It also states that Germany needs prior consent of the Bundestag for all adjustment programmes
20 September: Commission, Council and European Parliament agree on the reform of the EU economic governance, the so-called Six-pack (see chapters 3 and 4)
31 October: Mario Draghi becomes President of the ECB, after Jean-Claude Trichet
3-4 November: G20 Summit in Cannes, where informal discussions focus on the announcement by the Greek Prime Minister to hold a referendum on the rescue programme
23 November: Commission proposes a deepening of the economic governance, the so-called Two-Pack and launches consultations on the feasibility of introducing Stability Bonds
8 December: ECB announces measures to support bank lending and liquidity, the Long Term Refinancing Operations (LTROs)
8-9 December: Eurozone Leaders agree on the Treaty on Stability, Coordination and Governance (TSCG), often referred to as the Fiscal Compact, an intergovernmental treaty that tightens the rules of the Stability and Growth Pact (SGP)
13 December: Six-Pack enters into force

2012

Eurozone macroeconomic indicators	
Real GDP growth rate	−0.9%
Inflation rate (annual average)	2.5%
Unemployment (% of active population)	11.3%
Budget balance (% of GDP)	−3.7%
General government debt (% of GDP)	90.7%
Current account balance (% of GDP)	1.0%

2 February: Amended ESM Treaty signed incorporating the decisions taken since July 2011 and increasing the firepower to €500 billion
21 February – 14 March: Second Adjustment Programme for Greece (see

chapter 38). In total, Euro area countries pledge €142 billion and the IMF €12 billion

2 March: Eurozone members sign the TSCG

26 June: Four Presidents' Report on completing the architecture of EMU (see chapter 30 and 38)

29 June: European Council agrees to complete Banking Union and strengthen the measures to fight off the financial crisis (see chapter 8, 9, 10, 19, 21, 22, 26, 27)

20 July: Spain is granted financial assistance to recapitalise banks, following the country's request on 9 June

26 July: Mario Draghi, in a speech at the Global Investment Conference in London, pledges to do "whatever it takes to preserve the euro," a turning point in the Eurozone crisis (see chapter 38)

6 September: Technical features of Outright Monetary Transactions (OMT) announced by the ECB

12 September: Commission publishes roadmap to complete Banking Union (see chapters 5 and 7)

12 September: German Constitutional Court allows ratification of the ESM and TSCG Treaties

8 October: ESM formally starts operating; Klaus Regling becomes Managing Director

2013

Eurozone macroeconomic indicators	
Real GDP growth rate	–0.2%
Inflation rate (annual average)	1.3%
Unemployment (% of active population)	12.0%
Budget balance (% of GDP)	–3.0%
General government debt (% of GDP)	92.6%
Current account balance (% of GDP)	2.1%

25 March: Cyprus is granted financial assistance following the country's requests on 25 June

May: Two-Pack enters into force

5-6 September: G20 Summit in Saint Petersburg, where Leaders welcome the incipient recovery in the Eurozone. However, they also recognise that despite their actions the global recovery is weak (see chapter 26)

December: Ireland (13 December) and Spain (31 December) exit their assistance programme

2014

Eurozone macroeconomic indicators	
Real GDP growth rate	1.4%
Inflation rate (annual average)	0.4%
Unemployment (% of active population)	11.6%
Budget balance (% of GDP)	–2.5%
General government debt (% of GDP)	92.8%
Current account balance (% of GDP)	2.4%

17 May: Portugal exits the assistance programme

22-25 May: European Parliament elections. Turnout lower than 50%

22 August: Mario Draghi's speech at the Jackson Hole Symposium, where he advocates for a more appropriate policy mix addressing both demand and supply, with fiscal policy having a larger role (see chapters 29 and 38). He also hints at the start of Quantitative Easing

4 October: Greece returns to the financial markets issuing €3 billion Eurobonds

1 November: Beginning of Juncker's Commission; Valdis Dombrovkis appointed as Vice-president for the Euro, Social Dialogue and Financial Stability, and Pierre Moscovici as Commissioner for Economic and Monetary Affairs

4 November: Start of the Single Supervisory Mechanism (SSM), the first leg of Banking Union (see chapters 1, 5, 9, 10, 39, 41)

November: Launch of the Juncker investment plan (see chapter 29). It aims at mobilizing at least €315 billion in additional investments on key sectors across the EU by 2018, raising €440 billion as of October 2019

1 December: Donald Tusk appointed as European Council President: the focus of the European Council moves from economic to foreign and strategic political matters

2015

Eurozone macroeconomic indicators	
Real GDP growth rate	2.0%
Inflation rate (annual average)	0.2%
Unemployment (% of active population)	10.8%
Budget balance (% of GDP)	–2.0%
General government debt (% of GDP)	90.9%
Current account balance (% of GDP)	2.8%

1 January: Lithuania joins the Eurozone bringing membership to the current 19 countries
1 January: Single Resolution Board (SRB), the second leg of Banking Union, becomes operational (see chapter 41)
13 January: Commission communication on making the best use of the flexibility within the existing rules of the SGP
22 January: ECB announces Quantitative Easing that will eventually start on 9 March (see chapter 15 and 37)
16 June: European Court of Justices declares the OMT legal
22 June: Five President Report on completing EMU (see chapter 5, 6, 15, 16 and 22)
26 June: Greece's Prime Minister Tsipras announces referendum on Greece bailout package
29 June: Greece imposes capital controls
5 July: Referendum in Greece rejects the Memorandum of Understanding with the Troika
July: German Finance Minister, Wolfgang Schäuble, suggests Grexit as a possible scenario (see chapter 1 and 38)
19 August: Start of the third adjustment programme for Greece. ESM approves €86 billion stability programme
24-30 September: Commission proposes action plan for the Capital Markets Union
21 October: Commission publishes a roadmap for moving towards a more consistent external representation of the Euro Area in international fora (see chapter 22)
9 November: European Council debates the migration crisis (see chapter 39)
24 November: Commission proposes European Deposit Insurance Scheme (EDIS) as the third leg of Banking Union (see chapters 8, 36, 39, 41)

2016

Eurozone macroeconomic indicators	
Real GDP growth rate	1.9%
Inflation rate (annual average)	0.2%
Unemployment (% of active population)	10.0%
Budget balance (% of GDP)	–1.5%
General government debt (% of GDP)	90.1%
Current account balance (% of GDP)	3.1%

31 March: Cyprus exits the adjustment programme. Only Greece is left under the programme

23 June: United Kingdom votes to leave the European Union (see chapters 1, 22, 23)

4-5 September: G20 Summit at Hangzhou, where Leaders reiterate the commitment to use all policy tools to achieve strong, sustainable, balanced and inclusive growth (see chapter 34)

20 October: The European Fiscal Board, an independent advisory body to the Commission, starts operating; Niels Thygesen appointed as Chairman (see chapter 8)

16 November: Commission releases a communication on a positive fiscal stance for the Euro Area (see chapters 6, 15, 16)

2017

Eurozone macroeconomic indicators	
Real GDP growth rate	2.6%
Inflation rate (annual average)	1.5%
Unemployment (% of active population)	9.0%
Budget balance (% of GDP)	–0.9%
General government debt (% of GDP)	87.7%
Current account balance (% of GDP)	3.1%

1 March: Commission publishes a White Paper on the Future of Europe (see chapter 6)

25 March: Rome declaration on the 60th anniversary of the creation of the EU outlining a way forward after the UK referendum (see chapter 6)

31 May: Commission publishes a Reflection Paper on deepening EMU (see chapters 6 and 7)
26 September: Macron speech at the Sorbonne on new frontiers of European integration
11 October: Commission communication on completing the Banking Union (see chapter 7 and 9)
6 December: Commission sets out roadmap and makes concrete proposals for deepening EMU (see chapter 7)

2018

Eurozone macroeconomic indicators	
Real GDP growth rate	1.9%
Inflation rate (annual average)	1.8%
Unemployment (% of active population)	8.1%
Budget balance (% of GDP)	−0.5%
General government debt (% of GDP)	85.7%
Current account balance (% of GDP)	2.9%

2 May: Commission proposes to create the InvestEU Programme as a successor to the Juncker investment plan, which aims at triggering at least €650 billion in additional investment
23-26 May: European Parliament elections. Increase in the turnout to 50.7%. A quarter of the seats in the European Parliament are taken by anti-EU parties (see chapter 1)
31 May: Commission proposes to establish a European Investment Stabilisation Function (see chapter 8)
20 August 2018: Greece concludes the ESM Programme. €61.9 billion of EU support has been mobilised over three years
5 December: Commission puts forward proposals for strengthening the euro's international role, reversing the attitude of benign neglect (see chapter 36)

2019

Eurozone macroeconomic indicators	
Growth	1.3%
Inflation rate (annual average)	1.2%
Unemployment (% of active population)	7.5%
Budget balance (% of GDP)	–0.6%
General government debt (% of GDP)	83.9%
Current account balance (% of GDP)	2.3%

14 June: Spain exits the Excessive Deficit Procedures (EDP). It is the last Eurozone country to do so since the beginning of the financial crisis

18 June: Mario Draghi's speech at the ECB Forum on Central Banking, Sintra, where he underlines that monetary policy needs to remain patient, persistent and prudent (see chapter 38)

1 November: Christine Lagarde takes over from Mario Draghi as President of the ECB

1 December: Beginning of Von der Leyen Commission; Valdis Dombrovskis appointed as Executive Vice-president for the euro, and Paolo Gentiloni as Commissioner for the economy

1 December: Charles Michel appointed as European Council President

1 December: Marco Buti appointed as Head of Cabinet of Commissioner for the Economy, Paolo Gentiloni. Subsequently, Maarten Verwey appointed as Director-general of ECFIN

11 December: Commission proposes the EU Green Deal as Europe's new growth strategy (see chapter 41)

2020

Eurozone macroeconomic indicators	
Real GDP growth rate	–6.6%
Inflation rate (annual average)	0.3%
Unemployment (% of active population)	7.8%
Budget balance (% of GDP)	–7.2%
General government debt (% of GDP)	98.0%
Current account balance (% of GDP)	2.3%

31 January: United Kingdom formally leaves the EU

March: Pandemic crisis begins sending shockwaves thorough the European and global economies (see chapters 39 and 41)

18 March: ECB announces the Pandemic Emergency Purchase Programme (PEPP). The Governing Council increased the initial €750 billion envelope by €600 billion on 4 June and by €500 billion on 10 December, for a new total of €1.850 billion (see chapter 41)

20 March: Activation of the General Escape Clause of the SGP and adoption of Temporary Framework for State aid measures (see chapters 39 and 41)

6 April: Commissioners Gentiloni and Breton publish an op-ed with proposal for setting up a European recovery fund to tackle the economic fallout of the pandemic

9 April: Eurogroup approves SURE, ESM Pandemic Crisis Support and EIB credit totalling €540 billion of cheap loans (see chapter 39)

18 May: President Macron and Chancellor Merkel announce a joint proposal for a European recovery programme of €500 billion of transfers

27 May: Commission publishes a staff working document on Europe's recovery needs and proposes Next Generation EU of €750 billion, with the Recovery and Resilience Facility (RRF) at its heart. The programme is to be financed via issuance of common debt by the Commission (see chapters 39, 40 and 41)

17-21 July 2020: European Council finds an agreement on the Next Generation EU and the EU multi-year budget (see chapters 39 and 41)

21 October: First issuance under SURE, where bonds were more than 13 times oversubscribed

2021 – Spring Economic Forecast of the Commission, May 2021

Eurozone macroeconomic indicators	
Real GDP growth rate	4.3%
Inflation rate (annual average)	1.7%
Unemployment (% of active population)	8.4%
Budget balance (% of GDP)	–8.0%
General government debt (% of GDP)	102.4%
Current account balance (% of GDP)	3.1%

22 January: Commission publishes guidelines on the RRF (see chapter 40)
19 February: Regulation establishing the RRF enters into force (see chapter 40)
3 March: Commission publishes fiscal policy guidelines where it calls for the continuation of the expansionary fiscal policy and proposes to maintain the General Escape Clause until 2022 (see chapter 41)
21 April: German Constitutional Court gives green light to government for the ratification of the Own Resources Decision, an essential step to allow the Commission to borrow to finance Next Generation EU
30 April: Target date for the submission of the Recovery and Resilience Plans. Twelve countries submitted plans by end of April
8 May: Launch of the Conference on the Future of Europe
June-July: The Commission raises EUR45 billion by issuing EU bonds to finance Next Generation EU
July: Based on the proposals by the Commission, the Council approves the first RRPs
August: Disbursment of the 13% advance payment to the countries whose RRP was adopted by the Council

Part A.
EMU: Past, Present and Future

By historical standards, the euro is still in its infancy. Its architecture has evolved much over its lifetime, but it remains incomplete. The chapters in this section look back at the first ten years of the euro, which ended as the financial crisis hit the world in Autumn 2008, and at the end of its second decade, in the aftermath of the Great Recession. They also examine key reform proposals that have been put forward and partly adopted over the last several years.

Whilst the survival of the euro and the integrity of the Eurozone have challenged the critics of the single currency, the economic and financial crisis laid bare the weaknesses of EMU's initial construct. Throughout the financial crisis, some features of EMU's institutional setting have been reconsidered and, in recent years, considerable efforts have been made to strengthen the Eurozone. However, its architecture is still incomplete: Banking Union and Capital Market Union still require decisive progress whilst the debate on Fiscal Union struggles to gain ground. The proposals to finalise the Eurozone emphasise the benefits of deeper integration of financial markets to smooth economic fluctuations and diversify risks, and the need for a central fiscal capacity to respond to large shocks.

Completing EMU is a political, not a technical choice. It requires accepting sharing sovereignty in key areas and building trust between member countries and between the latter and EU institutions. A key condition to make decisive progress is to overcome the pernicious division between creditor and debtor countries, with the first focussing on risk-reduction and the latter calling for risk-sharing. Rebuilding trust is essential in this endeavour. Institutionally, this requires pushing back on the tendency to introduce intergovernmental elements in EMU. While such an approach may have been warranted during the financial crisis, it cannot become a permanent feature of the economic governance framework.

In order for the single currency to succeed, Member States need to reduce national biases in decision-making that lead to an inefficient equilibrium for the Eurozone as a whole and ultimately for its individual members. The financial crisis, by sharpening the North-South divisions, has made clear who gains from the possible reform options. In the aftermath of the crisis, it is essential to recreate a "veil of ignorance" which prevents countries from processing in advance the relative gains and losses. This will require refocusing on their common goals and lowering the "political discount rate" knowing that, if EMU's fundamental issues are left lingering, the winners of today may be the losers of tomorrow.

2 The First Ten Years of the Euro*

December 2008

"It is in the nature of beginning that something new is started which cannot be expected from what may have happened before. This character of startling unexpectedness is inherent in all beginnings."
– Hannah Arendt, *The Human Condition*, 1958

1 Introduction

January 1st, 1999 marked the beginning of the Eurozone. The euro became the single currency for more than 300 million people, living in eleven countries, speaking different languages, characterised by different historical memories, traditions, customs, habits, behaviour patterns, cultures and institutions. The introduction of the euro ten years ago is a defining moment in the history of European monetary, financial, economic and political integration. It was an event of world significance.

Meanwhile, the process of enlargement of the Eurozone is on-going. Of the ten Member States that joined with the fifth enlargement, four have already joined the Eurozone, with Slovakia – which will join the Eurozone on 1 January 2009 – being the first member from the former Soviet bloc.

The Eurozone was designed to become an area of macroeconomic stability. It provides a coherent framework for stability-oriented macro-

* Co-author: Vitor Gaspar (European Commission), Vox CEPR, 24 December 2008.

economic policies. The institutional set-up of the Maastricht Treaty is centred around a single monetary policy, assigned to an independent central bank – the European Central Bank – with the primary objective of maintaining price stability over the medium-term, and national but coordinated economic policies, most notably rules aimed at ensuring budgetary discipline. Stability-oriented macroeconomic policies, in conjunction with open market economies with free competition, were considered to provide the best environment for sustainable growth and development.

2 Uncertain beginnings

Nevertheless, in the beginning, success could not be taken for granted. Otmar Issing (1999, 2008) conveys the message most vividly:

> "As a central banker involved in monetary policymaking, I have been dealing with uncertainty and its consequences for a large part of my professional life. From my experience as a member of the Board of the Bundesbank, I have vivid memories of the challenges posed by German reunification and the turbulence surrounding ERM crises. But never have I felt the impact of uncertainty as acutely as in the weeks that preceded and followed the introduction of the Euro and the birth of the single monetary policy. (...) when the Governing Council made its final announcement on the monetary policy strategy and was getting ready for the Changeover Weekend, the uncertainty was at its peak. Nothing could be taken for granted, no matter how careful the preparatory work had been."

The text transmits the "startling unexpectedness of all beginnings," to use the words of Hannah Arendt. But the challenges involved in the creation of the Eurozone went well beyond the irrevocable fixing of the exchanges rates. It is important to insist that the Eurozone is characterised by an unprecedented institutional architecture. The single monetary policy and the European Central Bank interact with a large number of EU Member States, with their own competences in the areas of economic and fiscal policies. The relationship between the single monetary policy and the multiplicity of economic and budgetary policies constitutes a novel feature of the Eurozone. Elements of tension could not be excluded – and did actually occur occasionally. Many other questions loomed large at the beginning. For example, would the transition from eleven national currencies to the euro proceed smoothly? Would the single monetary policy be perceived as credible? Would the fiscal rules – embodied in the Stability and Growth Pact – ensure budgetary discipline? Would the institutional architecture of the Eurozone prove flexible enough to withstand the pressure of unforeseen change? Would a monetary union be sustainable in the absence of a political union?

After ten years, it is clear that the conduct of monetary policy has been successful.

3 A decade of success

During the first decade, inflation in the Eurozone was, on average, close to but not below 2%, as the definition of price stability by the Governing Council prescribes. Specifically, excluding 1999 (on the ground that given transmission lags the ECB could not be held responsible for the outcome) inflation averaged 2.2% over the period. However, the deviation can be attributed to unforeseen (and sizeable) oil and commodities price developments. Excluding energy and unprocessed food prices, the average inflation rate would have been 1.8%. Perhaps more importantly the ECB has maintained well-anchored inflation expectations. Moreover, expectations have been largely unaffected by temporary price developments, that, unavoidably, affected both headline inflation and short-term inflation forecasts. The degree of credibility of the ECB is particularly remarkable given that it was, at the beginning, a new institution without a track record. Although the cash changeover, in January 2002, is estimated to have led to a temporarily higher inflation by 0.3% and created disconnect between inflation and inflation expectations, such misperception did not affect public trust on the ability of the ECB to deliver price stability.

Clearly, the success of the Eurozone goes beyond price stability.[1] During EMU's first decade, all nominal variables have displayed remarkable stability compared with previous decades (including, for example, short-term and long-term interest rates which have been low and stable). At the same time, volatility of real variables, like output, has also moderated. Although real GDP growth average has remained virtually unchanged at slightly more than 2%, during the period since 1999, more than 18 million jobs have been created (much more than in the previous decade): while it would be incorrect to attribute job creation mainly to the euro, the environment of macroeconomic stability and the ensuing labour market reforms in the run-up to EMU contributed to making the labour market more flexible.[2] Monetary unification has also been associated with important integration dynamics. Those relate to increased trade and financial integration. They derive from "One Money, One Market" mutually reinforcing virtuous circles.[3]

One of the acid tests for the macroeconomic architecture of the EMU was the interplay between the single monetary policy and decentralised fiscal policies. Would the removal of the "carrot" of Eurozone entry lead to opportunistic fiscal policies especially in traditionally undisciplined countries? Or, would the implementation of the Stability and Growth Pact imply a suboptimal degree of fiscal stabilisation? Neither fear was realised. Public sector budget deficits fell to a record low of 0.6% of GDP in 2007. This compares well with averages of close to 4% in the 1980s and 1990s. Fiscal discipline improved in particular after the reform of the Stability and Growth Pact in 2005, which strengthened the political ownership of EMU's budgetary rules. This went hand-in-hand with a correction of the pro-cyclical fiscal behaviour that traditionally affects EU countries. Indeed, the room for manoeuvre created in many countries in the past several years will allow fiscal policy to play an expansionary role in the current economic crisis.

4 The challenges ahead

Most observers deem the euro a resounding success. However, in doing so, they often forget the magnitude of the original challenge. In this short article, we tried to look at the first decade of the Eurozone going back to its beginnings.

The story is not over. Significant challenges lie ahead. As we write the world is living a financial and economic crisis of truly global proportions. For the Eurozone, the global crisis brings into sharp focus the challenges of maintaining macroeconomic stability and financial stability.

During the crisis, the role of the ECB and the Eurosystem in managing liquidity has been very visible. Liquidity management strived to maintain orderly market conditions in money markets and more broadly to contribute to orderly market conditions. It aimed, at the same time, to mitigate financial stability risks and disturbances. By doing so, it has muted the effects on economic activity. Membership of the Eurozone also contributed to insulating participating countries from some adverse effects that the crisis might otherwise have had on their economies.

The financial and economic crisis is leading to unprecedented co-operation and co-ordination at European and at global levels. One particularly telling example is the cooperation between the Federal Reserve, the ECB, and other major central banks to manage liquidity provision globally. However, it is also clear that the crisis made apparent the need to enhance co-operation and surveillance at the European and at the global level. One important example is the need to strengthen co-operation between supervisory authorities responsible for large cross-border financial institutions. Crisis prevention – including the overall framework of regulation and supervision – and crisis management are also sharply in focus.

Since December 2007, the US has been declared in recession whilst the Eurozone has recorded two consecutive quarters negative growth, and the slowdown in economic activity is spreading globally. It is a unique, unprecedented historical development. Uncertainty is unusually high. Clearly, the crisis constitutes a major challenge for the Eurozone. The first decade was truly a decade in between two major challenges. It is worth remembering the magnitude of the original challenge in order to use the crisis as an opportunity to strengthen governance at the European and global level. It has often been the case that crisis and uncertainty broke free from the resistances of the past and begat the wonders of the unexpected new.

Notes

[1] For a comprehensive assessment of the first decade of the euro, see European Commission (2008).

[2] As shown by Buti, Röger and Turrini (2009), the tightening of the fiscal rules after the launch of the second phase of EMU in 1993 – culminated in the adoption of the Stability and Growth Pact in 1997 – boosted the incentives to adopt labour market reforms for electorally motivated governments.

[3] See contributions to Buti, Deroose, Gaspar and Nogueira Martins (2010). Mongelli (2008) provides a critical overview of the argument.

3 The Commission's Proposals for Stronger EU Economic Governance*

October 2010

1 What are the main goals?

In September 2010, the European Commission adopted a comprehensive set of proposals to reform and to broaden EU economic governance. The reform package is a step in a much broader effort to incorporate the lessons of the crisis in the EU policy framework, to prevent economic instabilities and, ultimately, to protect workers and taxpayers.

Yet while recent comments have focused on individual sections of the package, in this chapter we provide an overview of all elements and clarify the thinking behind them.

The Commission's legislative package is a blueprint to tackle the weaknesses of EU fiscal and macroeconomic surveillance revealed by the Great Recession. Some of these weaknesses were difficult to anticipate, others had been more or less visible. While we all would have preferred avoiding the financial crisis, there is an equally broad agreement that this crisis should not be wasted – there are lessons to be learned. It may also be worth noting that public finances did not cause the crisis, yet stronger rules are needed now to put public finances back to a sustainable path.

The Commission's deliberations only mark the beginning of a more involved legislative process. It is up to the Council and the European Parliament, in line with the responsibilities assigned to them by the Treaty, to review the Commission's proposals and consider amendments.

Assuming the main thrust of the initial package is preserved, EU governance will undergo important changes. Changes that will make it more

---

* Co-author: Martin Larch (European Commission), Vox CEPR, 14 October 2010.

effective in important areas of surveillance: first, detecting potentially harmful fiscal and economic developments, and, second, enforcing the agreed set of rules.

The onset of the financial crisis has triggered a lively debate in both the academic and policy arena on how to improve EU economic governance. Four distinct areas of discussion have emerged: 1) monitoring of fiscal developments, 2) the link between macroeconomic imbalances and public finances, 3) the enforcement of EU rules, and 4) crisis management and resolution.

Reflecting these main areas of discussion, the Commission had already outlined the key directions of its reform plan in May 2010 followed by a more detailed plan at the end of June 2010 (European Commission 2010a, c). The concrete reform package adopted in September 2010 comprises six pieces of draft legislation that can be divided into two pillars (European Commission 2010d). The first relates to fiscal governance, the second to broader macroeconomic governance. Within each of the two pillars, proposals can in turn be split into two groups: one is related with new surveillance tools, both European and national, the second with new tools of enforcement. A schematic representation of the whole package is provided in Figure 1.

Figure 1 Schematic overview of the Commission reform proposals

	Fiscal governance	Macroeconomic governance
Surveillance	• Preventive arm of the SGP: principles of prudent fiscal policy making (amendment to Regulation (EC) 1466/97) • Corrective arm of SGP: benchmark for sufficiently diminishing debt ratio (amendment to Regulation (EC) 1467/97) • Minimum requirements of national fiscal frameworks (new draft directive)	New procedures for monitoring, preventing and correcting macroeconomic imbalances (new draft regulation)
Enforcement	New disincentives/sanctions in case of noncompliance in preventive and corrective arm of SGP (new draft regulation)	New disincentives/sanctions in case of non-compliance with new macro surveillance procedure (new draft regulation)

Source: European Commission.

The only element not covered by the Commission's legislative package, but mentioned in the broader reform plan outlined in the Commission communication of 12 May 2010, is the crisis resolution mechanisms. Specific instruments dealing with crisis resolution had already been deliberated there as a direct response to the mounting sovereign debt crisis.[1]

2 What is new and why do we need it?

On the surface, each individual element encapsulates a response to weaknesses revealed by the crisis. Starting with fiscal surveillance, the Great Recession indicated, not for the first time, that Member States had missed an opportunity to take advantage of the good years preceding the crisis to create fiscal space. Important revenue windfalls were partly used to increase spending just to find out shortly after that expenditure levels were not sustainable.

In order to avoid such unfortunate patterns in the future, the intention under the preventive arm of the Stability and Growth Pact is to use a prudent rate of medium-term economic growth as benchmark for assessing the sustainability of government expenditure growth. Departures from such a benchmark are allowed if they are matched by discretionary revenue measures (rather than by temporary revenue windfalls); uncovered deviations would be in conflict with prudent fiscal policymaking.

Prior to the crisis, but especially during the crisis, the dynamics of government debt were increasingly driven by elements other than the deficit. It also became clear that with declining average economic growth it would no longer be sufficient to respect the 3% of GDP reference value to ensure a declining debt ratio. As a result of this, and in a bid to control debt developments, the legislative package proposes a benchmark for sufficiently diminishing debt ratios.

Still under the heading of fiscal surveillance, the package encourages Member States to improve domestic fiscal frameworks. The rationale for this proposal is twofold: a) as evidenced by past experience, the enforcement of EU fiscal rules cannot be expected to derive only from EU rules. Domestic budgetary arrangements need to be consistent with the obligations under the pact. And b) there is abundant empirical evidence that fiscal performance tends to improve with the quality of domestic fiscal governance.

The most important extension of EU economic governance implied by the Commission's legislative package relates to the prevention and correction of macroeconomic imbalances. The respective proposal addresses the most serious and particularly bitter lesson of the crisis – a lesson for the economic profession as a whole – namely that fiscal discipline, coupled with low and stable inflation, is not sufficient to guarantee overall macro-financial stability. The new surveillance framework mapped out in the package aims at detecting, as early as possible, macroeconomic imbalances so as to allow a timely formulation of corrective policies.

Finally, the package encompasses a new battery of graduated disincentives and sanctions. While media coverage has mostly, if not exclusively, focused on this aspect it is important to stress that sanctions should not be seen in isolation. They are an integral part of the whole set of proposals in both the fiscal and the macroeconomic pillar and are meant to strengthen the enforcement of the rules. The degree of deterrence of existing sanctions, those under the provisions of the corrective arm of the Stability and Growth Pact, was low because they can kick in only at the very end of the surveillance process.

3 Would the new tools have made a difference?

Once implemented, it will take a number of years before we will be able to form a solid judgement on the merits of the reformed EU economic governance. This notwithstanding, there are a number of elements that give us sufficient confidence about the effectiveness of the new set of rules, especially when compared with the current Stability and Growth Pact framework.

As regards macroeconomic surveillance, simulations on past data provide encouraging evidence of the potential utility of the proposed instruments. In particular, an alert mechanism based on thresholds for a scoreboard of relevant macroeconomic variables (the current account balance, net foreign assets the real effective exchange rates house prices, the government debt ratio and private sector credit as a percentage of GDP) would have signalled emerging imbalances in Spain and Ireland already in 2004, and even more clearly in 2007.

Figure 2 shows how changes in the external balance ahead of the crisis went along with increases in government debt during the crisis. The exclusive focus on fiscal developments did not capture the mounting risks for public finances, inter alia because revenue windfalls embellished the actual budgetary stance.

Figure 2 External imbalance and government debt

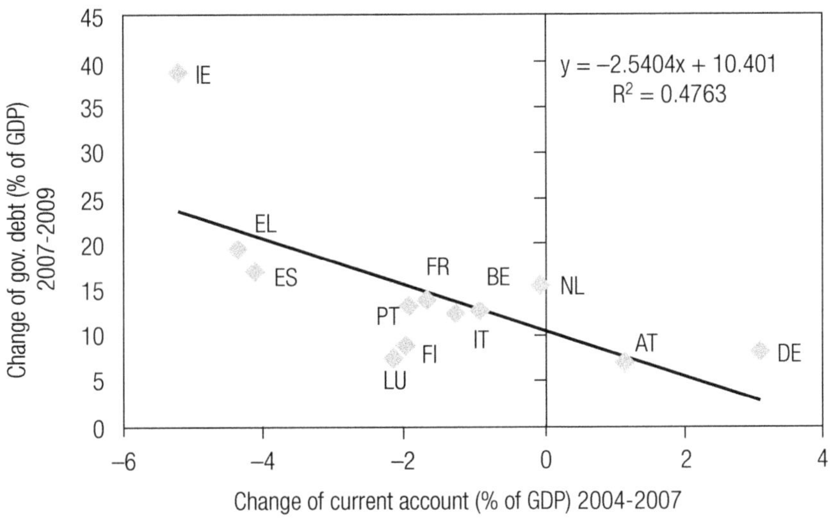

Source: European Commission.

In practice, the scoreboard-based alert mechanism would not automatically lead to EU policy recommendations. According to the Commission's proposal this would happen only after an in-depth analysis of the country concerned. But the alert mechanism would constitute a first important step in the new surveillance mechanism and seems to give useful and timely signals.

Turning to the concept of prudent fiscal policymaking, the main reform proposal under the preventive arm of the Stability and Growth Pact, a simple exercise on past data also provides some interesting insights. Taking again the two emblematic country cases, Spain and Ireland, Figure 3 sets out the annual rate of growth of real government primary expenditure in 2000-2007 against a benchmark of prudent medium-term economic growth, where the benchmark is defined as the ten-year forward-looking average of the long-term projections (covering a horizon of 50 years) used by the Commission to assess the long-term sustainability of public finances of its Member States (details of the projection can be found in European Commission and the Economic Policy Committee 2008).

The two graphs clearly show that in both countries primary expenditure outpaced a sustainable rate of medium-term economic growth in most years, especially in the 2-3 years preceding the crises when public coffers benefited from extra revenues linked to a housing and an asset price boom. If the concept of prudent fiscal policymaking had been part of the formal surveillance process, concerns would have been raised earlier and, more importantly, the respective surveillance instruments would have been deployed to correct deviations. Under current provisions no formal steps were possible because both Ireland and Spain had achieved their medium-term budgetary objectives and/or were running a budgetary surplus.

The Great Depression marked a clear break in post-WWII economic history. It brought to a sudden and, for most observers, unexpected, close to a period which was, with the benefit of hindsight, ironically dubbed the "Great Moderation."

According to the commonly accepted paradigm underpinning the "Great Moderation," keeping the fiscal house in order and inflation low and stable was sufficient to safeguard overall macroeconomic stability. By these standards, most European countries were doing just fine in the years preceding the crisis. In 2007, government deficits in EU Member States had reached the lowest levels in more than two decades and inflation was generally low and stable almost everywhere, especially in the Eurozone.

Admittedly, the 2005 reform of the Stability and Growth Pact, the EU's fiscal governance framework, had revealed some weaknesses, especially in the area of monitoring and enforcement; yet following the 2005 reform, things seemed to be working pretty smoothly.

Then came the crisis. It imposed a sobering assessment of not only macroeconomic prospects. It also called for a fresh look at macroeconomic policymaking as a whole including economic policy coordination in the EU. While there is no doubt that existing EU instruments helped stave off a full-scale depression, the Great Recession has revealed scope for improving and broadening economic governance in the EU. The legislative package of draft reform proposals presented in this contribution is the Commission's response to the gaps and weaknesses in economic and budgetary surveillance exposed by the crisis.

Figure 3 Expenditure growth vis-à-vis a prudent rate of economic growth

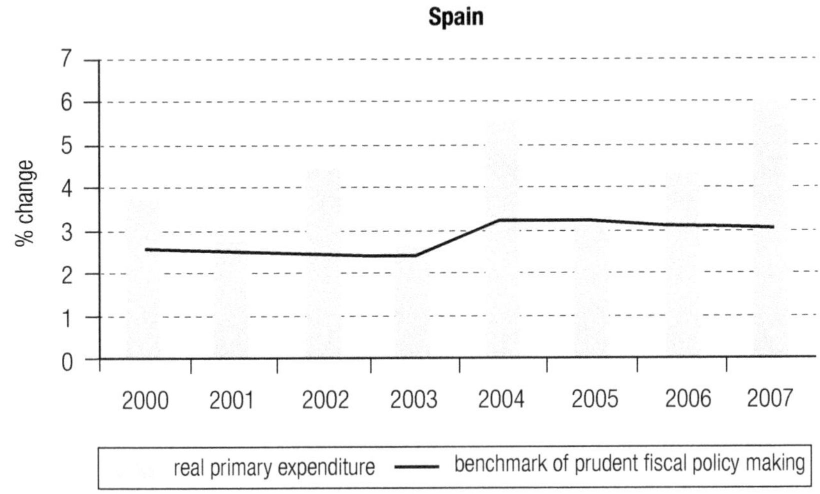

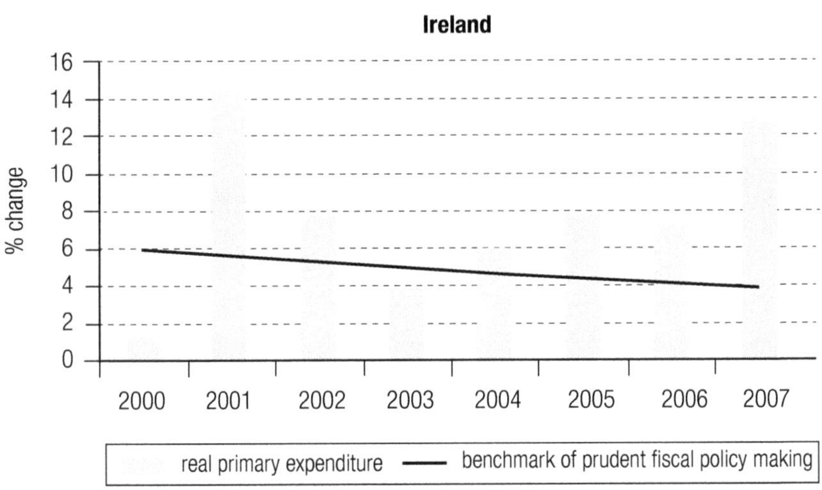

Note: The reference for the benchmark of prudent fiscal-policymaking is the 10-year forward-looking average of the long-term projections of potential output growth used by the European Commission to assess the long-term sustainability of public finances. The benchmark is set equal to this 10-year forward-looking average if a country has already achieved its medium-term objective (MTO). It is set one percentage point below the 10-year forward-looking average if a country has not achieved its MTO yet.

Source: European Commission.

4 Will it work this time?

Like all real-life reforms, the Commission's proposal can be described as the result of constrained optimisation. First, after the very difficult and, above all, lengthy adoption process of the Lisbon Treaty, the work underpinning the reform proposals took the provisions of EU primary law as given. Second, and linked to the first, although the crisis proved beyond any doubt that more economic policy co-ordination is needed, there is little appetite among Member States for more centralisation in the area of fiscal policymaking.

Keeping these constraints in mind, the legislative package represents a fairly encompassing and daring reform of EU economic governance. Moreover, the package is not the only improvement in EU economic governance deliberated in the recent past. Other important steps include: a) the new EU financial supervision framework adopted in early 2010; b) measures to deal with sovereign debt crises agreed by the Council and the Commission in May 2010; and c) a more effective annual calendar for assessing economic policymaking in the EU Member States, the so-called "European Semester."

When finally implemented, the actual performance of the new set of rules will also depend on how Member States exercise their responsibility under the provisions of the Treaty. At the end of the day, the reform cannot obviate one of the pivotal features of EU economic governance which Peter Sutherland, a former EU Commissioner, succinctly described as the inherent tension between acknowledging the obvious inadequacy of national procedures to confront continental and global challenges while preserving absolute national sovereignty in fiscal, budgetary, and macroeconomic matters.

Nevertheless, in addition to the sound and comprehensive nature of the proposals, what makes us reasonably confident about their effectiveness going forward is that they will interact with an increased degree of attention on the part of financial markets. In fact, the crisis has invited back an older player, which for a long time – as long as the existing rules were backed by results – had taken a back seat. In the aftermath of the crisis there is sufficient awareness that, unless we prefer the merciless judgement of market forces, the credibility vis-à-vis markets can only be re-gained by following agreed rules.

Note

[1] On 9/10 May 2010 the ECOFIN Council decided on a comprehensive package of measures. It approved the rescue package for Greece, the European Financial Stability Mechanism, worth up to €60 billion, and the European Financial Stability Facility, worth up to €440 billion.

4 Stronger EU Economic Governance: A Response to the Critics*

October 2010

1 Common analysis but diverging conclusions

Severe crises trigger reforms, and reforms trigger controversy. The ongoing reform of EU economic governance is no different. It is an inevitable and necessary consequence of the worst financial and economic dislocations Europe has witnessed in decades. The legitimate and most pertinent question is: Has the Commission found the right answers?

A number of prominent observers have serious doubts. They either believe the Commission's proposals aim at the right targets but use the wrong tools, or aim at the wrong targets. Here we examine the main points of criticism in turn.

In their contribution of 14 October 2010, Francesco Giavazzi and Luigi Spaventa (2010) focus on the so-called "excessive imbalance procedure," a new mechanism that, if eventually adopted, would broaden EU economic governance with a view to identifying potentially harmful macroeconomic imbalances.

While they remain silent about the other elements of the reform package, they do not leave the slightest trace of doubt about what they think of the proposed excessive imbalance procedure. They call it "an empty and useless exercise." This harsh judgement is motivated by two considerations. First, Giavazzi and Spaventa believe that monitoring and correcting macroeconomic imbalances will be a difficult and potentially contentious exercise. Second, they maintain that instead of monitoring

---

* Co-author: Martin Larch (European Commission), Vox CEPR, 25 October 2010.

an indicative scoreboard of macro variables, attention should focus on credit growth, which, if unchecked, is, in their view, the main source of macroeconomic instabilities.

Interestingly, we broadly agree with these two points yet strongly disagree with their conclusions.

To start, if one accepts that fiscal discipline alone is not enough to ensure the stability of the euro – and Giavazzi and Spaventa would seem to do so – one also needs to accept the respective challenges. Arguing that monitoring and correcting macroeconomic imbalances would be difficult cannot really prevent us from addressing the challenge.

True, the institutional and procedural side of the macro surveillance mechanism put forward in the Commission's proposals is new, and we may not be able to fully anticipate all practical difficulties or pitfalls. Nevertheless, it should also be stressed that the Commission is not a complete novice in the field.

When taking stock of the first ten years of the Economic and Monetary Union in 2006/07, the Commission, on top of reviewing the upsides of the project, also – and unmistakeably – pointed to the accumulation of macroeconomic imbalances in the Eurozone arguing even then in favour of a broader economic surveillance process (European Commission 2008). As political economists would have predicted, it took a serious crisis to gather the necessary consensus to broaden economic surveillance.

We also agree with Giavazzi and Spaventa when they say that credit growth should be closely monitored. In fact, we read that part of their contribution as providing support to the plan for broader macroeconomic surveillance. As indicated in the Commission communication of 30 June 2010, private-sector credit growth would indeed be one of the key indicators of the proposed mechanism (European Commission 2010c). The more general idea is to monitor private debt alongside public debt to the extent that the former, if out of hand, carries the risk of becoming a liability for governments.

2 The big picture

If the tone chosen by Giavazzi and Spaventa is rather defiant, we can only ascribe it to the fact that they may have taken a partial view of the ongoing reform process. In chapter 3, we made a clear point: the legislative package adopted in September 2010 is just one element of a more comprehensive blueprint that seeks to strengthen economic surveillance along various dimensions including, in particular, financial surveillance.

The same reminder goes to Guido Tabellini (2010), who on 5 October 2010 seems to have taken a fairly narrow reading of the Commission's reform proposals of 29 September. He suggests that the Commission, rather than trying to mend the Stability and Growth Pact, which he believes has failed, should focus on financial supervision.

There is no mention of the significant work carried out by the European Commission since the end of 2008 to build a new supervisory architecture. And there is no mention either that as a result of this work the Parliament has, earlier this year, given its green light to a new system of financial supervision in Europe addressing many of the shortcomings revealed during the crisis. By way of example, the European Systemic Risk Board (ESRB), one of the key actors in the new supervisory framework, will also serve as interface between a broader macroeconomic surveillance and financial developments.

Maybe in Tabellini's view the new system does not go far enough. Perhaps he is of the opinion that sovereignty in the field of financial supervision should be further centralised, and we tend to agree. At the same time, it should be acknowledged that, in view of the extent and the depth of the crisis, the Commission and the Council are working on different fronts.

In actual fact, improving financial supervision has been one of the very first preoccupations at the EU level. This is why the respective legislative works are more advanced than those on fiscal and economic governance. Moreover, and at the risk of repeating ourselves, the reform proposals of September 2010 are not meant to provide universal solutions to all possible ills; they are to be considered in conjunction with the overall response to the crisis.

3 Enforcement, yes please. Sanctions, no thanks

Several observers, including the three mentioned above, question more or less categorically the effectiveness of the proposed system of sanctions; the main argument is that, at the end of the day, Member States can always find a majority to block fines. This is a fair point, and we may even agree with Charles Wyplosz (2010), who on 4 October 2010 said that "imposing a fine on a friendly sovereign state with a democratically elected government is an unknown experiment" and that imposing sanctions may give rise to anti-European sentiments.

On the other hand, sanctions or disincentives are part of the institutional history of all EU Member States. Admittedly, they are easier to apply at the national level than at the supranational level, but they are not entirely new. In the area of competition policy, the Commission regularly obliges Member States to undo certain policies if they are not compatible with EU law. In the area of regional policy, Member States are frequently asked to return EU money in case of irregularities. Of course these measures are not popular, but they are necessary.

The strictest reservation concerning new sanctions was advanced by Paul De Grauwe (2010). Going well beyond any justifiable doubt about whether fines will ever be applied in practice, in his Vox column of 4 October 2010 he raises a fundamental issue of legitimacy. In particular, he contests the proposed system of graduated sanctions on the ground it would conflict with the principle of "no taxation without representation."

Unfortunately, questioning the democratic legitimacy of EU institutions has become a frequent and cheap way of criticising things that originate in Brussels. But then, one should keep in mind that, with the Lisbon Treaty, the Commission President is elected by the European Parliament and that the Commission as a whole is responsible to the same Parliament. Moreover, the new Treaty also vests the assembly of directly elected representatives with the right to vote the Commission out of office (see Art 17.8). Clearly, such provisions are not likely to impress hardcore Eurosceptics, but they certainly disqualify the claim the Commission lacks democratic legitimacy. Besides, sanctions would not be imposed by the Commission. They would be linked to a decision of the Council in all steps of the surveillance procedure.

Finally, if taken to the letter, De Grauwe's argument would, of course, question many existing rules and institutions, first and foremost the independence of central banks, including that of the ECB.

4 What is not "empty and useless"

To be fair, there are elements in the Commission's reform package that were received somewhat more favourably, at least in principle. These elements include: (i) the idea of asking Member States to upgrade their domestic fiscal frameworks with a view to making them consistent with the obligations under the treaty; (ii) the plan to use a prudent rate of medium-term economic growth as benchmark for assessing the sustainability of government expenditure plans; and (iii) the intention under the corrective arm of the Stability and Growth Pact to have an operational definition of when a debt ratio in excess of 60% of GDP is considered to be sufficiently diminishing.

Charles Wyplosz, for instance, explicitly welcomes the idea of strengthening national fiscal frameworks yet thinks the Commission proposal does not go far enough. In fact, the corresponding legislative act lists what we call minimum requirements to domestic fiscal frameworks, not optimal configurations. There are two good reasons for choosing this approach. First, since national fiscal policymaking remains a national prerogative, the legal basis for deliberating budgetary institutions and procedures at the EU level is fairly narrow. Asking for more than minimum requirements would only be possible with a Treaty change, an avenue few are ready to consider (although the Franco-German agreement of 18 October 2010 would seem to qualify this judgement). Second, budgetary frameworks need to allow for national idiosyncrasies; one-size-fits-all solutions do not exist.

On the proposed benchmark for a sufficiently diminishing debt ratio, in his 7 October 2010 Vox column, Paolo Manasse (2010) sees a major practical difficulty. The application of the benchmark, he warns, would lead to pro-cyclical fiscal policies – something the Commission has always condemned and tried to avert. While Manasse is right about the Commission's concern with pro-cyclical policies, he overlooks an important element of the proposed benchmark: it would not be applied in a mechanical way. The Commission has always been clear about this. If approved, the benchmark would not automatically trigger surveillance procedures. It would simply serve as a first point of reference followed and complemented by an assessment of other relevant factors, including in particular cyclical conditions. The risk of trading off diminishing debt ratios for pro-cyclical policies is, therefore, fairly remote.

5 Macroeconomic policy analysis in flux

Taking into account the type and size of challenges we are facing in the aftermath of the financial crisis, it would have been truly surprising if the Commission's proposals for stronger EU governance had been received with unconditional praise.

One important part of the criticism originates in the frustration with past experience. The crisis laid bare weaknesses that cannot simply be dismissed as teething problems, especially since the system underwent a first major reform just five years ago. There is a palpable scepticism about whether, under current institutional arrangements, the system can be mended at all. We tend to condemn the devil we know.

Another important part of the controversy surrounding the Commission's proposals clearly has to do with the fact that the crisis invalidated important building blocks of the prevailing macroeconomic paradigm. The economic profession is rethinking macroeconomic policymaking. For the moment, there are only painfully established facts. Fiscal discipline in combination with low and stable inflation is not enough to guarantee overall macroeconomic stability and economic policy needs new instruments of supervision and new instruments of surveillance. The scope for reform is blatant.

To pretend the legislative package tabled by the Commission in September 2010 was the perfect and only answer to the lessons of the crisis would be foolish. However, as we have repeatedly pointed out, the package has to be seen in conjunction with the other reform initiatives undertaken by the Commission and the Council in the recent past. Some of these other initiatives go into the direction vindicated by the some of the critics; possibly not as far as some may wish, but nevertheless.

Symptomatically, the sharpest criticism is levelled against the proposals aimed at occupying virgin surveillance territory, that is, against monitoring and correcting macroeconomic imbalances. For sure, this new arrangement will confront us with difficulties. With the benefit of hindsight we will find out it was not perfect and adjustments will have to be made. But then, few can afford the luxury of hindsight. Policymaking remains an exercise carried out under uncertainty.

5 Smoothing Economic Shocks in the Eurozone: The Untapped Potential of the Financial Union*

August 2016

1 The importance of resilience to shocks in the Eurozone

The prime objective of Europe's Economic and Monetary Union (EMU) is to foster stability and economic growth. But for this to happen, the EMU needs to be able to: first, better prevent crises by fostering sustainable fiscal and economic policies in each of the participating Member States; and second, better absorb shocks – individually and collectively – whenever they occur.

Most idiosyncratic economic shocks can be smoothed through the normal operation of national fiscal stabilisers. This requires suitably resilient economies, and the maintenance of appropriate fiscal buffers over the economic cycle. However, when large shocks occur, market pressure can deprive individual countries of their fiscal stabilisers, as was the case during the recent debt crisis, which in turn affects the Eurozone as a whole. This is the reason all mature monetary unions also involve mechanisms for cross-border shock absorption. These stabilisation mechanisms can take the form of temporary fiscal transfers (public risk-sharing) or of financial flows linked to the operation of credit and capital markets (private risk-sharing). In the EMU, preventing unsustainable policies and absorbing shocks individually and collectively did not work well before or during the crisis, leading to significant economic and social divergence across the Eurozone.

* Co-authors: José Leandro and Plamen Nikolov (European Commission), Vox CEPR, 25 August 2016.

This is illustrated in Figure 1 below. It shows that the difference in the cyclical positions of the Eurozone Member States shrank immediately after 1999, the year the single currency was launched. This was a welcome effect of the euro.

Figure 1 Output gap dispersion in EZ19 (%)

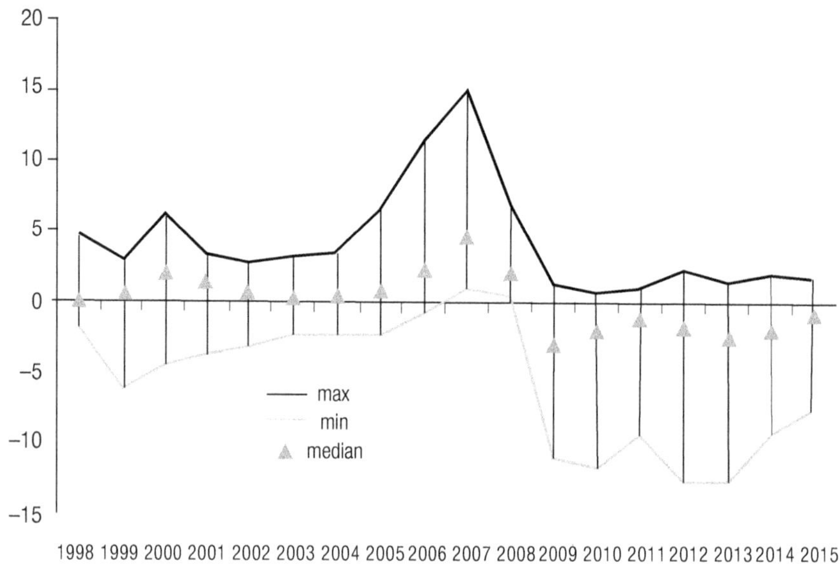

Source: European Commission.

But the boom years preceding the Global Crisis and the subsequent bust led to a widening of the output gap differences among the Member States, suggesting an increased exposure to asymmetric shocks. These legacies from both the boom and the bust years call for efforts to mitigate their negative economic impact.

Shock absorption across state borders is a very important element in reducing the negative impact of large asymmetric shocks. The proper functioning of cross-border risk-sharing reduces the impact of output loss on consumption and prevents disparities from becoming entrenched.

This is the reason why different channels of cross-border risk-sharing feature prominently in the so-called Five Presidents' Report, the roadmap towards the completion of the EMU, issued in June 2015 (Juncker et al. 2015). The report pays particular attention to enhancing the shock absorption capacity of the Eurozone, both through better integrated financial and capital markets (private risk-sharing) and through a mechanism of fiscal stabilisation among Eurozone Member States (public risk-sharing).

Below, we evaluate how cross-border risk-sharing has functioned in the Eurozone and compare it with the US, a fully-fledged monetary, fiscal and financial union. We conclude that cross-border mechanisms for shock absorption in the Eurozone are comparatively weaker. This means that an equivalent loss of output in the US and the Eurozone leads to a much deeper decline in consumption for the latter. Furthermore, the evidence shows that better consumption smoothing in the US is mainly due to well-functioning capital and labour market cross-border channels. Therefore, enhancing private risk-sharing among the Eurozone Member States, especially through deeper capital markets (e.g. by developing equity and securitisation markets), remains a policy priority.

2 Cross-border risk-sharing channels

Cross-border risk-sharing is linked to integration between countries – first and foremost, economic and financial integration, but also at least to some extent, political and institutional. The channels of cross-border risk-sharing can be divided into two broad categories: private and public.

The private channels of cross-border risk-sharing work through access to foreign financial markets, including through foreign capital markets and cross-border loans and deposits, as well as through labour compensation generated across borders.

The cross-border provision of financial services by financial institutions and markets is one of the main ways that private risk-sharing operates. Residents of a country that experiences a negative output shock can smooth their consumption through income streams generated by financial assets held in another jurisdiction, which is unaffected by the shock. This is the capital market channel of risk-sharing. It operates *ex ante* because when the shock hits foreign capital, market income is already available to those who have invested in a market shielded from the shock.

Alternatively, residents of a country hit by a negative output shock can secure consumption levels by borrowing. This can also be done indirectly, for example when public borrowing is used to compensate for the loss of tax revenues after asymmetric shocks in order to sustain government expenditure levels and, in turn, smooth household consumption. This is called the credit market or savings channel of risk-sharing. It operates *ex post*, since those affected apply for and receive funds from a location that is unaffected by the shock before being able to smooth consumption.

The operation of both capital and credit market channels is greatly facilitated by integrated financial markets and competition among financial institutions. This requires the adoption of a legal framework for competitive cross-border financial intermediation (notably insolvency laws and accounting standards), the creation of an efficient financial infrastructure, and the institutional safeguards to ensure stable financial systems—most notably single bank supervision, single bank resolution and a common bank deposit insurance. Only under such conditions can money be truly single in a monetary union.

Another private channel of risk-sharing that operates through streams of cross-border income is the cross-border labour compensation channel. Residents of a country in which there is a negative shock to output could smooth their consumption with labour income generated in another jurisdiction. This channel requires free movement of labour as well as the prerequisites for a high degree of labour mobility, among which are investment in human capital and the portability of social security rights.

Naturally, these private channels are present among Eurozone Member States, but, as we will argue, their role for cross-border risk-sharing needs to be augmented.

The public channels of cross-border risk-sharing involve some form of fiscal redistribution between countries. Such redistribution can take the form of, for example, cross-border transfers, social protection, including a common unemployment insurance scheme, or cross-border financing of public investment.

The public channels naturally involve a higher degree of political and institutional integration between participating countries, including a system of common decision-making that ensures democratic legitimacy and accountability.

The initial EMU design did not envisage a substantial role for cross-border public risk-sharing through common fiscal support. Fiscal and political union were assumed, or hoped, to develop over time. To date, the EU budget remains quite small in comparison to the sum of the Member States' national budgets and is mainly designed to support structural convergence rather than to smooth shocks across countries.

3 What is the size of the various risk-sharing channels in the Eurozone and the US?

A recent study by the European Commission evaluates the relative roles of private and public risk-sharing in the Eurozone in comparison to the US (European Commission 2016c). The results of the study clearly show that the Eurozone lags significantly behind the US in insuring against asymmetric shocks, and highlights the untapped potential of private channels of risk-sharing.

A comparison with the US is relevant because the US can be seen as an economic and monetary union that has developed the necessary institutional framework for insuring against large localised shocks by cross-border means. It is a functioning banking and Capital Markets Union and it also has provisions for smoothing of shocks by fiscal means.

Risk-sharing between states in the US is well-studied, including in a canonical paper by Asdrubali et al. (1996). The European Commission's study uses the same methodology to gauge the relative importance of the different channels of risk-sharing in the Eurozone and the US. Figure 2

Figure 2 Cross-border risk-sharing through different channels (% of total asymmetric shock to output)

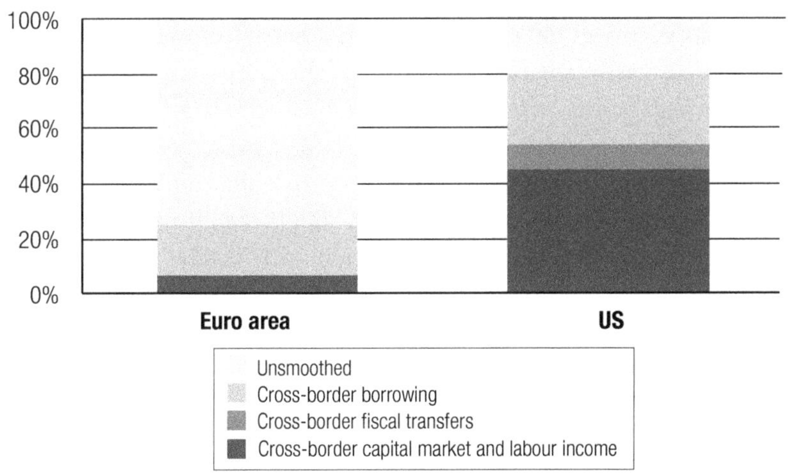

Source: European Commission.

summarises the key results. First, the direct impact of output shocks on consumption is almost four times bigger in the Eurozone – close to 80%. In other words, a 1% decline in GDP leads to a decline of about 0.8% in consumption in the Eurozone, against only 0.2% in the US. This shows the huge potential for improving cross-border shock absorption in general, including by completing the architecture of the EMU.

Second, cross-border risk-sharing through fiscal means is virtually non-existent in the EMU, though neither is it particularly strong in the US. This does not mean that fiscal policy does not have a stabilisation role within each Eurozone member state. The opposite is in fact true, since the average size of government in the Eurozone is larger than in the US. However, the results show that fiscal shock absorption takes place almost exclusively through national fiscal stabilisers. When large idiosyncratic shocks occur, as they did during the financial crisis, this can lead to a sub-optimal level of stabilisation not just for each Member State individually but also for the Eurozone as a whole.

Finally, the difference with the US is particularly striking in terms of the cross-border capital and labour income channels. Shock absorption through these channels in the Eurozone amounts to around 6% of the shock, while in the US it represents over 40%. So far as the labour income channel is concerned, there is a relatively high share of commuter workers in the US who cross state borders to work, whilst in the Eurozone this phenomenon is common only in Luxembourg. In addition, the US has very well developed capital markets that operate across state borders, whilst firm financing in much of the Eurozone is still predominately through banks, often based on established relationships with local branches.

Underpinning the high share of private risk-sharing in the US is the Federal Deposit Insurance Corporation, supported by a public backstop. This is crucial for a complete integration of financial markets and to maximise the shock absorption role through the private channel.

4 Conclusion

The public debate on risk-sharing in the Eurozone largely revolves around the role of the public sector. Views are highly divided. There are those who, in the spirit of solidarity, strongly argue in favour of a centralised fiscal capacity to allow for the temporary transfer of funds to countries in case of large shocks. Others strongly oppose the idea, underscoring the risk of moral hazard and permanent transfers. While fiscal risk-sharing can and, in our view, should play a more prominent role in the Eurozone going forward, this debate misses the main point. Even if the Eurozone had the same degree of cross-border fiscal risk-sharing as the US, the overall degree of shock absorption would still lag significantly behind. The more important deficiencies are in the banking sector and the capital markets. This is where we should prioritise our policy efforts in the near term.

In the aftermath of the crisis, the EU has taken ambitious steps towards a Banking Union. Key elements of the project – notably the Single Supervisory Mechanism, the European Systemic Risk Board, and the foundations of the Single Resolution Mechanism – have been put in place. But other crucial elements are still missing mainly due to political hesitations in some Member States. We need faster progress towards a common backstop to the Single Resolution Fund and an agreement on a common deposit insurance scheme. This should go hand in hand with a further reduction of risks in the financial sector, strengthening the availability of "bail in-able" funds and further steps in eliminating the scope of national options and discretions in prudential requirements. Only then will the Banking Union be completed, creating the necessary conditions for more cross-border provision of financial services and a higher level of shock absorption in the Eurozone.

Equally important are the measures to create a Capital Markets Union in Europe. It will reduce firms' dependence on bank financing and will allow access to cheaper sources of funding. This will improve financial integration by cross-border ownership of financial assets and increase the role of cross-border risk-sharing on capital markets.

A financial union – a fully-fledged Banking Union and unified capital markets – is the most effective way to increase the resilience of the Eurozone as a whole, and each of its Member States, to economic shocks while at the same time reducing the need to resort to public risk-sharing.

6 Completing EMU*

July 2017

1 EMU has been reformed but is still in an unsustainable equilibrium

Despite reforms during the crisis, EMU remains incomplete. There is by now consensus in both political circles (see the Rome Declaration of March 2017) as well as academic ones (e.g. Enderlein, Letta et al. 2016, Bénassy-Quéré and Giavazzi 2017) on the need to take further steps to complete EMU. There are, however, still diverging views on the problems that need to be overcome and, partly as a consequence, on the measures to be taken. Against this background, the Commission has re-launched the debate, with a Reflection Paper on the deepening of the EMU (European Commission 2017c).[1] It builds on the proposals in the Five Presidents' Report (Juncker et al. 2015) and suggests a series of concrete steps on how to complete EMU by 2025. But it also marks an important shift in one important aspect: the need for a better balance between common tools for shock absorption (i.e. risk-sharing) and a greater role for markets as incentives for fiscal and financial discipline (i.e. risk-reduction).

Despite the progress in recent years, EMU today continues to rest on an unsustainable equilibrium (Figure 1): the incomplete nature of the financial union (Banking Union and Capital Markets Union) and the absence of a fiscal stabilisation function for the Eurozone as a whole imply insufficient mechanisms for the absorption of shocks (both via private and public channels). At the same time, the combination of the current asymmetric

---

* Co-authors: Servaas Deroose, José Leandro and Gabriele Giudice (European Commission), Vox CEPR, 13 July 2017.

Figure 1 EMU today: An unsustainable equilibrium

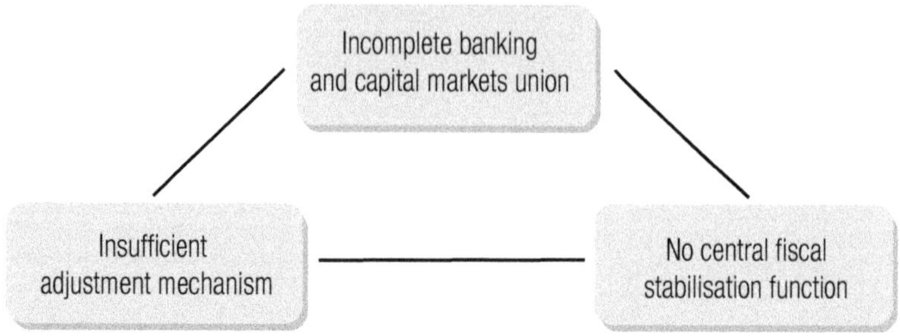

Source: Own elaboration.

nature of the surveillance processes – which put more emphasis on correcting fiscal or external deficits and has less influence on how to handle significant surpluses – coupled with the absence of a central fiscal stabilisation mechanism, means that it is impossible to achieve simultaneously an appropriate fiscal stance for the Eurozone as a whole and an optimal distribution of the fiscal effort enabling the right balance to be struck between stabilisation and sustainability at the national level.[2] This combination leads to an overburdening of monetary policy for stabilisation purposes and an inappropriate policy mix, especially at the zero lower bound for policy interest rates. This equilibrium is even more precarious as high debt and insufficient reforms in several countries make them vulnerable and hamper adjustment, within and across countries. In addition, it has been achieved as the product of several *ultima ratio* decisions, with agreements often partial and not entirely owned by all the sides.

There is no consensus on the way forward. The debate so far has been dominated by two main camps with significantly different views on the interplay between solidarity and responsibility, risk-sharing and risk-reductions, with tones so strong that this has been dubbed "a battle of ideas" along the "Rhine-divide" (Brunnermeier, James and Landau 2016). One camp calls for a "return to Maastricht," entailing the strict implementation of a rules-based fiscal framework with sanctions, the re-affirmation of the no-bailout clause, and an emphasis on risk-reduction. The other camp highlights the need for smarter rules with greater discretion, accompanied by the introduction of common risk-sharing instruments, both public and private.

But solidarity and responsibility should in fact be seen as two faces of the same coin and should be addressed together by finding a balanced agreement on the way forward. Building bridges between the two polar options is important, not only from a political, but also from an economic and financial perspective. Without appropriate risk-sharing arrangements, risk-reduction – namely, in the financial area – may actually result in higher risk of market instability. Conversely, risk-sharing without an effective risk-reduction strategy would enhance moral hazard and ultimately increase risk.

The Reflection Paper therefore attempts to bridge the two dominant narratives by identifying realistic and desirable solutions on which agreement can be more readily found in the short-term, while acknowledging that some other elements needed for the successful completion of EMU could be delivered over the longer run. A new institutional balance will also be needed, for example combining integration or centralisation in some policy fields with more scope for manoeuvre in other fields (Pisani-Ferry 2015). The Reflection Paper proposes advances in three areas: first, completing a genuine Financial Union; second, achieving a more integrated Economic and Fiscal Union; and third, strengthening Eurozone institutions and accountability (Figure 2).

Figure 2 Elements for a new political synthesis

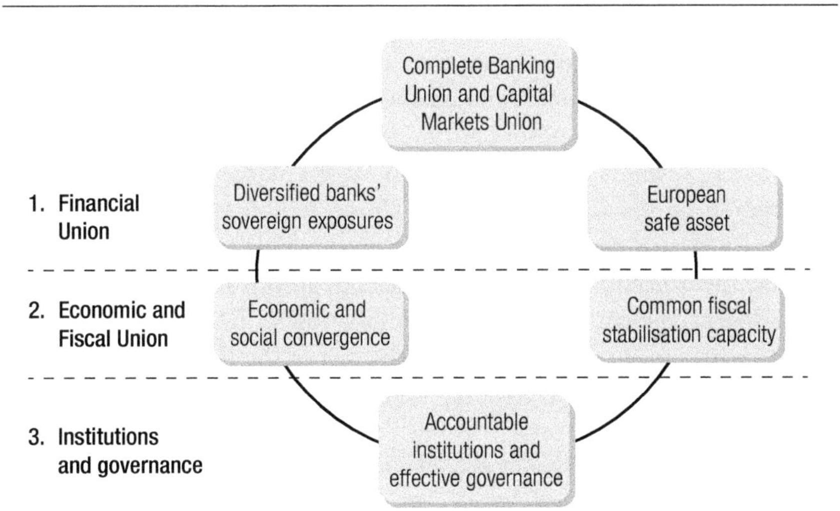

Source: Own elaboration.

2 Completing Financial Union to increase risk-sharing and reduce legacy risks

An integrated and well-functioning financial system is essential for an effective and stable EMU. Building on what has already been achieved in recent years, a consensus needs to be found on the way forward, including implementation of the elements agreed already, deciding quickly on the other elements that are on the table, and agreeing on additional steps to take until 2025.

Reducing risks from and increasing stability in financial markets

The first priority should be to complete the Banking Union. The package to reduce risks in the banking sector put forward by the Commission in November 2016 represents a priority and needs to be concluded swiftly. An agreement on the backstop to the Single Resolution Fund is essential to make the new EU framework for bank resolution effective. Equally crucial is the creation of the European Deposit Insurance Scheme to ensure that bank deposits are protected to the same extent across the Eurozone. The two measures should be adopted as soon as possible – ideally by 2019 – to be in place and fully operational by 2025. Other elements of the Financial Union should also be achieved by 2019. First, a comprehensive strategy to reduce the non-performing loans should be agreed and implemented. Second, the Capital Markets Union shall be further developed to provide more innovative, sustainable, and diversified sources of funding for households and businesses. As part of this process, a review of European Supervisory Authorities should be undertaken as well as first steps towards a single European capital markets supervisor.[3] The acceleration of the Capital Markets Union will contribute to creating a more integrated capital markets in Europe. This would be helpful to increase the capacity of financial markets to absorb shocks (risk-sharing through private channels), which is still too low in EMU, and to recycle excess savings in surplus countries to the rest of the Eurozone via equity rather than debt, thereby reducing the risk of financial instability

Addressing risks from sovereigns to banks as well

While the Banking Union and the Capital Market Union will reduce the stress that the banking sector can create for the public sector, the other direction of the "doom loop" – from sovereigns to banks –remains only partly addressed. Sound fiscal policies and the reduction of public debts will reduce the risks that sovereign bond developments can generate for banks. However, in the presence of a single monetary policy and full capital mobility, keeping the European financial system based on national bond markets creates the scope for sudden shifts of capital between these markets, which puts at risk the stability (and convergence) of the Eurozone (van Riet 2017).

Greater diversification of banks' balance sheets would help to address the problem of interconnection between banks and their "home country." The Reflection Paper suggests that one possibility of promoting more diversification could be the development of so-called sovereign bond-backed securities (SBBS), as explored by Brunnermeier, Langfield et al. (2016). Nevertheless, the Reflection Paper acknowledges that SBBSs are unlikely to become sizeable enough to become the benchmark for European financial markets with the potential to be comparable to US treasuries or Japan's government bonds.

A possible reform of the regulatory treatment of sovereign exposures (RTSE) has been raised in the discussions on how to deliver the Banking Union as an additional measure to sever the bank-sovereign loop. Several options have also been considered to that end (ESRB 2015). However, a possible reform of the RTSE could only be considered once the Banking Union is completed with a functioning backstop to the Single Resolution Fund and a common deposit insurance, in addition to a suitable common European safe asset being in place (changes to RTSE should be compatible with and supporting the safe asset). In addition, such a reform should be coordinated at the global level to ensure a level playing field.

A truly European safe asset

Experience has shown that at times of stress, the current structure of the sovereign bond markets in Europe, and the large exposure of banks to their national sovereign, have amplified market volatility, affecting the stability of the financial sector and the real economies of the Eurozone Member States.

Hence, to fully eliminate the "doom loop," a more ambitious solution changing the structure of the European bond markets itself is necessary. This would require, in the medium-term, the development of a genuine

Eurozone safe asset (Moscovici 2017). That will also help develop a Eurozone yield curve, important to facilitate both the conduct and transmission of the monetary policy and foster long-term investment and risk capital. It is also essential that the Eurozone be equipped with an asset class that matches more closely the weight of its economy, and offers an alternative investment opportunity for third countries currently investing in the EU mainly in equities. A truly European safe asset should preserve the capacity of governments to finance themselves at reasonable costs and with continuous market access, but at the same time it should improve the incentives for sound budgetary policies.

To deliver its full potential, first, the European safe asset should carry the lowest possible credit, market, liquidity, contagion, and supply risks – compared to other such assets in Europe and globally – and have a sufficiently transparent structure to allow investors to price it with ease and to be considered of the safest standard. Second, the European safe asset should be sizeable enough to become the reference bond for collateral and liquidity purposes in the Eurozone and to meet global demand. Third, it should encompass a wide maturity structure that can serve the objectives of various investors, including those with a very long-term horizon.

In recent years, several proposals have been put forward with different design features to create a European safe asset, ranging from full to partial or common issuance, some based on mutualisation and others entailing no joint liabilities (European Commission 2011c). Figure 3 illustrates the various options put forward in the literature and how they fare in the trade-off between liquidity, stability, and governance on the one hand, and incentives and discipline on the other hand. Eurobonds – with full mutualisation of liabilities – have significant potential benefits in terms of size, liquidity, and pooling of risks, but could have large drawbacks in terms of distribution of legacy debt and incentives for future national policies. Partly mutualised common issuances such as the "Blue Bonds" (Delpla and von Weizsäcker 2010) could attenuate both positive and negative effects of a full mutualisation. Pooling of sovereign bonds and tranching of the common issuance – as the SBBS mentioned above – could avoid mutualisation by shifting all risks to private holders, but may not be sufficiently sizeable. A reverse approach – doing first the tranching of sovereign bonds and then the pooling of the common issuance within a reasonable size – would also avoid the transfer of risks and mutualisation across Member States.[4] Proposals of this type include

Figure 3 Possible options for new forms of safe assets in Europe

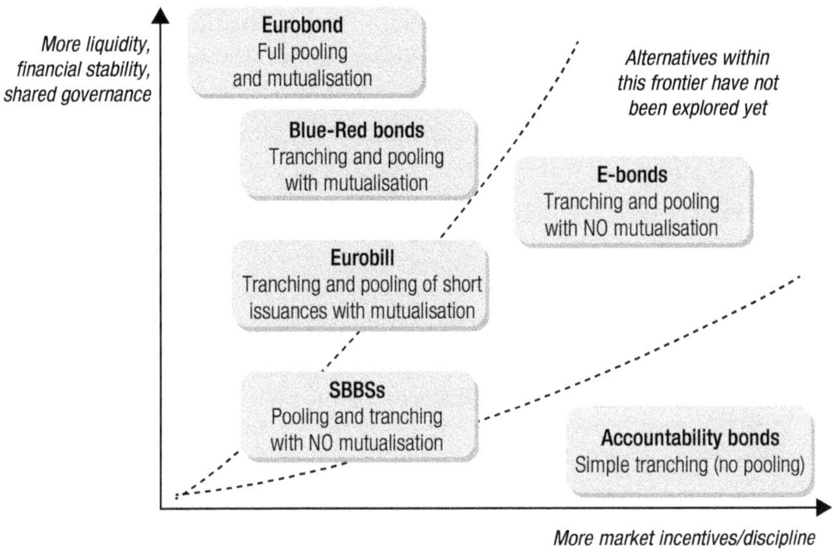

Source: Own elaboration.

E-Bonds (Monti 2010) and the Eurobills (Philippon and Hellwig 2011, Bishop 2013). Any further reflections in this area – which has been announced by the Commission – would need to focus on the necessary features of such an instrument, to make potential benefits materialise.

Achieving a better balance between market discipline and fiscal surveillance to promote reforms and fiscal responsibility

Achieving a more effective market discipline could allow a better balance in the way governance in EMU works. This requires first of all addressing the uneven stringency with which markets have been exercising their role in disciplining fiscal policies over time and across the Eurozone. The need to revive market discipline should be addressed without creating the risk of sudden stops (Philippon 2015). The recent evidence is that market discipline operates too late and in an abrupt fashion under the current framework. A new institutional regime (including a truly European safe asset) compared to the current (crisis) and pre-crisis regimes could increase the degree of "linearity" in financial market reactions and help avoid "cliff effects" in interest rates generated by perceptions of redenomination risks. The completion of the Banking Union and the creation of a common Eurozone safe asset could allow risks pertaining to excessive exposures to sovereign bonds to be recognised and – supported by stronger economic, fiscal, and financial integration over time – would also open the door to simplifying the current EU fiscal rules based on the Treaty concept of avoiding "gross policy errors" (Article 126.2).[5]

3 Achieving a more integrated Economic and Fiscal Union

The Five Presidents' Report (along with others, such as Enderlein, Letta et al. 2016) already recognised the convergence towards more resilient economic and social structures in Member States as an essential element for a successful EMU in the long-run. There exist several instruments that could be used better to achieve this goal, such as: (i) strengthening coordination of economic policy under the European Semester; (ii) reinforcing links between national reforms and existing EU funding; and (iii) further developing technical assistance to Member States to support capacity development.

Convergence towards resilient economies – able to withstand shocks and recover quickly to potential – is fundamental for improving the functioning of EMU. The experience of the past years has shown how lack of resilience in one or several economies of the Eurozone can have persistent effects not only on those countries concerned, but also on other Member States and the Eurozone as a whole. Resilience also fosters cyclical convergence and the effectiveness of the single monetary policy. Ultimately, policies identified as having a material impact on economic resilience in EMU could become part of the convergence standards – advocated by the Five Presidents' Report and the Reflection Paper. Compliance with these standards would be a requirement to access the new stabilisation capacity.

Creating a central stabilisation capacity

The concept of Fiscal Union being intimately connected to national sovereignty creates strong emotional reactions. In reality, a minimalistic interpretation is warranted, without transfer of competences in the areas of allocation and distribution, which would remain under national control. The Fiscal Union could be built on a set of fiscal surveillance rules codified in a simplified Stability and Growth Pact, on a fiscal backstop for the Single Resolution Fund, and on a stabilisation capacity.

The Five Presidents Report made a case for a central fiscal capacity in the Eurozone to improve macroeconomic stabilisation of the Eurozone[6], providing guiding principles: it should not lead to permanent transfers, should minimise moral hazard, and be strictly conditional on clear criteria and continuous sound policies; it should be developed within the EU framework; and it should not duplicate the role of the ESM. There are several options for setting up this function, which the Commission will look into, that are not mutually exclusive:

- A European Investment Protection Scheme would protect investment in the broad sense in the event of a downturn, by supporting well-identified priorities and already planned projects or activities at a national level, such as infrastructure or skills development.
- A European Unemployment Reinsurance Scheme would act as a "reinsurance fund" for national unemployment schemes. The scheme would provide more breathing space for national public finances and help economies to emerge from the crisis faster and stronger. The unemployment reinsurance scheme would, however, probably require some prior convergence of labour market policies and characteristics.[7]
- A rainy day fund could accumulate funds on a regular basis. Disbursements from the fund would be triggered on a discretionary basis to cushion a large shock. The rainy day fund, however, would normally limit its payments strictly to its accumulated contributions.

Stabilisation from these instruments should be delivered in the case of large shocks – it should not be a fiscal fine-tuning exercise. To increase its stabilisation effects, the function should be equipped with the capacity to borrow. This would need to be accompanied by a design that clearly provides for savings at other times and limits indebtedness. Finally, a Eurozone budget could ensure broader objectives, covering both convergence and stabilisation, and would need a stable revenue stream. More importantly, though, it implies a more significant transfer of competences to the European level. It is therefore a far-reaching option for which further integration progress would seem needed before it can become a concrete possibility.

4 Strengthening Eurozone institutions and accountability

For EMU to be stronger, Member States must accept to share more responsibilities and decisions on Eurozone matters, within a common legal framework. There is a need for a "quantum leap in institutional integration" (Draghi 2015). Completing the EMU means greater democratic accountability and higher transparency about who decides what and when at each and every level of governance. The European Parliament and national parliaments need to be equipped with sufficient powers of oversight, including by extending and formalising the dialogue between the European Parliament and the other institutions acting on behalf of the Eurozone, starting with the Eurogroup, whose members remain accountable to their national parliaments. Further political integration could involve a rethinking of the functioning of the Eurogroup as a formal and more transparent decision-making body and could justify the appointment of a full-time, permanent Eurogroup chair, which could be merged with the Member of the Commission in charge of EMU. The unification of the Eurozone's external representation should also proceed. Several competences and functions could be regrouped under a single umbrella provided by the Eurozone Treasury, as the institutional envelope for the functions of the Fiscal Union, within the EU framework. The Treasury – possibly with a Eurozone budget – could be responsible for the economic and fiscal surveillance, the macroeconomic stabilisation function, and the issuance of the European safe asset (including all issuances currently made by European institutions).

The ESM in its current form provides liquidity assistance to Member States and in the future could act as a common backstop to the Banking Union, which needs to be put in place as soon as possible. The ESM could evolve into a European Monetary Fund (EMF) to give the Eurozone more autonomy from other international institutions when it comes to financial stability. Different possible designs can be envisaged in the more general framework of the possible creation of a Eurozone Treasury. For instance, the EMF could be the financial stability arm of the Treasury. As a pre-condition, it is important that the ESM or this evolved EMF is integrated into the EU legal framework to improve the efficiency of its decision making and to allow adequate oversight by the European Parliament.

Overall, these institutional changes would be an important development which could take place at a later stage of the deepening of EMU.

5 Conclusions

We have highlighted a number of key elements in the Commission Reflection Paper, and developed the reasoning behind them. All the ideas face their own challenges and criticisms, which, as expected, have been aired again after the release of the paper. But when the various options are considered as a comprehensive package, their merits are more evident and their limits more nuanced. Besides the choice among options for deepening EMU, what is key is an appropriate sequencing for their implementation. The Commission proposed to move forward in two steps: a first phase, which runs to the end of 2019; and a second phase, over 2020-25, for completing the EMU architecture. A window of opportunity for forging a consensus and delivering concrete steps is opening with the approaching completion of the electoral cycle in the main Member States of the Eurozone and will likely close around the end of 2018, when the final stage of the mandate of the European institutions approaches. This period will also coincide with the timeframe expected by markets for the end of the accommodative policy of the ECB, which could – in the absence of further steps to deepen EMU – expose once again the vulnerabilities still faced by some Eurozone countries. This is a relatively short timeframe in the context of the typical pace in the history of European integration. But it could be sufficient to provide the needed momentum for discussing and agreeing a comprehensive package, and set the basis for launching Treaty changes required by several key reforms to complete EMU. The first reactions to the Reflection Paper are cautious but appear constructive. This window of opportunity should not be missed.

Notes

[1] The paper follows up the European Commission's White Paper on the future of Europe (COM 2017(2025), 1.3.2017 (European Commission 2017a).

[2] This dilemma was discussed by the European Commission (2016f).

[3] Another important aspect, although not discussed in the Reflection Paper, concerns changes to the current set up for the provision of Emergency Liquidity Assistance (ELA). This is still provided by national central banks, albeit after authorisation by the ECB. In our view, there should be symmetry between the level at which the ELA is provided and at the level at which supervision is carried out. This means that for banks under the SSM supervision, which would be typically operating across Eurozone countries, the responsibility for providing ELA should be at the European level, by the ECB.

[4] Tranching of national issuances could be done, for example, by maturity (national issuer does not cover specific maturities), creditor ranking (national issuer provides seniority to the common issuer), or ranking among bond issues (national issuances are divided into junior and senior bonds and the common issuer only pools the latter). Proposals which follow an approach of just "tranching" without pooling, such as "accountability bonds" (Fuest and Heinemann 2015), are not able to deliver a European safe asset.

[5] Some academics have been arguing that a truly credible framework requires not only changes in the RTSE, but also a mechanism which delivers a default of sovereign debt, possibly linked to a strengthened sovereign lending framework for the ESM (Gros and Meyer 2010, Corsetti et al. 2015). However these steps could backfire even if a full set of pre-conditions to ensure financial stability would be in place, as they could generate self-fulfilling prophecies.

[6] The case and proposals for a Fiscal Union are also made in, for example, IMF (2013b) and Thirion (2017).

[7] For overview of the discussions on a stabilisation mechanism based on unemployment benefits see, for example, Beblavy and Lenaerts (2017).

7 Deepening EMU Requires a Coherent and Well-Sequenced Package*

April 2018

1 Building on the progress made

The debate on EMU deepening is entering a critical stage. The contribution of 14 French and German economists (Bénassy-Quéré et al. 2018) is therefore timely. It suggests ways for reconciling risk-sharing with market discipline – where the biggest divisions lie. Their initiative overlaps in spirit and with much of the substance of the European Commission's May 2017 Reflection Paper on Deepening EMU (European Commission 2017c) which identified indispensable components of a comprehensive reform of EMU (see chapter 6) and underpins the subsequent Commission's initiatives (European Commission 2017e).

Bénassy-Quéré et al. put forward several attractive ideas on how to reform EMU. At the same time, the mix of proposals seems unbalanced and carries significant risks. The diagnosis of the crisis overlooks crucial issues such as macroeconomic imbalances and adjustments within the Eurozone and the redenomination risk connected to acute liquidity and credibility crises. As such, the proposals are mainly geared at increasing market pressure on fiscal policies, and are aggregated without appropriate sequencing necessary to contain macroeconomic and financial risks.

As a starting point, the progress made in reducing risks in Europe – in parallel with, or ahead of more risk-sharing – should be more clearly recognised. Achievements at both the EU and national level are in

---

* Co-authors: Gabriele Giudice and José Leandro (European Commission), Vox CEPR, 25 April 2018.

line with, and sometimes surpass, the ECOFIN Council's June 2016 roadmap for the Banking Union (BU) and the July 2017 Action plan to tackle non-performing loans (NPLs), as also acknowledged by the Eurogroup in February 2018. Several packages have been tabled and are being implemented to further reinforce banks' prudential management and strengthen market discipline, to improve insolvency frameworks, restructuring and second chances, to define a more gradual path to risk-sharing reflecting progress in risk-reduction, and to support the ongoing fall in non-performing loans (see Figure 1) and prevent their resurgence.[1]

2 Preserving financial stability is of the utmost importance

Bénassy-Quéré et al. aim at making the "no-bailout" clause (Article 125 TFEU) more credible, which is a desirable objective. A country not respecting its fiscal targets would face heightened market pressure, as ultimately it would be forced into outright default. They focus therefore on defining "when" or "how" default should take place, through the equivalent of a Sovereign Debt Restructuring Mechanism, or SDRM (Corsetti et al. 2016): governments missing their expenditure targets would issue junior national debt, which would be automatically restructured should the country require ESM crisis support.

But market forces must be handled with caution. Financial markets tend to operate along horizontal (benign neglect) and vertical (overreaction) lines. The proposals by Bénassy-Quéré et al. concentrate both liquidity and credit risks on a very narrow tranche of national debt. This would take Europe into uncharted waters and raises significant questions.[2] While in theory the proposals concern only the flow of debt, the crisis showed that markets fail with critical spillovers across assets issued by a country, and across jurisdictions. These proposals could generate self-fulfilling prophecies, with uneven market reactions to changes in perceptions and credibility of governments, destabilising financial markets.

As costless defaults are an illusion, rather than forcing defaults it would make more sense to work to reduce the economic, financial, and political costs in the extreme and unlikely case that a sovereign debt default becomes inevitable in the Eurozone. This alternative approach would involve: (1) making the financial system more resilient to such a default event (see below); (2) improving the EMU architecture to make defaults

Figure 1 Evolution of non-performing loans in selected countries and the EU

	Non-performing loans in % ot total loans in selected countries		
	Q3 2016	Q3 2017	% change
Cyprus	36.8	32.1	–12.7%
Spain	5.8	4.7	–19.7%
Greece	47.4	46.7	–1.5%
Ireland	14.4	11.2	–22.5%
Italy	16.1	12.1	–24.9%
Portugal	17.7	14.6	–17.3%
Slovenia	14.4	10.8	–24.8%

Non-performing loans in the EU
EU total gross non-performing loans and advances,
in % of total gross loans and advances, end of quarter values

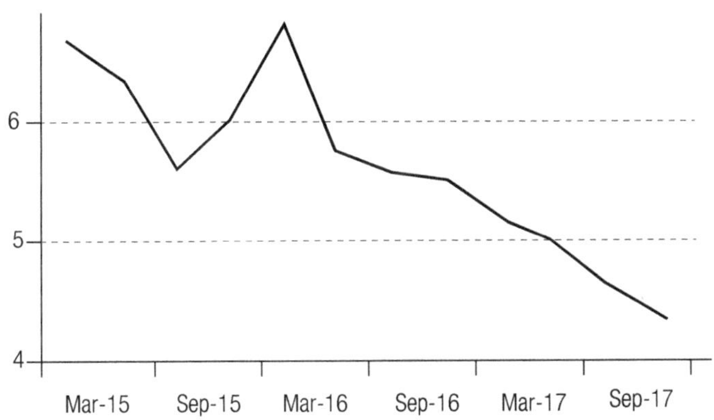

Source: European Central Bank.

even less likely; and (3) clarifying *ex ante* "who" would bear the cost of a government default.

Sovereign bonds have a particular role in funding public expenditure and as benchmarks for national financial systems, which explains why they enjoy a risk-free status across all advanced economies. If the regulatory treatment of bank sovereign exposures were to be changed in isolation, or with an inappropriate combination or sequencing, the consequences could be material and unpredictable for financial stability.

A regulatory reform to reduce excessive concentration of sovereign bonds in the banks' balance sheets could reduce the impact of government defaults, improve incentives for governments and avoid any possibility of indirect financing, but only if such reform were implemented wisely, gradually, and as part of a well-sequenced package. The right sequencing would depend not just on having a deal on the deposit insurance, as proposed by Bénassy-Quéré et al., but on key steps to improve the functioning of financial markets: completing Banking Union, progressing towards the Capital Markets Union and reaching an agreement to launch a genuine European safe asset. This should not be seen as a way to delay progress but rather as an argument that all these elements of the package should be considered as soon as possible.

3 A stone that could hit many birds

A genuine European safe asset would create a large, homogenous, and hence liquid Eurozone-level bond market; it would avoid "sudden stops" and reduce the financial fragmentation that blunts the transmission of monetary policy; it would replace sovereign bonds on the banks' balance sheets, hence mitigating the sovereign-bank loop; and it would increase the total supply of European and global safe assets. It would therefore improve debt dynamics across the Eurozone. Mutualised solutions such as Eurobonds (De Grauwe and Ji 2018) or Blue-Red bonds (Delpla and von Weizsäcker 2010), while appealing, have limited political traction at this juncture and would require a change to the EU treaties. Sovereign bond-backed securities (Brunnermeier, Langfield et al. 2016, ESRB 2018), while increasing diversification and the supply of safe assets, are unlikely to fulfil all the objectives of a genuine European safe asset, as many market analysts, academics and sovereign debt managers have highlighted, even if regulatory barriers are removed. In addition, introducing SBBS alongside Accountability bonds, as proposed by Bénassy-Quéré et al., would also dangerously fragment bond markets even more.

A recent paper (Leandro and Zettelmeyer 2018) concludes that safe assets could be produced without mutualisation in sufficient quantities to replace the Eurozone banks' current holdings of sovereign bonds, which would make them more immune to defaults. Among the non-mutualised options, so-called E-Bonds (Monti 2010: 61-65, Juncker and Tremonti 2010) – whereby the whole national debt is subordinated to any funding received from the common issuer, which may well be the ESM or the EIB – could directly exert fiscal discipline (by raising the marginal cost of sovereign debt issuance, without raising the average costs for lower-rated borrowers). Against the current lack of trust among European countries, an option balancing and indissolubly binding significant common issuance with market discipline could overcome the reciprocal fear among Member States that others may backtrack on agreed reforms (see Figure 2). Its introduction would facilitate a progressive implementation of concentration charges, the prospect of which could help a rapid agreement on both the deposit insurance and the backstop, while it may also smoothen the reduction of the ECB's balance sheet.

Figure 2 Possible forms for a European safe asset

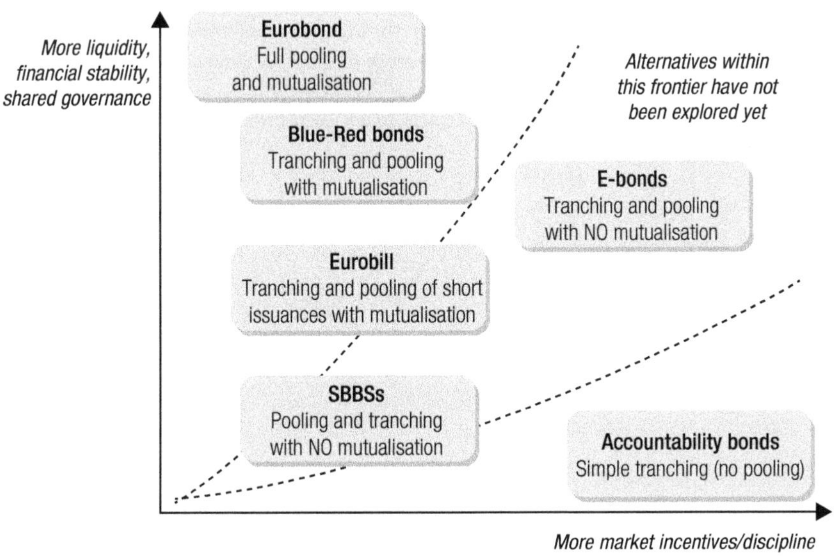

Source: Chapter 6.

4 Conclusion

The proposals in Bénassy-Quéré et al. (2018) are welcome and the main message should be heard loud and clear: there is a need to strengthen EMU through parallel risk-reduction and risk-sharing, complementing each other within a package of reforms. Risk-reduction has to continue, but one should avoid changing the goalpost before risk-sharing takes place.

In the paper the exact sequencing is however unclear, not all necessary elements are covered, and some proposals create risks. The diagnosis overlooks some key aspects of EMU (internal imbalances, liquidity flows, redenomination risks) and the focus of the proposals on reducing fiscal risks could rather lead to financial distress ultimately requiring more, not fewer, rescues. After all the effort to regain financial stability, there is a need to advance without delay, but with a coherent and well-sequenced package, avoiding unsafe steps in the dark.

Notes

[1] See European Commission (2016i, 2017d, 2018a).

[2] Such as: What happens if fiscal targets are missed because of forecast errors or surprise elements, rather than wrong policies? If bonds are meant to be issued only rarely (as countries would normally stick to the fiscal targets), how easy will it be to issue them in a very thin market? Who would enforce their issuance? What happens if there is no buyer at any price (something that we also experienced during the last crisis).

8 The Case for a Central Fiscal Capacity in EMU*

December 2018

1 Introduction

Following the outbreak of the financial crisis important governance steps have been taken to bolster the resilience of the European Economic and Monetary Union (EMU). The changes include putting in motion a Banking Union, establishing the European Stability Mechanism (ESM), and strengthening the surveillance framework. However, there is broad acceptance that the current set up remains prone to shocks that could damage its functioning and even imperil its integrity. Further progress is therefore needed for a stable EMU (e.g. Bénassy-Quéré et al. 2018).

In general the remaining "problem" can be described as a lack of adjustment channels to large shocks, given the incomplete nature of the financial union and the absence of common fiscal instruments. Key ingredients to overcome these gaps are the completion of Banking Union and Capital Markets Union (CMU) as well as the introduction of a stabilisation function. And, as argued in this chapter, a financial union is not a substitute for a stabilisation function – they are in fact complementary.

However, while the achievement of a full financial union is relatively consensual in principle, the value added of a central fiscal capacity is sometimes put in doubt (Heijdra et al. 2018, Feld 2018).

Critics of the fiscal capacity make several points. They claim that: i) sizeable asymmetric shocks are infrequent; ii) private risk-sharing mech-

---

* Co-author: Nicolas Carnot (European Commission), Vox CEPR, 7 December 2018.

anisms, including as enhanced by the completion of Banking Union and CMU, could provide considerable shock absorption; iii) fiscal stabilisation can in any event rely on national budget stabilisers, provided that Member States properly adhere to fiscal rules of the Stability and Growth Pact (SGP).

Finally, critics claim that any common fiscal tool could only be an incentive to moral hazard and a door for non-legitimised permanent transfers. They conclude that the risks of a fiscal capacity outweigh its advantages.

We beg to disagree with this analysis. So too do the international organisations, which strongly favour the introduction of a fiscal capacity (e.g. Lagarde 2018, Draghi 2018, OECD 2018).

In the rest of this chapter, we take the points of the critics in turn. Hence, we examine four analytical questions:

a. Is there evidence of large cyclical fluctuations in EMU, including country-specific components?
b. Does private risk-sharing via the completion of Banking Union and CMU eliminate the case for a central fiscal capacity?
c. Do national automatic stabilisers within the SGP suffice to smooth the remaining shocks?
d. Does a central fiscal capacity necessarily entail moral hazard and permanent transfers?

We finally recall, in conclusion, how together with other contributions, the Commission has proposed to move forward by tabling a balanced proposal.

2 Is there evidence of large cyclical fluctuations in EMU, including country-specific components?

Business cycle fluctuations have remained sizeable since the inception of the euro. Interestingly, simple decompositions of the cycle suggest that output fluctuations comprise both a common component and country-specific developments, with the two weighing similar proportions. The average standard deviation of output gaps is about 3% of GDP (Figure 1), implying that output gaps bigger than that are not infrequent.

Moreover, when measured relative to the average of the zone, the average standard deviation of relative output gap is over 2% of GDP. National business cycles are imperfectly correlated and when they are, their amplitudes may considerably differ.

Cyclical fluctuations in EMU countries therefore reflect about as much a common component and country-specific fluctuations. This is confirmed by a more formal analysis relying on a principal component method, which finds that at most 60% of fluctuations can be ascribed to the common component, and thus, at least 40% is the result of idiosyncratic shocks or of the asymmetric transmission of common shocks (European Commission 2018f). In addition, there is no empirical evidence of greater cyclical convergence over time. In other words, it is incorrect to consider that large asymmetric cyclical developments are irrelevant.

Figure 1 Standard deviations of output gaps, 2000-2017 (% of GDP)

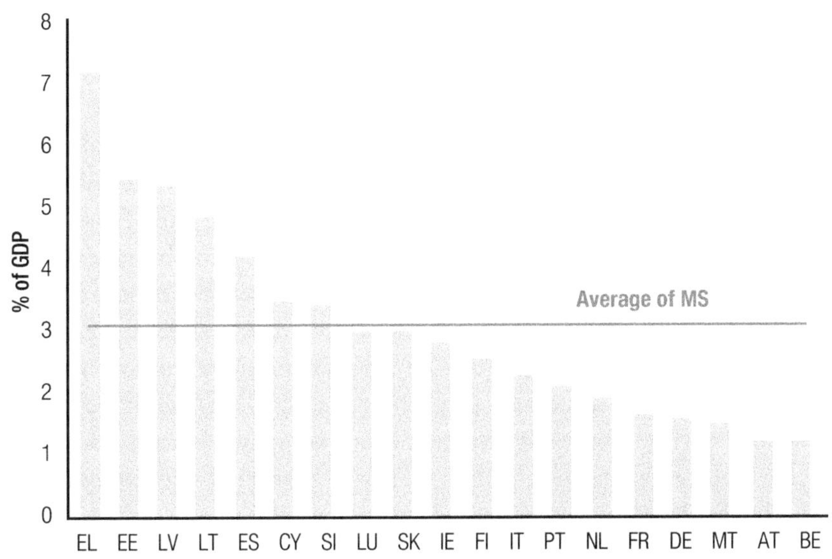

Source: AMECO database, authors' calculations.

Overall, there remain significant asymmetric shocks, or at least asymmetric cyclical developments, across EMU countries, which by definition cannot be addressed by the single monetary policy. In fact, the monetary stance may contribute to cyclical differentials, as it is likely to be too supportive for countries in more favourable cyclical positions than the average and vice versa.

The presence of a relatively large common business cycle component also has implications. It justifies attention to the overall Eurozone fiscal stance, at least in circumstances such as the lower bound where the ECB may benefit from an aligned fiscal policy for counteracting large shocks, as happened during the early 2010s. While this possibility was largely ignored at EMU inception, the experience has dramatically shown it to be relevant in the environment of the 2010s, and it is likely to remain relevant in the future. This means that conceptually, a common stabilisation capacity may not just be focused on asymmetric shocks, but may also usefully cater for large symmetric shocks, thereby also overcoming the limitations of coordinating the aggregate Eurozone fiscal stance from national fiscal policies.

3 Does private risk-sharing via the completion of Banking Union and CMU eliminate the case for a central fiscal capacity?

Private risk-sharing remains underdeveloped in the EU, as highlighted by comparisons with the situation in the US (see chapter 5). Private risk-sharing works by the combined effects of cross-border ownership of assets and labour compensation as well as credit markets (saving and borrowing). In the Eurozone the effect of cross border factor incomes (capital and labour) has so far been to smooth a meagre 6% of asymmetric shocks, compared with over 40% in the US (Figure 2). The potential for improvement in this area is therefore large, and a well-functioning CMU would definitely contribute to this. The credit channel, which actually is better understood as consumption smoothing rather than risk-sharing *stricto sensu* (Alcidi and Thirion 2016), is also more developed in the US.

Full financial integration is unlikely to be reached in the short or even medium-term, as it requires deep structural changes. For instance, it will take time to diversify cross-border holdings, and a certain degree of home bias may persist even in the long-term in the presence of asymmetric information. This alone could be enough to justify a central fiscal capacity at least as long as the degree of financial integration remains limited. But more fundamentally, the question is whether a complete fi-

Figure 2 Cross-border risk-sharing (% of output shocks)

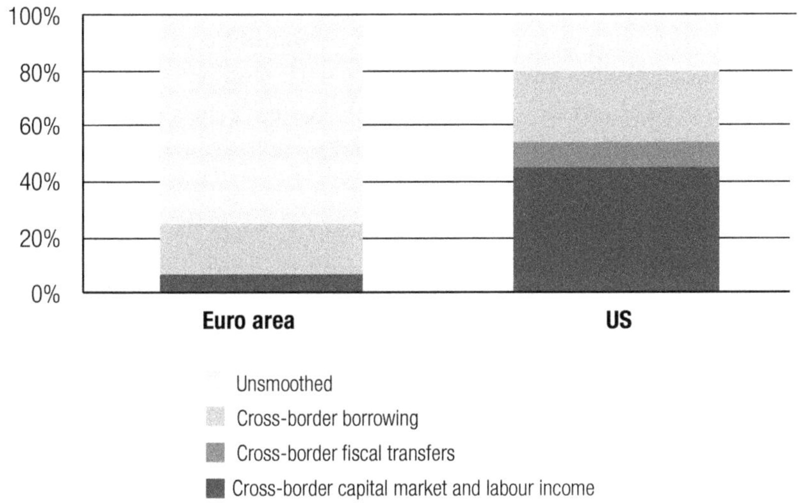

Source: European Commission.

nancial union can be seen as a substitute to a targeted fiscal capacity, or whether the two act as complements that strengthen each other, as is the case in the US. The evidence suggests that financial and fiscal unions may substitute as shock absorbers in normal times but need each other in bad times. In other words, in times of acute market stress, the shock absorption function of the financial union will depend on the existence of a credible and effective central fiscal capacity.

Specifically, there is evidence that private markets behave pro-cyclically when left entirely on their own. In the case of EMU, cross-border financial flows increased somewhat in the run up to the crisis before collapsing afterwards. In other words, the credit channel for smoothing shocks froze during the Eurozone crisis and actually worked in reverse (Furceri and Zdzienicka 2015). Private risk-sharing is more effective when working in conjunction with public sector risk-sharing. Some studies also point out that financial markets are not Pareto-efficient as private agents fail to hold the kinds of portfolios ensuring proper risk-sharing in large shocks (Fahri and Werning 2017).

The pro-cyclicality may in part be explained by an inadequate structure of financial flows, such as the proportion of debt versus equity. And progress in financial supervision and more effective macroprudential policies should help. At the same time, it would be perilous to assume that financial booms and busts together with flights to safety and sudden stops are behind us in the Eurozone. Instead, the risk of a re-run of mechanisms similar to those experienced in the past crisis seems hardly negligible.

The experience in Europe and elsewhere suggests that these risks are attenuated with a public tool that acts as a catalyst for confidence (Kalemli-Özcan et al. 2014). In this context, the existence of a fiscal risk-sharing tool can actually foster risk-reduction by preventing excessive market volatility and full-blown financial crises.

Moreover, moving to a genuine financial union will require a more comprehensive approach than implied by some authors, including Heijdra et al. (2018). The experience during the financial crisis and discussions clearly indicate the difficulties in going ahead to complete the Banking Union as there is no agreement yet on even the technical elements which should allow political negotiations to start on a European Deposit Insurance Scheme.

The Banking Union needs to be completed with the backstop for the Single Resolution Fund and the European Deposit Insurance Scheme. The introduction of these forms of public risk-sharing is crucial in order to make the system robust by strengthening financial stability, reducing pro-cyclicality, and maximising its capacity to smooth asymmetric shocks via private sector risk-sharing. While prudential and bail-in rules will help to contain and reduce risks and prevent them from having a fiscal impact, this does not eliminate the need for a public backstop. In this respect, an excessive focus on risk-reduction measures would, ironically, lead to increasing risks. For instance, there are good reasons to proceed very cautiously to avoid the risk of financial instability when considering any changes to the regulatory treatment of bank sovereign exposures. Should such a proposal be contemplated, one would also need to consider a broader set of measures including a credible backstop to the Single Resolution Fund, the creation of EDIS and the introduction of a suitable common European safe asset to take a central role in the financial system (see chapter 6). By reducing the risk of flight-to-safety and sudden stops in times of market stress, such a common safe asset would also reinforce the shock-absorbing role of the financial union through private sector channels.

4 Do national fiscal stabilisers within the SGP suffice to smooth the remaining shocks?

Contrary to the US, the EMU does not have a large central budget which provides stabilisation as a "by product" of its allocative and redistribution functions. At the same time, Member States of the EMU have very large national budgets with significant stabilisation capacities. The rules of the SGP, while primarily focused on ensuring fiscal discipline, have been crafted and evolved in a manner that aims at preserving stabilisation role of national fiscal policy. In principle, adherence to the balanced budget rule in structural terms, the medium-term objective (MTO), provides room for the automatic stabilisers to play out in ordinary cyclical situations without breaching the 3% reference value for excessive deficits. Preserving prudent fiscal positions including by constituting buffers in the good times is essential for this work.

Hence there is in general agreement that national automatic stabilisers should constitute the primary fiscal line of defence against demand shocks.[1] The disagreement is on the need for a central fiscal tool in addition to that. Here, we believe that the sceptics miss three points that tilt the case.

First, the frequency and magnitude of country-specific shocks is relatively large, as noted above. Admittedly, this is especially true for the more volatile economies of the Eurozone. The Baltic economies offer a good example.

Second, the gyrations in the public finances triggered by exogenous shocks are often far stronger than conventionally measured. The standard measurement of cyclical deficits based on the output gap relies on average values for fiscal elasticities (Mourre et al. 2014). In practice, growth composition effects and residual technical factors imply that the sensitivity of the budget to economic shocks can be considerably greater. As an illustration, Figure 3 reports the distribution of tax windfalls and shortfalls that come in addition to conventionally measured cyclical deficits. In a downturn changes in headline balances will reflect variations in these windfalls and shortfalls together with the change in conventional

Figure 3 Distribution of tax revenues windfalls (+) and shortfalls (–) in Eurozone Member States (% GDP)

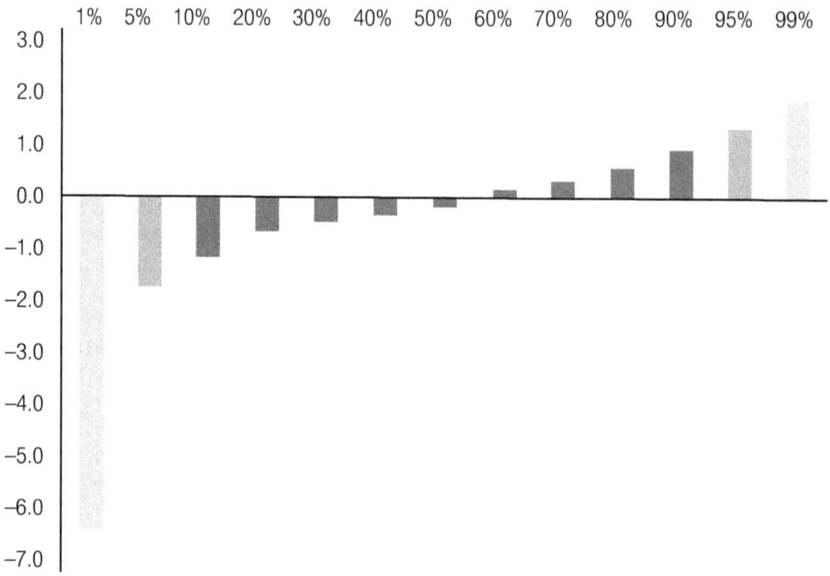

Source: AMECO database, authors' calculations.

cyclical balances. Putting these factors together, the evidence is that cyclical changes in headline fiscal balances typically exceed 3% of GDP every 10 years, and 5% of GDP every 20 years. This goes beyond the protection offered by medium-term objectives, especially when the latter are met in good times by flattering temporary windfalls, as was the case in previous cycles.

Third, the legacy of high debts in some countries greatly complicates the use of stabilising national fiscal policies. Member States with high levels of debt are in an especially fragile position. When faced with a significant slowdown accompanied by large revenues shortfalls, they may very quickly come under the suspicion of markets, even when actually adhering to the agreed spending policies. These countries may be facing an unpalatable choice between tightening policy at the wrong time to reassure markets and risking a self-fulfilling spiral of higher deficits and interest costs.[2] In those circumstances, an element of fiscal risk-sharing can tip both policies and expectations towards a better equilibrium and prevent the materialisation of self-destructing austerity or a full-blown meltdown. This is not mutualisation but insurance for the benefit of the whole Union.

These considerations make the case for completing the economic architecture of EMU, including in particular a common fiscal capacity to top up the national automatic stabilisers in the event of large shocks. To be sure, the design of such an instrument needs to be well conceived in order to be timely and effective, while preserving against the risk of degenerating into a hidden transfer union. Several worthy proposals have been made in this respect (e.g. Carnot et al. 2017, Arnold et al. 2018, Lenarcic and Korhonen 2018).

It is important to also stress that a stabilisation capacity would complement the fiscal rules framework and could actually strengthen it, by encouraging the build-up of fiscal buffers in good times and making it easier to implement rules of fiscal discipline (European Fiscal Board 2018). In due time, the fiscal rules framework could also be simplified and strengthened, for example by focusing on a debt anchor and a proper operational target.

5 Does a central fiscal capacity necessarily entail moral hazard and permanent transfers?

The design features are essential in this respect. The Commission proposal for a European Investment Stabilisation Function (European Commission 2018e), which was tabled in May 2018, includes strong safeguards.

First, the rules for activating support are targeted exclusively on large shocks of a cyclical nature. The triggering criterion relies on a "double condition" on observed unemployment rates whereby unemployment must at the same time be historically high and strongly increasing (by over 1 percentage point). Moreover, payments are tied to changes in unemployment rates, precluding by construction indefinite support.

Second, Member States are eligible to support only if they have delivered effective action on recommendations under the corrective procedures of the SGP and of the Macroeconomic Imbalance Procedure.

Third, the support takes the form of the provision of loans, possibly at concessional rates, but does not involve outright transfers. The provision of direct transfers could be more powerful in terms of stabilisation but admittedly would open more risks of permanent transfers. By definition loans would entail permanent transfers only under the extreme assumption of a default by a Member State vis à vis the Union.

Simulations using real time data over the past three decades confirm that the proposed mechanism would have been timely and would have potentially benefited all Member States at a certain point. They show that the support would have been concentrated in the most severe downturns and would have extended to a maximum half of the area at peak points, that is, in 2009-10 and 1993-94 (Figure 4).

Figure 4 Share of Eurozone countries supported under the EISF proposal (%)

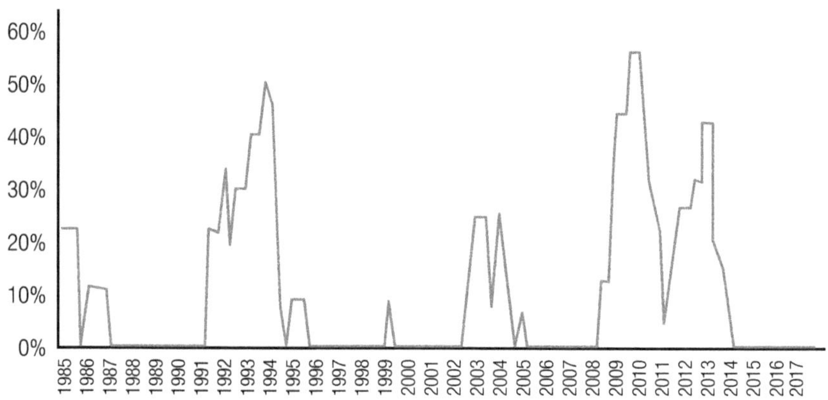

Source: European Commission (2018f).

6 Conclusions

From the inception of the euro it has been asked whether the EMU set-up offered enough space for macroeconomic stabilisation. This question arises naturally as countries in a monetary union lose channels of adjustment to asymmetric shocks by giving up their own monetary policy and the possibility of nominal exchange rate changes. The initial understanding at Maastricht was that this loss might be "compensated" by a natural convergence of business cycles within the union. In addition, national fiscal policies remained available in order to absorb country-specific shocks.

However, the experience suggests that these assumptions were too optimistic. Even if they are partly synchronised, business cycles remain sizeable in EMU. They reflect both a common component and substantial idiosyncratic cyclical developments in Member States. National fiscal stabilisers have functioned at times and in some countries, but have also exhibited serious limitations. Market mechanisms have not been a reliable shock absorber either and the importance of financial markets was underestimated. Indeed, recent evidence shows that markets can have a pro-cyclical effect in times of stress if not complemented by a credible fiscal risk-sharing set up.

Looking forward, the two priorities to deepen the EMU are the completion of the financial union as well as the introduction of targeted and effective common budgetary instruments. They complement and reinforce each other.

The debate on the nature of further budgetary instruments is gradually gaining traction. Germany and France have recently proposed in the Meseberg declaration the creation a Eurozone budget within the EU budget to support convergence, competitiveness, and stabilisation. Other ideas have also been suggested such as unemployment reinsurance funds. The Commission has proposed new tools as part of the next Multiannual Financial Framework for 2021-2027, including a Reform Support Programme to promote reforms for national resilience and a European Investment Stabilisation Function. The latter has been designed to prevent any risk of mutualisation and to complement national fiscal stabilisers only in the event of large cyclical shocks. These various proposals from Member States and the Commission are non-exclusive and could actually be combined. They should go hand in hand with further financial integration and sound implementation of the fiscal rules.

Notes

1 It may also be useful to enhance national automatic stabilisers (see chapter 14).

2 Note that while the SGP provides for escape clauses in exceptional circumstances, activating those would not fundamentally change the terms of this dilemma.

9 The Euro, a Tale of 20 Years: The Priorities Going Forward*

February 2019

1 Coming of age

Flashback to January 1999. On 2 May 1998, European leaders agree to start the third and final stage of the Economic and Monetary Union (EMU) on 1 January 1999. As of 1999, the exchange rates towards the common currency are fixed and the ECB becomes responsible for the monetary policy of a currency union made up of eleven countries and 293 million people. Three years later, the first euro coins and banknotes enter in circulation. The culmination of decades of European economic integration, the euro represents a historic milestone and much more than a monetary reform.

Fast-forward to January 2019. Nineteen countries belong to the Eurozone with a total population of 340 million. The euro has become the second currency used in world markets under any metric.

In spite of the existential crisis in 2011-13, membership to the Eurozone has continued to grow. In its short life span, the euro has become an anchor of economic and financial integration. In late 2018, the Eurobarometer survey (European Commission 2018h) showed that around two-thirds (64%) of Eurozone citizens think the euro is a good thing for their country and about three quarters (74%) think that having the euro is a good thing for the EU, the highest level since the question was first asked in 2004. At the same time, more than two-thirds (69%) in the

---

* Co-authors: Maya Jollès and Matteo Salto (European Commission), Vox CEPR, 19 February 2019.

Eurozone also think that there should be more economic policy coordination.

The 20th anniversary provides a good occasion to reflect on what the EMU has achieved and what remains to be done. This requires first recalling the initial objectives set for the euro and how these have changed over time, notably due to the weaknesses which came to the fore throughout the recent crisis. This also puts into question the policy taken during the crisis and the priorities going forward.

2 The Maastricht assignment

The original motivations for creating a common currency in Europe were both economic and political in nature. These are rooted in the collapse of the Bretton Woods world in the 1970s. From an economic standpoint, the common currency was considered a necessary complement to the Single Market that would remove exchange rate risks and conversion costs. As early as June 1982, Tommaso Padoa-Schioppa identified an "impossible quartet": free capital movements, free trade, and exchange rate stability are jointly incompatible with independent national monetary policies. The Delors report (Delors 1989) laid down the operational ground to build the Economic and Monetary Union and realise Tommaso Padoa-Schioppa's vision. Shortly after, the *One Market-One Money* study commissioned by the European Commission evaluated the benefits and costs of forming an economic and monetary union (European Commission 1990). These economic arguments were soon reinforced by political imperatives: the reunified Germany had to be firmly anchored in the EU (Buti, Deroose et al. 2010).

The EMU institutional setting was based on a "strong" version of the policymaking consensus that prevailed in the 1980s (Buti and Sapir 1998) and considered macroeconomic stability as the overarching goal. A centralised and independent monetary policy would credibly bring down inflation (Barro and Gordon 1983, Rogoff 1985) and keep output close to potential. In order to avoid "fiscal dominance" and possible government bailout (Sargent and Wallace 1981), excessive government deficits and monetary financing of government deficit would have to be banned. Moreover, in line with the tax smoothing theory (Barro 1979), tax rates would be held constant over the business cycle. Hence, fiscal policy was to be limited to automatic stabilisation during normal cycles. Financial markets were expected to allocate resources efficiently within and across Member States. Finally, the EU competencies in competition and trade policies, as well as the progress in the internal market (European Commission 1988) would increase market efficiency gains, notably through increased competition. These were expected to spread across the economies while trade integration was set to make the Eurozone eventually satisfy the Optimum Currency Area (OCA) criteria endogenously (Frankel and Rose 1998).

These principles were enshrined the Maastricht Treaty, which notably set the convergence criteria required for Member States to join the common currency. These criteria focus on price stability, government budget deficits, government debt-to-GDP ratios, exchange rate stability and long-term interest rates. While the convergence criteria ensured Eurozone Member States would nominally converge prior to adopting the euro, the Stability and Growth Pact, adopted in 1997, aims at maintaining and enforcing fiscal discipline in the EMU over time. The independence of the European system of central banks (the ECB and the national central banks of Member States) and its focus on the primary objective of price stability aimed to achieve macroeconomic stability. Finally, competition policy, with its unicum of state aid policy, was meant to ensure efficiency and, together with macroeconomic stability, economic convergence.

3 The Eurozone throughout the crisis: weaknesses of EMU's architecture come to the fore

During its first ten years, the Eurozone grew on average at the same level as the US in terms of GDP per capita and the ECB quickly gained credibility and was able to bring inflation in line with its target of "below but close to 2%." At the same time, structural reforms stalled and the benefits of lower interest rates and easier access to credit – both in the public and private sector – gave rise to an "anaesthetic effect," slowing down reform efforts and fiscal consolidation in peripheral countries. The financial crisis which started in the summer 2007 stands as the first major test case for the Eurozone. The crisis, at least in Europe, was triggered by a conjunction of factors and unfolded through many channels: current-account imbalances, sometimes related to productivity developments, banking sector shocks and their relation with sovereign debt. It was thus a strong catalyst to test the solidity of the Maastricht institutions and revisit the validity of the underlying assumptions. The financial crisis brought to the surface the weaknesses of the initial EMU architecture and the policy divergences of the first ten years of the euro.

First, in the absence of exchange-rate risks, investors did not take into account country-specific risks both in the banking and in the government sector. Second, economies in the periphery (like Ireland, Portugal, Spain, or Greece) were expected to rapidly converge with core Eurozone countries thanks to capital and credit inflows (Baldwin and Giavazzi 2015), as counterparts of sustained current account deficits. However, part of those inflows went into government sovereigns and in non-tradeable sectors (Figure 1), driving prices up, eventually resulting in an appreciation of their real exchange rates (see chapter 30). While at the Eurozone level, the current account was broadly in balance, divergences between creditors and debtors aggravated. In relative terms, the periphery became more intensive in non-tradeable while core countries gained competitiveness. The resulting changes in industrial structure resulted in agglomeration effects and, over time, contributed to diverging social and political preferences.

During the crisis, the negative effects of capital misallocation and excessive debt levels built over the preceding years came to the fore with the sudden stops of capital flows towards the periphery. These countries corrected their external accounts, but the adjustment was asymmetric as surplus countries did not boost domestic demand. As a result, the current account rebalancing proved considerably more painful in terms of output losses. The collapse in flows among banks gave rise to a sovereign problem, while, in the opposite direction, tensions on the sovereign weighed on banks' balance sheets. The sovereign-bank "doom loop" amplified financial distress and was responsible for deepening the recession, notably through worsened lending conditions in the economy.

Upon sudden stops, the only institution that had the mandate and the means to intervene – namely, the ECB – did take action and inter-banking short-term flows were replaced by central bank lending (Figure 2). This provided the space for EMU governments to create the institutions necessary to deal with Members faced with extreme difficulties. However, the absence of a lender of last resort in the EMU construction made

Figure 1 Imbalances and resource allocation

a) Increasing imbalances

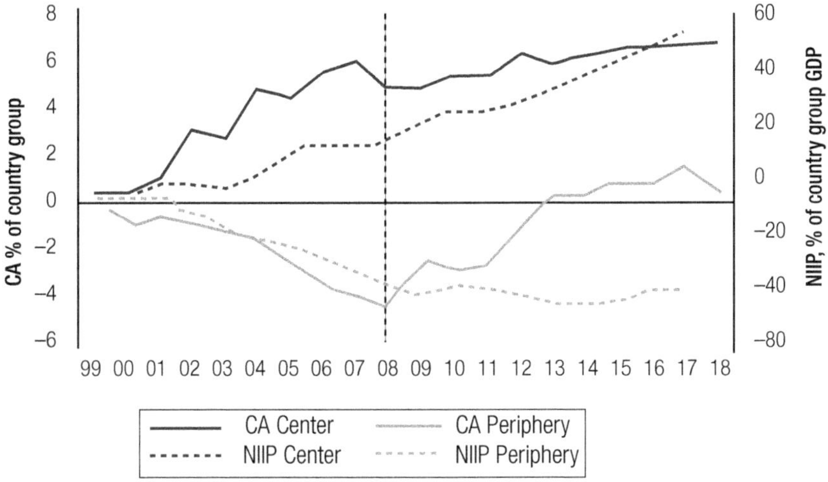

b) Cumulative growth rate of non-tradeable/tradeable value added

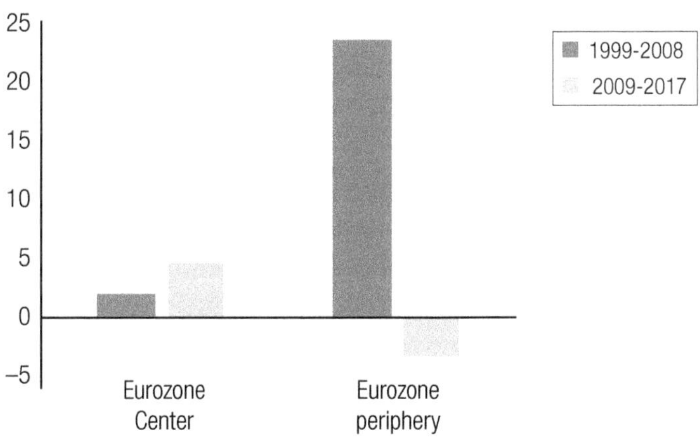

Notes: Centre includes Austria, Belgium, Finland, Germany, Luxembourg and the Netherlands. The periphery includes Cyprus, Estonia, Greece, France, Ireland, Italy, Latvia, Lithuania, Malta, Portugal, Slovakia, Slovenia, and Spain. Centre and periphery Eurozone countries grouped according to their external position. Updated from Buti and Turrini (2012).

Source: Authors' calculations based on AMECO.

it impossible to prevent the geographically contained sovereign crisis to morph into a general crisis of the Eurozone. It was only in July 2012, when monetary policy transmission was completely impaired by the sovereign crisis, that, in order to restore market confidence, ECB President Mario Draghi announced: "Within our mandate, the ECB is ready to do whatever it takes to preserve the euro. And believe me, it will be enough."

Figure 2 ECB policy and euro overnight rates, Eurosystem Balance Sheet size

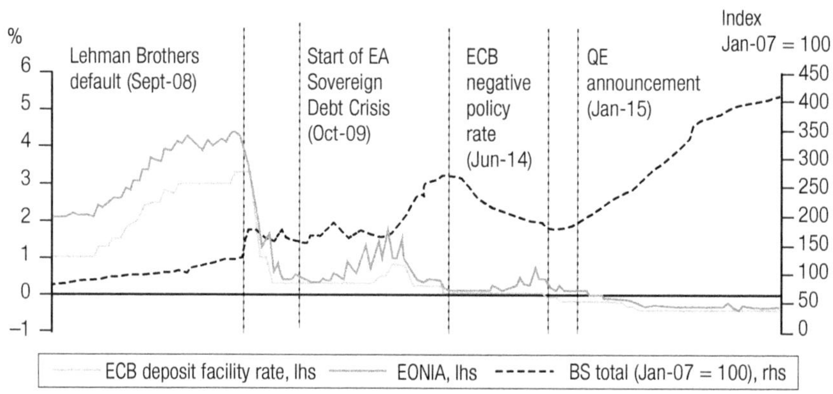

Source: Macrobond, European Central Bank.

The pre-conditions for such a statement were laid out in the European Council conclusions of June 2012, in which leaders committed "to do what is necessary to ensure the financial stability of the Euro area" and agreed to set up the Banking Union with the ultimate objective of tackling the negative loop between sovereign and bank risks.

Whilst the financial crisis was not fiscal in origin (apart from Greece), the lost opportunity of reducing public debt in the first ten years of EMU and the lack of central fiscal stabilisation contributed to aggravate the slump. After the initial coordinated fiscal expansion in 2008, the lack of fiscal buffers at national level meant that, in many countries, fiscal policy was no longer available to respond effectively to the demand shortfall. As a result, the aggregate Eurozone fiscal adjustment became pro-cyclical from 2011 to 2014 (Figure 3). In such a context, a common stabilisation fiscal instrument for the currency union could have played an important role. Indeed, the presence of a Eurozone fiscal capacity allowing to fully compensate for the contractionary policy made by Member States in 2012 and 2013 (represented by the red dashed lines in Figure 3) would have sensibly reduced the output gap during the crisis leading the output gap to almost reach 2016 levels three years in advance.

Figure 3 Fiscal stance over the economic cycle, Eurozone, 2011-2018

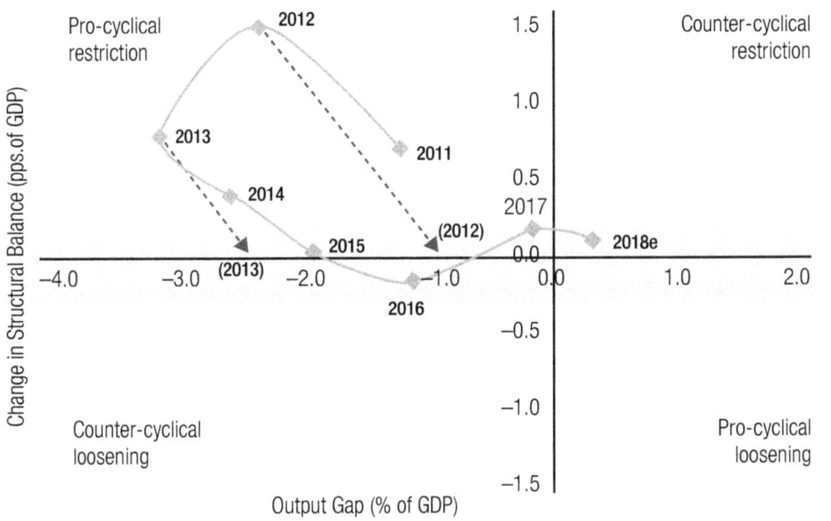

Note: This is computed with a multiplier equal to 1, with monetary policy at zero lower bound, large underutilized capacity and high private debt.

Source: Authors' calculations based on AMECO.

4 Reforms during the crisis, but job still not completed

Because of shortcomings in the construction of the EMU, countries in the Eurozone entered the financial crisis with too high government debt and excessive bank leverage, and without the institutions or mechanisms to manage shocks. Since then, reforms have aimed at preventing the repetition of this crisis and have led to overhauling the toolbox of EMU (European Commission 2017c). Efforts have notably been made to detect and correct macroeconomic imbalances, to better coordinate economic and fiscal policies and to provide financial assistance to Member States in financial difficulties through the European Stability Mechanism.

One of the salient actions was to initiate a Banking Union in 2012. The Single Supervisory Mechanism became responsible for supervision of banks throughout the Eurozone.

The Single Resolution Mechanism was designed to sever the links between bank and sovereign stress by unifying the bank resolution and restructuring frameworks across countries and providing a common, industry-funded backstop. These two pillars of the Banking Union rest on the foundation of the single rulebook, which applies to all EU countries. The completion of the Banking Union requires a credible backstop and a common deposit guarantee (European Commission 2017d).

Progress towards private risk-sharing requires the completion of the Banking Union, overcoming the remaining fragmentation, and the advancement in the Capital Markets Union. The latter will allow the excess savings in some Eurozone members to be recycled via equity rather than via debt, which will considerably reduce the risks we witnessed in the pre-crisis period. In the medium-term, a genuine Eurozone safe asset will also need to be considered (see chapter 6).

On the fiscal side, more reforms to improve the stabilisation capacity of the Eurozone economies are needed (see chapter 8). A central investment scheme could provide enough liquidity to compensate the effort made by the Eurozone members. To help monetary policy, some insurance mechanism would be necessary to manage the impact of large shocks and ensure that Eurozone Member States are not constrained to carry out pro-cyclical fiscal policies in a downturn. (European Commission 2017c). The first concrete proposal for a Eurozone fiscal capacity in the context of a multi-annual financial framework (2021-2027) came in May 2017 (European Commission 2017e).

5 Conclusion

Europe's currency union is still in its formative years. The foundations of the EMU were laid down in the Treaty of Maastricht in 1992 and, in 2019, the euro celebrates its 20th year of existence.

While important reforms were undertaken during the European sovereign-debt crisis, this does not mean that the job is complete. The deepening of the Eurozone is unfinished business. Two Euro summits took place in 2018 (in June and then in December). Leaders have endorsed the terms of reference for the common backstop to the Single Resolution Fund and the term sheet on the reform of the European Stability Mechanism. They have agreed on next steps to pursue the work on a European deposit insurance scheme. They also mandated the Eurogroup to work on the design, modalities of implementation, and timing of a budgetary instrument for convergence and competitiveness for the Eurozone going forward. While such reforms are important steps, a unified approach on EMU's "final equilibrium" is still missing.

To bridge competing visions on the way forward, mutual trust has to be rebuilt. In order to move to a genuine EMU, we need to restore the veil of ignorance (Rawls 1999) under the consideration that the creditors (and debtors) of today are not necessarily the creditors (and debtors) of tomorrow. This will require policy authorities to develop a vision of the common interest and a low discount rate in the decision-making. The upcoming campaign for the European Parliament election is an opportunity for a mature debate on the euro's next frontier.

10 Should the Eurozone Be Less Intergovernmental?*

August 2019

1 Intergovernmentalism versus Supranationalism

The question whether different areas of cooperation are characterized by intergovernmental or supranational elements goes back to the inception of the European Union and the different communities preceding it. Different theories of integration attempt to explain the process and the key drivers of integration based on two different perspectives: From an intergovernmental point of view, national governments are the central actors of the integration process whereas from a supranational angle, integration triggered by sovereigns evolves independently of national governments (Bache et al. 2015).

Structures and institutions within the EU are neither purely intergovernmental nor supranational and the balance of intergovernmental and supranational features can change over time. Different areas of cooperation can therefore entail varying degrees of intergovernmental or supranational elements. In a number of areas, decisions are subject to unanimity, to preserve "vital" interests of individual Member States while discussions take place within a supranational framework. This is for example the case for common foreign and security policy (with some exceptions requiring qualified majority, e.g. appointment of a special representative), EU finances and the harmonisation of national legislation on indirect taxation.[1]

---

* Co-author: Martina Krobath (European Commission), Luiss SEP, 30 August 2019.

The recent economic and financial crisis highlighted the need for more coordination and brought about further integration but also revived the discussion on how competences should be divided between the EU institutions and its Member States. In this respect, the binary choice seemed to be between the intergovernmental method and the community method; the latter is characterized by the sole right of the European Commission to initiate legislation, co-decision by the Council and the European Parliament, and qualified majority voting in the Council. However, the German Federal Chancellor, Angela Merkel, in 2010 shaped the concept of a new "Union method" which she defined as "coordinated action in a spirit of solidarity."[2] EU institutions and Member States are supposed to act in accordance with the competences assigned to them by the Treaties, with the main goal being the achievement of a common position notwithstanding which method is used.

With the EU Treaties largely unchanged through the crisis, and limited scope for action in some areas through secondary legislation, further integration led to increased policy coordination of Member States. While there has been a strengthening of supranational institutions in particular in the area of banking supervision and the implementation of the Stability and Growth Pact (Dehousse 2016), overall, the revisions in the framework of economic governance in Europe largely followed an intergovernmental approach. This led to an integration paradox and what some scholars define as "*new intergovernmentalism*": Member States pursued more integration but resisted further supranationalism (Bickerton et al. 2015).

2 The "new" economic governance framework

The recent economic and financial crisis led to a considerable improvement of the economic governance architecture while preserving the fundamental principles of the Treaty of Maastricht: centralized monetary policy and decentralized but coordinated economic policies.

In order to safeguard the financial stability of the Eurozone and its Member States, the European Stability Mechanism (ESM) was based on an intergovernmental treaty, following its temporary precursor (the European Financial Stability Facility, EFSF). This treaty is currently under revision following an agreement by Member States to strengthen the role

Figure 1 New economic governance framework

1. Crisis Management			
Crisis Resolution Mechanism	European Financial Stability Facility (SFSP)	International Treaty	Intergovernmental
	European Financial Stabilisation Mechanism (EFSM)	EU regulation	Supranational
	European Stability Mechanism (ESM)	International Treaty	Intergovernmental
2. Financial Union			
Banking Union	Single Supervisory Mechanism (SSM)	EU regulation	Supranational
	Single Resolution Mechanism (SRM)	EU regulation and International Treaty	Supranational and intergovernmental (Financial arrangements of Single Resolution Fund, SRF)
European System of Financial Supervison (ESFS)	European Systemic Risk Board (ESRB)	EU regulation	Supranational
	European Supervisory Authorities (EBA, ESMA, EIOPA)	EU regulation	Supranational
3. Economic Surveillance			
Fiscal coordination	Stronger preventive and corrective arms Stability and Growth Pact	EU regulation	Supranational
	Introduction of an annual process for economic and budgetary policy coordination	EU regulation	Supranational
	Requirements for national fiscal frameworks	EU directive	Supranational
	Treaty on stability, coordination and governance	International Treaty	Intergovernmental
	Establishment of independent advisory European Fiscal Board	Commission decision	Supranational
Economic coordination	New procedure for correcting macroeconomic imbalances	EU regulation	Supranational
	Establishment of National Productivity Boards	Council recommendation	Supranational

Source: Own elaboration.

for the ESM in financial assistance programmes, develop further its precautionary instruments and to cater for the provision of the backstop to the Single Resolution Fund (SRF). One of the main achievements of the past years was the agreement to set up a Banking Union comprising a Single Supervisory Mechanism (SSM) and a Single Resolution Mechanism (SRM) for banks, both being part of the community framework. At the request of the Council – due to legal uncertainties related to the legal base of the SRM – the transfer of the contributions to the SRF and the mutualisation of the financial resources in the national compartments were regulated through an Intergovernmental Agreement (IGA). However, the agreement included a clause that steps would need to be taken to incorporate the IGA into the legal framework of the Union within ten years of its implementation. Economic policy coordination, as well as the underlying rules, were strengthened considerably. Heads of States and Governments of the Eurozone also agreed on a new Fiscal Compact, which complemented the revised EU fiscal framework. Due to the absence of unanimity among Member States to include the Fiscal Compact in the EU legal framework, including by means of a Treaty change, it was adopted as an intergovernmental treaty. The so-called Treaty on Stability, Coordination and Governance (TSCG) was signed by all EU Member States except for the United Kingdom and the Czech Republic and foresees the eventual incorporation of its substance into Union law. The Commission made a proposal to this end.

There are a number of reasons behind the shift towards an intergovernmental working mode during and after the crisis. In many instances, this approach was the only option during the turmoil since the EU Treaties and the budget did not provide the necessary competences to safeguard the stability of the Eurozone within a very tight timeframe and under extreme stress. This was exacerbated by the fact that changing the EU Treaties would have required unanimity. The response to the crisis was also shaped by an increased role of the European Council and the Council in economic governance. Since the start of the economic and financial crisis, the European Council has not only provided the necessary impetus for the Union's development and defined the general political directions and priorities but it also played an increased role in day-to-day politics. Furthermore, informal working methods started to prevail. Key strategic policy discussions have increasingly taken place in the Eurogroup, instead of the ECOFIN Council,[3] with the latter essentially becoming primarily a law-making forum (Puetter 2012). Importantly, the use of the intergovernmental approach was also favoured since Member States pledged significant new national resources in the framework of assistance programs which needed to be matched with the adequate accountability on the national level.

3 Is the new intergovernmental model successful?

Undoubtedly, the Eurozone crisis has laid bare multiple compromises, which were the result of the integration process and were motivated by the need to preserve the Union's unity. As Fabbrini (2014) pointed out, Denmark's and the United Kingdom's decision to stay out of the Euro reflects the existence of diverse preferences concerning the economic and monetary integration and more broadly economic policies: in this case, agreement on the goals – economic growth and price stability – but not the same means. Intergovernmental agreements can therefore help to pursue integration of those willing to cooperate more closely or at different speeds and be a strategic opportunity and a catalyst for a deepened EU.

Various scholars advocate for a multi-speed Europe consisting of different clubs or clusters in particular in light of a further enlargement of the EU. Schmidt (2019a) suggests an EU "as soft-core of multiple clusters of Member States, in which any duo or trio of Member States would take leadership in any given policy community." Member States could therefore intensify cooperation in policy fields in which they have an interest in working together while participation in the Single Market and the respect of fundamental social and democratic rules as well as common institutions and legal systems are a perquisite. Voting would be restricted to policy areas in which Member States participate. Similarly, Demertzis et al. (2018) presented a new structure for Europe that should break the existing stalemate. Member States would be part of a "bare-bones EU" consisting of a set of policies and could then choose to integrate further and participate in multiple clubs open to all.

Challenges related to differentiated integration can be eased if such a cooperation is organized within the EU legal framework. However, under certain circumstances enhanced coordination outside the EU legal framework can be beneficial if it follows the notion of "intergovernmental avant-garde." This means that that intergovernmental agreements should fulfil the following criteria: all Member States have the opportunity to join, the role of EU institutions is strengthened, no new parallel institutions are set up outside the EU legal framework and there is the willingness to integrate such structures into the EU framework as soon as possible (Emmanouilidis 2012). Looking at the reform initiatives of the past years, not all the intergovernmental structures fulfill the last two criteria. While intergovernmental features have been and will continue to be a part of the EU framework, the question arises whether the current economic governance framework works efficiently and whether the status-quo should be preserved.

We see several drawbacks linked to this system.

1. *The new system is perceived as being complex and difficult to understand.* Due to the reforms in the past years, the current system is criticised as too complex and opaque and therefore difficult to apply (Tuori and Tuori 2014). Whereas monetary policy is centralized and assigned by the EU Treaties to the ECB which regularly reports to the European Parliament, economic and fiscal policy is decentralized. Economic and fiscal policy remain national competences, although thoroughly coordinated at the Union level in various fora, often with the involvement of different stakeholders: these fora and institutions have their own Chairpersons and Presidents, their own accountability and in some cases accounting systems (European Commission 2017c).
2. *The decision-making, including the principle of unanimity, might delay or hamper processes.* The decision-making process under an intergovernmental method usually requires a consensus, and often involves additional national procedures which make it difficult to reconcile with the speed needed for ensuring effective crisis management. This is illustrated by the use of the European Financial Stability Mechanism (EFSM), a temporary crisis mechanism backed by EU budget guarantees, to provide bridge finance to Greece in July 2015: amending an EU Regulation and deciding to use it proved in practice to be quicker than taking an ordinary ESM decision of disbursement.
3. *Democratic accountability is not always ensured at the appropriate level.* The basic principle of democratic accountability is that accountability should be ensured at that level where the respective executive decision is taken, while taking into account the level where the decision has an impact (European Commission 2012d). As chapter 22 shows, it is hard to achieve effective democratic checks and balances when decisions

Figure 2 Stakeholders in the economic governance framework

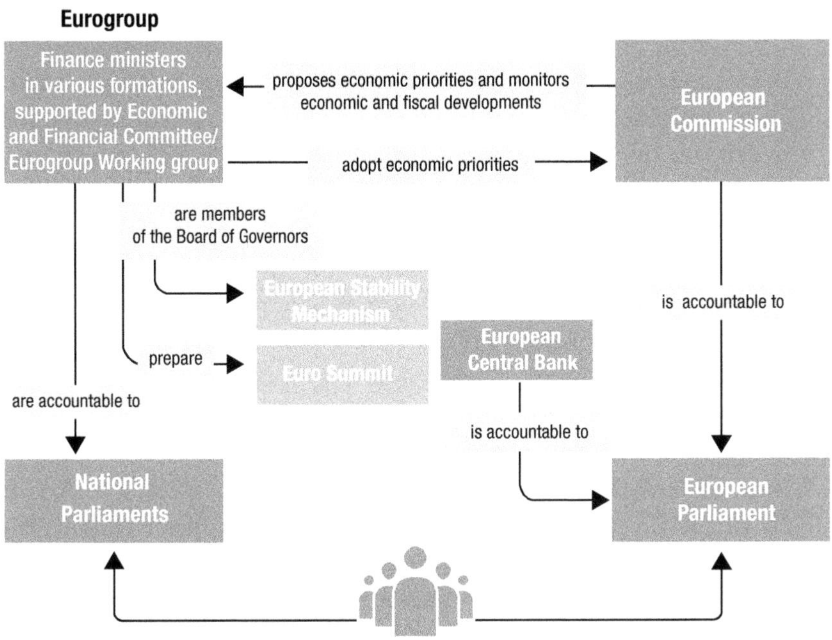

Source: European Commission (2017c).

affecting the Eurozone as a whole are taken by national institutions. While democratic accountability of intergovernmental institutions such as the ESM is ensured on the national level, albeit not in a uniform way across countries, the ESM only has an informal relationship with the European Parliament although decisions on granting financial assistance affects the Eurozone and its Member States as a whole.

4. *Intergovernmental features can lead to imbalances between state equality and state power.* The community method tries to reconcile the principle that all states are equal while acknowledging the role of larger states and, through various checks and balances, normally delivers an agenda in the interest of all. The increased role of the European Council - and hence intergovernmentalism - changed that balance by providing room for the domination of larger states (Fabbrini 2015). However the dividing line did not only run between small and large Member States but also between conflicting preferences of debtors wanting

more risk-sharing and creditors pushing for more risk-reduction. The outcome of negotiations in an intergovernmental setting is directly related to the bargaining power which favoured creditor countries since the immediate consequences resulting from the crisis would have hit debtor countries much more. Furthermore, intergovernmental negotiations are characterized by brinkmanship bargaining behavior leading to delaying rescue initiatives and adjustment policies (Schimmelfennig 2015). In the absence of a unified view on how to improve the architecture of the EMU, Member States adopted a piecemeal approach, fixing the parts of the architecture of the Economic and Monetary Union essential for its "survival" instead of agreeing on a roadmap for its medium-term evolution (Pisani-Ferry 2015) which would be in the common interest of all. The current framework therefore reflects an accumulation of decisions based on "*ultima ratio*."

5. *Intergovernmental institutions and bodies do not have the same transparency standards that are in place for EU institutions.* According to Article 15 of the Treaty on the Functioning of the European Union, "the Union's institutions, bodies, offices and agencies shall conduct their work as openly as possible." This means that citizens have the right of access to documents of the institutions unless disclosure would undermine the protection of the public interest as regards the financial, monetary or economic policy of the Community or a Member State, or the privacy and the integrity of the individual amongst others. Such requirements are not in place for example for intergovernmental institutions and bodies.

4 The way forward: recreating the "veil of ignorance"

As Schmidt (2019b) highlights, the politicization of the EU – defined as the process of political awareness and the engagement in politics – has increased over time which expanded the influence of national politics on the position of Leaders in the European Council. However, there is a conflict between national interests mainly between creditor and debtor countries on the distribution of the adjustment burden (Delatte 2018) which together with a lack of trust between countries as well as in the EU institutions (Demertzis 2018) can stall necessary reform efforts, produce an inefficient equilibrium and lead to outcomes and structures that are in many instances complex, lack transparency and democratic accountability is based solely on national institutions. Intergovernmental negotiations fail to give convincing and durable responses to challenges, which in turn lead to additional integration steps to correct deficiencies related to previous action (Piattoni 2017). The result is a "failing-forward" approach (Jones et al. 2016) leading to institutional incompleteness because agreements are based on the lowest common denominator. Advancing integration through a sequence of incomplete reforms can make the economic adjustment more difficult and lead to permanent output losses. In turn, the weaker economic performance undermines public support for the European project in the long-run and influences national preferences on which basis decisions are taken in the European Council.

In order to overcome this problem, Member States need to recognize and acknowledge the links and benefits between the national and the EU level and revert back to the community method. Against this background, the Commission has proposed a number of reforms in the past years to address the deficiencies related to the current system. The aim of the reforms was to favour solutions within the Treaties, in order to deliver democratic accountability at all levels and they contributed to the Eurozone speaking with one voice. In December 2017, the Commission presented a proposal to develop the ESM into a European Monetary Fund anchored within the EU's legal framework and to integrate the substance of the Treaty on Stability, Coordination and Governance into EU law. Furthermore, it presented a Communication to establish a European Minister of Economy and Finance who could serve as Vice-President of the Commission and chair the Eurogroup and would amongst others pursue the general interest of the EU/Eurozone economy. In the past few months, intense discussions have taken place on the issues addressed by the Commission, but only in some cases the supranational approach has been followed.

The use of intergovernmental solutions was certainly unavoidable during the crisis. However, an ad hoc model of integration based on an *ultima ratio* approach, which does not rely on the EU Treaties and does not use the EU institutions, contains important risks for its stability. As pointed out in chapter 9, a shared narrative is necessary to rebuild trust. In this respect, recreating Rawls' "veil of ignorance" can help Member States to revert to the common goals and leave behind their national resentments and narrow self-interest. The cooperative approach on which the Community method is built can bring wins for all.

Notes

[1] There is an ongoing debate whether unanimity could be overcome in some of these fields. In particular, in the area of taxation the Commission presented a Communication in January 2019 to move gradually from unanimity voting to the ordinary legislative procedure.

[2] Text of the full speech: https://www.coleurope.eu/events/mrs-angela-merkel-delivered-opening-address-opening-ceremony (Merkel 2010).

[3] This, however, has changed lately since the Eurogroup in inclusive format (all EU Member States except for the United Kingdom) has allowed EU Member States to come back to the table.

Part B.
Fiscal Policy and Fiscal Rules

Credible fiscal rules aiming at ensuring public debt sustainability have been at the heart of EMU since the very beginning. The Stability and Growth Pact is probably the most contentious and hotly debated component of EMU's architecture. The chapters in this section explore the evolving role of fiscal policy in EMU, the appropriateness of numerical rules and the quest for a balanced monetary-fiscal policy mix. The Pact is often associated to "austerity," a word like no other that has come to embody the political divisions between Member States and heated popular feelings.

Ensuring fiscal sustainability is a "conditio sine qua non" for a well-functioning currency area. Whilst most economists agree that many European economies share the need to reduce their high public debt, the controversy rages on the speed of consolidation and on how state-contingent it should be. At the height of the financial crisis, the fragility of EMU's construct required very prudent fiscal policies as a "signalling device" to financial markets. However, a gradual rethinking of the interplay between public debt sustainability and fiscal stabilisation has started to emerge, eventually leading to a fundamental reassessment of the role of fiscal policy in EMU.

It is increasingly acknowledged that national fiscal policies must contribute to a balanced policy mix, taking into account that fiscal space is heterogeneously distributed across the Eurozone. This implies that some countries are able to exploit their ample fiscal scope whilst others need to pursue a more prudent approach of gradual debt unwinding. A common stabilisation capacity would help for managing shocks that cannot be smoothed by national stabilisers alone. The considerations on the appropriate fiscal stance need to be complemented with a much stronger emphasis on the quality of public finances, in particular investment and other targeted programmes supporting sustainable growth and high-quality employment.

As the focus on underlying budgetary conditions and the fiscal stance acquired prominence, measurement problems have come to the fore. Focussing on the structural balance is, in principle, the correct way to assess the fiscal position of countries. However, the reliance on unobservable variables in the calculation of the structural balance makes its use controversial when applied to fiscal surveillance. Many of the criticisms focus on an excessive role of potential output in the EU fiscal framework. However, in practice, unlike what sceptics tend to suggest, fiscal surveillance has moved away from the exclusive reliance on structural balances.

11 Fiscal Austerity and Policy Credibility*

April 2012

1 Introduction

Most economists agree that European economies share the need to reduce public deficits and debts. This chapter stresses that while gradual consolidations are in general more likely to succeed than cold-shower ones, the superiority of a gradual strategy tends to evaporate for high levels of debt and is also less pronounced for consolidation episodes following a financial crisis.

The renewed phase of tension in Europe, and the Eurozone in particular, since the second half of 2011, with the prospect of a double-dip recession alternating with that of a sovereign-debt crisis, has reignited the debate on fiscal austerity, to which European governments have been committed since the end of the most acute phase of the crisis in 2009.

Before entering the debate, it is important to stress that there should be little question that European economies share the need to reduce public deficits and debts from levels that, as confirmed by a growing strand of empirical literature (Reinhart and Rogoff 2009a, Kuhmar and Woo 2012), are likely to be harmful for growth in the medium-term, and even more so if one factors in the large implicit government liabilities linked to ageing. In fact, a striking feature of the financial crisis compared to previous comparable episodes in industrial economies is not so much the increase in public debt from the onset of the crisis, which appears to have

---

* Co-author: Lucio R. Pench (European Commission), Vox CEPR, 20 April 2012.

followed a well-trodden path, but the (much) higher level from which the increase started (Figure 1). This heightens the concern for threshold effects.

The debate on fiscal austerity is therefore also about the timing and speed of consolidation, not only its overall size.

Figure 1 Gross public-debt crises (% of GDP)

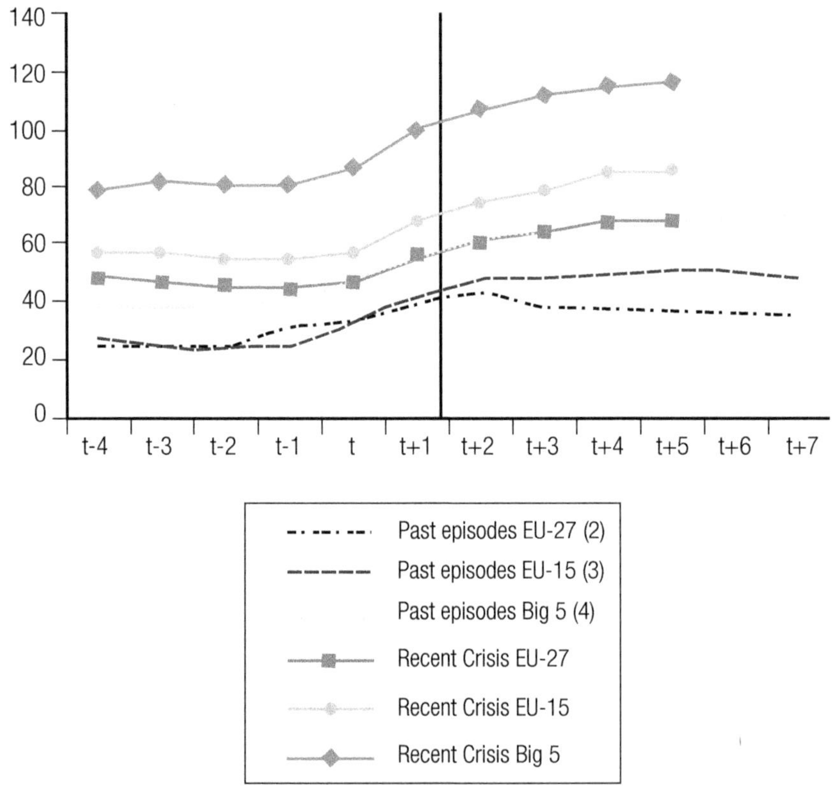

Notes: (1) Based on 49 crises episodes. Unweighted country averages. t = start of the crisis. (2) Includes crisis episodes in Czech Republic, Finland, Hungary, Latvia, Poland, Slovak Republic, Spain and Sweden. For new Member States data from 1991. (3) Includes crisis episodes in Finland, Spain and Sweden. (4) Includes crisis episodes in Finland, Norway, Sweden, Japan and Spain.

Sources: Calculations based on IMF International Financial Statistics and AMECO.

2 The debate on fiscal austerity: a stylised representation

In economic terms, it can be seen as revolving around the size of the fiscal multipliers – the higher the multiplier, the more costly, in terms of growth, the austerity. The following stylised representation (borrowed from Röger and in't Veld 2012) may help to illustrate the matter.

For a given composition of the fiscal adjustment, the multiplier can be expressed as:

$$\text{Multiplier} = \frac{1 - \text{“confidence”}}{1 + \text{monetary policy} \times \text{competitiveness} - \text{financial constraint}}$$

The "confidence" term refers to i) "non-Keynesian" wealth effect on consumption and investment stemming from the expected reduction in future taxes, and ii) the credibility effect on the real interest rate stemming from the reduction in risk premia (both effects are supposed to follow an adjustment that is, and perceived to be, permanent and successful, hence the "confidence" label). "Monetary policy" and "competiveness" stand, respectively, for the accommodating reaction of monetary policy to, and the gains in international competitiveness from, the negative impact of adjustment on inflation, which partially offset its negative impact on private demand. Finally, the proportion of households and firms that are liquidity- or credit-constrained will increase the multiplier, by making it difficult or impossible for the private sector to compensate by borrowing the impact of adjustment on current income.

The composition of fiscal adjustment interacts with the multipliers' determinants to produce different growth outcomes depending on the choice of the instrument, with the ranking inverting, however, when one moves from the short to the medium-to-long-term. In particular, (exhaustive) expenditure cuts have more negative short-term output effects, but positive effects in the long-term (through the non-Keynesian confidence channel); the short-term output loss of tax increases is smaller, but persistent over time (for a summary set of simulations of the effect of different instruments using the Commission QUEST III model, see European Commission 2010e).

Last but not least, the effects of adjustment are likely to differ depending on whether the economy is in a recession or expansion phase. The response effect of output is likely to be larger in a recession, reflecting the presence of unused resources.

If one compares this stylised representation of the effects of fiscal adjustment with the current situation in the Eurozone, the following conclusions stand out.

First, the state of the economy can be characterised as a balance-sheet recession, namely, a major financial-cycle bust following a boom against a backdrop of low inflation (Borio et al. 2011). This implies that the multipliers determinants are working in different directions.

Second, the debt and capital overhang in the private sector and the corresponding impairing of the financial sector make further borrowing to offset the impact of fiscal adjustment on current income a difficult, if not impossible, proposition. The very low level of inflation and interest rates constrain the room for accommodating monetary policy and for achieving competitiveness gains (under fixed exchange rates).

Third, ballooning public deficits and debts, largely a consequence of the unrecognised unsustainable nature of revenues and build-up of contingent liabilities during the long boom phase preceding a balance-sheet recession, raise doubts on government solvency, thereby increasing the "confidence" term, working through the sovereign-risk channel linking public and private borrowing costs.

Fourth, conventional fiscal stimulus measures fail to address directly the debt overhang and balance-sheet repair problem. Addressing balance-sheet repair problems head on is instrumental to reducing the size of the multipliers in the adjustment process and ultimately unlocking a "virtuous cycle" of self-sustained recovery (see chapter 25).

Finally, as a consequence of the above, while economies share the need for reducing deficit and debts, the appropriate pace of consolidation should differ across countries. Countries with very high and/or rapidly rising debts may be well-advised to pursue a fast adjustment, in spite of an unfavourable economic environment, if the alternative of a sovereign-debt crisis is sufficiently plausible. While the composition of the adjustment should be tilted towards expenditure, which typically would have risen too much throughout the period when windfall revenues were flattering public accounts, a mix of expenditure cuts and tax rises is likely to be inevitable. Besides considerations of political economy, it may also produce a smoother response of output to consolidation.

These conclusions find support in an analysis of successful fiscal consolidations focusing on the probability of reducing the public-debt ratio relative to its pre-consolidation levels (European Commission 2010b). In particular, it shows that while gradual consolidations are in general more likely to succeed than cold-shower ones, the superiority of a gradual strategy tends to evaporate for high levels of debt and is also less pronounced for consolidation episodes following a financial crisis.

It has been argued that fiscal consolidation can be "self-defeating" if, for example, risk premia respond positively to the debt-to-GDP ratio and the latter increases instead of diminishing as a result of consolidation. While this result is plausible in the short-term for a range of values of the multiplier and the debt ratio, the reaction of risk premia presupposes myopia on the part of financial markets, since the initial increase in the debt ratio would be followed by a movement in the opposite direction as the multiplier effect fades away and the primary balance is permanently improved by the adjustment (Gros 2011).

3 How the EU fiscal framework fits in the policy debate

The EU fiscal framework is sometimes characterised as imposing a "one-size-fits-all" fiscal-consolidation model, which ignores the need for differentiation outlined above (Wolf 2012). This characterisation is less than accurate. Admittedly, the EU fiscal framework is rule-based, which implies a presumption of reaction on the part of the budgetary authorities when certain trigger indicators of unsound fiscal policies are activated. In turn, for the rules to be workable, the triggers need to be easily readable. Hence the choice of "reference values" for the government deficit (level) and debt (level and change) for triggering the excessive deficit procedure (in fact, considerations of simplicity led, until recently, to privileging the deficit indicator at the expense of debt dynamics). At the same time, the framework leaves considerable scope for modulating the fiscal policy reaction, both in terms of the initial prescription of the adjustment path and its subsequent adaptation to economic shocks. These characteristics have been accentuated by the recent reform of the Stability and Growth Pact (European Commission 2011a, 2012a) and are borne out by the fiscal exit strategy that EU countries commonly agreed in 2009 and subsequently confirmed with some modifications. The strategy revolves around three pillars.

First, countries are given a multi-year horizon, ranging from two to five years, to correct the excessive deficit position. Setting a deadline for the correction is a requirement of the excessive-deficit procedure, but also serves the economic purpose of anchoring expectations of return to sound public finances.

Second, the speed of adjustment and the degree of frontloading broadly reflect the availability of fiscal space and economic conditions. Specifically, countries facing market pressures were already recommended to start their (typically larger) adjustment in 2010, while for the others adjustment should effectively start from 2011. Consolidation is generally gradual, albeit substantial.

Third, countries are encouraged to pay attention to the quality of the adjustment, in terms of composition and accompanying structural reforms. Policy recommendations in these areas, which already figure prominently in adjustment programmes, are to be sharpened for all countries through the implementation of the macroeconomic imbalances procedure, which complements the recent reform of the Stability and Growth Pact.

Concerning the response to shocks, it needs stressing that the Stability and Growth Pact explicitly allows for the playing of automatic stabilisers around the adjustment path, that is, the adjustment is formulated in structural terms. Acknowledging the problems inherent in the measurement of structural balances, the framework calls for an "in-depth analysis" of the reasons behind a country' s failure to meet the budgetary targets, including revisions in potential growth and endogenous changes in revenue elasticities. To these elements of flexibility, the recent reform has added the possibility of extending deadlines for the correction of the excessive deficits irrespective of a country's individual predicament, if the situation of the Eurozone or the EU as a whole calls for a relaxation of fiscal policy.

It should also be noted that the operationalisation of the debt criterion of the excessive-deficit procedure through the "1/20" debt-reduction benchmark - possibly the most visible innovation of the reform - is accompanied by greater allowance for an economic reading of the debt trigger. Of particular interest in the current context is the provision whereby capital injections to preserve the stability of the banking sector are counted as mitigating factors when assessing a breach of the benchmark.

4 Conclusion

The greater-than-commonly-appreciated flexibility afforded by the Pact entails a considerable room for discretionary judgement when it comes to its application. In particular, while the occurrence of economic shocks allows for an extension of the deadline for the correction of the excessive deficit, on condition that the prescribed structural effort has been delivered, it is left to the discretion of the Commission and the Council whether an extension should be effectively granted. In this connection, the second pillar of differentiation of the EU fiscal exit strategy, namely, differentiation according to fiscal space, comes into play. It may be necessary to ask for an additional fiscal effort from a country facing the risk of a debt interest spiral, while longer correction deadlines certainly make sense for countries where sovereign risk is subdued.

The attention drawn by a few problematic cases should not obscure the fact that most countries in the Eurozone and the EU made steady progress towards the correction of the excessive deficit in line the multi-year adjustment path defined by the Council in 2009. For these countries, the EU framework has provided an anchor, in the absence of which adjustment might have less credible and hence even more costly, according to the stylised discussion presented above. Nor is it clear, including from the revealed preferences of national authorities, that even the minority of countries that are struggling to meet the deadlines would necessarily benefit from a generalised relaxation of the current targets.

A differentiated application of flexibility, trading the risk to stabilisation against those to financial stability, may in fact be the preferable approach. Nor should the quest for flexibility be concentrated on the relaxation of deficit targets. When balance-sheet repair is the pre-condition for the restoring of normal economic relationships, it may be preferable to concentrate the limited fiscal firepower on the recapitalisation of the banking sector rather than on conventional tax and expenditure programmes (for model simulation lending support to prioritising bank recapitalisation see Kollmann et al 2011).

To sum up, the EU fiscal framework can certainly be criticised. As with every rule-based framework, it represents an imperfect answer to the basic credibility problem of economic policy. Depending on their overall persuasion and their reading of the current situation, critics may blame a lack of flexibility or even an excess of it. The framework is not, however, disconnected from the economic debate on austerity. In fact, it can be rationalised as being broadly consistent with the view that "weak growth in countries facing precarious fiscal positions is not sufficient evidence against fiscal austerity" (Corsetti 2012).

12 Fiscal Policy in Europe: Searching for the Right Balance*

March 2013

1 Introduction

The debate on the fiscal strategy in Europe seems at times like a war of religions. This is unfortunate because the objective disagreements in substance (e.g. see VoxEU debate: Has austerity gone too far?) are in our view less pronounced than is sometimes depicted.

In this chapter, we lay out the main tenets of the EU's approach to current fiscal adjustments. It is not a dogmatic call for austerity at all costs. Rather, it is a delicate balancing act between implementing credible adjustments, keeping flexibility against shocks, and factoring in institutional constraints.

We proceed by examining more closely some of the accusations levelled against fiscal policy recommendations adopted by the Council under the EU framework. Our claim is not that recommendations have always been "just right," or that they could not be improved upon in any specific aspects. But we would say that more often than not, these recommendations have been and remain sensible and in line with those advocated by other institutional organisations such as the IMF or the OECD.

* Co-author: Nicolas Carnot (European Commission), Vox CEPR, 14 March 2013. This chapter is adapted from Buti and Carnot (2013).

2 Allegations and rejoinders

Allegation 1: There was irrational panic in the sovereign-bond markets of vulnerable European countries, and this led to the imposition of unnecessarily harsh consolidation (see in particular de Grauwe and Ji 2013).

There is agreement that markets are prone to excessive swings. Yet, this need not imply that markets acted purely out of irrational fear in the sovereign-bond crisis. Some investors did lose money on Greek bonds after all. And though arguably excessive at times, sovereign spreads have remained loosely correlated with the underlying fundamentals. So even though they may not reflect only objective factors, spreads are not unrelated to them either.

Clearly the announcement of the OMT programme by the ECB did much to mitigate the threat of a self-fulfilling liquidity crisis. However, the OMT announcement does not address the underlying sustainability concerns. Vulnerable countries have sustainable positions, but this holds under the condition that they adjust.

Thus, the fact that the reduction in spreads coincided with the announcement of the OMT is no sufficient evidence that the concomitant consolidation efforts were not necessary. In fact, fiscal adjustment and the possibility to activate the OMT are arguably strongly complementry. And a growing perception that adjustments are underway, as evidenced by significant progress in reducing deficits and restoring external positions, probably also contributed to the improvement in markets.

Now, it may be argued that consolidation efforts, while necessary, were not needed to the extent prescribed. This leads to the next point.

Allegation 2: The adjustment is too frontloaded.

There is widespread agreement that fiscal consolidation should be pursued in most European countries. This is the view of the IMF, the OECD and the Commission. It is important to underline this area of agreement. Once it is admitted that fiscal adjustment is due, the issue becomes not one of principle, but one of degree.

Many commentators say the problem is rather that adjustment is overly frontloaded, especially for the Eurozone periphery (e.g. Wolf 2013). When setting the pace of fiscal adjustment, one important consideration is the economic outlook, including what we know of the short-term effects of consolidation (the multiplier). As compared with usual circumstances, there are reasons to expect higher multipliers in an environment of weak activity, lack of room for a supportive monetary policy, and tight financing constraints for private agents. All else equal, this calls for spreading out adjustments over time. The argument, also inspired by the Japanese experience (Koo 2008), is to sequence private and public deleveraging.

There are several opposite considerations however. First, one cannot be sure by when and how much the fiscal multiplier could fall in the future (Wolff 2013). Then, while consolidation may be now more costly than in normal times, no or limited consolidation may in some cases have even worse consequences, notably if it triggers market expectations of a sovereign default and a liquidity crisis (Corsetti 2012). This risk might have been lowered with the possibility of the OMT, but as noted above, this does not remove the need to demonstrate early commitment to fiscal consolidation,

Another point is simply basic arithmetic: when the scope of required adjustment is large in the medium-term, even a gradual consolidation strategy spreading out consolidation over several years in broadly equal instalments will translate in not-insignificant fiscal effort from the beginning. Public sustainability gaps are at historic highs in a number of countries (European Commission 2012e). In addition, stressed Eurozone countries face a big overall external challenge, unlike Japan in the 1990s. That requires an adjustment of the nation as a whole that is bound to be painful, whatever the exact distribution between public and private deleveraging.

Overall, the policy implications require treading a fine line. The IMF considers a structural adjustment pace of 1% a year as a useful guideline, with needed differentiation according to the country situation (IMF 2012b). The Stability and Growth Pact (SGP) requires an annual structural adjustment of 0.5%, and more in the case of vulnerable countries. Country-specific features are important to consider as well (Gros 2013).

In practice, policy prescriptions under the EMU framework have struck a balance between the conflicting considerations. It should be recalled that the fiscal exit strategy originated in the early response to the crisis in the form of a fiscal stimulus in 2009/2010. Many initial recommendations under the excessive deficit procedure (EDP) were drafted in this period, where it was agreed that the initial fiscal relaxation should be followed by fiscal retrenchment to stabilise and reduce debts. Recommendations set out at the time, of which a number remain in place, charted a path of sustained but spread out adjustment over several years, and with more effort required when the sustainability challenge is bigger.

The international consensus is that fiscal consolidation needs to continue at a gradual and sustained pace, with fiscal adjustment in most advanced economies broadly appropriate (IMF 2013a). The precise pace of consolidation remains a delicate balance in each country specific cases, and may always be discussed. For example, future recommendations could better factor in the consequences of changes in growth models (such as rebalancing towards the tradable sector) in terms of lower tax elasticities.

Allegation 3: The Commission follows an inflexible approach.

In a sense, this criticism comes at a paradoxical time. The Commission has taken the initiative by proposing to extend deadlines for correcting the excessive deficit in several countries: Ireland, Portugal, Greece and Spain have already benefited from such flexibility. When recently presenting its 2013 winter forecast, the Commission made clear that other extensions could be considered this spring.

An important aspect of the EU fiscal framework is the weight given to structural targets, rather than just the overall deficit of a country (see chapter 11). The reliance on structural targets provides both predictability and flexibility. The predictability stems from the fact that countries can embark on a "steady structural approach." The flexibility lies in allowing the automatic stabilisers to play out around the (structural) path of adjustment. Unless warranted by an overwhelming financing constraint, there is generally no need to chase nominal targets when growth disappoints.

Of course cyclically adjusted balances are not without limitations either, based as they are on partly conventional assumptions. The surveillance framework is being developed to cope with these limitations (European Commission 2012a).

The simple allegation that the Commission pursues austerity inflexibly does not hold. Nor does the opposite accusation that the framework is being weakened by downplaying the role of headline balances. The size of the fiscal adjustment already produced in vulnerable countries and elsewhere is testimony against that.

Allegation 4: Fiscal consolidation is not politically or socially sustainable. There is no denying that the adjustments undergone by stressed countries are severe. This may strain social cohesion. However, a lot can be done both to soften the consequences of adjustments, and accelerate the return to sustainable growth.

The composition of fiscal adjustment warrants attention. One needs to pick-up growth-friendly measures in an encompassing manner. Spreading the costs across the population and confronting vested interests help generate a sense that everyone pays their fair share. Some fiscal reforms, such as pension reforms, can improve sustainability and medium-term growth without weighing on aggregate demand.

Structural reform is another aspect, which goes hand in hand with fiscal consolidation in the present juncture (see chapter 25). Structural reforms improve efficiency, but are also important when it comes to sharing the cost of adjustment in an equitable manner (Cœuré 2013). For example, flexible work arrangements reduce the impact of downturns on outright layoffs. Reducing rents in product markets fosters the pass-through of wage restraint to prices, supporting household purchasing power. In other cases (e.g. employment protection legislation), reforms would not cushion the impact of negative shocks, but favour a stronger upturn.

On the financial front, the deleveraging drag will be lowered by efficient bankruptcy procedures and genuine financial repair that allows lending to dynamic parts of the economy to go unhindered. Ensuring the effectiveness of monetary policy and restoring credit channels soften the costs of consolidation too.

In countries inside or outside the Eurozone under a EU-IMF programme, the governments concerned and the troïka (Commission, IMF, ECB) have made efforts to embed equity considerations into fiscal adjustment plans. Tax measures have focused on higher income brackets, and cuts in government wages or social benefits have often spared the lowest income levels. In some of the countries, the internal and external imbalances were so large and deep-rooted that radical choices had to be considered to rebuild their economic and policy credibility.

Allegation 5: The Commission's approach is one-sided. It puts all the burden of adjustment on debtor countries.

Several observers have pointed to the spillover implications of fiscal policies, and possibly insufficient policy coordination in the EU (e.g. Holland and Portes 2012). We would agree that the symmetry of the adjustment is a legitimate concern. There are ways to favour a coordinated approach to rebalancing, but the tools currently available also present limitations.

For vulnerable countries of the Eurozone that face a large external sustainability gap, external growth is the only sustainable way to grow out of their debts. They must undergo rebalancing. But their adjustment should not be hampered, and ideally be fostered by concomitant changes elsewhere. The improved current balances in the periphery thus have to be matched by rebalancing trends also in Eurozone countries that feature large current account surpluses.

Policies and reforms supporting demand in these countries have a role to play. In Germany, the fiscal stance is now broadly neutral, hence consistent with the call for a differentiated fiscal stance according to the budgetary space. Reforms advocated by the Commission and the Council in labour and product markets or the tax system should contribute to raising domestic demand. There is also an increasing willingness to allow wages to reflect the higher productivity in surplus countries. And since fiscal consolidation-cum-deflation is likely to be self-defeating, re-establishing competitiveness across the area implies higher than average inflation in stronger countries, provided price stability in the Eurozone and inflation expectations remain well anchored.

3 Broader implications

The discussion above has also implications for the long-run improvement of EMU architecture. The current situation appears as a cas d'école for the potential attraction of a "fiscal capacity" at the central level, in the form of a stabilisation instrument, which the Commission has proposed in its Blueprint on the future of EMU (European Commission 2012d). A dedicated stabilisation fund could improve the conduct of fiscal policies throughout the cycle by enforcing tighter policies in good times and providing additional leeway for cushioning downturns. Such a tool could strengthen the existing automatic stabilisers while maintaining a credible rule-based framework. It would be particularly useful in the current predicament characterised by large cyclical differentials across the zone as well as a not insignificant average output gap. The potential of such an instrument needs to be further explored analytically, even if the Commission blueprint considers it as a long-run prospect following deeper integration, rather than as a tool for tackling the current crisis.

13 What is a "Responsible" Fiscal Policy Today for Europe?*

February 2015

1 Introduction

What direction should fiscal policy take in Europe in the aftermath of the sovereign debt crisis? On the one hand, stocks of public debt are higher than ever, calling for long-run fiscal adjustment. On the other, doubts about the subdued recovery push for slowing fiscal consolidation and providing short-term stimulus. There doesn't exist a clear compass to balance these considerations. And the balance of course may differ with specific country situations.

The European Commission has adopted "fiscal responsibility" as a key pillar of its growth strategy, together with boosting investment and a renewed commitment to structural reforms (European Commission 2014g). Fiscal responsibility has to do with appropriately confronting the current dilemmas, since the Commission at the same time stresses that Member States "still need to secure long-term control over deficit and debt levels" while underscoring that consolidation should be "growth-friendly." The Commission has also judged that concerning the Eurozone as a whole, a broadly neutral stance emerges from the analysis of country budgetary plans for 2015 (European Commission 2014h). Moreover, while this is deemed to strike an appropriate balance for the overall zone, the country distribution of fiscal policies is judged to be sub-optimal, as "some Member States are called to increase their efforts

---

* Co-author: Nicolas Carnot (European Commission), Vox CEPR, 24 February 2015.

to comply with the SGP, [which] implies a degree of fiscal support coming from the exploitation of the fiscal space available elsewhere."

These judgments beg a number of analytical questions: a) How to characterise the notion of fiscal responsibility? b) Can the conclusion of appropriateness of a broadly neutral fiscal stance for the Eurozone at the current juncture be substantiated? c) How to make consistent assessments between the Eurozone taken in its entirety and the needed country differentiation?

The theoretical background to this discussion is being shaken by the debate over the possibility of secular stagnation (Summers 2014). Economists have generally agreed that keeping debt at prudent levels is a sensible long-term objective, if only to preserve space for firing countercyclical ammunition in downturns. Secular stagnation in a deep sense has the potential to unravel this wisdom (Eggertsson and Mehrotra 2014). A permanent (or at least persistent) shortfall in desired private investment relative to saving can – and arguably should – be countered by permanent fiscal support. This may in turn imply a growing stock of public debt – but without much concern for financing as there is a large pool of savers craving safe assets. However, the implications of low interest rates for policy depend on the underlying causes. Chronic private underspending is one explanation, yet another one is an increasingly feeble supply side (Gordon 2014).

2 Navigating in a grey reality

Models offer stylised descriptions within particular paradigms, but reality combines features of different models. This "grey reality" has crucial implications. For one, we are unlikely to receive unambiguous signals as to which kind of world we live in. At best, we modify with new information the subjective plausibility that we attach to each of the "visions." But fundamental uncertainty about key features of the economy is bound to remain. This applies to the current European predicament, which combines an interaction of supply and demand weaknesses.

From a policy perspective, uncertainty has deep implications that are not always sufficiently acknowledged (Aikman et al. 2014). An important one is the need for robust policy strategies – strategies that are not optimal under a given state of the world, but which perform acceptably well across a broad range of plausible worlds.

In the fiscal field, the premium on robust strategies is increased by the political economy complexities of budgetary policy-making. Today, running fiscal policy is a bit like steering a big tanker that is lost at sea under changing weather conditions. One needs to maintain a steady course while acknowledging the uncertainties. One also needs to think deep about coordinating the short-term with the long-term (Borg 2014). To this end it is useful to keep an eye on a "fiscal compass" that can act as a consistent guiding principle.

Carnot (2014) explores a rule of thumb that puts at its core a balancing act between fiscal sustainability and macroeconomic stabilisation. Fiscal sustainability is anchored in a long-run debt objective. For each budgetary period, the rule suggests a fiscal impulse that trades off the fiscal gap with a summary measure of economic conditions. This "rule of thumb" is both temporally consistent and geographically consistent. Moreover – and crucially in the context of European discussions – it delivers a consistent prescription for both the aggregate stance of a group of countries (e.g. the Eurozone) and each participating country of the group.

3 Heading north or south?

The 2015 fiscal map (Figure 1) shows that overall, the Eurozone still retains a fiscal gap of about 2% of GDP compared with what would be needed for a smooth reduction of debt in the long-run (although this gap has been already significantly reduced in past years). On the other hand, while not as acutely dramatic as in the Great Recession of 2009, economic conditions clearly remain depressed, albeit with signs of improvements (European Commission 2015a). There is also significant country differentiation around this average picture. In particular, Germany has "fiscal space" in the sense that its primary surplus overachieves what is needed for gradual debt reduction, while other large countries have sizeable fiscal gaps, though to varying extents.

What guidance does this imply for current budgets? The rule of thumb combines the primary gap and the summary of cyclical conditions to determine the desirable fiscal stance – like how a Taylor rule blends the inflation and output gaps for gauging policy interest rates. Our specific formulation gives equal weights to the primary gap and the economic score.

Figure 1 The fiscal map: primary gaps and economic conditions in 2015

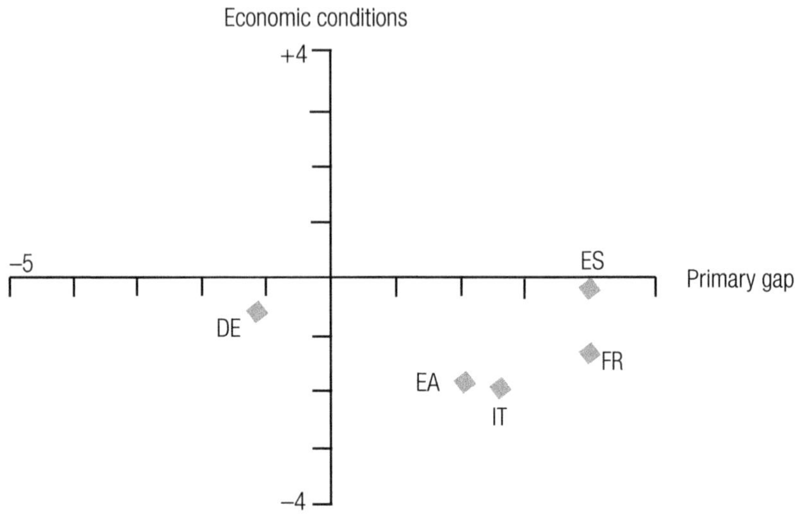

Note: The primary gap (in percent of GDP) summarises the long-run sustainability challenge. It is the distance between the actual primary balance and one that would put debt on a gently declining path. A negative sign indicates the existence of "fiscal space." The score on economic conditions summarises business cycle conditions based on the output gap and the change thereof. A zero score corresponds to broadly neutral conditions. See Carnot (2014) for details.

Source: European Commission.

We find the following (see Figure 2): A) as a whole, the Eurozone should conduct a close-to-neutral fiscal stance. This reflects the fact that, at the current juncture, the contributions from the fiscal gap and from the economic outlook broadly cancel out. This was absolutely not a forgone conclusion enshrined in the nature of the rule. Over the past decade, the same rule of thumb would have prescribed both expansion and retrenchment, depending on circumstances. B) Confirming a common insight, this overall stance should be differentiated across the zone. Pursing moderate consolidation appears warranted in both France and Spain (reflecting the still very large primary gaps). The case of Italy is more in-between, given the relatively smaller fiscal gap and

Figure 2 Fiscal stance according to the rule of thumb for 2015 (in % of GDP)

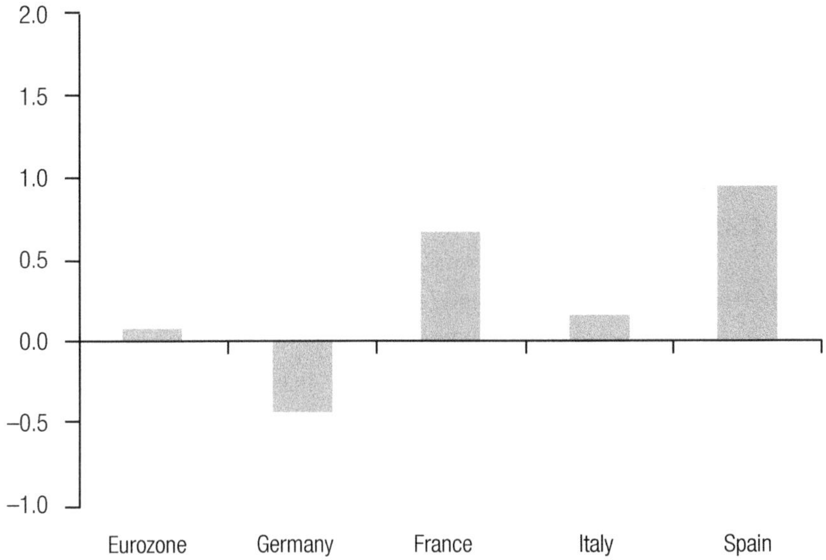

Note: The desirable fiscal stance is determined as Ft = ¼(Pt + St), where P is the primary gap and S the economic score. The rule of thumb is used in the version giving equal weights to the primary gap and economic conditions in terms of their possible contributions to the desired fiscal stance.

Source: European Commission.

the still very depressed environment (in contrast to better momentum in Spain). C) Meanwhile, the rule of thumb is consistent with a moderate fiscal stimulus in Germany. This, it should be stressed, reflects the conditions of Germany only, and should thus not be done "for the sake of others" but primarily as a result of a balanced judgment of Germany's situation.

These messages are in line with the Commission's conclusions over the 2015 round of budgets. Indeed, as formalised in the rule of thumb, the advice from the Commission on an appropriate fiscal stance takes into account the cyclical conditions of a fairly fragile recovery and sustainability concerns from high debt levels.

When the recovery gains strength, the rule of thumb will point towards resuming differentiated consolidation for the Eurozone and most countries until the remaining primary gaps are eliminated and positions are on par with steady debt reductions. This reflects the premise that public debt should be contained at prudent levels in the long-run for individual sovereigns, in line with the EU fiscal framework.

4 Conclusion

In a deeply uncertain environment, the fiscal policy debate would benefit from simple benchmarks that help steer a responsible and time-consistent course, explicitly acknowledging conflicting considerations. This is especially the case in a Europe which faces the additional challenge of coordinating decentralised fiscal policies. Indeed, as also underlined by the ECB President, there is a need and scope within the Stability and Growth Pact for "stronger coordination among the different national stances … to achieve a more growth-friendly overall fiscal stance for the Euro Area" (Draghi 2014).

Our fiscal compass offers a tool to explore these considerations. At the current juncture it suggests differentiating fiscal policies around a broadly neutral overall stance in the Eurozone. The results are partly parameter-sensitive but nevertheless suggestive. They bring analytical support to the recent judgement over the aggregate stance carried out by the European Commission as part of its assessment of budgetary plans (European Commission 2014h). In addition, the composition of fiscal policies also needs to be considered, as fiscal changes offer the opportunity to improve the quality of public spending and of the tax structure.

14 Designing Fiscal Policy for Steady, Enduring Growth*

December 2015

1 Why fiscal stabilisation?

Several years after the peak of the Global Crisis, substantial risks to the global economy abound. Prospects for economic growth have been repeatedly marked down. Public debt to GDP ratios in many Eurozone countries are at levels not seen since World War II. Several countries are significantly out of step with their medium-term fiscal targets. Monetary policy in several major economies is constrained by the zero lower bound. China, the largest economy in the world in purchasing power parity terms, is undergoing an epochal economic rebalancing and ensuing growth moderation, with important spillovers.

Against this background of heightened risks and uncertainties, constrained monetary policy, and limited budgetary space, how can fiscal policy contribute to steady and enduring growth? Here, we argue that fiscal stabilisation through automatic stabilisers can play a prominent role.

Fiscal policy can influence medium-term growth through its support of macroeconomic stability. A large body of theoretical and empirical work has shown that high macroeconomic volatility dampens output growth. For example, in a sample of 92 countries as well as a sample of OECD countries, Ramey and Ramey (1995) find that countries with higher volatility have lower growth. This suggests that lower volatility can increase growth insofar as it helps avoid wasteful fluctuations in em-

---

* Co-author: Vitor Gaspar (IMF), Vox CEPR, 10 December 2015.

ployment and growth. Lower macroeconomic uncertainty also provides a favourable environment for physical and social capital, thereby supporting medium-term growth.

Fiscal policy has a stabilising effect on an economy if the budget balance increases when the output gap rises, and decreases when the output gap falls. The April 2015 Fiscal Monitor introduced the "FISCO," a fiscal stabilisation coefficient that measures the systematic response of a country's overall fiscal deficit to changes in the output gap, whether the response is automatically driven or resulting from discretionary actions. If the fiscal stabilisation coefficient is equal to one then, when the output gap increases by one percentage point of GDP, the general government deficit also increases by one percentage point of GDP. The Monitor estimates that the average fiscal stabilisation coefficient is 0.7 for advanced economies (Figure 1), most of which as a result of automatic stabilisers. For advanced economies, a significant – but plausible – increase in the fiscal stabilisation coefficient by 0.1 (equivalent to one-standard deviation of cross-country variation in the sample) is estimated to reduce output volatility by 15% and increase growth by 0.3 percentage points.

Figure 1 Advanced economies, fiscal stabilisation coefficients

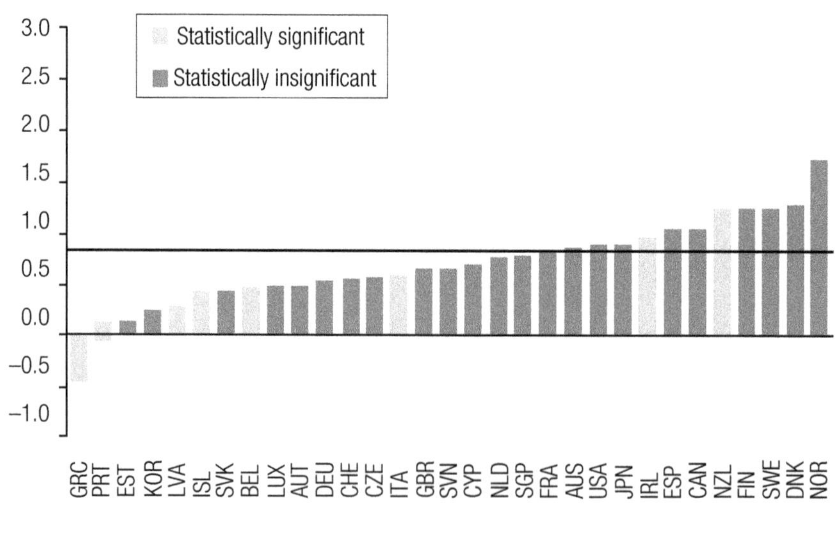

Source: Own elaboration from IMF Fiscal Monitor, April (IMF 2015a).

In the EU, automatic fiscal stabilisation is traditionally measured as the semi-elasticity of the overall fiscal balance to changes in the output gap, as described in Mourre et al. (2014) and used in the EU fiscal framework. The aggregate semi-elasticity is derived from the sensitivities of individual tax and expenditure categories to output fluctuations. The size of automatic stabilisers appears strongly and positively correlated with the ratio of government expenditure to GDP (Figure 2). However, in practice the influence of automatic stabilisers can be larger or smaller than suggested by the expenditure ratio depending on the country's tax and spending structures. For example, if the output gap decreases by 1 percentage point, the headline budget balance would deteriorate automatically by around 0.3%-0.6% of GDP, depending on the country.

Figure 2 Government size and automatic stabilisers

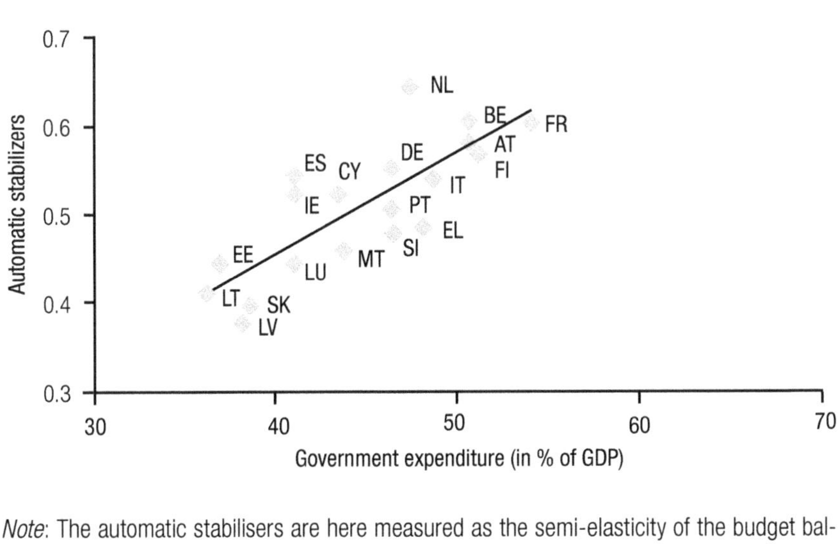

Note: The automatic stabilisers are here measured as the semi-elasticity of the budget balance to the output gap, as found in Mourre et al. (2014) for EU countries.

Source: European Commission and OECD.

2 The importance of automatic stabilisers

How, then, can the stabilisation properties of fiscal policy be enhanced? Adapting (discretionary) fiscal policy continuously to economic circumstances seems impossible in practice. It requires good answers to a panoply of questions. How to gauge the state of the economy in real time? How to calculate the required fiscal policy response? How to ensure timely legislative or executive decisions? How to implement policy actions on time? Empirically, Fatás and Mihov (2003) find that countries with the most volatile public consumption also tend to have the most volatile business cycles. The aggressive use of discretionary fiscal policy may therefore harm economic growth through the amplification of business cycle fluctuations. This may arise either because fiscal policy interventions are poorly designed and react untimely to the business cycle, or because they are also driven by objectives unrelated to stabilisation (i.e. equity, resource allocation, electoral motivations).

Automatic stabilisers – by acting in real time – solve the problem of recognition, design, decision and implementation lags. By design, automatic stabilisers also automatically reverse when the business cycle improves, which is not necessarily the case for discretionary policies.

But, in practice, this has not always been the case. Fiscal policy decisions often undermine the functioning of automatic stabilisers, especially in good times. In good times politicians are tempted to spend the (temporary) revenue windfall. The pro-cyclical bias not only contributes to macroeconomic volatility, it also creates an upward drift in public debt over time. Letting automatic stabilisers operate fully would ensure a symmetric response to the business cycle. It would ensure that in "good times" fiscal space is gradually built up.

Clearly, long-term sustainability of public finances is crucial if fiscal policy is to play a larger role in stabilising the economy. Protecting credibility with the public and financial markets is essential. Prudent public finances are particularly called for in countries that value large welfare states and have a strong dislike for macroeconomic volatility. As former Swedish finance minister Anders Borg (2014) put it, "surplus Keynesianism still works."

3 How to improve automatic stabilisers?

Automatic stabilisers were not designed with macroeconomic stability and growth in mind. They are the by-products of policies put in place to serve other objectives. From the perspective of Musgrave (1959), automatic stabilisers reflect political and/or societal choices regarding insurance and redistribution. Therefore, there may be room to improve substantially on the design of automatic stabilisers. It should be possible to do so without undermining their original purpose; creating a form of structural fiscal policy that can be designed in a budget neutral way.

That said, there is also evidence of decreasing returns to fiscal stabilisation above certain size of government, e.g. through disincentives to supply labour, high marginal tax rates, deadweight effects or misallocation of resources. Buti et al. (2002) show in the context of the Eurozone that, if the initial level of government expenditure and thus of the tax burden is high, reducing the tax burden may lead to higher output stabilisation, reaping a double dividend of market efficiency and stabilisa-

Figure 3 Avenues for increasing automatic fiscal stabilisation

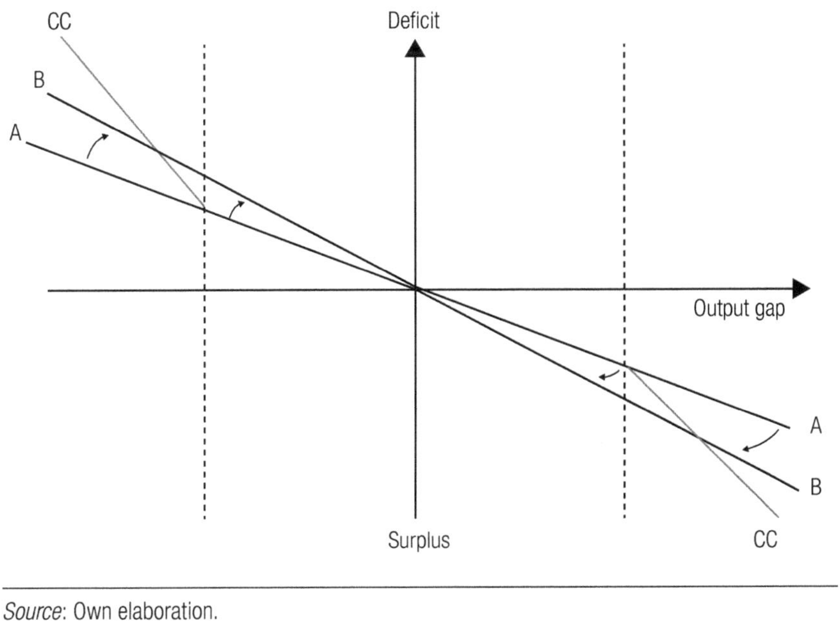

Source: Own elaboration.

tion. Debrun et al. (2008) find that the marginal effect of an increase in government size is negligible for expenditure levels above 40% of GDP, increasing the likelihood that the gains in terms of stabilisation are offset by efficiency losses. This suggests that in the majority of advanced countries any further increase in government size would not increase the effectiveness of automatic stabilisers. In a context of high debt levels, this raises a key policy issue, namely how to boost automatic stabilisers without increasing the size of the government.

The effectiveness of "traditional" automatic stabilisers in smoothing output fluctuations can be enhanced by adjusting the features of selected revenue/expenditure categories to increase their response to economic activity. In Figure 3, this corresponds to rotating line AA clockwise to BB.

Introducing automatic changes to tax and expenditure parameters in response to macroeconomic developments may further enhance fiscal stabilisation. In a nutshell, this will consist in automating adjustments in policy levers (such as tax rates and the replacement rate or duration of unemployment benefits) rather than simply letting budgetary aggregates respond to tax bases or the number of people entitled to social transfers. It can also mitigate the shortcomings of discretionary policy action already discussed. In Figure 3, automatic triggering of parameter changes beyond a certain threshold of output gap (or employment) corresponds to introducing a kink in the curve so that line AA shifts after a certain point to line CC. This pattern may be particularly suited for countries which enjoy little fiscal scope. Triggers would need to be carefully designed and clearly defined in advanced to ensure predictability.

On top of avoiding pro-cyclical provisions in the tax code (for example tax loss carry-forward), possible avenues, combining both strategies, include:

- *Personal income tax*. A budget-neutral shift within personal income taxation with higher rates for top incomes and lower rates for lower incomes can increase stabilisation. However, consideration needs to be given to possible effects on incentives for work. For countries with collection lags (e.g. income tax based on actual income of the previous year), moving to an estimated income for the current year would strengthen the link between tax payments and the economic cycle.

- *Corporate income tax.* Pre-payments based on the estimated profits for the current year would allow linking tax payments to the current state of the economy more closely.
- *Unemployment benefits.* The design of unemployment benefits can be enhanced to increase their generosity or coverage during recessions. This raises disposable incomes of constrained households with a high marginal propensity to consume, and boosts total consumption. However, reform would need to avoid possible disincentives to work. One option is to include stronger tapering over time.
- *Automatic investment tax deductions during recessions.* Automatic tax deductions reduce the cost of capital and ease credit constraints. This in turn helps stimulate investment.
- *Cyclical loss-carry backward.* This measure allows deduction of corporate tax losses against past profits and provides companies immediate tax refunds during recessions.
- *Automatic transfers to local governments.* Subnational governments are often bound by balanced budget requirements, which fuels pro-cyclicality. Making transfers to local governments counter-cyclical would mitigate this effect.

4 Conclusion

The complexities, risks and uncertainties associated with the current global developments suggest the need for an upgrade in fiscal policy. Such upgrade amounts to structural change in fiscal policy. We propose to strengthen automatic stabilisers in a budget-neutral way. This is particularly important in the Eurozone countries, as fiscal policies have the responsibility of smoothing country specific disturbances, when their finances are relatively constrained.

Reforming automatic stabilisers, nonetheless, represents a difficult political challenge. Substantial changes to tax and expenditure structures may affect vested interests. Such changes could also be seen as removing too much discretionary authority from policymakers in the future, which is likely to face significant political resistance. Furthermore, during the economic upswing, there may be political pressure to prevent the automatic unwinding of supportive policies intended only for low cyclical conditions. This would result in pro-cyclicality in good times and economic distortions, which would in turn compromise the rebuilding of fiscal buffers and lead to, or aggravate, macroeconomic imbalances. However, overcoming these political challenges will foster fiscal policy for steady and enduring growth.

15 Fiscal Space and Low Interest Rates: A Eurozone Perspective*

November 2016

1 The basic arithmetic of debt, growth and interest rates

Some observers have called for more aggressive fiscal policies, arguing that fiscal space is increased by historically low interest rates (Furman 2016). There are also calls for 'living with the debt' (Ostry et al. 2015) as long as debt is "safe." Debt should be stabilised, not reduced.

This chapter asks how far these arguments can be taken, in particular in the specific setting of the Eurozone. The European Commission has called for a fiscal stance more supportive of the recovery and of monetary policy in the Eurozone (European Commission 2016f). However, the Commission has also highlighted the tensions between the desirable fiscal stance when considering the Eurozone as a single entity, as if there were a Eurozone finance minister, and the limitations of the current EU fiscal framework, including fiscal sustainability concerns that are particularly relevant for certain Member States. The implications of the low interest rates environment should thus be tailored to the peculiarities of the Eurozone.

Over the past decades, interest rates have steadily fallen and have now reached historic lows. Super-low nominal interest rates reflect the fall in (expected) inflation and a decline of the natural interest rate. While there is great uncertainty on future evolutions and a moderate rebound from

* Co-author: Nicolas Carnot (European Commission), Vox CEPR, 28 November 2016.

current lows is likely at some point, the mainstream view is that generally low interest rates are to stay for a while (e.g. Fisher 2016).

Low interest rates push back the boundaries of government debt sustainability. Debt stabilisation requires generating a primary surplus for servicing the debt burden. If there is a maximum feasible primary surplus p^{max}, there is a corresponding debt limit $b^{max} = p^{max}/(r^*-g^*)$ where r^*-g^* is the interest rate growth rate differential (Blanchard 1984). In this stylised framework, a durably lower interest rate implies a higher debt limit.

Stronger growth is also conducive to additional fiscal space. However, when lower rates are accompanied by equally lower growth, the inter-temporal budget constraint is basically unchanged. Put differently, it is the difference (r^*-g^*) that plays out in the debt limit equation. Therefore, one needs to examine the evidence on r^*-g^*, now and going forward, when assessing fiscal space.

2 What is the empirical evidence and prospects?

The average r-g on Eurozone government bonds fell to -0.3% in 2015 and is on course to fall further in 2016 (Figure 1a). This contrasts with an average r-g of 1.4% since the start of EMU. Negative values of r-g allowing Ponzi-type schemes may not last forever. However, even assuming a medium-term uptick, an r-g lowered to say 0.5% together with moderate primary surpluses would be consistent with relatively high debt limits, e.g. 200% of GDP for just a 1% of GDP primary surplus.

The ability of Eurozone countries to generate primary surpluses is backed by past evidence (Figure 1b). Looking forward, ageing-related pressures and expanding needs in public services will constrain that ability. This makes it all the more necessary to pursue structural improvements in the quality of public finances for raising the efficiency of tax and spending.

At the global level, the critical question is how long the current exceptional financing conditions will continue. The full effect of exceptionally low issuing rates still has to materialise on average borrowing costs, and governments can “lock in” the currently favourable terms by increasing the maturity of emissions, as several sovereigns are doing. Rates will go up at some point however. Besides, forces that have weighed down on the natural rate such as demography may start working in reverse (Bean 2015).

The bottom line is that r-g is currently low, is likely to go up at an indeterminate horizon, but could nevertheless remain a little lower than past averages indicate. Policy-wise, the optimal response is to spend now on growth-boosting but non-permanent programmes. This advice should be followed. The challenge is to find initiatives that are efficient and add up to a significant macroeconomic total (Blinder 2016). Maintenance investment and spending on active labour market policies, as well as targeted investment tax credits and cuts in labour costs, can take priority. Big ticket infrastructures that carry long lags would support growth in a longer-term perspective. A sound institutional framework is however necessary to ensure the quality of projects. Similarly, a credible fiscal framework helps raise the commitment to needed for medium-term adjustments.

Figure 1a Distribution of growth-adjusted implicit rate

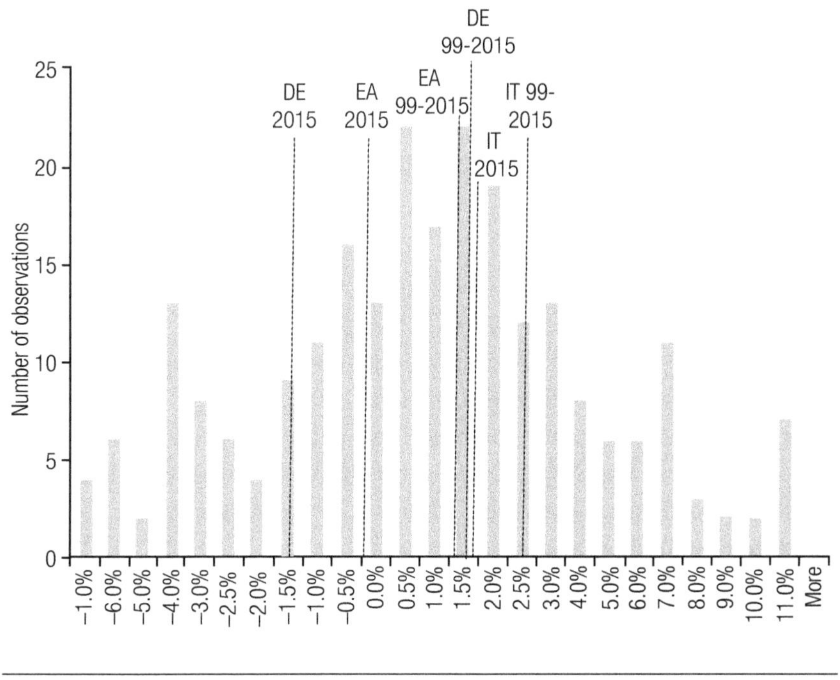

Figure 1b Distribution of primary surplus

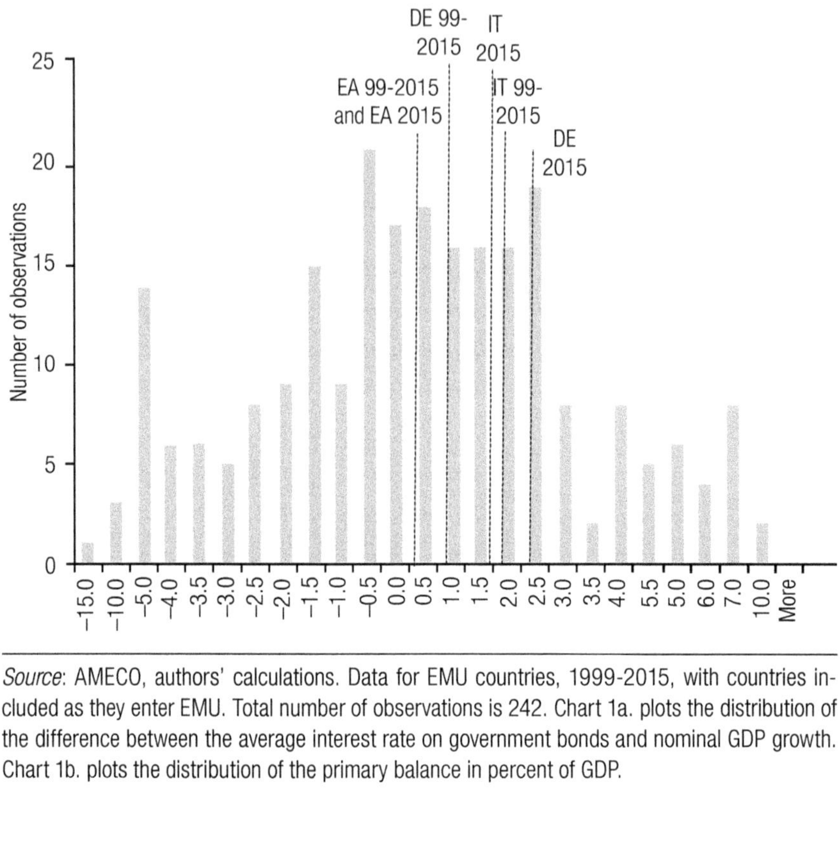

Source: AMECO, authors' calculations. Data for EMU countries, 1999-2015, with countries included as they enter EMU. Total number of observations is 242. Chart 1a. plots the distribution of the difference between the average interest rate on government bonds and nominal GDP growth. Chart 1b. plots the distribution of the primary balance in percent of GDP.

The empirical evidence also points to a large heterogeneity of countrys' situations including within the EU. Debt levels, growth prospects and borrowing rates all differ. At the national level, there is something that looks like a vicious circle and a virtuous cycle. Broadly speaking, one group of countries tend to combine high debt, low growth and higher borrowing rates. These factors are mutually reinforcing. Another group has the opposite characteristics. This is a loose categorisation. But it is suggestive – a basic Blanchard criterion uses the same r-g for all. In reality, there is multi-dimensional endogeneity.

One implication is that there is no one size fits all. Policy prescriptions must be differentiated. Interestingly, while r and g may be strongly connected worldwide, there is room for national differences in r-g. Free moving capital implies common trends in r (Gros 2016), but national factors affect national r, including on liquidity and perceived sustainability.[1] Differentiation of g is even more evident. In particular investments and reforms sustaining growth remain largely national.

3 Eurozone specificities

In advanced economies, sovereign debt is typically regarded as risk free in nominal terms. This is because the central bank can always ensure the cash payment of debt obligations, while keeping the option to raise interest rates to preserve a low inflation regime.

The Eurozone has a more complicated setting with a single central bank, 19 national budget authorities and legally enshrined clauses of no bail out and no monetary financing. This makes it impossible for the central bank to backstop governments unconditionally. The instruments that have been introduced by the ECB within its price stability mandate recognise this reality. For example, the Outright Monetary Transactions programme is conditional on a sustainability-restoring programme with the European Stability Mechanism. Similarly, quantitative easing by the ECB incorporates only limited cross-border risk-sharing.

The current institutional setting in the Eurozone implies that government debts cannot be consolidated in a single "federal" balance sheet (Cœuré 2016). Fiscal space has to be evaluated on a national basis. Moreover, like for example US states, there is a case for a more conservative debt strategy at the country level than in an environment where direct monetary control would fully eliminate the rollover risk on sovereign debt (Fall et al. 2015). At the same time, if the Eurozone were to deepen its fiscal integration in the future, it may be able to sustain a higher level of public borrowing overall than is presently the case as the sum of individual Eurozone countries.

4 Which "debt anchors" in the EU?

One way to devise a credible debt strategy is to keep a long-run debt objective serving as an anchor to the fiscal framework. Stabilising debt around its current level is a viable strategy when far away from debt lim-

Figure 2 Operationalising fiscal space: A Blanchard (1984)-inspired framework

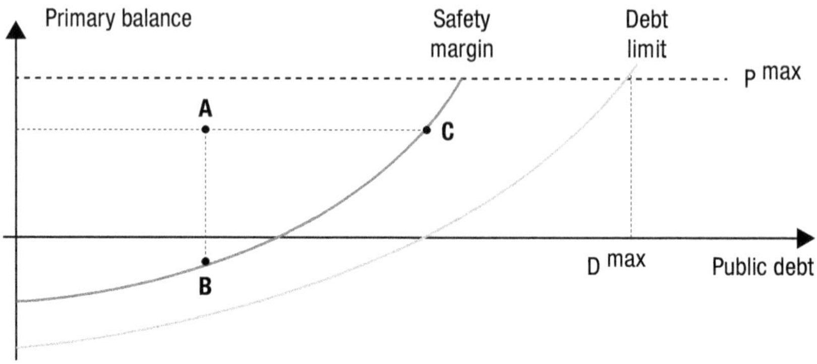

Note: Points A, B, C describe stylised positions of hypothetic countries. Point A corresponds to moderate debt and moderate primary surplus: there is ample fiscal space. Point B: debt remains moderate but the current primary position is low. In a prudent approach taking into account a safety margin there is little fiscal space. Point C: debt is relatively high. The country has adjusted somewhat in terms of "flows," i.e. a moderate primary surplus. It is therefore still in the safety space (note it would not be if had the same primary balance as country B). However, in a prudent approach taking into account a safety margin there is little fiscal space.

Source: Own elaboration.

its. When closer to those limits, some gradual reduction may be necessary. That implies a long-run debt anchor that is below the current level.

One rationale for aiming at reducing debt when starting from high levels is uncertainty. Medium to long-run projections of debt are sensitive to many risks. One is uncertainty on the future values of r-g. Other risks tend to be positively (debt enhancing) biased. In particular, debt shocks are largely asymmetric, *inter alia* because of contingent liabilities (Escolano and Gaspar 2016). In addition, implemented fiscal policy tends to be looser than planned.

In a risk-based approach, aiming at debt stabilisation *ex ante* may not be enough to be reasonably confident that debt will not increase *ex post*. For this reason, highly indebted countries may need to aim *ex ante* for some pace of debt reduction, just in order to have sufficient assurances that debt will at least stabilise ex post. As an illustration, one can calculate the targeted debt reduction in a median scenario so that one has a

Figure 3 Fiscal space and adjustment needs at country level

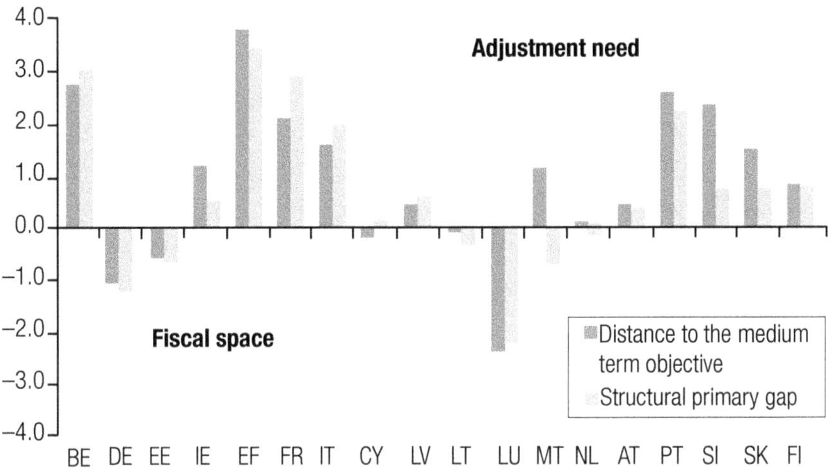

Note: The distance to the medium-term objective is the difference between the level of the structural balance in 2016 and the medium-term objectives of the country within the Stability and Growth Pact. The structural primary gap is the difference between the level of the structural primary balance in 2016 and a primary balance norm. The latter is the primary balance that generates an annual reduction of 5% of the excess of debt over 60% of GDP. For countries with debt levels below 60%, the primary balance norm stabilises debt at its current level. The calculations of the primary balance norms assume a positive but low growth adjusted interest rate of 0.5%.

Source: European Commission.

90% chance that the debt ratio at least does not increase *ex post*, given the historical variance of shocks on r and g.[2]

To give a more operational characterisation of fiscal space, one must consider the information on both "stock" (debt) and "flow" (balance). In a stylised "Blanchard framework" (Figure 2), the debt limit curve (red curve) depicts the frontier between initial combinations of debt and primary balances that are sustainable and those that are not. In the real world, nearing the debt limit may not be prudent enough for the above reasons. Thus, for debt to be regarded as safe, one needs to incorporate a security margin (green curve) vis à vis the debt limit.

In practice, a basic measure of available space can be derived by comparing the current level of the primary balance with a primary balance norm consistent with a long-run debt anchor. The difference between the two is suggestive of fiscal space, or remaining adjustment needs. Figure 3 illustrates on the basis of a conservative choice of debt criterion in line with EU fiscal rules. The results are cross-checked with another criterion directly drawn from the Stability and Growth Pact, i.e. the distance between current positions of the structural balance and medium-term objectives.

Using this simple criterion, one sees that there is fiscal space in some EU countries, but there remains an adjustment gap in others. Some Member States have significant fiscal space (e.g. Germany). Other countries including France, Italy and Spain still show a need for further adjustment from the perspective of debt stabilisation cum gradual reduction.

5 Conclusions

The extraordinary conditions in the aftermath of the financial crisis call for a supportive fiscal policy. However, the consequences for the inter-temporal budget constraint may be less than meets the eye. They depend on uncertain future evolutions (in particular of r-g) as well as on policies. In any event, the case is strong for spending now on investment and other targeted programmes supporting growth and employment.

However, fiscal space is heterogeneously distributed. In the Eurozone some countries have a clear margin and should use it. Others that may be pushed closer to the debt limits should pursue a more prudent approach of gradual debt unwinding. The sustainability risks attached to Eurozone individual countries may in fact prevent the Eurozone from pursuing an adequately supportive fiscal policy in unusual circumstances. A common stabilisation capacity would help for managing shocks that cannot be absorbed by national stabilisers alone, as advocated in the Five Presidents' Report (Juncker et al. 2015).

Notes

[1] In practice liquidity and risk premia are also strongly influenced by overall market conditions.

[2] The Fiscal Sustainability Report explores such an approach over a five-year horizon by introducing the notion of "non increasing debt caps" (European Commission 2016a, see section 2.3).

16 Why We Need a Positive Fiscal Stance for the Eurozone and What It Means*

November 2016

1 Introduction

The Eurozone aggregate fiscal stance has been an issue of increasing importance since its introduction into the Two Pack. Reinforcing the Eurozone dimension in budgetary policy and surveillance is one of the main objectives of this piece of legislation. In particular, the Two Pack requires the Commission to present an overall assessment of the budgetary situation and prospects for the Eurozone as a whole on the basis of the national draft budgetary plans and their interaction. In response to this request, the Commission annually adopts a Communication providing horizontal Eurozone context to the national budgetary decisions.

The fiscal stance is usually understood as the orientation given to fiscal policy by governments' discretionary decisions on tax and expenditures, noticeably with a view to their contribution to the economy.

Growth is still weaker than desirable in the Eurozone. Downside risks remain and challenges originating from geopolitical developments further complicate the economic outlook. Responsible, growth-friendly fiscal policy needs to play a bigger role in supporting demand in the Eurozone today. This is a concern shared by the global community: at its September meetings, the G20 reiterated its members' commitment to a three-pronged growth strategy, stating their determination to "use all

* Co-author: Lucía Rodríguez Muñoz (European Commission), Vox CEPR, 28 November 2016.

policy tools – monetary, fiscal and structural – individually and collectively to achieve our goal of strong, sustainable, balanced and inclusive growth."

In this context, the Commission has adopted a Communication on Eurozone fiscal policy, which outlines what a "positive fiscal stance" for the Eurozone would look like (European Commission 2016f).

2 Why a positive fiscal stance for the Eurozone?

As the Communication explains, the role of fiscal policy is now given more prominence than usual because the combination of three factors makes the economic environment exceptional. First, as often observed following financial crises, the Eurozone has experienced a more protracted period of slow recovery than after other kinds of crises. This is characterised by unusually high long-term unemployment and low investment, with a corresponding low level of internal demand and inflation. Figure 1 illustrates the degree of slack in the Eurozone economy: persistently low inflation and a large external surplus are associated with weak internal demand. Second, there are large outstanding risks which call for pushing to support stabilisation based on internal demand, notably investments. External demand cannot be relied upon to buttress the economic recovery in the current circumstances. Third, monetary policy is facing constraints as the interest rates have reached the zero lower bound and unconventionally measures have been intensively used, while credit demand remains subdued despite the low credit costs.

Against this background, a responsible fiscal policy reaction is to act decisively, rather than reluctantly, in support of demand. While the Brainard principle suggests that policy should exhibit conservatism in the face of uncertainty (Brainard 1967), exceptions to this principle are found in the literature, particularly when the uncertainty involves a high degree of inflation persistence. This exception may very well characterise today's context, making a vigorous response – rather than a conservative response – optimal in these circumstances.

Devising the adequate response is not about adjusting short-term demand through fiscal policy fine-tuning, but instead to adequately face unusual circumstances that require a decisive growth stimulus. Two elements in particular speak to this need.

Figure 1 Eurozone current account balance and inflation compared to their respective benchmarks

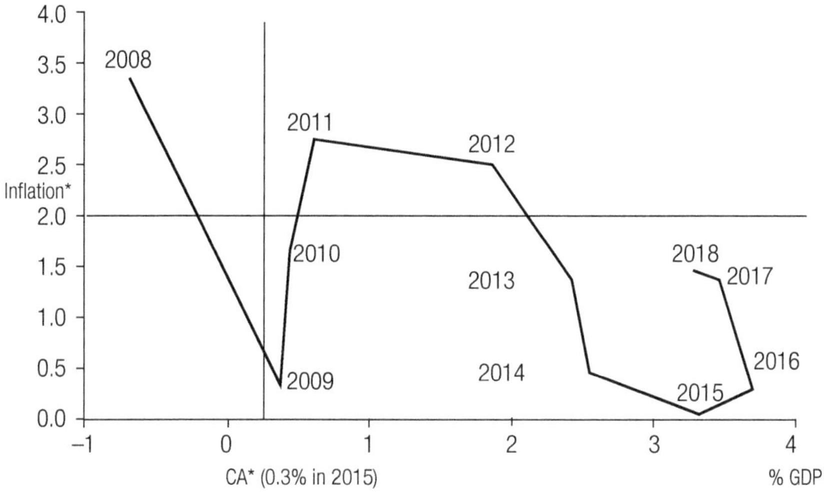

Note: Inflation* and CA* respectively denote the benchmark inflation and current account balance. The benchmark current account balance represents the current account balance implied by fundamental determinants (such as demographics and ageing, relative income, resources, reserve currency status, and manufacturing intensity) with respect to the rest of the world. The estimates are derived from panel regressions for 67 countries representing 95% of world GDP, akin to the IMF's EBA model (European Commission 2015c).

Source: European Commission.

First, the likelihood of abrupt negative effects on the macroeconomic side is now assessed to be higher (these abrupt negative effects are also referred to as "cliff effects"). The need to address the cyclical lethargy by promoting an increase in aggregate demand appears urgent. Otherwise, crisis legacies, such as low investment or high unemployment could eventually become structural with long-lasting effects on potential growth (hysteresis effects) or on the social fabric.

Second, the efficiency of fiscal policy to attain the desired stabilisation goal is now judged to be higher than in normal economic times. In a situation where monetary policy is constrained by the zero lower bound, fiscal stimulus is found to be more effective to stabilise the economy than usual.

The need to preserve the sustainability of public finances also calls for supporting demand in the Eurozone as a whole in the current context. Whether stabilising or receding, government debt ratios still stand at high levels in a number of Eurozone Member States. Reducing debt levels becomes a strenuous task when low real GDP growth is coupled with low inflation for a significant period of time. At the same time, sustainability is a key issue for some Member States, for which prudent fiscal policy in compliance with EU fiscal rules will be necessary. However, as mentioned in the last section of this chapter, stimulus in countries with fiscal space will not only boost their GDP, but also have a beneficial impact on the sustainability of other Eurozone countries.

Figure 2 shows that an expansionary fiscal stance such as the one advocated by the Communication would leave the Eurozone economy closer to its potential growth in 2017. Compared to that, the fiscal stance that results from Member States' 2017 draft budgetary plans (DBPs) is suboptimal: Member States' national fiscal policies add up to a broadly neutral overall fiscal stance which would be insufficient to properly address current stabilisation concerns.

Figure 2 Eurozone fiscal stance over 2011-2017

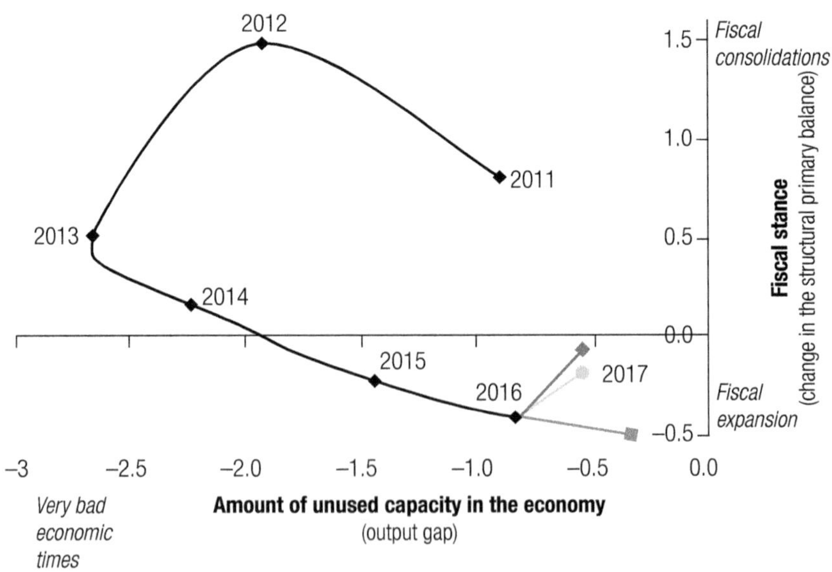

Source: European Commission.

3 The desirable fiscal stance from a Eurozone standpoint

What is the desirable fiscal stance in the Eurozone for 2017? Thinking of the Eurozone as a single entity, the size of desirable expansion should provide a meaningful fiscal impulse to the economy and help lift inflation.

As shown in Table 1, assuming a multiplier of 1, the Eurozone's output gap can be expected to half in 2017 following a fiscal expansion of 0.3% of GDP. Conversely, the output gap will close if the fiscal expansion would amount to 0.8% of GDP. A multiplier of 1 is deemed to best characterise the growth impact of fiscal policy in the current context. This is both compatible with a high quality stimulus and a zero-lower-bound monetary environment. The Communication calls for prioritising budgetary variables with the largest growth impact, such as public investment. Well-designed fiscal expansions result in stronger growth effects, as captured by larger multipliers. Moreover, as stated above, fiscal stimulus is most effective in an accommodative monetary environment.

In all, a fiscal expansion of up to 0.5% of GDP, within the range identified in Table 1, appears appropriate for the Eurozone as a whole; still a tension remains between considering the Eurozone as a single entity and the decentralised fiscal policy across the 19 different Member States.

Table 1 Fiscal stance consistent with different closures of the output gap and different multipliers

Fiscal multiplier	Fiscal stance consistent with a closure of the output gap by		
	25%	50%	100%
0.8	−0.1	−0.4	−1.0
1	−0.1	−0.3	−0.8
1.2	−0.1	−0.3	−0.7

Note: Fiscal stances expressed as a change in the structural primary balance as a share of GDP, derived from the analysis based on Eurozone numbers.

Source: European Commission.

4 Toward a better composition of the Eurozone fiscal stance

The Communication also stresses that the current fiscal situation is sub-optimal from a geographical point of view. In other words, the repartition across Member States of the neutral fiscal stance that results from the aggregation of 2017 DBPs is clearly not appropriate. Paradoxically, some countries facing higher sustainability challenges seem to privilege stabilisation needs, while Member States with fiscal space do not use it to address stabilisation concerns.

Thus, the Eurozone would not only benefit from a more supportive orientation of overall fiscal policy, but also from its more appropriate geographical repartition. This is especially so in the current context where spillover effects are higher than usual (In't Veld 2016). Similarly to fiscal multipliers, the literature finds spillover effects (the impact of fiscal policy on other countries' GDP) to be also much larger if monetary policy operates in a zero interest rate environment, compared with normal times. In addition, larger spillover effects are associated with an intensification of government spending on the most productive categories, such as public investment, as opposed to other categories of government expenditure.

QUEST simulations suggest – in line with other studies on infrastructure investment – that additional government investment in Germany and the Netherlands could substantially raise both domestic and other Eurozone regions' GDP. In the case of high efficiency of public investment, QUEST simulations run by DG ECFIN illustrate that additional government investment of 1% of GDP in Germany and the Netherlands, sustained over 10 years, could raise domestic GDP by 1.1% and 0.9%, respectively (In't Veld 2016).[1] Over a 10-year horizon, real GDP in Germany and the Netherlands would increase by more than 2% thanks to a positive supply effect, that is, government investment raises the productivity of private capital and labour over a sustained period of time. The real GDP in other Eurozone regions (France, Italy, Spain and the rest of the Eurozone) would increase by around a range of 0.3-0.5 percentage points after only one year. These spillovers derive from the trade channel (the demand boost in Germany and the Netherlands will partly leak out to other countries via increased demand for imported goods) and some depreciation of the exchange rate (which will increase demand from the rest of the world for goods exported from the Eurozone).

Crucially, such a fiscal stimulus would have a very modest impact on these two countries' public finances and could actually decrease their debt ratios in the long-run. The impact on public finances in Germany and the Netherlands is small, as higher growth would also boost tax returns. Government debt would in fact be less than 2% of GDP higher in Germany after ten years, and a bit more in the Netherlands, while debt ratios in the rest of the Eurozone would actually fall by around 2 percentage points due to the positive spillovers. In case of a permanent increase in public investment, debt ratios in Germany and the Netherlands would actually decline in the long-run and the stimulus would become self-financing.

At the same time, intensified government investment efforts are vital to keep the existing infrastructure stock in good working conditions, without hampering its long-run service to the economy. The perceived quality of existing infrastructure stock in the Eurozone has considerably declined. Survey data shows that this is particularly the case in several Eurozone Member States, including Germany, where this declining trend has been ongoing for more than a decade already (World Economic Forum 2015). Furthermore, the decline in the perceived quality of existing public capital stocks concerns all categories of core infrastructure such as roads, railways, air transport and ports infrastructure.

5 Concluding remarks

The debate on the appropriate fiscal stance of the Eurozone is an essential one and it constitutes an important milestone in the deepening of the EMU. The Communication recently adopted by the Commission says that every Member State should take into account the objective of the Eurozone as a whole in the definition of its own national fiscal stance.

The design of an appropriate fiscal stance for the Eurozone remains the collective responsibility of its Member States. In the absence of rules or instruments to directly manage the aggregate fiscal stance of the Eurozone, attaining a sound macroeconomic policy mix requires close coordination of national fiscal policies, within the requirements of the Stability and Growth Pact.

As advocated by the Five Presidents' Report for stage 2 of EMU deepening, the Eurozone needs an autonomous fiscal stabilisation capacity in the medium-term. This stabilisation capacity can be for smoothing out country-specific shocks, common shocks to the area as a whole, or both kinds of shocks. Indeed, the recent experience suggests that the EMU setup may not allow for stabilising large economic shocks. In particular, the impossibility to force Member States with fiscal space to use it and the soft nature of the recommendations on the composition of public expenditure constrain the possibility of reaching a "positive fiscal stance."

Note

[1] There is a somewhat smaller positive GDP effect for the Netherlands, as the country is characterised by larger trade openness, which implies stronger demand leakage to imports.

17 Potential Output and EU Fiscal Surveillance*

September 2019

1 Introduction

Any economic evaluation of the public finances must rely on some notion of potential output. However, potential output must be estimated, and the way these estimates are produced and then used in policy, including in EU fiscal surveillance, is frequently criticised. One such vocal criticism is the "Campaign against 'nonsense' output gaps"[1], or CANOO (Tooze 2019).

In this chapter, we firstly recall the role of potential output and structural (cyclically adjusted) balances in the EU's fiscal surveillance processes, and re-state why their introduction in the EU's rules constituted progress, compared with the cruder, much more pro-cyclical, nominal rules. We then acknowledge the issues and challenges from the use of the "unobservable" potential output variable in isolating the cyclical component of actual GDP and why, in order to avoid having too many estimates of potential, the EU agreed, 20 years ago, to have a commonly agreed methodology (CAM) for calculating it. Despite acknowledging the ongoing challenges, we dispute some of the criticisms, including from the CANOO, by showing the plausibility of the EU's output gap estimates compared to other business cycle indicators. Finally, we put the role of potential output in EU fiscal surveillance into its appropriate context: far from being mechanical, the practice of surveillance has given space to the

---

* Co-authors: Nicolas Carnot, Atanas Hristov, Kieran Mc Morrow, Werner Röger and Valerie Vandermeulen (European Commission), Vox CEPR, 23 September 2019.

use of constrained judgment in specific situations, while simultaneously trying to increase predictability in fiscal assessments.

2 The structural focus of the SGP's "second generation" fiscal rules has improved EU fiscal surveillance

To appreciate the role of potential output and structural balances in EU fiscal rules today, one has to remember that the fiscal surveillance apparatus has come a long way from its original design. The Maastricht Treaty refers to "headline" nominal reference values for deficits and debt-to-GDP ratios (3% and 60%, respectively). EU surveillance and the original Stability and Growth Pact (SGP) largely focused on headline deficits. It was the difficulties that the SGP[2] ran into in its first economic cycle, culminating in the controversy over Germany's and France's deficits in the early 2000s, which led to a stronger emphasis on cyclically adjusted measures, with the first evolution of the Pact in the mid-2000s.

From there on, the EU's fiscal framework evolved as a perfect illustration of what has been dubbed "second generation fiscal rules" (Debrun et al. 2018). The role of structural balances was confirmed in the "Six-Pack" and "Two-Pack" reforms of the early 2010s (together with other innovations such as the introduction of a net expenditure rule). In the SGP, the medium-term objective (MTO) now serves as the target of reference in the preventive arm. It is conceived to allow the automatic stabilisers to play out, both in upturns and downturns, without breaching the 3% value for the deficit (European Commission 2019). Also in the corrective arm of the Pact (i.e. the Excessive deficit procedure, or EDP, arm), structural balances play an important role in setting the pace of fiscal adjustments.

From an economic perspective, the more "intelligent" fiscal rules of the second generation, which rely heavily on notions of potential output and cyclically adjusted fiscal balances, represent clear progress compared with the simpler, but overly crude, rules which relied on headline nominal numbers. The difficulty, however, has now shifted from one of nominal naivety to one where the significant consequences from having to accept the "unobservability" of potential output have to be sensibly dealt with.

3 The issue of potential output unobservability and recent criticisms of the EU's output gap estimates

Potential output is, and always will be, an unobservable variable and consequently has to be estimated. In order to ensure equal treatment and to obtain transparent and unbiased estimates for all of the EU's Member States, a CAM has been employed over the last 20 years in order to calculate the potential growth and output gap estimates which are used in the EU's policy surveillance processes. Given the importance of the CAM – in particular, its estimate of the amount of economic slack in the EU's economy at a given point in time – to the conduct of the EU's fiscal policy, it is understandable, and indeed welcome, that it is the subject of sustained interest and criticism from the economics profession and the wider public.

Currently, criticisms of the economic plausibility of the output gaps produced by the EU's CAM focus on the following three broad themes: First how is it possible that the EU's CAM is suggesting that we have a closed output gap and yet the EU has still almost no inflation? Second, what is the link between the output gap and external imbalances? And finally, how is it plausible that Germany and Italy have the same level of the output gap in spite of their very different growth dynamics?

Below we sequentially address these three criticisms, first at a conceptual level and second by providing empirical evidence. We will show that a lot of these criticisms draw heavily on specific inflation indicators (such as headline or core inflation) or on indicators of external imbalances[3], which do not perform well as indicators of the cycle and consequently should be used with extreme caution by policy makers.

(i) Is a closed output gap consistent with almost no inflation?

The inflation rate is often used as a plausibility check for output gap estimates. There is a significant correlation between the output gap and inflation, and limited inflation acceleration in the Eurozone has been a reason for questioning the speed in which the output gap is closing (Cœuré 2018a). However, one should be aware that a one-to-one relationship between inflation and the output gap should not be expected and that there are a number of plausible explanations for the so-called missing inflation puzzle. The first explanation is that inflation is not only driven by demand pressure but also by supply shocks. In recent years, there has been little wage pressure in the Eurozone. In Germany, real unit labour costs have remained stable despite a continuous decline of the unemployment rate, which suggests that the NAWRU (trend unemployment rate) has been falling. Restrained domestic cost pressures to some extent reflect the fact that Germany's labour market problems are more skewed to supply-side or skill mismatch issues rather than to cyclical and labour demand issues. Other reasons for a divergence between the closure of the Eurozone's output gap and weak inflation developments are low raw material and oil price inflation, and low import price inflation in general, which reflects globalisation induced deflationary mechanisms, with knock on implications in terms of pricing power throughout the Eurozone (Forbes 2019).

In overall terms, therefore, there are lot of reasons why the output gap and inflation do not co-move, with the present combination in the Eurozone of having an output gap which is closed and with inflation staying low providing a strong reminder as to why a one-to-one relationship should not be expected. In fact, many aspects of recent Eurozone trends are consistent with the central elements of the secular stagnation debate, especially the evidence regarding increasing savings, higher risk aversion and falls in the natural rate of interest. The downward shift in actual GDP growth rates in the Eurozone between the pre-crisis and post crisis periods is perhaps heralding an era of both permanently lower potential growth and core inflation rates, similar to what has been experienced in Japan for some time now.

(ii) What is the link between the output gap and external imbalances?

Whilst measures of external imbalances such as the current account balance are, like inflation, linked to output gap developments, they are also similar to inflation in that they are not unequivocal cyclical indicators. The current account balance can incorporate a strong trend component, because it can reflect changes in household savings driven by shifts in demographic trends (e.g. Cheung et al. 2013). Moreover, the link to the cycle is not straightforward: the current account balance can be positive because of low domestic demand (small or negative output gap) or because of buoyant external demand conditions (which tend to push up the output gap).

(iii) How plausible is it that Germany and Italy have the same level of output gap despite their very different growth patterns?

The level of the output gap is simply the difference between the level of actual and potential output at a given point in time. Differences between countries therefore depend on their actual and potential growth rates and the location of a country in their own respective economic cycle. Transitory country specific shocks, which the individual countries have been exposed to, determine cross-country differences. If one focuses in on the longer term evolution of economies, rather than on their shorter business cycles, one can see clearly that over the last 20 years Germany's actual and potential growth rates have both grown at around three times those of Italy, with the unsurprising, mechanical, result that average output gaps over this 20 year period have been broadly the same. Consequently, commentators should not really focus on the fact that Germany's and Italy's output gap in 2019 are, in both cases, forecast by the CAM to be around -0.25% (and therefore that the fiscal policy response should be broadly the same). The real issue is why are German and Italian potential growth rates so different (a structural, not a fiscal, policy question).

In relation to the question of weak Italian potential growth (which ultimately determines the sustainable, non-inflationary, pace of Italy's actual GDP growth), the CAM is consistent with the central thrust of the academic literature which pinpoints the set of structural factors which can explain Italy's relatively disappointing growth performance. First, there is Italy's negative trend productivity growth (this negative trend was already firmly established before the crisis), which has been highlighted in various studies (e.g. Calligaris et al. 2016, Gopinath et al. 2017, OECD 2017) and is often attributed to capital misallocation (with one indication of this misallocation being the high share of non-performing loans). Associated with capital misallocation, the investment rate in Italy has been very low (leading to a negative contribution from capital growth to potential growth). In addition, the population of working age is only growing at a very low pace (and growth has been negative in recent years). Though real unit labour costs have been declining, the decline was smaller than in other countries struck by the Great Recession in 2008/2009, such that Italy did not manage a turnaround of unemployment of the same order of magnitude as other EU countries.

4 Are recent criticisms of the EU's CAM based on solid empirical evidence?

Recent research by Commission staff (Röger et al. 2019) suggests caution using specific business cycle indicators for estimating output gaps and confirms the plausibility of the EU's output gap estimates. It shows that a lot of the criticisms of the EU's CAM are not only flawed conceptually but also empirically. It shows how most of the critiques use indicators of the economic cycle that have a poor track record in terms of explaining changes in the amount of cyclical slack in the EU's economy.

Röger et al. (2019) analysis explains that if one was to use only specific business cycle indicators, such as price inflation and the current account balance, then one would have expected to see a significant negative output gap in the Eurozone as a whole (and in specific Eurozone Member States) in 2018, as claimed by the CANOO. Instead, the EU's CAM shows a small positive output gap for the Eurozone in that year. The authors explain this discrepancy by demonstrating that specific business cycle indicators may only be capturing partial dimensions of the business cycle (i.e. they only provide a cyclical signal for either the product or labour market dimension but not both dimensions). Moreover, they may not be unambiguous cyclical indicators since they contain strong non-cyclical and trend components.

Röger et al. select seven of the most widely used business cycle indicators – price inflation, wage inflation, current account balance, GDP growth, short-term unemployment rate, sentiment indicator for economic slack, and capacity utilisation – and try to find a common cyclical signal amongst them by performing a principal component analysis (PCA). The analysis confirms the cyclical ambiguity of the inflation and CAB indicators. The paper derives a PCA output gap shown in Figure 1. The PCA and CAM output gap for four Eurozone countries are highly correlated, with the two output gaps following a similar pattern over the period 2000-2018.

The most important conclusion to be derived from Röger et al.'s analysis is that one needs to be very careful in selecting business cycle indicators, since an excessive reliance on individual indicators might lead to wrong conclusions about the business cycle position of a country. Some indicators might be ambiguous and might contain trend as well as cyclical variations, with the price inflation and CAB variables being classic examples of this. This is why one should always look at a broad range of indicators in order to get a balanced and plausible view of the current cyclical position. Preferably, one should combine indicators that exploit the cyclical signal from both the labour and product market sides of the economy, which is exactly what the CAM does.

Figure 1 "PCA output gap" and the EU's "CAM output gap" for Germany, Italy, Spain and Portugal, 2000-2018

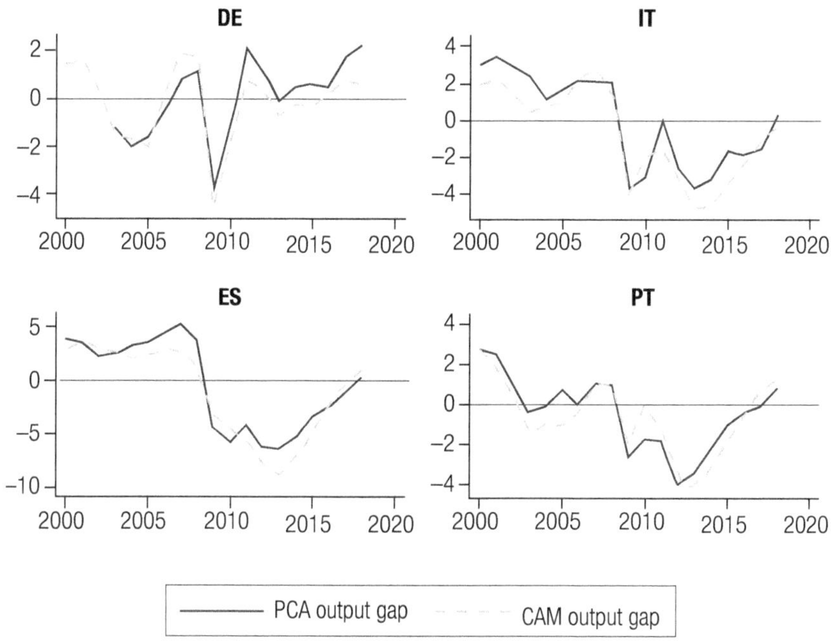

Source: European Commission.

5 Dealing with potential output unobservability in EU fiscal surveillance must involve an element of constrained judgement

Whilst the EU's fiscal surveillance system is an essentially rules-based system, the fact that it is based on an unobservable variable – and could, in extreme circumstances, lead to the imposition of legally binding sanctions on a specific country – makes it clear that the EU never intended it to be used for the taking of automatic decisions. This essential need to include a judgemental component in the EU's fiscal surveillance system was underlined in the 2002 ECOFIN Council decision which introduced the CAM, with the Council stating clearly that they welcomed "the Commission's intention to apply this method in a non-mechanistic, transparent and consistent way." This clear signal from the Council has placed the role of potential output in EU fiscal surveillance in its proper context, with a joint focus on ensuring non-mechanistic, yet broadly predictable, fiscal assessments.

In practical terms, beyond the ongoing research efforts of the OGWG to produce more robust estimates, quite a few steps have been taken in the EU's fiscal surveillance framework itself in order to mitigate the implications of potential output unobservability. In particular, efforts have been made both to reduce the amount of dependence being placed on the potential output estimates in order to increase predictability, as well as retaining an element of judgement in the implementation of the SGP.

The following elements are worth stressing:

The emphasis is on the change in the output gap rather than on the level of the output gap

Within the assessment of the Stability and Convergence Programmes, it is not so much the output gap as such which is important, but the change in the output gap. As long as a Member State is not at it's MTO, it must be on an appropriate adjustment path towards the MTO. This adjustment is measured as an improvement in the structural balance, and is thus influenced by the change in the output gap.

The SGP's overall dependence on potential output estimates has been reduced

More emphasis is given to the so-called expenditure benchmark in the preventive arm of the SGP. It compares the growth of primary expenditure to a smooth notion (10-year centred average) of potential growth (the indicator also corrects for revenue measures, hence it is a "net" expenditure rule that doesn't take "sides" with respect to the size of government). The expenditure benchmark still relies on an evaluation of potential growth, but not on the level of potential output, as the MTO does. This makes a considerable difference in practice, as uncertainty on potential growth is almost an order of magnitude smaller than level uncertainty. Finally, any assessment of the correction of excessive deficits in future EDPs should also focus on policy delivery in terms of tax and expenditure measures.

An element of judgement has also been introduced into the fiscal surveillance process

The Commission, with the backing of the Council of Ministers, has introduced elements of flexibility and judgement in the implementation of the rules to deal with specific circumstances. In particular, where the potential output estimates depart from plausible estimates based on other cyclical indicators (Hristov et al. 2017, European Commission 2018d), constrained judgement is used when setting the pace of adjustment to the MTO. In addition, a range of country-specific changes have been approved to the CAM over recent years, with specific attention also being paid to countries where the need to consolidate has had to be weighed up against a fragile recovery. Due to the existence of these provisions, reduced fiscal requirements, compared with the standard rules, were approved for countries including Spain and Slovenia.

6 Conclusion

The overall outcome from the above considerations is that the reality of the implementation of fiscal surveillance in recent years is a long way from a rigid, mechanical approach based solely on an evaluation of output gaps. In fact, some commentators actually consider that the Commission has gone too far in taking an overly flexible approach.

In conclusion, what emerges from the analysis in this chapter regarding potential output and EU fiscal surveillance is a small number of deeper and more subtle challenges. First, while the EU's fiscal framework has become more sophisticated, it is now widely seen as too complex – and the above considerations make this clear. Second, there is some tension between the need for predictability (and consistency across countries and over time) and the need to retain discretion in particular circumstances. This is not to say that further improvements might not be conceivable, possibly building on a "third generation rule" such as the so-called single expenditure rule with a debt anchor. It will in any event remain a tall order to find an economically sensible and politically viable compromise given the complex trade-offs involved between the principles of simplicity, predictability and flexibility.

Notes

[1] See https://twitter.com/RobinBrooksIIF.

[2] The Commission does not apply its own methodology. It applies the rules and methods that have been commonly agreed, in the Output Gap Working Group (OGWG), by technical and academic experts from all of the EU's 28 Member States, as well as from the OECD and the IMF; with the OGWG also periodically drawing on assessments of the method which have been carried out by independent academic experts and institutions (European Commission 2018d).

[3] See https://twitter.com/RobinBrooksIIF and Tooze (2019).

Part C.
The Political Economy of European Integration

A well-functioning Eurozone requires root-and-branch reform at national and central level. However, the political incentives for governments to undertake such reforms are often lacking. The chapters in this section address the complex issues of the political economy of European integration from several angles.
European politicians fear that embracing reform means losing elections. This is behind the famed Juncker's dictum that "we all know what we need to do, but don't know how to be re-elected afterwards." However, empirical evidence does not support such statement. Actually, the analysis points to just the opposite – the odds of re-election are larger for reformist than for non-reformist governments. Two conditions underpin such conclusion: first, the financial system must function well (hence allowing smoother reallocation of resources across sectors and time) and, second, an adequate social safety net has to be present (thereby reducing the short-term negative impact of reforms).

"Impossible trinities" abound in economics. The most compelling one was actually at the root of the creation of the single currency: as one cannot have free capital mobility, fixed exchange rates and independent monetary policies at the same time, the creation of the Eurozone gave up the latter by pooling monetary sovereignty under the responsibility of the ECB.

I show that a "consistent economic trinity" and a "consistent political trinity" are key to improve the functioning of the Eurozone and the EU. The former encompasses structural reforms within countries, more symmetric macroeconomic adjustment across countries, and a Banking Union for the Eurozone. The latter requires overcoming the intergovernmental method that dominated EU decisionmaking during the financial crisis, avoiding the seemingly easy route of blaming all evils on "Brussels," and a more unified external representation.

With its current competences lacking the ability to address distributional effects, the EU is often seen as an agent of globalisation rather than a response to it. This exposes the Union to criticisms of undermining national autonomy, identity, and control. A number of principles should guide reform and should help foster a new, more positive EU narrative. These principles would include: focusing on EU public goods, re-establishing core values of the European social model, mainstreaming distributional considerations in EU policy design and the EU budget, and ensuring transparency and accountability in decision-making.

18 Can Governments Implement Structural Reforms and Yet Be Re-Elected?*

June 2008

1 Juncker's curse

Jean-Claude Juncker, a founding father of the Euro and one of Europe's leading policy makers, once famously quipped that "we all know what to do, but we don't know how to get re-elected once we have done it" (The Economist 2007). Politicians in Europe are deeply aware of the need for structural reform – in particular in the Eurozone where the pace of structural reform has been disappointing since the inception of the single currency (European Commission 2008, Duval and Elmeskov 2005) – and yet reluctant to bite the bullet out of fear of losing the next general election.

Of course, this fear is rooted in experience: structural reforms – ranging from the abolition of state monopolies to making labour markets more flexible – invariably meet strong opposition from vocal interest groups while the benefits of reforms are more diffused and are believed to arise only in the future – hence beyond the term in office of the current ruler. But does this also mean that the electorate punishes incumbent governments if they push through bold structural reforms? In a recent paper (Buti, Turrini *et al.* 2009) we argue that this fear is largely unfounded, particularly if a number of conditions are met.

---

* Co-authors: Alessandro Turrini (European Commission) and Paul van den Noord (European Commission), Vox CEPR, 17 June 2008.

2 Raw evidence

A *prima facie* examination of the electoral and structural reform records for 21 OECD countries over the 1985-2004 period shows that a small majority of incumbent governments (50 – 55%) are re-elected for a next term in office whether they are reformist or non-reformist. Figure 1 shows the fraction of governments that were not re-elected (first pair of columns) and those that were (second pair) for all elections and elections that were preceded by reforms.

This confirms findings from a recent series of case studies that reformist governments, even if they have to overcome initial resistance and misconception, tend to be re-elected (Munkhammar 2007). More sophisticated testing with a probit model indicates that the incumbent government's pursuit structural reform is not statistically insignificant for its re-election probability. The only statistically significant economic factor appears to be the business cycle: if the economy happens to be in an upswing, the incumbent's re-election probability clearly increases.

We could simply stop here, taking the view that structural reforms are apparently irrelevant for the re-election probabilities of incumbent

Figure 1 Probability of re-election and the occurrence of reforms

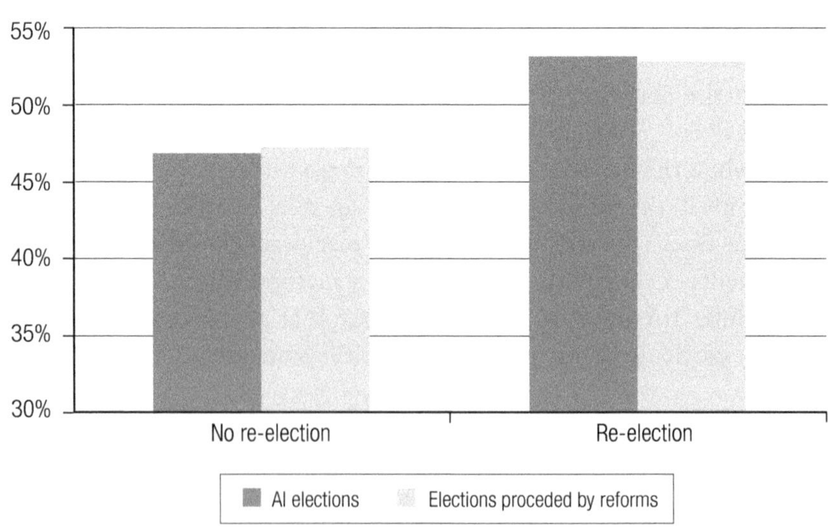

Source: Authors' calculations.

governments. But we want to go one step further by asking: under which conditions can structural reform raise the incumbent's probability of re-election? Our prior belief, and the hypothesis we extensively test in our paper, is that the stage of development of financial markets matters significantly for the re-election probabilities of reformist governments.

3 Finance, reform, and elections

Here is the story. Well-developed financial markets permit households to borrow against future income and smooth consumption over time. Moreover, the availability of a wider range of investment opportunities and income sources improves risk-sharing and permits consumption-smoothing across states of nature. In practice, well-functioning financial markets allow households to seize the opportunities created by structural reforms early and hence help bring forward their benefits.

This has implications for the political feasibility of structural reforms. Even in the presence of short-run costs, reforms would be perceived as bringing overall gains while making agents more resilient to reform-related temporary income loss. We therefore expect structural reforms to meet a more positive electoral reception if financial markets function well. In countries with poorly functioning financial markets, the electoral constituency in favour of reforms is bound to be smaller and hence the government carrying out reforms more likely to be punished at the next elections. Additionally, by reducing the share of liquidity-constrained households, well-functioning financial markets make the economy more "Ricardian" (Seater 1993). This means that fiscal policy is less effective, and hence the government will be less tempted to prop up demand by opening the public purse and more inclined to take the hard route of structural reforms.

The data show *prima facie* evidence that, of all reformist governments that have been re-elected, 65% were governing a country with relatively pro-competitive financial market regulations (according to the financial freedom indicator compiled by the Fraser Institute), whereas the corresponding share among non-reformist governments was only 50% (see Figure 2). More sophisticated testing in our paper strongly confirms this *prima facie* evidence. We find a highly significant positive effect of the interaction of the financial freedom index and structural reform on the

Figure 2 Probability of re-election and the occurrence of reforms by financial freedom

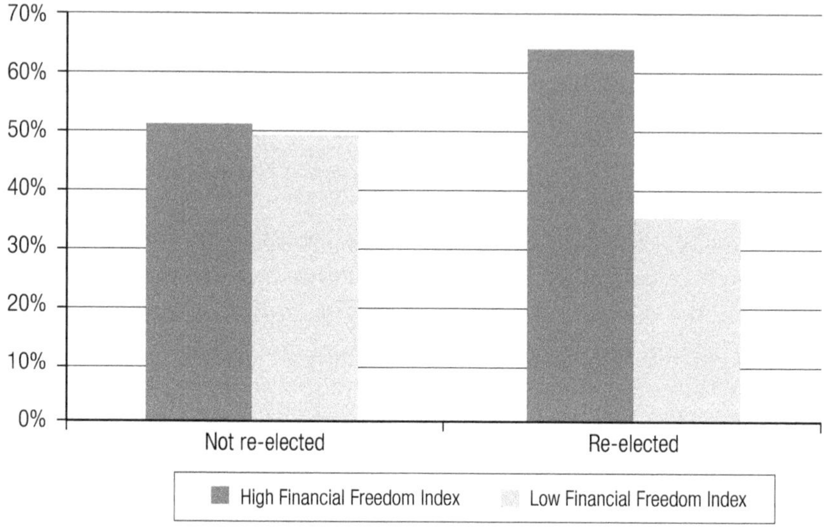

Source: Authors' calculations.

re-election probability of incumbents. An interaction between the cyclical position of the economy and structural reform is also highly significant, suggesting that an incumbent who pursues ambitious structural reform in an environment of financial market freedom while the economy is in an upswing is very likely to be re-elected.

Of course the consumption-smoothing and risk-sharing roles are not unique to financial markets. Social security can in principle also provide this. In fact, recent evidence shows that financial markets and automatic stabilisers can be alternative means to smooth output volatility (Debrun, Pisani-Ferry and Sapir 2008) or to promote the acceptance of globalisation (Bertola 2007). Thus, if well-designed, social security may be expected to strengthen and complement the role of financial markets in softening the resistance against structural reform. While there is little *prima facie* evidence that fiscal automatic stabilisers would play any role in making reformist governments more popular, the more sophisticated testing procedures reported in our paper do support this.

4 Conclusions

We think these findings are novel. To our knowledge - and surprisingly given the well-known quote by J-C Juncker – no attempt so far has been made to test empirically the impact of structural reforms on governments' re-election. The few existing cross-country analyses on the determinants of re-election, such as Powell and Whitten (1993) and Brender and Drazen (2008) do not include structural reform among their explanatory variables. Our work tries to fill this gap.

To sum up, our paper suggests that – in addition to the well-known implications of well-functioning financial markets for the growth potential and the resilience of economies to shocks – there is also an indirect political economy benefit. Financial development, neglected so far, strengthens the constituency in favour of reforms, thereby boosting the electoral incentives for governments to make progress with structural reforms in product and labour markets. As such, reforms improving the functioning of financial markets play an important role in defying, and defeating, the "Juncker curse." This has important implications for any advice regarding the optimal packaging of reforms: as indicated by the Commission communication on EMU@10 (European Commission 2008), upfront financial market reforms facilitate reforms in product and labour markets.

19 Reform and Be Re-Elected: Evidence from the Post-Crisis Period*

July 2014

1 Juncker's curse again

The former Eurogroup president allegedly said, "We all know what to do but we don't know how to be re-elected once we have done it" (The Economist 2007). In chapter 18, we argued that the presumed electoral risk for a reformist government – based on the statement by Mr Juncker – is largely unfounded, particularly if a number of conditions are met. Based on electoral and structural reform records for 21 OECD countries over the period of 1985-2004, we found that electorates generally do not discriminate between reformist and non-reformist governments, although the electoral approval of reforms is stronger when the financial system works effectively and an efficient social safety net is present. More sophisticated econometric testing broadly confirmed these findings (Buti, Turrini et al. 2010), which we interpret as follows: First, well-developed and properly regulated financial markets allow households and firms to seize the opportunities created by structural reforms at an earlier stage, bringing forward benefits that often materialise with lags. Second, they also help the reallocation of factors of production towards new activities spurred by structural reforms. Third, the availability of a wider range of investment opportunities improves risk-sharing and permits consumption-smoothing in the face of policy shocks, making agents more resilient

---

* Co-authors: Alessandro Turrini (European Commission) and Paul van den Noord (University of Amsterdam and ACES), Vox CEPR, 4 July 2014.

to reform-related temporary income or job losses (notably in the case of labour market reforms).

Of course, the consumption-smoothing and risk-sharing roles are not unique to financial markets. If well-designed, social security and social protection systems may play a similar role, and hence soften the resistance against structural reform.

2 The record before and after the crisis

Chapter 18 was based on pre-crisis data. Do our conclusions still hold when taking crisis period data into account? To examine this, we updated our dataset on 20 OECD countries to include the period 2005-2012, based on the same (but updated) sources, most prominently the World Bank Database on Political Institutions data (to determine when incumbent government chief executives were re-elected), various OECD structural reform indicators in the fields of pension, labour market, and product market (to define the reformist nature of governments), and the Fraser Institute indicator of financial freedom (our gauge of the role of financial markets).

Three stylised findings stand out: A) The popular perception that incumbent governments have been punished for the crisis is not rejected by the data. B) Pre-crisis – that is over the period 1987-2007 – there are 131 elections in our dataset, of which in 76 (58%) the incumbent government was re-elected, and in 55 (42%) it was not re-elected. Post-crisis – that is over the period 2008-2012 – there are 29 elections, of which in 14 (48%) the incumbent government was re-elected and in 15 (52%) it was not re-elected. So the (unconditional) probability of being re-elected appears to have fallen after the crisis, most likely as a consequence of the crisis itself, as supported by the econometric evidence indicating a significant effect of economic growth on the probability of re-election (Buti, Turrini et al. 2010). C) Another popular perception – that electorates have penalised reformist incumbents particularly hard in the wake of the crisis – is, however, disproved by our data.

Pre-crisis the re-election probability of reformist governments was slightly smaller than the probability of re-election of all governments taken together. Post-crisis it is the other way around – reformist governments were more likely to be re-elected than all governments taken

Figure 1 Probabilities of re-election and no re-election

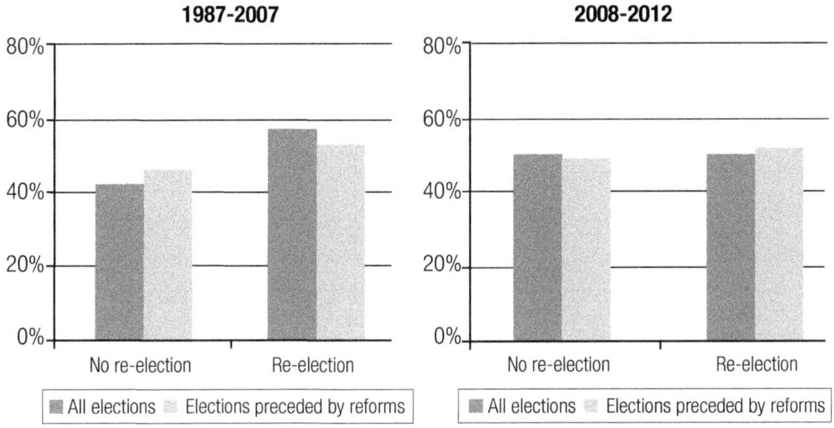

Source: Authors' calculations.

together (see Figure 1). The difference in probability is presumably not statistically significant, not least since post-crisis the number of reformist governments that faced elections is small – six in total, of which three were re-elected (all in the Eurozone). But it surely does not suggest that abstaining from, instead of embarking on, reform is the best route for the incumbent to win the next election. Such a presumption is corroborated by econometric tests: Updating the Buti, Turrini et al. (2010) probit model with post-crisis data, whether governments were reformist or not remains non-significant in determining the probability of re-election. Our earlier finding – that a reformist government is more likely to be re-elected if financial freedom and/or the social safety net is large – remains intact.

As shown in Figure 2 over the whole sample period high financial freedom and a large government size are both conducive to a comparatively higher-election probability of reformist governments.

Figure 2 Probability of re-election of reformist governments

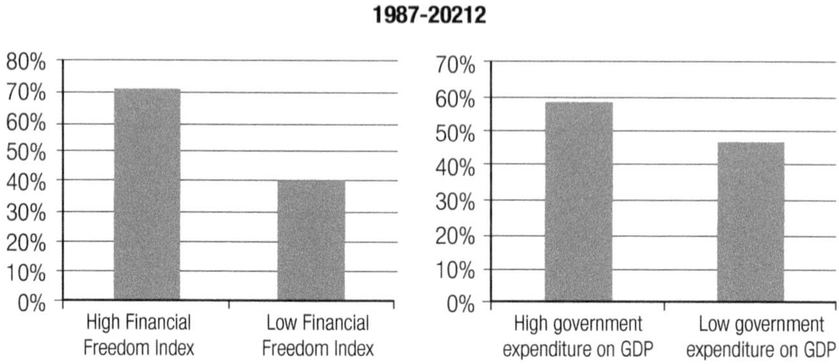

Source: Authors' calculations.

3 What lessons can we draw?

The creation of the Banking Union and the development of financial markets as a complementary channel to banks for financing the real economy are generally welcomed as an important step forward towards easing the fragmentation of the financial system in the Eurozone. This is an important achievement both from the point of view of economic efficiency – i.e. by promoting the effective flow of funds across the monetary union – and financial stability. Our findings add a – perhaps unexpected, but potentially very important – third dimension to the considerations of efficiency and stability. They suggest that improvements in the functioning of the banking and financial system promote the electoral reward for structural reform.

The above findings have an important implication. If reform activism indeed does not hinder the re-election of incumbent governments, further synergies within the "consistent trinity" of policies in the Eurozone – genuine Banking Union, symmetric macroeconomic adjustment, and deep structural reforms (see chapter 20 and chapter 21) – may emerge. The Banking Union and the better functioning of the financial system it will entail over time – by fostering the electoral incentives for incumbent governments to embark on structural reforms – would also support growth and macroeconomic adjustment. Moreover, growth would permit the sustainability of adequate welfare models, which, as our work suggests, would further heighten the electoral rewards for structural reform, thus reinforcing the virtuous circle.

Last but not least, a virtuous circle of this kind, once set in motion, would facilitate the task of the coordination of economic policies at the supranational level – e.g. in the framework of the Macroeconomic Imbalances Procedure and the European Semester. Indeed, the perceived conflict between "national" and "European" policy objectives would fade.

4 Conclusion

It may be true that governments are reluctant to embark on bold structural reforms for electoral reasons, but we find that those governments that dared to carry out reforms have not suffered worse electoral outcomes than those who did not. In fact, electorates tend to reward reformist governments in certain cases, notably if electorates can rely on effective welfare systems to protect them against social hardship, and if well-functioning financial markets help frontload the benefits of structural reform and diminish their short-run cost.

This suggests that, looking forward, financial system repair and the preservation of an effective welfare system would contribute to further contain the risk of reform inertia. We can, therefore, add a "consistent trinity" to the list: there are no conflicts between sustainable social welfare systems, well-functioning financial markets, and electoral support for structural reform.

20 A Consistent Trinity for the Eurozone*

January 2014

1 Post-crisis "inconsistent trinities"

While it would be premature to declare victory, owing to sustained policy efforts at all institutional levels, major progress was made during the financial crisis to put Economic and Monetary Union (EMU) on much firmer ground. All strands of economic policymaking have been working together to overhaul economic governance, to ensure the efficient transmission of monetary policy, and to create effective financial firewalls. What made this possible was the clear political determination to safeguard the integrity and future of EMU.

We have, however, not yet reached a steady state in which EMU's architecture can be considered complete and all economic challenges solved. There is still a risk that a new steady state will be characterised by economic stagnation and persistently high unemployment. Unless appropriate macroeconomic policy conditions are secured and ambitious reforms implemented, a slow, uneven and fragile recovery may become the central scenario. The Eurozone faces a number of concrete policy challenges, the responses to which will shape the Eurozone's ability to withstand future crises and asymmetric shocks. In this chapter, I explore three fundamental challenges that are open to a range of policy responses, some more EMU-friendly, others less so. Choosing the former kind

* Vox CEPR, 8 January 2014. This chapter is based on the author's opening remarks at the conference to celebrate the 30th Anniversary of CEPR held 21 November 2013 at the Bank of England.

of response is vital to underpin confidence and, hence, put the current recovery on a sustainable basis.

Three central challenges will act as a real-life test of EMU's coherence in the coming years, and these can be represented as three "inconsistent trinities," or trilemmas for the Eurozone. For each of these trilemmas there appears to be an optimal, EMU-friendly solution; deviations from this optimal solution would imply trading-off indispensable policy objectives against each other.

2 Structural reforms to safeguard European welfare systems

In the current slow growth environment and given ubiquitous high debt levels, there is little choice other than to maintain a prudent fiscal stance, though with stronger differentiation among Member States according to their fiscal space. Slow growth also makes unemployment more persistent, thereby raising the spectre of depreciating human capital, as well as social unrest at a juncture where the European social model is increasingly under strain. There are considerable equity implications of the ongoing adjustment and reform process that demand a rethink of Europe's welfare systems accordingly.

A first inconsistent trinity, therefore, exists between conducting sound fiscal policies and achieving sustainable welfare systems while pursuing unambitious structural reforms that will keep EU economies locked in a "stagnation trap."

It is not possible to have fiscal discipline and at the same time maintain the European welfare model on a sustainable basis without structural reforms that are able to deliver job creation and generate growth in order to finance those welfare models. At the same time, if fiscal discipline is to be maintained without embarking on far-reaching structural reforms to increase growth, this will only come at the expense of dismantling, or at least gradually eroding the European welfare model.

Since our welfare model is a central safeguard of social cohesion, failure to seize reform opportunities will, by extension, risk undermining an important element of the inclusive European social market economy. Besides, social cohesion is a pre-condition for political viability of more integration. Therefore, ambitious structural reforms are the EMU-friendly resolution of this trilemma.

Figure 1 First inconsistent trinity: Political and social viability

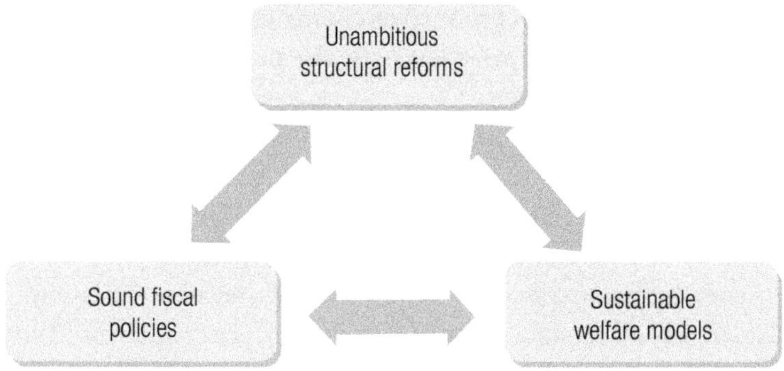

Source: Own elaboration.

An ambitious agenda of structural reforms should be pursued with policies focusing on competitiveness gains within sustainable and inclusive growth models. Balanced growth will require an acceleration of reforms in the core and semi-core countries, not only in the vulnerable countries which have shown greater "reform responsiveness."

3 Reclaiming macroeconomic policy space for greater adjustment symmetry

The Eurozone faces a fundamental challenge to support the nascent recovery and deal with macroeconomic vulnerabilities. Modest real growth – partly resulting from ongoing and inevitable adjustment in private sector balance sheets after such a major financial crisis – will be compounded in its effect on nominal GDP growth by slowing Eurozone inflation, which is forecast at around 1.5% for 2014 and 2015 (European Commission 2013d). Slow nominal GDP growth becomes a particular concern when economies have to deal with a large debt overhang, as is currently the case for many parts of the Eurozone.

Besides ensuring debt sustainability in a low-inflation environment, Eurozone members face a simultaneous challenge in ensuring a rebalancing of competitiveness and external accounts. In the absence of nominal exchange rate adjustment, meeting these challenges can only be achieved via changes in relative prices across the Eurozone. Restoring competitiveness in vulnerable economies will generally require a negative inflation differential with respect to surplus countries located in the Eurozone core, so as to ensure that price levels in the periphery rise more slowly than in the core.

The objectives of debt sustainability and external rebalancing in the Eurozone may conflict, as long as actual Eurozone inflation remains persistently low – well below the 2% inflation target of the ECB. This is because competitiveness rebalancing for the periphery would dictate much lower inflation rates, or even outright negative inflation. This would adversely affect debt dynamics in the periphery and would create a deflationary bias in the Eurozone as a whole. This conflict is particularly acute for highly indebted countries in the Eurozone, which tend to have greater competitiveness adjustment needs, notwithstanding their progress made to date (Pisani-Ferry 2012).

This conflict of policy objectives and economic realities can be represented as a second inconsistent trinity – that vulnerable countries cannot simultaneously reduce their high debt burdens and gain competitiveness in an environment of persistently low Eurozone average inflation.

As both debt sustainability and competitive rebalancing lie at the very heart of macroeconomic stability in the Eurozone, the EMU-friendly resolution of this trilemma, therefore, is to reject inflation being persistently below ECB target. Doing so would widen the range of possible

Figure 2 Second inconsistent trinity: Adjustment objectives in the Eurozone

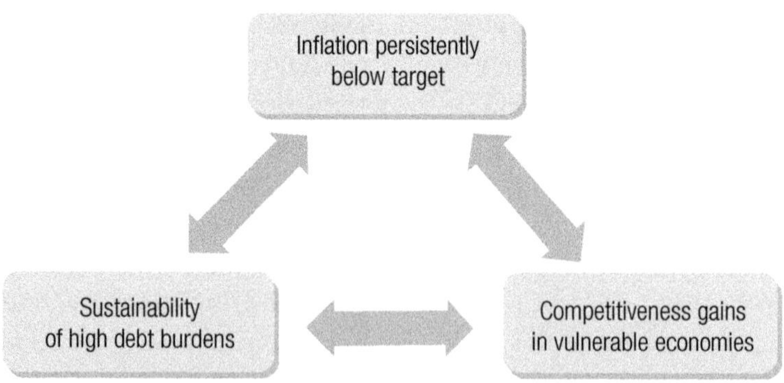

Source: Own elaboration.

inflation differentials between the core and periphery that would still ensure non-deflation in the periphery.

Crucially, this is not to argue for a change in the ECB's inflation target, but rather to argue in favour of the ECB's continued efforts to meet its mandated target. Besides the risk of dislodging well-anchored inflation expectations, persistently low inflation may bring the Eurozone close to a Japanese-style nominal depression, the costs of which have become all too evident during Japan's "lost decade." But stemming the disinflationary momentum in the Eurozone cannot be done by the ECB alone, though making full use of both conventional and unconventional tools can contribute to this goal.

Instead, ensuring different inflation rates in a diverse economic region consistent with aggregate price stability such as the Eurozone is also about ensuring appropriate demand conditions in both the core and periphery. Tremendous reform efforts are already underway in vulnerable countries at a particularly weak point in the business cycle. Part of a durable resolution of this trilemma will also involve core countries undertaking reforms to boost domestic sources of growth resulting in higher domestic demand, in particular by supporting public and private investment. This balanced approach to Eurozone macroeconomic policy may also be thought of as a more symmetrical form of adjustment that would make tackling the main vulnerabilities in the Eurozone less onerous to deliver.

4 Effectively combatting systemic financial sector vulnerabilities

The third challenge, closely connected with the two previous ones, relates to the Eurozone's highly integrated financial system in the context of large banking sector vulnerabilities and limited national fiscal space.

Many banking systems are both fragile and too large for any sovereign state to comfortably backstop. This is the root of what has been termed the "deadly embrace" between banks and their sovereigns (De Grauwe 2013). A related problem has been the fragmentation of the Eurozone's financial systems. Credit conditions have become highly divergent across the Eurozone, thus constraining recovery, especially in the more vulnerable economies, and impairing monetary transmission channels. This policy challenge represents another inconsistent trinity, relating to the fact that financial stability and integrated financial markets cannot be achieved unless the deadly embrace between the banks and the sovereigns is broken (Obstfeld 2013).

Pisani-Ferry (2012) develops a related trilemma, which elucidates the role of the ECB's lender of last resort function in a "deadly embrace" context without common fiscal backstops for banks.

Figure 3 Third inconsistent trinity: Restoring financial integration and stability

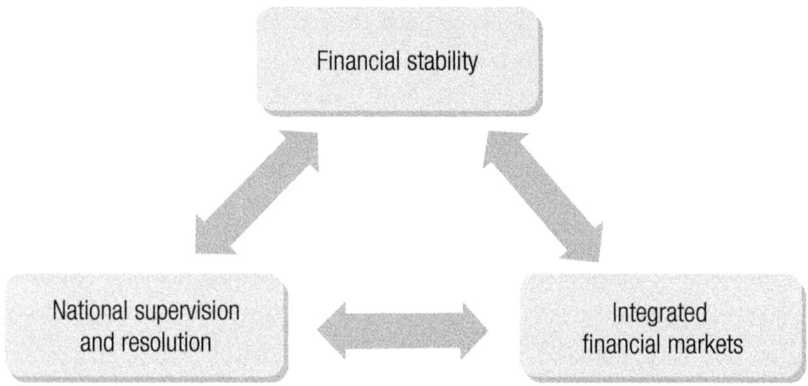

Source: Own elaboration.

This trilemma suggests that the aims of achieving financial stability within an integrated, competitive, and dynamic single financial market can only be satisfied by allowing for greater mutual responsibility for banking sector problems. This provides an intellectual underpinning to a genuine Banking Union, which has been developed and implemented since 2012. While several initiatives have been taken on the regulatory front, completing a full Banking Union with a mutual backstop remains a clear priority.

5 Overcoming the policy conflicts

The current economic and political realities suggest a need for policymakers to reflect on a new paradigm for economic integration in Europe. Resolving the three aforementioned inconsistent trinities through

EMU-friendly solutions can achieve a superior outcome that benefits all Eurozone members. These respective solutions form yet another trinity, which this time is consistent and self-reinforcing.

Figure 4 A consistent trinity

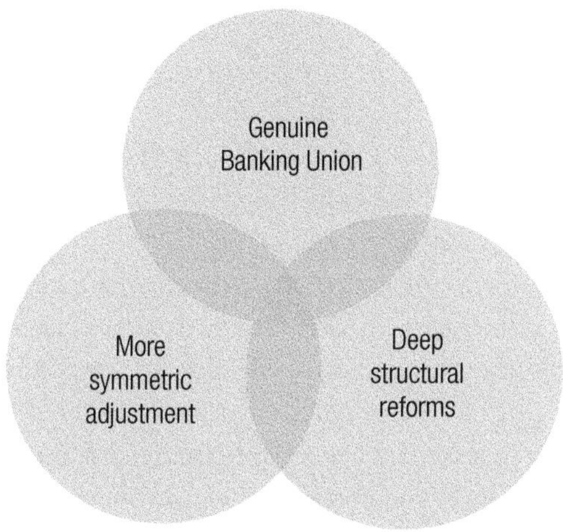

Source: Own elaboration.

Slow growth would be tackled by bold structural reforms both in the core and the periphery, which in turn would help maintain sustainable welfare systems. Appropriate structural reforms would also increase domestic demand in the core, which would in turn have a positive effect on internal demand in vulnerable countries through exports, and would facilitate rebalancing. Higher demand would help bringing overall Eurozone inflation closer to its target and, hence, provide room for higher inflation differentials between the core and the periphery, giving margin for competitive gains in vulnerable countries, and at the same time alleviating debt sustainability problems. If coupled with a full and effective Banking Union, financial fragmentation would recede, and credit conditions could support growth and reforms through spurring investment, while important fiscal and financial risks would be reduced by severing sovereign-bank links.

What does this imply in concrete policy terms? Vulnerable Member States have recently pushed through impressive structural reforms, which can be expected to deliver growth dividends in the medium-term. Early signs of economic revival are visible already. These achievements notwithstanding, further progress is needed to rebalance their economies. Meanwhile, some other Member States, including those with current account surpluses, show signs of stronger domestic demand. Bolder reform efforts will help spurr domestic demand and will enhance the overall rebalancing process. Measures to encourage public and private investment would also not only help in rebalancing the EU economy but also increase potential growth in the medium-term.

Finally, a genuine Banking Union would help break the vicious link between the sovereign and the banks. A critical step towards repairing the financial system is cleaning up and strengthening bank balance sheets. The asset quality review and stress tests, ahead of the agreed launch of the single supervisory authority (SSM) will be instrumental in this respect. It will have to complement a Single Resolution Mechanism (SRM) and a Resolution Fund. The completion of a fully-fledged Banking Union remains critical to reverse the process of financial fragmentation and restore the flow of credit to the corporate sector, not only through its effect on fragmentation and the cost of borrowing, but also by providing a more stable, transparent, and predictable financial environment.

This "consistent trinity," whose elements gradually start to materialise, could be the basis for a new contract for the Eurozone.

21 Delivering the Eurozone "Consistent Trinity"*

March 2014

1 Introduction

As argued in chapter 20, the financial crisis exposed important economic inconsistencies in the way that EMU operated (see chapter 20, see also Pisani-Ferry 2012). Although progress has been made, the reality is that more needs to be done. A number of countries still need to consolidate their public finances further, and also implement structural reforms to promote growth and sustain satisfactory welfare systems. At the same time, there is a need for vulnerable countries to ensure consistency between regaining competitiveness and the sustainability of private and public debts. Finally, overcoming financial fragmentation is a *sine qua non* for promoting financial stability while ensuring the effective flow of funds across the monetary union. The institutional/policy mix that addresses these problems comes in the form of a "consistent trinity" that involves: (i) deep fiscal and structural reforms within countries, (ii) a rotation of demand that contributes to a more symmetric adjustment across countries, and (iii) a Banking Union at the level of the Eurozone as a whole.

The Commission has delivered its part of the consistent trinity. As the European Parliament, Council, and Commission reach important agreements on the Banking Union, the Commission has been monitor-

* Co-authors: Maria Demertzis and João Nogueira Martins (European Commission), Vox CEPR, 30 March 2014.

ing progress made by countries in terms of the two first aspects of the consistent trinity.

2 Changing challenges: structural reforms and rotation of demand

Integrated surveillance of fiscal and structural issues

On the fiscal field, the Commission is implementing the reformed Stability and Growth Pact, and ensuring that each country delivers the appropriate fiscal efforts effectively. After the analysis (for the first time) of the draft budgetary plans prepared by the Eurozone governments in autumn 2013, a continuous monitoring of developments led the Commission to address formal recommendations to France and Slovenia on 5 March 2014, as risks have accumulated that these two Member States could fail to reach their headline and structural targets. Moreover, the Commission has published "in-depth reviews" (IDRs) carried out for 17 Member States, under the Macroeconomic Imbalance Procedure, which is the new coordination process introduced in 2011 in the aftermath of the financial crisis (European Commission 2014a).[1] The IDRs focus on the structural features of the economies which may constitute imbalances and generate macroeconomic risks and harmful spillovers.

Structural reforms for competitiveness and sustainability

Before the outbreak of the financial crisis, the main policy issues related to unsustainable current-account deficits, worrying losses in competitiveness linked to very dynamic labour costs, increasing private debts, and high housing prices. The main challenges of a cross-country nature in the aftermath of the sovereign debt crisis concern the lingering impact that deleveraging pressures in many countries have on medium-term growth, the sustainability of private and public debts in a context of competitive disinflation, and the need to provide credit to viable investments in the vulnerable economies, under a convalescent financial system.

Figure 1 shows that unsustainable current-account deficits have been corrected (see Spain and Portugal in the left-hand panel, but similar developments also took place in Ireland, Greece, and Slovenia). However, the figure (right-hand panel) also shows that while flows have adjusted, the stocks remain problematic for the peripheral countries that are left with a large debt overhang. The dichotomy between "deficit countries" and "surplus countries" has been replaced by one between "net debtors" and "net creditors." In order to reduce their debts and the burden that they cause in terms of negative income flows, the peripheral countries will have to run current-account surpluses for several years – the ongoing reorientation of the productive system towards exports and the recovery in competitiveness will have to be maintained. From a policy perspective, this emphasises the need to continue with structural reforms to encourage real growth and facilitate the reallocation of labour and capital to the tradable sectors.

Figure 1 External rebalancing in the Eurozone: stocks and flows

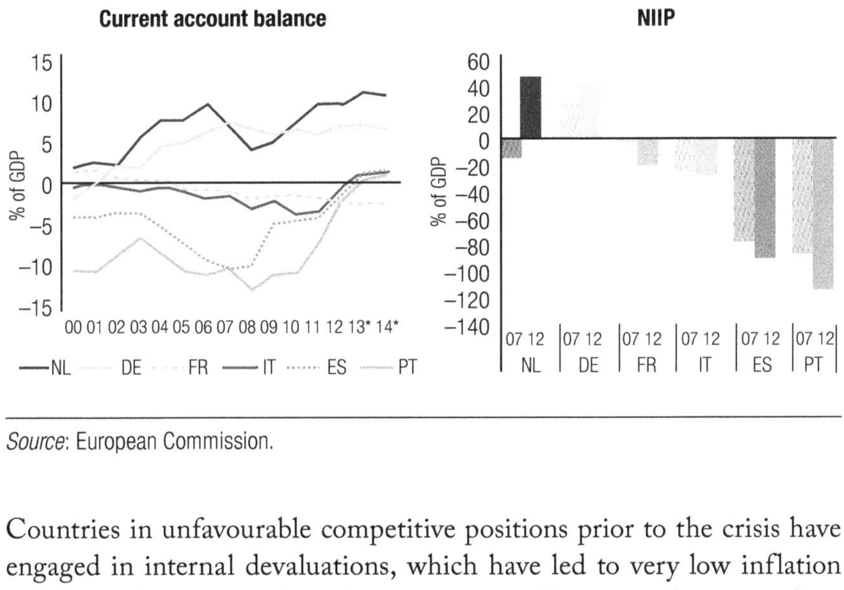

Source: European Commission.

Countries in unfavourable competitive positions prior to the crisis have engaged in internal devaluations, which have led to very low inflation or even reductions in their domestic prices. However, the pace of internal devaluation needs to be made consistent with debt sustainability, since low nominal growth may conflict with the need to reduce private and public debt ratios, while the reduction in wages compresses domestic demand. Figure 2 illustrates this, as the countries with lower inflation (and nominal GDP growth) given the initial competitiveness position are those with higher debts and facing higher financing costs (Merler and Pisani-Ferry 2012). Over and above this, an environment of persistent low inflation across the Eurozone – below the ECB's definition of price stability of an inflation rate below, but close to, 2% – makes the relative price adjustment between countries, which is so necessary to the peripheral countries, all the more difficult. Moreover given nominal rigidities, the persistence of very low inflation might also be a hurdle to the necessary adjustments in real wages, which has important consequences for employment and unemployment.

Figure 2 Low inflation and debt

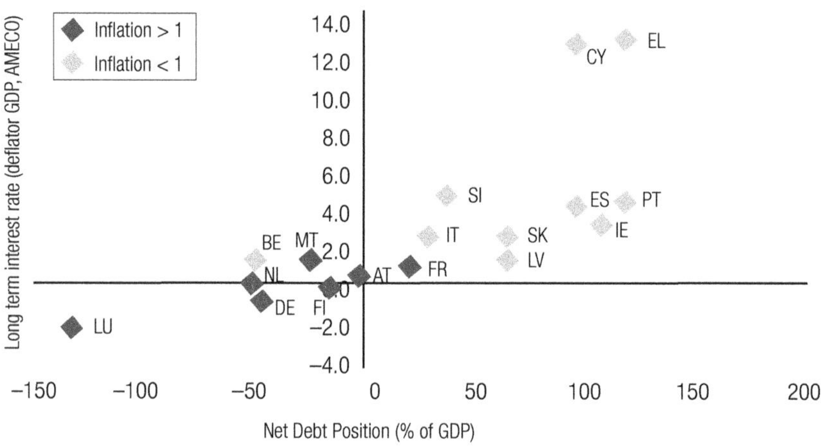

Notes: The x axis is Net International Investment Position (NIIP) multiplied by -1, i.e. positive numbers reflect debt. NIIP value of 2013Q3, except FR and MT (2012Q4), and IT (2013Q2). Inflation based on EC Winter forecast for 2014.

Source: Eurostat, AMECO.

Structural reforms for investment, rotation of demand, and symmetry in adjustment

The correction of the large current-account deficits means that, since creditor countries are not adjusting sufficiently, the Eurozone is registering a large and increasing current-account surplus. The risks arising from such a surplus are the strain on domestic demand and therefore on the ability of the Eurozone to grow, but also the possibility of a euro appreciation that could erode peripheral countries' efforts to regain competitiveness. Preventing this from happening is very important for the peripheral countries themselves, but also for the Eurozone as a whole.

Appropriate reforms in core countries and a greater symmetry in adjustment would be good for stimulating domestic demand in the creditor countries, as well as in the whole Eurozone, and facilitate the periphery's efforts to restore competitiveness and to grow. Policies that contribute to an increase in investment are particularly critical, as they boost demand in the short-term and increase potential growth in the future.

Chapter 27 shows how the reform dynamism has paid off in terms of potential growth, and therefore contributed to sustainable and long-lasting gains. In turn, higher potential growth contributes to the sustainability of private and public deft, and protects welfare systems in times of fiscal consolidation. Figure 3 shows that the reform dynamism and responsiveness to policy recommendations have differed among the Eurozone countries, with progress registered by the vulnerable countries, where the need was acute, but much less so by the largest or core Eurozone economies.

Figure 3 Responsiveness to policy recommendations across the Eurozone, 2011–2012

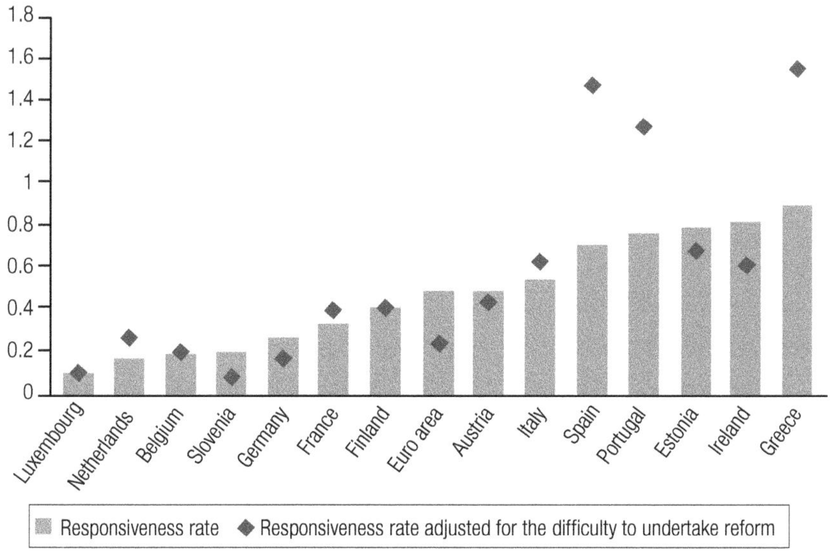

Source: Adapted from OECD (2013a).

3 Eurozone governance coming of age

The Commission's integrated analysis has acknowledged the important progress made in a number of countries, but also clarified the changing nature of the challenges remaining. In its third year of operation, the Macroeconomic Imbalance Procedure as a new governance tool has allowed granularity and greater differentiation in the way countries are evaluated – discussing both the remaining competitiveness issues in the periphery and drawing attention to the inefficiencies that are behind the large external surpluses in the core. The country assessments are based not only on a snapshot of their present economic position, but also on the country's dynamics and interaction within the monetary union. In addition, the analysis takes into account the country's capacity to adjust and efforts made to implement necessary policies.

The Commission's approach in 2014 assessed how macroeconomic risks and imbalances have evolved. In the case of Italy, the risks were deemed higher than the previous year, leading to the identification of "excessive imbalances." The opposite result has been identified for Spain and Ireland, where reforms have contributed to the reduction of existing risks and the successful completion of their programmes supported by international financing. The Commission surveillance has discussed country-specific inefficiencies, such as low levels of investment (Germany) or losses in competitiveness (France), but also what their synthesis implies for the Eurozone as a whole.

In the middle of a broadening but still fragile recovery, a boost to economic activity and the medium-term outlook is expected to come from continuing structural reforms aimed at boosting competitiveness and adjustment in the vulnerable economies. For the larger and less indebted Member States, policies to increase demand and potential growth would provide both benefits domestically and ensure greater symmetry in adjustment. Among the largest Eurozone Member States, the policy priorities should focus on: strengthening domestic demand, including investment, and medium-term growth in Germany; addressing bottlenecks to medium-term growth while working on structural reforms and fiscal consolidation in France and Italy; and continuing the orderly deleveraging and structural transformation of the economy in Spain that will contribute to sustainable growth, while addressing social issues.

At the Eurozone level, progress on the Banking Union, including the asset quality review and the stress tests, is crucial to minimise the feedback loops between banks and sovereigns, restore confidence in the banking system, and tackle financial fragmentation in the Eurozone. The current benign market conditions should not lead to the relaxation of reform efforts, as happened all too often in the past.

Note

[1] See European Commission (2014a). This is the second step in a three-step process. The first step starts with the Alert Mechanism Report (COM (2013) 790 of 13 November 2013) in the Autumn that decides which countries will be subject to an in-depth reveiw. The third step comes in Spring when the Commission issues Country Specific Recommendations following countries' submissions of their national reform and stability programmes; these recommendations will then be adopted by the Council.

22 Europe's Incompatible Political Trinities*

September 2016

1 EU economic policy coordination: where we come from

The economic and financial crisis that started in 2008 took a taxing toll on European economies. The cost has not only been economic, but also political. In the wake of this crisis, political scepticism has grown, as shown by the number of ruling parties and coalitions that lost elections during the height of the crisis. Meanwhile, populist parties with an anti-European, anti-Euro stance have emerged and turned out stronger in recent elections. The discontent with the present state of the EU culminated with the outcome of the Brexit referendum (O'Rourke 2016).

Chapter 20 stressed that a number of inconsistent economic and financial trinities emerged since the outset of the crisis. We build on this here by looking at current challenges from a political economy point of view, and identify three elements that are key to adapting our vision of subsidiarity to the current times: overcoming the intergovernmental method that has dominated EU decisionmaking since the crisis (an EU task); refusing the seemingly easy solution to blame all evils on Brussels, including for the costs of tough but inevitable reforms (a domestic task); and moving towards a more unified external representation in global economic governance (a global task).

At the core of the concept of monetary union created by the Maastricht Treaty in 1992 was the "impossible trinity" proposition by Mundell

* Co-author: Muriel Lacoue-Labarthe (European Commission), Vox CEPR, 7 September 2016.

– a group of countries cannot pursue simultaneously a fixed exchange rate, complete capital mobility, and autonomous monetary policies. This was even truer in the context of free trade, as emphasised by Tommaso Padoa-Schioppa in his "inconsistent quartet" (Padoa-Schioppa 1987). His report on the consequences of the Single European Act called for the evolution of the Community's responsibilities for the three branches of public policy defined as allocation, stabilisation, and redistribution (Musgrave 1959). As the Single Market would have major consequences for allocation efficiency, monetary policy centralisation was key for stabilisation, and an evolution of the EU budget towards economic convergence and social cohesion would contribute to addressing distribution issues across EU countries.

In institutional terms, the principle of subsidiarity at the core of the Maastricht Treaty of 1992 led to centralisation of monetary policy, but left budgetary and economic policies as a "matter of common concern" in the competence of Member States, within a macroeconomic policy coordination framework including a specific set of minimum rules against fiscal profligacy. While the adoption of framework rules remains grounded in the traditional Community method, which implies majority voting and co-decision between the Council and European Parliament on the Commission proposals and recommendations, their implementation and the adoption of Council recommendations to Member States belong to the Council alone.

2 The EU after the financial crisis: policy challenges and their political consequences

The institutional setting laid out in the Maastricht Treaty has been put to a trying test from 2008 onwards. In the wake of the crisis, key policy challenges have emerged in terms of Eurozone internal rebalancing, structural reform efforts to increase growth, and financial stability and integration, all of which still need to be fully addressed (see chapter 20). Besides Eurozone economic issues, protecting public goods such as security, defence or asylum requires joint policy responses from the EU, rather than at the level of each Member State. In the meantime, institutional and political challenges have arisen, raising the question not only of what should be done in policy terms, but also how it can best be delivered. This requires addressing legitimacy issues that have arisen over the crisis years and considering their consequences for how the EU's and its Member States' competences should be articulated at the current juncture.

Political inconsistent trinity

A first inconsistent trinity appears when decisions to be taken at the European level rely on democratic checks and balances based only on national institutions.

The response to the crisis was dominated by the shift to an intergovernmental process in decisionmaking, based on unanimity. The European Council, often in its EA formation and based on pre-agreement between some Member States, defined not only broad policy orientations – which is the role entrusted to the European Council by the Treaties – but also detailed arrangements. Examples of this include the negotiation of financial assistance programmes to vulnerable Member States, or the details of the reform of economic and budgetary surveillance procedures set out in the Van Rompuy Task Force. The intergovernmental method also played a major role in the creation of financial assistance mechanisms. Both the European Financial Stability Facility (EFSF) and the European Stability Mechanism (ESM) rely on a mutual consent procedure. The Banking Union, launched in 2012 to address the incompatibility of national financial supervision with the objective of financial stability in a context of integrated financial markets (Schoenmaker 2011), was in key respects based on intergovernmental agreements, although most of its founding texts and new institutions are anchored in the Community method.

Unanimity, which entails the possibility of a veto, still has the same drawbacks that led to its replacement by a majority voting rule in the Single European Act of 1985. Participants are accountable to their domestic constituencies in the way they have upheld domestically defined priorities in decisions that will also apply to other constituencies. While a majority voting rule helps define a joint narrative and common interest beyond the mere average of individual objectives, unanimity leads to compromises based on a minimum common denominator or, as in the heat of the crisis, the relative bargaining powers of creditors and debtors. What ensues is the "ultima ratio" logic where a consensus is eventually achieved, but often too late and at much higher costs. Not being based on genuine ownership, consensus proves difficult to sustain as soon as the market pressure abates.

In political science terms, this means that not only was the output legitimacy of the Eurozone in question, but also the ability of its decision-making to reach a balanced solution ("throughput legitimacy") and its responsiveness to the public debate, which was mostly held at domestic level (input legitimacy), as stressed by Schmidt (2015a, 2016).

Similar to the "globalisation trilemma" developed by Rodrik (2000), this complex process can be summarised in a first inconsistent political trinity, whereby democratic checks and balances over deeply integrated political decisions cannot be achieved by institutions based solely on national sovereignty. Democratic institutions at the national level are adapted to decision-making regarding domestic public goods. But combining democratic requirements with decision-making at the level of the EU or the Eurozone, to ensure public goods such as its integrity and stability, must also involve institutions that are representative and accountable to this wider constituency.

In institutional terms, this calls for overcoming "intergovernmentalism" and returning to the Community method as an adequate setting for multilevel governance. It does not suppress national sovereignty but complements and shares it, with accountability commensurate to the level where decisions are made, based on a renewed subsidiarity assessment.

Figure 1 First inconsistent trinity: Political integration

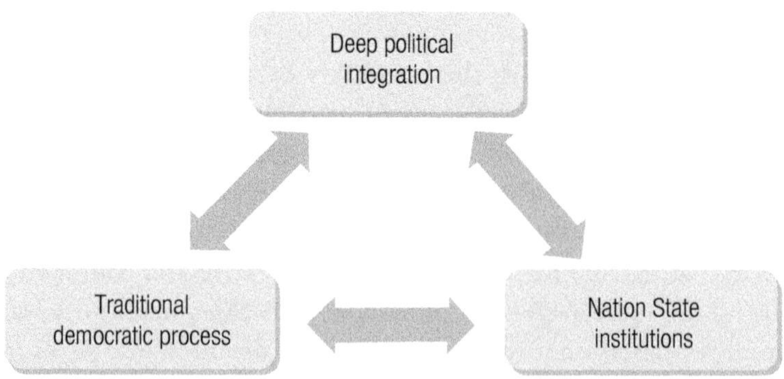

Source: Own elaboration.

This was recognised by the Five Presidents' Report in June 2015, which, among other elements, calls for the creation of a Eurozone Treasury accountable at the European level, and the integration of the ESM into the Community framework, as parts of the second step of completion of the EMU (Juncker et al. 2015).

Institutional inconsistent trinity

At the national level, blaming "Brussels" is inconsistent with the relevant degree of subsidiarity, but also fuels domestic political instability.

One of the impacts of the crisis has been to deepen divergences between Eurozone economies, with deeply ambitious reform efforts still to be endeavoured, while revealing a larger extent of interdependence and spillovers from economic and fiscal policies.

In the current context of slow recovery, one of the key challenges is to ensure more symmetry in rebalancing efforts, in order to support the ECB's inflation objective of price stability while vulnerable economies are restoring their competitiveness and reducing their high debt burdens. This requires Member States that have the necessary margin to support domestic demand and investment more than they are doing now, and more vulnerable economies to run prudent fiscal policies and implement deeply ambitious reforms at the national level to recreate conditions protective of their social model, while restoring their public finances. In other words, this requires reorganising domestic priorities in recognition of deep economic interdependence.

Political parties have two choices in this respect. They can either create a narrative explaining why certain decisions are better taken at the central level and set out a European policy agenda, or blame an abstract Brussels that is unable to cater for domestic priorities and reluctantly implement the outcome of decision-making despite their involvement in the process.

The negative option appears frequently in periods of distress, not just in populist forces but also mainstream parties. The length of the crisis, ensuing rising inequalities between and within Member States, and the prospect of difficult reforms make political choices more difficult to accept and defend. However, blaming Brussels for the implications of difficult but inevitable choices entails negative consequences in public opinion, for which the result of the UK referendum on the EU should serve as a cautionary tale. First, it weakens the ability to effectively achieve the adequate level of subsidiarity-based devolutions at the European level, thus hindering the definition of mutually stabilising solutions. Second, it lends credibility to the anti-European, anti-Euro stance of populist parties, even though none of their alleged solutions addresses the question of how isolated states would resolve the larger challenges of globalisation better than a union that shares core values of a European social and political model. This eventually creates instability in the domestic political landscape, making stable ruling coalitions more difficult to achieve, and eventually making the prospect of populist parties in governing positions more likely.

Hence, the institutional relations setting needs to overcome an inconsistent trinity, where taking the EU as a general scapegoat for the consequences of the crisis prevents the achievement of both domestic political stability and the adequate level of subsidiarity required to deliver EU-based solutions to EUrelevant problems.

Figure 2 Second inconsistent trinity: Institutional relations

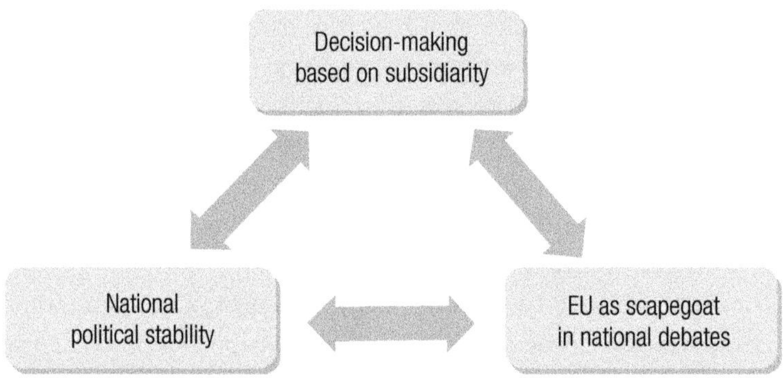

Source: Own elaboration.

The inconsistent trinity in global governance

While European integration should help address economic challenges linked to globalisation, poor coordination weakens Europe's voice in global debates.

A logical consequence of deeper EU integration, namely the creation of the EMU, was the ability to increase its influence on the functioning of the international economic system. The Union must be able to speak with one voice to make full use of its position, not just to adapt to growing globalisation but also contribute to shaping it. Again, this requires a balancing act between integrated and national policies and institutions for their representation in multilateral forums (Buti 2016).

While an important degree of integration has been reached in the field of trade policy, EU representation remains dispersed in multilateral forums – such as the IMF, the G20 and the Financial Stability Board – on issues of key importance for global economic governance, such as the stability of the international economic system and the need to rebalance economies.

Again, there is a choice to be made within an inconsistent trinity, whereby it is not possible to achieve an important role in global governance if representation in multilateral forums remains that of Member States alone. In other words, fragmented external representation undermines the European message to the world, or it weakens the effectiveness of the multilateral global governance framework via a web of state-to-state bilateral agreements. Only a single external voice, at least at the Eurozone level – along the lines of the proposition of the Five Presidents' Report and the proposal by the Commission (European Commission 2015b) – can be conducive to a greater influence in global decisionmaking.

Figure 3 Third inconsistent trinity: Global governance

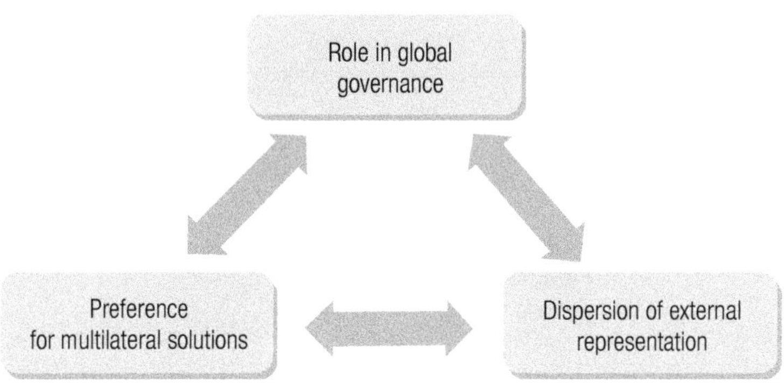

Source: Own elaboration.

3 Overcoming inconsistent trinities to achieve a new political synthesis

Lessons learnt over the financial crisis, and the need to respond faster and more effectively to secure the recovery, shed light on the importance of taking a fresh look at the degree of subsidiarity that is relevant today. Solving the three political trilemmas discussed here is instrumental to achieving better policy outcomes. The solution lies in a new trinity based on three elements – at the domestic, European, and global level – that would be mutually reinforcing, this time in a consistent manner.

At the domestic level, it is up to civil society, and chiefly mainstream parties, to develop a positive narrative on European integration, explaining why certain decisions are better taken at the central level and developing a vision for its integration.

At the European level, intergovernmental decision-making must be overcome in order to reach faster and more transparent solutions grounded in the common interest, by returning to and adapting the Community method to the requirements of the post crisis environment.

At the global level, the EU should be enabled to make full use of its position as one of the largest economies in the world, and, via a more unified representation in multilateral forums, bear more weight in pro-

Figure 4 A new political synthesis

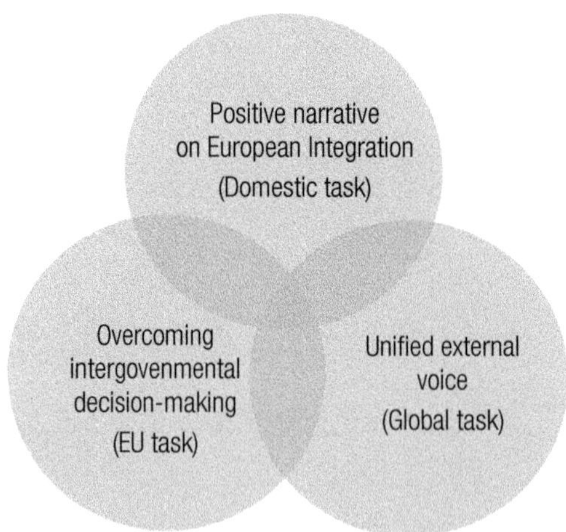

Source: Own elaboration.

moting the core values of a European social and economic model that is unique in the world.

Gathering these three elements would, in turn, strengthen the conditions necessary for policy reform, both at the domestic and European level. While pundits and media commentators often emphasise the growing Euroscepticism in several EU countries, one should not underestimate the profound understanding of and attachment to the European project that European citizens have, and their own readiness to take further steps for the EMU, even in the aftermath of this challenging crisis. Results from a recent poll in Germany, Italy, France, Spain, Belgium, and Poland showed, for instance, that 59-89% of respondents considered belonging to the EU as a good thing, and 57-75% were opposed to returning to domestic currencies. Moreover, 58-67% were in favour of the creation of the position of Finance Minister for the Eurozone, and 63-71% would be favourable to an EU President directly elected by citizens (IFOP 2016).

While polls are obviously different from an actual vote, this only shows that there is solid ground to provide a rigorous and unbiased narrative of the implications of European integration, and to propose a renewed subsidiarity model whereby the respective responsibilities at each level are identified more clearly, and decisions are taken at the relevant level with commensurate democratic checks and balances.

23 European Integration and Populism: Addressing Dahrendorf's Quandary*

February 2017

1 The tide has turned

EU institutions and policy settings are prone to populist attack from both the purely economic and the more cultural "nativist identity" angle. Current competences, mostly confined to organising markets and lacking the ability to address distribution effects, make the EU appear as the agent of globalisation within Europe, rather than a joint European response to globalisation. At the same time, it is charged with undermining national autonomy, identity, and control. Against that background, we set out five guiding principles for policy articulation at the EU level for a new positive EU narrative.

After a decades-long process where national economies became more and more entangled and interdependent at both the international and regional level, increasing strains to economic integration are evident both at the global and the European level. Examples abound – even without mentioning Brexit or the 45th US president – from rising stress in international capital and currency markets to protectionist pressures of all sorts on domestic markets coupled with a rising tide of nationalistic, actually often nativist, go-alone policy approaches. What is at stake is huge as the spectre of disintegration is raising its ugly head and, in fact, an integration process that has been the bedrock of a half-century of peace and economic development can no longer be taken for granted.

---

* Co-author: Karl Pichelmann (European Commission), Vox CEPR, 22 February 2017.

The current rise in populist parties is a wake-up call resembling what the late Ralf Dahrendorf – a major scholar of the 20th century and a former member of the European Commission – summarised in the mid-1990s as a quandary between globalisation (as a means towards growth), social cohesion and political freedom:

> To stay competitive in a growing world economy [the OECD countries] are obliged to adopt measures which may inflict irreparable damage on the cohesion of the respective civil societies. If they are unprepared to take these measures, they must recur to restriction of civil liberties and of political participation bearing all the hallmarks of a new authoritarianism (…) The task for the first world in the next decade is to square the circle between growth, social cohesion and political freedom.[1]

Indeed, the EU integration process has traditionally been conceived as a means to square the circle, allowing for catching-up economic growth and convergence (the EU as a great "convergence machine"; Gill and Raiser 2012), while preserving Europe's social model(s) as reflected in the EU social acquis. However, while the deepening globalisation and integration process has generated overall income gains via higher static and dynamic efficiency, in combination with skill-biased technical progress, it has almost certainly not been Pareto-optimal, creating winners (take-it all) and losers in an age of massive transformation. The financial crisis and its fall-out have only fuelled an already existing undercurrent of discontent and fading trust in democratic institutions and the so-called "elites" to deal with the (real or imagined) unfair distribution of gains and burdens in society. In this context, EU institutional settings and policies have been increasingly perceived as being pro-market, paying little attention (if any) to their social impact, and undermining cohesion, solidarity, autonomy, and governability at the national, regional, and local levels. Put succinctly, in Musgrave's Three Functions of Government, the EU is seen as dealing with the allocative and, subordinately the stabilisation function, while not caring about the redistribution function which was largely left to Member States.[2]

2 A populist backlash with economic and cultural roots

The backlash against globalisation and integration runs deeper than cheap populism, as it is nurtured by economic and cultural roots that should not too easily be dismissed.

New trade agreements face fierce opposition almost everywhere. TTP, TTIP, CETA – acronyms such as these, once only known by specialists in the field, have become household names and prominent issues in election campaigns. And unfettered market opening policies have lost a lot of their appeal with a growing recognition that the rising tide has not lifted all boats; on the contrary, in some cases perhaps even only a few super-yachts. Losers in the globalisation process have become clearly visible, while the middle classes have seen scant evidence of the gains once promised. Over the past decade, political scientists and economists have amassed a considerable body of survey evidence shows that ordinary peoples' attitudes towards globalisation and integration are exactly what Heckscher-Ohlin economics would predict (Figure 1). Thus, while globalisation may not actually be the main culprit, there is nothing populist about noticing that the past decades have seen the top 1% grab an ever-larger share of national income and wealth – a trend particularly pronounced in the US – while median incomes have stagnated.[3]

Protectionism, if not to say outright hostility, already rules the day when it comes to immigration. The arrival of migrants is perceived as threat that diminishes or dilutes the locational premium enjoyed by citizens of host countries, which includes not only possible direct economic impacts on jobs and wages, but also good health and education services, and public goods like the preservation of national culture and language. Arguably, the fears about "native identity" posed by immigrants from a different ethnic, cultural, and religious background largely dominate the public debate and are often ruthlessly exploited by populists; thus, pro-immigration arguments that it may have long-run positive economic effects tend to fall on deaf ears.

It has to be acknowledged that some populist lines of attack are derived from a response to real grievances; and not everyone who criticises elites is a populist, and not everyone who worries about immigration is a racist. But populists do not talk in terms of disagreement over policy, which in a democracy is the very point of politics; rather they claim that they and they alone speak in the name of what they tend to call the 'real people' as

Figure 1 Working class and low-skilled people tend to see globalisation as a threat

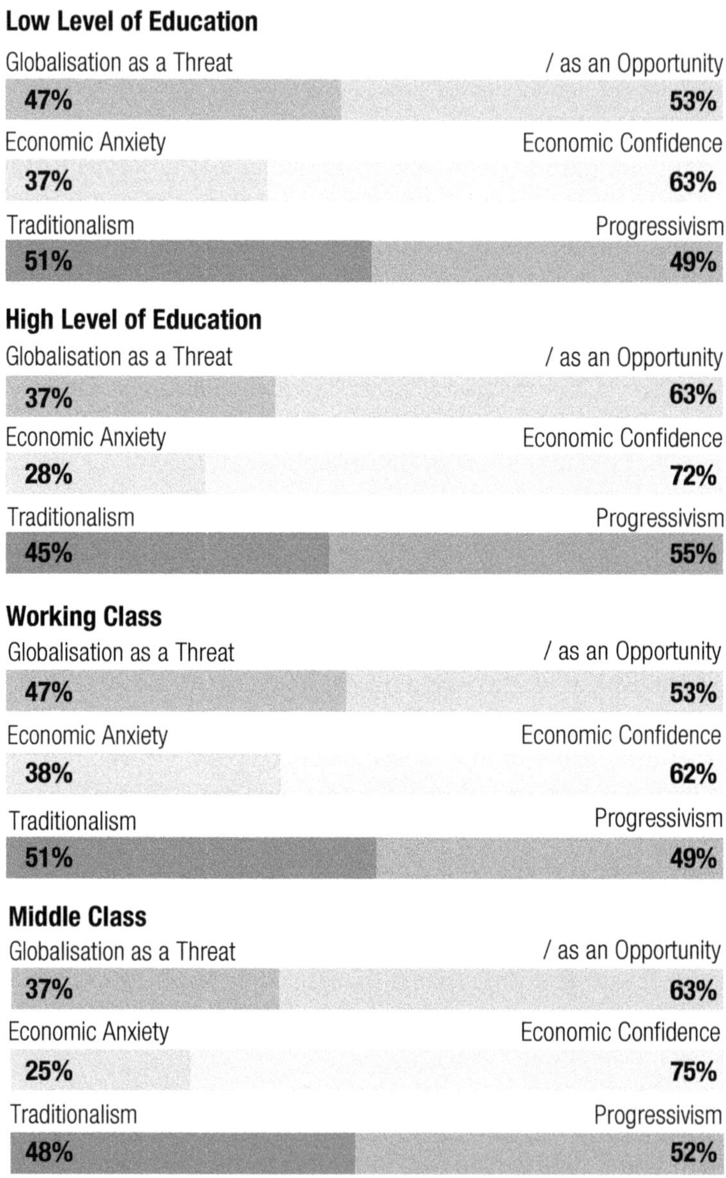

Source: data provided by eupinions, EU-wide public opinion research by the Bertelsmann Stiftung. See also de Vries and Hoffmann (2016).

opposed to the "establishment" (Müller 2016). This is coupled with assurances to restore autonomy, identity, and control, which were taken away from citizens by hostile forces. The identity offer of the "us, the honest (native) ordinary people, versus them, the corrupt elites" is very powerful and tempting in an era of massive transformation where, to use a term coined by Zygmunt Bauman, many people are left to lead a "liquid modern life" amidst multiple insecurities threatening the social fabric.[4]

The populist promise to restore autonomy, identity, and control typically comes with disrespect for rules and procedures, disparaging the inbuilt checks and balances of representative democracy while propagating referenda and other elements of direct democracy to implement "the true will of the people." In this context, ridiculing expert opinion (admittedly sometimes made all too easy) and denouncing statistical evidence as abstract and not in line with the experience of ordinary people ("numbers are liberal") belongs to the standard repertoire. Populists have also been quick to realise the potential of social media given their (partly real, partly imaginary) offer to create a space of common identity and understanding, and to establish a direct link of identification between the individual and its alleged true authentic representative.

3 The EU and European integration as an easy target for populist onslaught

The EU has become a popular "punch bag," an easy target and prey. It is of little comfort that the EU is often not really the main concern of many of its critics. They use opposition to European integration as a vehicle for their ultimate objective: to strengthen their influence and power at home. But we need to acknowledge that EU institutions and policy settings are prone to populist attack from both the purely economic and the more cultural "nativist identity" angle (Müller 2016).

From an economic perspective, the established policy allocation and the distribution of responsibilities between the EU institutions and the Member States (Padoa-Schioppa 1987) – with the central level being predominantly focused on growth and efficiency (free trade, open markets, the four freedoms, competition, etc.), while the social dimension was largely left to Member States – have made "Brussels" an easy scapegoat, accused of ignoring the social consequences of its policies and, even worse, undermining the capacity of the nation state to deal with them. The EU and populist forces collide as they operate in the same sphere, namely, the market, with the EU aiming at opening and integrating markets internally (Schengen, the single market, labour mobility, competition policy) and externally (trade policies), and populists aiming at closing them. In consequence, the EU is seen as the agent of globalisation, rather than the response to it.

The distributional fault lines are easily identifiable, impacting upon all three dimensions: the pre-market distribution of endowments, the distribution of gross market incomes, and the post-market distribution of net disposable incomes. Integration and open market policies affect the relative scarcities of production factors, with free (embedded) factor flows in integrated markets favouring mobile factors; they propagate (skill-biased) technical progress associated with a globalisation/digital divide, favouring capital and high-skilled labour; they may also enhance dynamic agglomeration effects, thereby increasing high/persistent regional disparities. EU policies and deeper economic and monetary integration increase competitive pressures and enforce higher market flexibility which, if left unattended, may negatively affect working conditions and protection in the market and undermine established rent-seeking and rent-sharing practices. At the same time, the room for re-distributional manoeuvre at the national and local level becomes more limited due to a reduction of discriminatory and enforcement power, enhanced system competition effects, and, last but not least, the perception of fiscal rules as a straight-jacket rather than as a safety vest. Identifying the EU exclusively with the market dimension and disregarding its potential role in the pre-market and post-market field would accentuate the distance with citizens and open the way for the populist attack.

Similarly, a number of elements fuel anti-EU sentiments from a nativist-identity perspective. Charges of "homogenisation" undermining, or even erasing, national specifics and identity are commonly brought up by populists mainly on the right side of the political spectrum. At the same time, the transfer of national autonomy and decision rights to EU institutions and bodies evidently shifts democratic control further away from national electorates. This is associated with a significantly higher complexity of mediation and, thus, intransparency of decision-making at the EU level, thereby increasing the distance to the ordinary citizen. A rules-based and institutions-based system, instead of being perceived as a guarantee for equal treatment and protection of minorities, is seen as an additional layer between ruler and the people. The inevitable loss of input-legitimacy[5] from a national perspective can easily be transformed into allegations of eroding the sovereignty of the Member State and the will of its citizens, eventually leading to the populist call "to take back control." Moreover, the often highly technical issues to be resolved at the central level make it easy to depict EU policies as designed by soulless technocrats detached from the life of ordinary people and accused of "fake" policy-based, pre-determined evidence-making. It is of little consolidation in this context that trust in the EU has actually held up better than trust in national institutions.

Figure 2 Trust in the EU versus national institutions

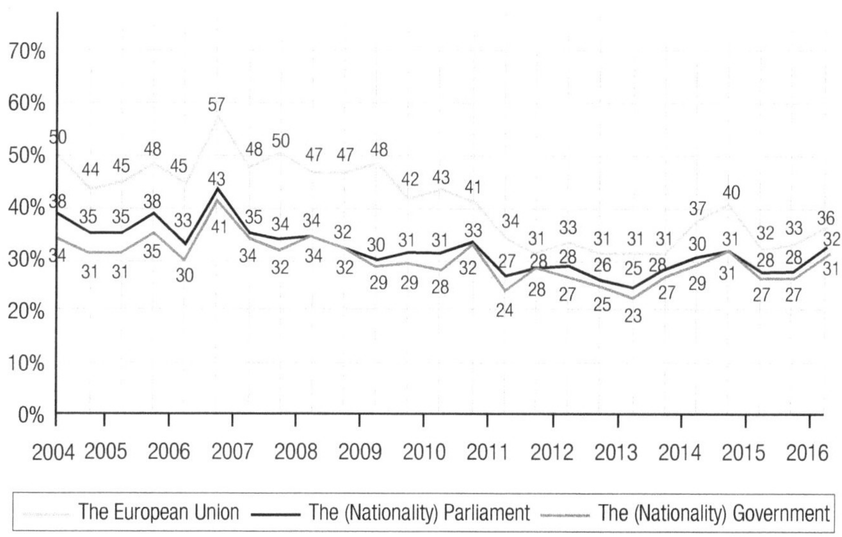

Source: Own elaboration from Eurobarometer December 2016, European Commission (2016l).

Output legitimacy has clearly suffered as well, given the hesitant and still incomplete reaction to the financial crisis and its fallout, or the difficult handling of the migration/refugee issue. Protection of minorities and upholding the rights of citizens such as free movement of people – a stronghold of EU policies – can without much difficulty be construed as running against the will of "the no longer silent majority." Enhanced by national politicians' tendency to blame "Brussels" for some of their own failings and their reluctance to give the EU credit for its successes, we witness widespread frustration with the EU's ability to tackle the poly-crises we are confronted with.

4 Some guiding principles for a new positive EU narrative

Unfortunately, there is no quick fix. A sustained period of growth and rising incomes would help. So, too, would proactive policies to cushion the impact of liberalisation on the losers. But the present politics of middle class discontent demands a broader response to restore the trust in the European project. As long as EU integration is seen as a project of the political elites and the rich, it will carry the seeds of its own destruction. The growing polarisation in our societies needs to be addressed by finding better ways to combine the benefits of open markets and integration with democratic inclusion, social protection and fairness. Rebalancing is even more complicated in the EU integration context, where the divide between winners and losers does not merely follow the traditional fault lines along the functional and the personal distribution of income and wealth, but often also carries strong nationalistic connotations of north-south and east-west conflict.

Today's reality requires a rethinking of the requirements of the subsidiarity principle in the EU, aiming to ensure that decisions are taken as closely as possible to the citizen and correctly identifying and redefining the areas where action at EU level is justified and needed in light of the possibilities available at the national, regional, or local level.

Against that background, we set out five guiding principles for policy articulation at the EU level to foster political stability, social cohesion and integration.

(i) *Focus on delivering the common public goods in need of well-defined EU value added*

This involves strengthening security both at Europe's external borders and internally, including a shared migration, asylum, and refugee policy worthy of the name. Tackling the environmental challenge is another area where go-alone policies are obviously bound to fail. International cooperation will also be required to fend off protectionist tendencies, wherever they originate, and to defend European interests in the global economy. And obviously, economic security starts at home with safeguarding and extending the Single Market achievements, completing the Banking Union, and taking the necessary steps to ensure the sustainability of EMU.

(ii) *Re-establish the core values of the European social model as a joint response to globalisation*

The EU's social acquis already provides a floor of social rights, protecting worker's health and safety, equal treatment and job security. However, in response to remaining gaps, allegations of "social dumping," and the many new demands in a rapidly changing world of work, a critical reflection is needed. Consequently, work on establishing a European Pillar of Social Rights is under way.

(iii) *Mainstream distributional considerations into EU policy designs*

While acknowledging that social fairness is primarily a domestic challenge, in the EU's monitoring and surveillance processes more focus needs to be given to distributional issues. Stronger emphasis on the quality of public finances also contributes to higher intergenerational fairness and more tangible and intangible investments. The EU has become a strong actor in strives for fairer taxation systems, as evidenced, for example, by current efforts to tackle profit shifting, tax evasion and the erosion of tax bases, and the use of competition policy instruments to address tax benefits granted selectively to companies.

(iv) *Embody the new requirements derived from the subsidiarity principle in the EU budget*

The EU budget, albeit limited in size, is one of the main tools for the EU to achieve its objectives. Thus, it is vital to ensure "vertical consistency" between European and national actions budgets (Buti and Nava 2003). The recent crises have put extra pressure on the EU budget but they have also pointed to areas where EU action and delivery of common public goods is the most pertinent (see principle (i)). A dedicated fiscal capacity for the Eurozone could not only add to the macroeconomic stability properties of EMU, it could at the same time serve distributional functions, be it in support of social investment or in the form of unemployment benefit funds.

(v) *Ensure transparency and democratic accountability over the course of decision-making*

The EU's activities today affect millions of European citizens' lives. As such, these decisions should be taken as openly as possible. Admittedly, this is easier said than done, and despite many efforts to increase transparency, the perception of EU decisions as being driven by lobbying activities and backroom deals is widespread. There are many ways to streamline decision-making processes, making them more easily comprehensible. It is also essential that responsibilities of "Brussels" and the national legislators are clearly identified, so that accountability – ultimately, the decision of citizens to re-elect officials – can be exercised at the right levels.

Implementing these principles will not silence the populists, but it will hopefully take the wind out of their sails to some extent. Such an effort also requires that mainstream political parties across Europe do not give in to the populist version of "blaming Brussels" for difficult decisions to be taken domestically. Embracing the European project for what it is, namely a democratic endeavour to preserve and strengthen values shared by all European traditions, is even more essential in a time when international cooperation seems to be fading away.

Notes

1 Dahrendorf (1995).

2 Obviously, the EU budget and its associated net cross-country transfers also perform a redistrubutive function, but it is very limited and mainly geared at the regional, rather than the interpersonal level.

3 The "elephant chart" of income distribution has become a reference point for the debate on the global inequality (Milanovic 2016).

4 In the 1990s, Bauman coined the term "liquid modernity" to describe a contemporary world in such flux that individuals are left rootless and bereft of any predictable frames of reference. In books including Liquid Times and Liquid

Modernity, he explored the frailty of human connection in such times and the insecurity that a constantly changing world creates where traditional institutions no longer fill the wells of common understanding and experience.

[5] The term goes back to Fritz Scharpf (1999) who introduced the distinction between input legitimacy of governance, i.e. the responsiveness to citizen concerns as a result of participation by the people; and output legitimacy, i.e. the effectiveness of policy outcomes for people. Vivien Schmidt (2013) later added the concept of throughput legitimacy, i.e. the governance processes that happen in between input and output.

Part D.
Real Economy and Convergence During the "Great Recession"

Fostering real adjustment and the correction of external imbalances, creating the environment for stronger investment, ensuring conditions for adequate real wage growth proved intertwined challenges during the Great Recession. Tackling these issues effectively is key to promote lasting convergence. The chapters in this section explore such challenges.

Increasing external imbalances plagued the Eurozone in the run up to the financial crisis and were one of the factors that exacerbated its impact. For external adjustment to occur, decisive and credible policy action is needed to turn the economy around and bring it towards a "good equilibrium." This strategy encompasses reducing policy uncertainty, repairing the financial system, and creating new investment opportunities. Reforms of labour markets under duress in vulnerable countries, by increasing competitiveness, started to redress their external deficits. However, adjustment has to take place also in surplus countries so that they contribute as well to the correction of imbalances while avoiding a built-in deflationary bias.

Investment plays a particularly important role in fostering Europe's growth potential. Low investment reduces aggregate demand, thus lowering short-term growth, and hampers medium-term growth through its effect on the capital stock. There are three main ways of boosting investment in the Eurozone: increase public investment, address financial fragmentation, and reduce uncertainty.

An oft expressed view is that the Eurozone's straitjacket is a reason why income convergence in peripheral members has slowed, halted or reversed. This view is partial at best. What emerged during the financial crisis is structural divergence which reflects agglomeration effects and different patterns between tradeable and non-tradeable sectors within Eurozone members. Tackling structural divergence is key to underpin lasting real income convergence, but also to address the polarisation of political and social preferences between Eurozone members. For this to happen, the right institutions and policies need to be in place at both European and national levels.

Wage developments in the Eurozone play an important role both in supporting monetary policy and fostering external rebalancing. Exceptionally low aggregate wage growth has been at the heart of Eurozone "lowflation," while wage growth differentials have not sufficiently contributed to a symmetric rebalancing within the currency union. Although wage setting is a prerogative of social partners and not a policy under direct public control, the coordination of a number of government policies affecting competitiveness would bring sizeable benefits.

24 Slow but Steady? External Adjustment Within the Eurozone Starts Working*

November 2012

1 Introduction

There is a general perception in the policy debate that Eurozone imbalances are not adjusting. Deficit countries are stuck in an unsustainable equilibrium and surplus countries' growth is mostly based on exports. The most pressing concern is that a symmetric evolution of competitiveness between surplus and deficit countries is needed for rebalancing to be complete and durable. This will be something that is hard to achieve, most notably because the competitive disinflation processes that are required in deficit countries are painful. Further, strong incentives are not always in place to encourage surplus countries to reduce their excess savings (see Krugman 2011).

Recent evidence, however, provides some encouragement. External imbalances are coming down and labour cost developments are increasingly supportive of more rebalancing down the road. Most importantly, recent reforms in a number of Eurozone countries appear to be bearing fruit, although the extent of necessary adjustment for some deficit countries is still considerable. It now seems that there could be light at the end of the tunnel. Provided the process is supported by reforms that boost non-tradeable production, consistent wage developments in surplus countries, and a recovery in productivity growth in deficit countries. For this to happen, private capital will have to start flowing downhill again,

* Co-author: Alessandro Turrini (European Commission), Vox CEPR, 12 November 2012.

and thus overcome the current fragmentation of financial markets. In order to achieve all this, a fast and effective adoption of a Single Supervisory Mechanism and – eventually – moving towards a Banking Union will be crucial steps.

2 Wage and competitiveness adjustment, where do we stand?

Since the Euro's inception – and until the debt crisis – the adjustment to asymmetric shocks within the Eurozone worked, but at the cost of growing external imbalances (European Commission 2006, 2008). Conversely, following the debt crisis the sudden stop in private capital flows led to a prompt reduction in current account imbalances. This redirection of financial flows was a major driver of the recessions in the Eurozone periphery; capital flows stopped being a shock absorber and contributed instead to the widening of output divergences.

Looking forward, competitiveness will play a key role both in redressing external imbalances on a sustainable basis and in reducing the major output and unemployment divergences that have emerged within the Eurozone since the crisis.

Recent developments are somewhat encouraging. Current account deficits are below 3% of GDP in all Eurozone countries in 2012, with the exceptions of Greece, Cyprus, and Portugal (European Commission 2012c). Unit labour costs (ULCs) have fallen substantially in 2010 after increasing in all EU countries after the great recession because of productivity losses linked to labour hoarding.

Since 2011, a decoupling has been observed; growth is stronger in surplus than in deficit countries (Figure 1).[1] This is in clear contrast to the pre-crisis situation. The recent subdued growth rate of unit labour costs in deficit countries was not entirely linked to productivity gains from job shedding. Indeed, since 2010, wage growth started being slower in deficit countries by about one percentage point. Moreover, the deceleration in nominal compensations in deficit countries appears stronger in non-tradable sectors. This contrasts with the pre-crisis situation, and supports the argument for labour relocation from the non-tradable to the tradable sector (cf. Buti and Turrini 2012).

When assessed across countries, since the start of the financial crisis the downward adjustment in unit labour cost compared with competitors

Figure 1 ULC and nominal compensation per employee, % change

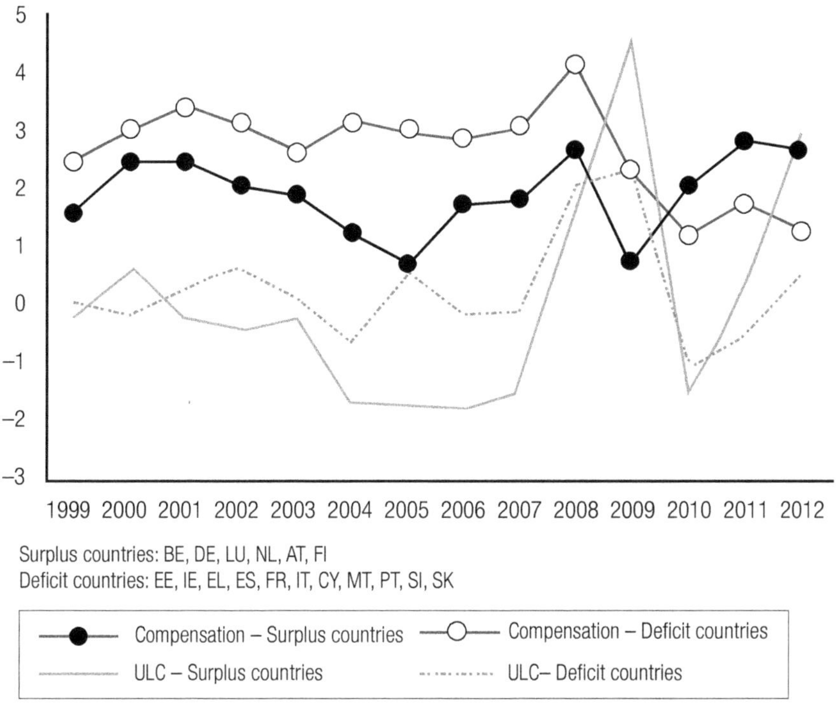

Source: European Commission, AMECO database.

– the ULC-based real effective exchange rate (REER) – seems proportionate to the external adjustment channel. More pronounced reductions in the REER were recorded in countries that were characterised by a wide gap between their underlying current account and that which is consistent with a sustainable position in the Net International Investment Position (Figure 2). Figure 2 suggests that for some countries, notably Greece and Portugal, the magnitude of the adjustment challenge is such that further competitiveness improvements will be needed. Symmetrically, despite some sizeable positive current account gaps in countries like Germany or the Netherlands, competitiveness in these countries has not changed substantially since the start of the crisis. Indeed, competitiveness gains were the rule rather than the exception.

Figure 2 Competitiveness gains and current account gaps

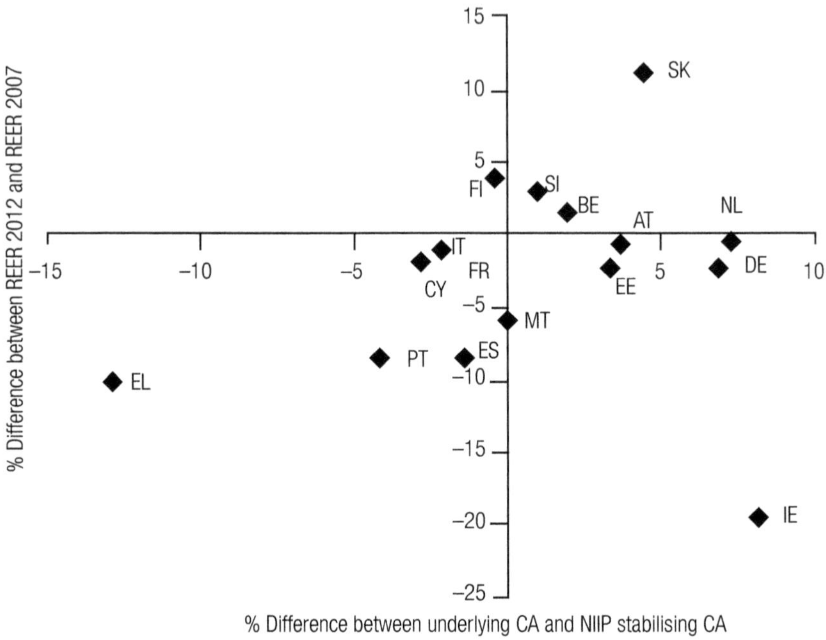

Note: The underlying current account includes both cyclical effects and lags in the impact of REER changes (Salto and Turrini 2010). The NIIP-stabilising current account is defined as the current account that stabilises the NIIP at the 2011 value on the basis of medium-term projections for potential growth.

Source: European Commission.

3 What's next?

The answer depends most notably on two factors: the market-based response of wages to the labour market slack-tightness and the impact of current and forthcoming labour market reforms.

Wage Bargaining

The market-based adjustment of wages appears to be currently working in a fashion that supports external adjustment. While in countries with low unemployment, real wages are growing above productivity, the opposite is occurring in countries characterised by high unemployment (Figure 3). This pattern of adjustment is consistent with the expected market reaction of wages to the labour market slack. It also contributes to a correction adjustment of output and unemployment divergences within the Eurozone. Since the countries with the lowest (or highest) unemployment rates also correspond to those with largest current account surpluses (or deficits), the process is expected to continue contributing to rebalancing until the large unemployment divergences are fully offset.

Figure 3 Real unit labour costs (% change 2010-2012) and unemployment rates, 2010

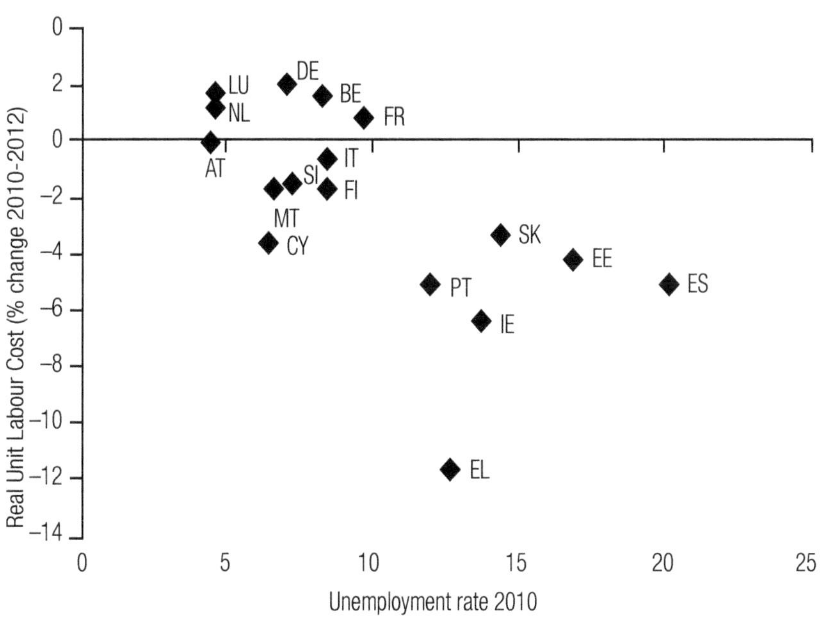

Source: European Commission, AMECO database.

For low-unemployment countries, there is no reason to think that wages cannot adjust upward in the absence of countervailing policies. For instance, the most recent evidence on collective contract negotiations in Germany suggests strong wage dynamics looking forward. In May 2012, IG Metall, the German trade union for the mechanical and engineering sector that traditionally plays a leading role in wage negotiations negotiated the highest pay increase in 20 years, with the renewed collective contract stipulating a 4.3% wage increase over 13 months (Sackmann 2012). Conversely, for high-unemployment countries, downward rigidities could kick in and hamper downward wage adjustment. This is where labour market reforms matter.

Other labour market reforms

In this respect, things do not look too gloomy. EU countries, notably those more severely hit by the debt crisis and major fiscal consolidations, have engaged in a number of courageous labour market reforms (European Commission 2012b). In particular, compared with years before the crisis, pro-competitive reforms aimed at revisiting the wage setting system became much more frequent (Figure 4).

Greece is the country where wage setting reforms were implemented first and where they went deeper. The decentralisation of wage bargaining was facilitated by firms being granted the ability to derogate from sectoral agreements and via the suspension of the faculty of extending collective contracts to non-signatory parties. The minimum wage negotiated at national level was cut, and measures were taken to reduce the inertia in the renegotiation of collective contracts. The most recent evidence from quarterly labour cost data suggests that these reforms are producing effects, as the speed of wage reduction accelerated in 2012, reaching levels above 10% on an annual basis (Figure 5).

Wage setting reforms in other Eurozone countries have not yet produced comparable effects to those carried out in Greece, but it can be reasonably expected that most recent and forthcoming reforms in a number of countries, including Portugal, Spain, Italy and Ireland, will bear fruit.

Figure 4 Selected measures affecting the wage setting system carried in EZ countries since 2010

	Measure	Surveillance framework
Greece	• Suspension of favourability clause for firm-level collective contracts and increased room for work councils to conclude firm-level collective contracts • Suspension of extension mechanism for sectoral collective contracts • Increased flexibility of working time management • Minimum wage reduction • Measures favouring the re-negotiation of collective contracts • Reduced non-wage labour costs • Reform of minimum wage system (ongoing)	Adjustment programme
Portugal	• Enhanced possibility for work councils to conclude firm-level contracts • Reduced cost of overtime and increased flexibility of working time management • Reform of extension mechanism	Adjustment programme
Spain	• Increased room for firm-level bargaining to derogate from sectoral contracts • Reduced room for survival of expired collective contracts	EU semester
Ireland	• Revised system for sectoral and professional minimum wages and registered collective agreements	Adjustment programme
Italy	• Agreement among social partners on criteria for representativeness in firm-level bargaining • Enhanced possibility for firm-level collective agreements to derogate from sectoral agreements and labour law in pre-defined matters • Enhanced fiscal incentives to wage elements linked to productivity at firm level (ongoing)	EU semester

Source: European Commission.

Figure 5 Labour cost index growth (% change compared with same quarter of previous year – working day adjusted)

Source: European Commission.

4 What is missing?

Are ongoing trends and the current reform measures sufficient? The answer depends on four conditions.

First, the improvements in cost competitiveness need to have an impact on current account balances. Relative unit labour costs have started adjusting, but this needs to be matched by a reduction in relative prices as well. Unfortunately, the evidence indicates that the recent improvements in labour cost competitiveness in deficit countries was not accompanied by proportionate gains in relative price competitiveness (cf. European Commission 2012b).

Second, to be sustainable, competitiveness gains cannot be based uniquely on wage and price restraints. Productivity and non-price export competitiveness need to grow again. This is the key pre-requisite to stabilise the high share of net foreign liabilities in a number of Eurozone countries. During the process of rebalancing, growth is inevitably subdued for some time because domestic demand needs to be moderate to favour the expenditure shift away from imports and non-tradables. However, if recessions are protracted for too long, the sustainability of external positions could be compromised and we risk turning competitive disinflations into a negative spiral of external debt deflation.

Third, competitive disinflations in deficit countries may need to be sustained over a relatively long period of time. This raises the general issue of the sustainablility of competitive disinflations from a social and political perspective.

Fourth, the adjustment needs to be symmetric, underpinned by consistent developments in surplus countries. In most surplus countries, it is only recently that wage growth has accelerated despite persistently high current account surpluses and largely positive net international investment positions. Looking forward, it is important that rebalancing implications of ongoing market-driven responses of wages to the tightening labour markets operate fully and is unrestricted. Reforms raising productivity in the non-tradeable sector would help further help rebalancing in surplus countries, as well as a fiscal stance which is not unduly restrictive.

5 Conclusions

A more supportive role of financial markets appears to be the single most important prerequisite for the fulfilment of the conditions for rebalancing. The re-direction of cross-border private capital flows away from deficit countries and towards surplus countries that followed the financial and debt crises contributed to the narrowing of current account deficits. However, this withdrawal of financial resources also implied reduced investment rates and reduced room for total factor productivity improvements. Moreover, by increasing non-labour costs, reduced investment rates contributed, together with lack of progress on product market reforms, to the incomplete pass through of labour cost competitiveness gains into price competitiveness gains.

Fragmented financial markets also imply delayed and reduced benefits from structural reforms in vulnerable countries. This is because part of the future gains from reforms can accrue much sooner, provided efficient and developed financial markets help bring forward these gains in terms of higher asset values (see chapters 18 and 19, and Buti, Turrini et al. 2009). Going forward, orderly investment conditions will be needed to compensate for the loss of capital and to get total factor productivity growing again. Orderly investment conditions are also needed for a durable adjustment of unit labour costs and for the political sustainability of protracted wage moderation.

Completing the monetary union with a Single Supervisory Mechanism for the banking sector – and eventually a Banking Union – will help redress the interwoven nature of sovereigns and banks, a relationship that segments financial markets and could help capital to flow downhill again. An effective framework for macroprudential policy as well as structural reforms in recipient countries will be needed to ensure that, unlike the pre-crisis period, capital is channelled towards productive uses.

Note

[1] The classification between deficit and surplus countries used in the paper is as follows: all surplus countries recorded a surplus over the 1999-2012 period (the only exceptions being DE and AT before 2002 and FI after 2010), while deficit countries recorded a deficit on average starting from 2000.

25 From a Vicious to a Virtuous Circle in the Eurozone: The Time Is Ripe*

March 2012

1 The need to focus on a strategic response to the crisis

The economic and financial crisis in the Eurozone dangerously evolved in late 2011 into a vicious circle of sluggish growth, tensions in sovereign debt markets and banking sector fragility. Investor confidence in the Eurozone seemed on the verge of collapse, many sovereigns and banks struggled to access market funding and the future of the Eurozone was widely questioned in financial markets and the policy debate.

While tensions have eased recently, the Eurozone is still in a situation in which multiple equilibria can materialise. In a vicious circle, confidence falls and financial market conditions deteriorate, jeopardising debt sustainability, more so in an environment of low growth. A bad equilibrium can establish itself (Padoan et al. 2012, Buti and Padoan 2012). To move from a vicious to a virtuous circle requires time, while markets tend to be impatient. By providing a confidence bridge, decisive and credible policy action can turn the economy around and bring it towards a good equilibrium of debt sustainability and sustainable growth. Securing a good equilibrium for the Eurozone is possible. Developments since the beginning of 2012 surprised on the upside. The ECB's provision of longer-term bank funding has had a powerful effect in boosting confidence. The fear of an imminent bank failure and the risk of a credit crunch have receded. Despite the downturn towards the end of 2011, there are signs of stabilisation and an increasingly likely recovery in the second half of

* Co-author: Pier Carlo Padoan (OECD), Vox CEPR, 27 March 2012.

2012. Sovereign debt markets have improved, as reflected in successful bond auctions and declining yields.

These favourable trends cannot be a cause for relaxing Europe's efforts, but offer the opportunity to focus on a more strategic response. It is essential that this opportunity is not squandered. Further measures are required to address unfinished business and avoid the establishment of a bad equilibrium. In the near term, contagion must be blocked and reverted. This would create space for strengthening the banking system without engendering a credit crunch – implementing structural reforms to strengthen growth and to address competitiveness problems, fiscal consolidation to restore the sustainability of public finances, adequate firewalls to prevent contagion, and Eurozone governance reforms will be required to prevent future crises. These policies need to be implemented as a coherent package – because of the systemic nature of the problem a partial solution is bound to be uneffective and lack credibility.

2 A five-point strategy to ensure a good equilibrium

A strategic response that will bring the Eurozone towards a good equilibrium is based on five mutually reinforcing points (European Commission 2011b[1]): 1) undertake credible economic adjustment in vulnerable Member States 2) establish an adequate firewall against contagion in sovereign-debt markets 3) ensure that EU banks are sufficiently capitalised 4) reform the framework for economic governance in the Eurozone and 5) implement policies to boost growth and address imbalances.

Substantial progress is being made on all five elements, with a decisive breakthrough achieved in the past three months. However, the pace of implementation is not uniform and failure to make sufficient progress on any single element – possibly motivated by complacency over recent developments - would undermine the overall strategy. The possibility of falling back towards a bad equilibrium is still uncomfortably high and requires strong determination at the national level and high vigilance by EU institutions.

3 Weak economic growth remains the key challenge

Of the five components of the strategy, in this chapter we concentrate on the need to boost growth. The unsatisfactory growth performance of, and imbalances in, the Eurozone over the past decade originated in poor structural settings that discouraged productive investments in some sectors, contributed to the instability of the housing market, and failed to keep wage and price developments in line with productivity. A credible and ambitious strategy of structural reforms that can address these weaknesses would have a tangible impact on economic growth and debt sustainability, particularly in vulnerable countries.

Often the fruits of reform are visible only over the medium-term. However, a credible reform package can also generate positive effects in the short-term in terms of confidence and performance, while short-term costs can be vastly overstated (OECD 2012).

Economic growth in the Eurozone remains subdued at best. The potential growth rate of the Eurozone is estimated to be around $1^{1/4}$%, with markedly lower rates in some of the countries facing intense market pressure. Stronger growth would restore confidence, improve debt dynamics and facilitate an exit from the crisis, particularly in countries with high accumulated debts.

Growth-enhancing policies must go hand in hand with appropriately paced fiscal consolidation. There are obvious reasons for this.

First, the extraordinary pre-crisis build-up of debt to largely unsustainable levels has left most Eurozone economies with the task of redressing imbalances and embarking on an unavoidable deleveraging. High debt permanently weakens economic growth.

Second, risk aversion and, with it, risk premia, have spiked since the financial crisis in 2008 and ended a long period of high risk appetite and compressed premia. Current heightened risk aversion makes deleveraging even more necessary and, at the same time, more painful in the short-term.

Third, low interest rates and the excessive lending and borrowing prior to the crisis had not only led to growing debt levels, but also to an allocation of resources that has proven unsustainable and that must be corrected.

Finally, in a situation of multiple equilibria, where confidence plays a crucial role, the distinction between short-term and long-term measures (suggesting the possibility of postponing action) is misleading and could be possibly dangerous. Short-term measures that weaken confidence would push the medium-term dynamics towards a bad equilibrium (Padoan et al. 2012).

This legacy defines and limits the role of active demand management and calls for sound fiscal policies. Clearly, the scope, pace and approach to fiscal consolidation should not be uniform across Member States but, rather, reflect the specific features of each country, its fiscal position and the strength of its economic conditions. In all cases, fiscal adjustment should be growth-friendly.

The reinforced governance framework of the Eurozone will help Member States stay on track towards these goals. Experience shows that fiscal discipline is especially at risk in countries where policies are more short-sighted, possibly driven by the electoral cycle. In such a setting, a strong external anchor, as provided by the recently reinforced fiscal governance rules in the Eurozone, can help keeping up necessary reforms (Buti, Röger and Turrini 2009). Available evidence points, remarkably, to the fact that structural reform efforts during the current crisis appear positively correlated with fiscal consolidation efforts. Moreover, reforms are taking place in countries that most require a boost in growth potential and adjustment within the Eurozone (OECD 2012).

Note

[1] Leaders of Eurozone States committed to these in October 2011 (European Council 2011).

26 How to Make Europe's Incipient Recovery Durable: End Policy Uncertainty*

September 2013

1 A subdued and fragile recovery

When leaders met for the G20 Summit in Saint Petersburg in September 2013, they welcomed the incipient recovery in the Eurozone. However, they also recognised that "despite our actions the [global] recovery is too weak" and fraught with risks. This is particularly relevant for the Eurozone, firstly because GDP growth in the area is still very weak and uneven, and secondly because, in the current external macroeconomic environment, the Eurozone economy can expect to get only a limited boost from external demand (in spite of its growing current account surplus). Addressing the weakness of domestic growth, exploiting the cyclical developments to make growth more sustained and sustainable, and therefore removing impediments to private investment, is vital.

In 2013, after six quarters of contraction, GDP surprised on the upside in the second quarter, expanding by 0.3% compared to the previous quarter. The latest GDP release also shows further progress in intra-Eurozone rebalancing, with a strong export performance in some vulnerable Member States and welcome signs of strengthening domestic demand in the core. Overall, the recession has now given way to a modest recovery, and key indicators are signalling a continuation along this path in the second half of 2013 and a recovery gaining traction in 2014.

However, this is no time for complacency. Short to medium-term growth prospects remain subdued and the recovery is fragile, surrounded

* Co-author: Pier Carlo Padoan (OECD), Vox CEPR, 12 September 2013.

by downside risks (see European Commission 2013a, OECD Economic Outlook, May 2013b). Lacklustre economic growth does not come as a surprise as it is in line with experiences from recoveries following systemic financial crises (see Reinhart and Rogoff 2009b and 2012). This reflects the needs for balance-sheet repair and sectoral rebalancing, the lack of which hold back demand and weigh on labour markets. Nevertheless, while this consideration applies to all advanced economies which entered the recession with significant financial imbalances, the growth shortfall of the Eurozone compared to the US is striking.

A notable difference with the US is the drawn-out contraction of investment in the Eurozone after the Great Recession. In the US, investment fell sharply in 2008-09, but has registered positive growth in 10 out of 14 quarters since the beginning of 2010. In the Eurozone, investment picked up briefly in 2010, but declined for 8 straight quarters thereafter (Table 1). The picture is similarly grim for employment, with the notable exception of Germany.

Table 1 GDP, investment and employment (annual % growth)

Gross domestic product							
	EA	FR	DE	ES	IT	UK	US
2009	−4.4	−3.1	−5.1	−3.8	−5.5	−5.2	−3.1
2010-2013	2.4	3.7	8.4	−3.3	−1.6	3.5	8.3
2009-2013	−2.0	0.5	3.3	−7.1	−7.1	−1.7	5.2
Total investment							
	EA	FR	DE	ES	IT	UK	US
2009	−12.8	−10.6	−11.7	−18.0	−11.7	−16.7	−16.1
2010-2013	−5.2	1	9.9	−25.5	−12.7	2.7	17.3
2009-2013	−17.9	−9.6	−1.8	−43.5	−24.5	−14.0	1.2
Total employment							
	EA	FR	DE	ES	IT	UK	US
2009	−2.1	−1.5	0.1	−6.5	−2.9	−1.6	−5.0
2010-2013	−1.8	0.7	3.5	−11.8	−3.1	2.4	2.6
2009-2013	−3.9	−0.9	3.6	−18.3	−5.9	0.8	−2.4

Source: European Commission.

This suggests that factors specific to the Eurozone and most of its Member States are adding to the usual obstacles to growth in the post-financial-crisis world. Deleveraging and bank balance sheet repair have been markedly slower in the Eurozone than in the US, and this lack of progress is weighing on both credit demand and credit supply, and thereby on investment. For instance, returns on banks' assets have recovered significantly in the US since their nadir in 2009 but have remained under pressure in the Eurozone, particularly in vulnerable countries (Figure 1).

Figure 1 Bank returns on assets (in %)

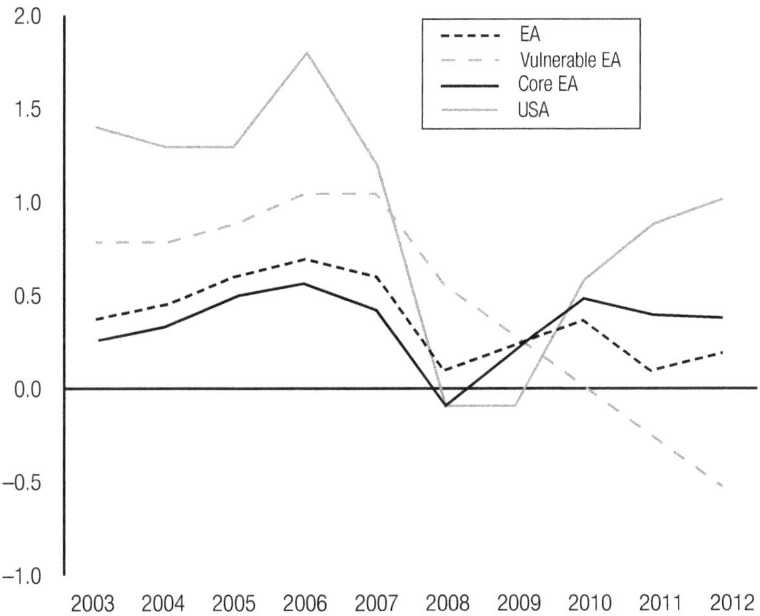

Source: Own elaboration based on IMF data.

Balance-sheet repair in the Eurozone has been hampered by what are now well-known faults in the Eurozone's architecture. In particular, in the absence of a proper Banking Union, uncoordinated national responses to banks' balance-sheet difficulties have led to a damaging degree of fragmentation of the single financial market that has pushed financing costs to very high levels in some Member States (Figure 2), triggered negative bank/sovereign feedback loops, and ultimately threatened the very survival of the single currency. Faults in the architecture of Eurozone have been compounded by deep macroeconomic and structural imbalances in many Member States that have slowed the adjustment of the economy, notably in terms of sectoral reallocations. This has been strikingly reflected in the widening gap in productivity growth between the US and the Eurozone since the crisis.

Figure 2 Interest rates on loans to non-financial corporations (maturity up to one year, in %)

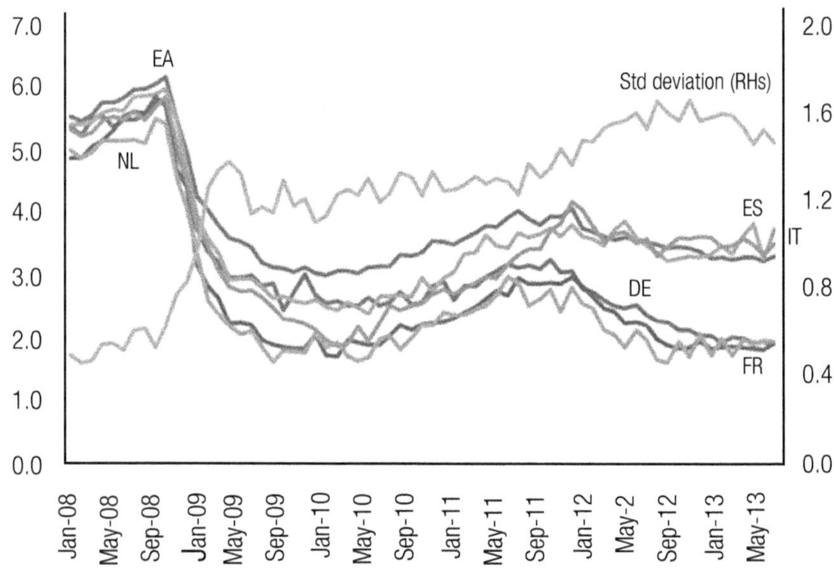

Source: ECB, European Commission, DG ECFIN calculations.

2 A targeted policy response to make the recovery durable

The incipient recovery reflects the disappearance of tail risks due to the determined action of the Eurozone governments and the ECB. The ensuing increase in confidence is evident in many early indicators. It is vital to build on such positive signs to foster a durable recovery. Key to this is creating the conditions for stronger investment and hence employment creation.

What has to be done to unlock investment in the Eurozone? We can think of three conditions that are necessary for investment to pick up: first, reducing policy uncertainty; second, repairing the financial system, and, third, creating new investment opportunities.

These conditions, if fulfilled, will be self-reinforcing and will enhance medium-term growth potential. For this to happen, action is needed at both the European and the national level, both on the demand side, by boosting investment demand, and on the supply side, by accelerating a much-needed structural change in the economy.

Reducing policy uncertainty

Announcing and implementing such a plan will address the exceptionally high level of economic and policy uncertainty, which is an impediment to investment decisions (condition 1). There is empirical evidence that uncertainty can significantly and negatively weigh on private spending and economic growth by offering agents an incentive to postpone investment, consumption and employment decisions (see QREA, Vol. 12, no. 2, European Commission 2013b) (Figure 3). At the current juncture, high uncertainty is all the more damaging for growth as it magnifies the effect of credit constraints and weak balance sheets, forcing banks to rein in credit further and companies to hold back investment, even if they are not liquidity constrained, to minimise the risks of irreversible decisions.

Ensuring a fully functional financial system

A critical step towards restoring full functionality of the financial system (condition 2) is the repair of bank balance sheets. This requires both transparency regarding the current health of bank balance sheets and proper recapitalisation where needed. The forthcoming asset quality review and stress tests, ahead of the move to a single supervision authority, will be instrumental in this respect and will have to be carried out earnestly and credibly. Recapitalisation will have to be underpinned by appropriate backstops.

Figure 3 Policy uncertainty and investment

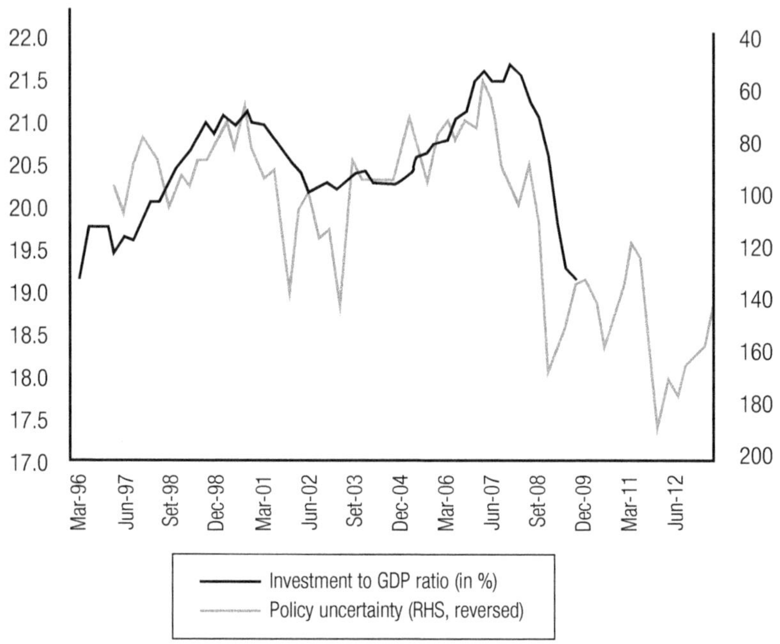

Source: Eurostat and Baker, Bloom and Davis at www.policyuncertainty.com.

Completion of a fully-fledged Banking Union is critical to ensure financial stability, reverse the process of financial fragmentation and restore the flow of credit to the corporate sector. The need for a single centralised mechanism for the supervision and restructuring of banks is clear, and a full Banking Union will require not only a Single Supervisory Mechanism but also a Single Resolution Mechanism with a common resolution fund and a common fiscal backstop. A full Banking Union will support investment not only through its effect on fragmentation and the cost of borrowing, but also by providing a more stable, transparent, and predictable financial environment.

Specific efforts should also be made to restore credit flow to SMEs, which are the main driver of investment and employment in Europe and have been overly hit by financial fragmentation. On-going joint work in that area by the Commission and the EIB, in liaison with the ECB, should be pursued.

Implementing an ambitious structural reform agenda

Measures to fix the financial sector will restore access to credit and are a precondition for investment, but they should be complemented by structural measures to boost investment opportunities and the economy's medium-term growth prospects (condition 3). Without a credible and ambitious structural-reform agenda at the Member State level, the recovery is unlikely to shift up a gear or even to repair the (still to be fully measured) damage that the crisis has caused to potential output. Conversely, failure to restore credit to the economy would limit the potential benefits of structural reforms by preventing firms from taking full advantage of new investment opportunities.

Although some progress has been made since the outbreak of the financial crisis, more can still be done to boost the Eurozone's growth potential (see chapter 25). Reforms in product markets in particular have the potential to unleash new investment opportunities, and evidence shows that they can have a significant positive effect on growth over the medium-term (Figure 4). Simulations carried out by the OECD (Johansson et al. 2013) also show that over the medium-term an ambitious structural-reform agenda, including both product- and labour-market reforms, would deliver large growth benefits in the Eurozone (Figure 5).

1. The gain in potential growth is the difference between the average annual rate of growth of per capita potential GDP in 2003-08 relative to the average for 1998-2003. Most countries experienced slower average per capita growth in the second five-year period, so the positive growth effect of product-market reform would generally mean that the growth slowdown would have been greater with less reform.
2. The OECD's Product Market Regulation (PMR) indicator is defined such that a higher number indicates more restrictive policy settings. Here the sign of the change is inverted, so that an increase indicates a move towards less restrictive policy settings.

Vulnerable Member States have recently pushed through impressive structural reforms. These achievements notwithstanding, further progress is needed to create investment opportunities that will help in shifting

Figure 4 Progress on product-market reforms is associated with better growth performance

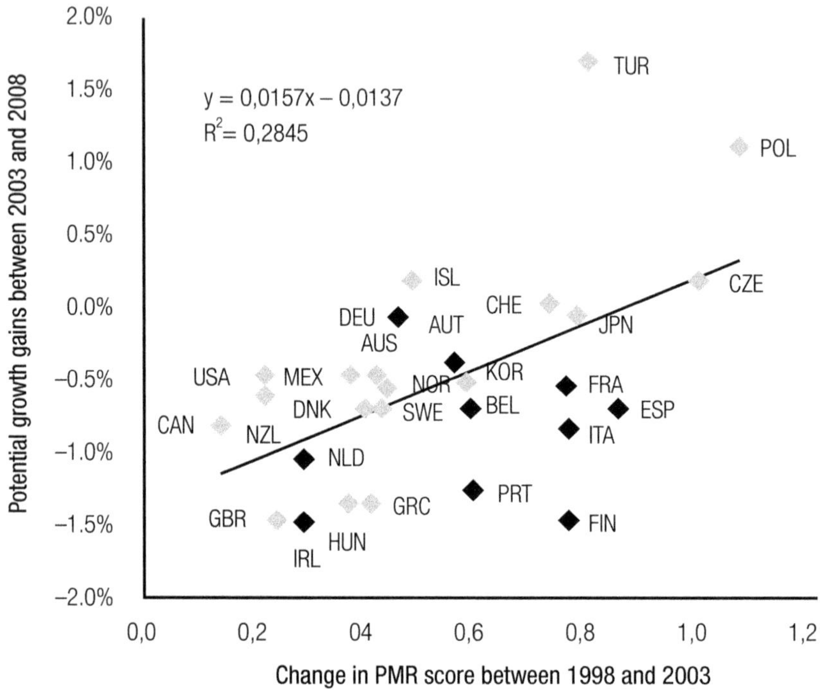

Note: Eurozone countries shown in blue, others in grey.

Source: OECD E093 database, and OECD calculations.

resources towards the production of tradable goods and services, raising external competitiveness and boosting productivity, and thus addressing the imbalances that were at the root of the Eurozone crisis. In Member States in the core area, reform efforts have generally been less ambitious so far, and product market reforms aimed at improving competition in non-tradable sectors would spur investment and facilitate the development of these sectors. By strengthening the role of domestic demand in the composition of growth, this would strengthen these countries' resilience to external shocks and make the adjustment in the Eurozone more symmetric.

Figure 5 Structural reforms raise long-run output - Difference in the level of GDP in 2025 (%)

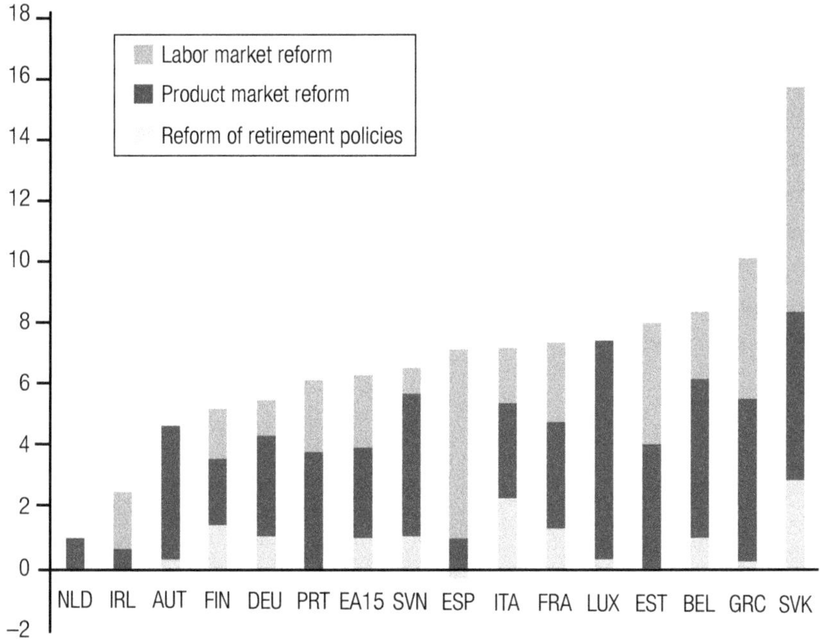

Note: The size of each bar shows the effect on GDP of each policy simulated in isolation. The reform of retirement policies assumes that the ratio of working-life to life-expectancy converges towards that of Switzerland. Labour market reforms are assumed to gradually reduce the structural unemployment rate to 5% in all countries where it would otherwise be above this level. Product market reforms move each country's regulations gradually towards best practice.

Source: OECD (2013b), Economic Outlook 93 long-term database.

3 Conclusion

Implementing the measures discussed here rapidly and credibly would boost confidence and reduce uncertainty while paving the way for more robust medium-term growth. Higher confidence, lower uncertainty, and better access to credit would support firms' investment and short-term economic growth, but would also make ambitious structural reforms easier to implement politically and allow economic agents to reap their full benefits. This is why there is no room for complacency. The cost of procrastination or dithering would be high, involving a double penalty on the economy as growth losses due to lack of reforms would be compounded by growth losses due to persistently high uncertainty and subdued confidence.

Procrastination is not inevitable, however, and policy action should be encouraged by the expected growth benefits. Such benefits and the strategy that will make them materialise should be well communicated so as to enhance consensus. It is essential that the vicious circles that have marred the Eurozone economy in the past are turned into a powerful virtuous circle where growth feeds confidence and confidence further reinforces activity.

27 How to Make Europe's Incipient Recovery Durable: A Rejoinder*

October 2013

1 Introduction

Chapter 26 triggered an interesting and lively debate (see for instance Krugman 2013, Fatás 2013, Watt 2013). In it, we argued that weak private investment is partly to blame for the growth shortfall in the Eurozone compared to the US since 2008, and that putting in place conditions for stronger investment was essential to turn the recent pick up of confidence and activity in the Eurozone into a robust and self-sustained recovery (see chapter 26). We further argued that a policy strategy to support investment and the recovery should be articulated around three mutually reinforcing elements – reducing policy uncertainty, repairing the financial system, and undertaking structural reforms.

We would now like to push further by providing a few additional arguments. While there seems to be a large consensus around the idea that repairing the financial system is a necessary condition to revive growth in the Eurozone, other aspects of our proposed policy strategy have been criticised by some commentators. Our reading of these criticisms is that they revolve around three major arguments.

First, differences in fiscal policy have been at the root of growth differences between the Eurozone and the US since 2008 and fiscal easing is the main policy advice to support an investment recovery.

Second, although policy uncertainty has been high, this is essentially a

* Co-author: Pier Carlo Padoan (OECD), Vox CEPR, 8 October 2013.

by-product of depressed economic conditions. Resolving policy uncertainty is unlikely to boost growth in a meaningful way.

Finally, while structural reforms are beneficial in the long-term, their short-term effect is unclear, especially in a context of depressed activity and when monetary policy is at the zero lower bound.

We will address these three arguments in turn.

2 Is fiscal consolidation at the root of the current investment-growth differentials between the Eurozone and the US?

It is undeniable that the front-loaded fiscal consolidation had a negative impact on Eurozone growth, and the factors that have aggravated the impact of consolidation on growth in the short-term are well known.

By contrast, the US had a somewhat larger fiscal expansion than the Eurozone in the early stages of the crisis (2008 and 2009), and consolidation started later (Figure 1). The jury is still out on the relative merits of a more front loaded consolidation, allowing a smaller adjustment later on, and a delayed consolidation (as in the US) requiring a more drastic effort when the recovery is still fragile. In any event, the bursting of the Eurozone sovereign-debt crisis left no choice but to undertake a front-loaded fiscal consolidation at least in some countries.

It must be stressed, however, that since 2012 the fiscal effort has been larger in the US than in the Eurozone. Therefore, while we naturally acknowledge that fiscal consolidation can have a detrimental effect on growth, this cannot be the main explanation behind investment and growth differentials between the Eurozone and the US over the past two years. Financial fragmentation, policy uncertainty and a weaker adjustment capacity in the Eurozone are more likely to be at the core of this differential.

Looking forward, the negative effect of fiscal consolidation on growth in the Eurozone should decrease gradually in the years to come as the additional fiscal effort that needs to be undertaken has peaked since 2011. By contrast, the US economy has only just embarked on its fiscal consolidation journey and therefore still faces large consolidation needs that will weigh on growth and investment in future years.

Figure 1 Annual change of cyclically adjusted fiscal balance (as % of GDP)

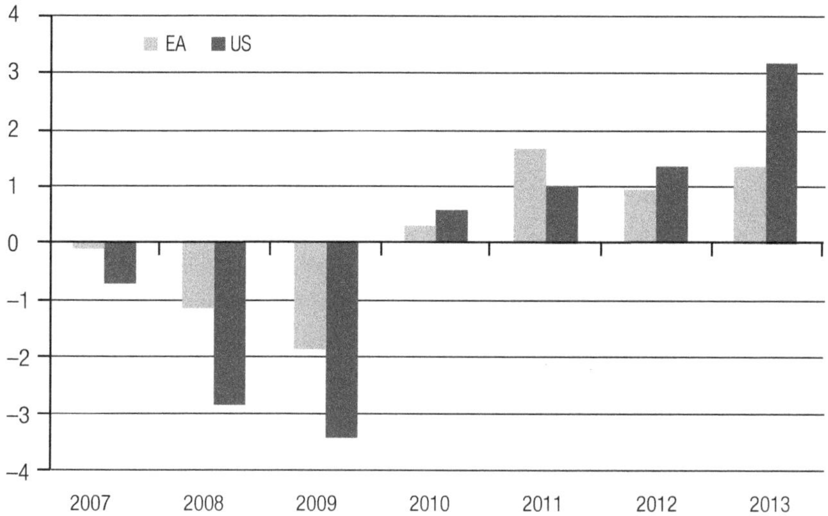

Source: OECD Economic Outlook 93 (2013b).

3 Have Eurozone-specific sources of uncertainty affected growth?

According to economic theory (see for instance, Bernanke 1984), uncertainty can depress economic activity through a number of channels: investment, consumption, employment, or risk-premia (Gilchrist et al. 2010). When investment, consumption or employment decisions are costly to reverse (e.g. due to fixed and adjustment costs), high uncertainty gives agents an incentive to postpone or cancel their decisions until uncertainty is resolved and more information is available. Moreover, in the current context, uncertainty is even more damaging for growth as it magnifies the effect of credit constraints and weak balance sheets, forcing banks to restrain credit further and companies to hold back investment, even if they are not liquidity constrained, to minimise the risks of irreversible decisions.

Most existing research (see for instance, Dixit et al. 1994) has established a negative correlation between uncertainty and growth, and the issue of the causal relationship between uncertainty and growth has been the subject of much academic discussion. There is now ample evidence showing that causality runs from growth to uncertainty, but also from uncertainty to growth. Regarding the latter, the results from both modelling exercises and econometric work based *inter alia* on the study of unpredictable shocks like natural disasters (see for instance, Bloom 2009), indicate that uncertainty shocks can have a substantial depressing effect on growth.

The unprecedented increase in tail risks in 2011 and first half of 2012, when the survival of the Eurozone was widely questioned, qualifies as such an uncertainty shock. Debt markets seized up, the financial system in the Eurozone became fragmented, and the transmission of an accommodative monetary policy was impaired. This has clearly heightened the amount of uncertainty with which economic agents have had to cope in the Eurozone.

Some US economists have argued that policy uncertainty is one of the factors which have made the US recovery sluggish by historical standards. It is, however, worth stressing, that the recent peaks of policy uncertainty observed in the US around the presidential election and in relation to the fiscal cliff, are not comparable in nature and scale with the uncertainty generated by risks of a collapse of the EMU.

Comparisons of levels of policy uncertainty between the US and the Eurozone should be interpreted with a lot of caution because indicators of policy uncertainty are not constructed in the same way in the two regions. With this caveat in mind, however, Figure 2 shows that policy uncertainty in the US was lower than the Eurozone during most of 2012, and has decreased during 2013 close to pre-crisis levels. By contrast, policy uncertainty in the Eurozone has remained elevated throughout this period, despite having receded in recent months. Furthermore, this recent decrease probably reflects expectations of bold policy measures being taken to reinforce EMU, notably in terms of the Banking Union. Failure to deliver could quickly bring uncertainty back to elevated levels. Overall, bold policy action is needed in the Eurozone to reduce uncertainty and restore confidence and thereby support investment and growth.

Figure 2 Policy Uncertainty Index (Baker, Bloom, and Davies), 2010=100

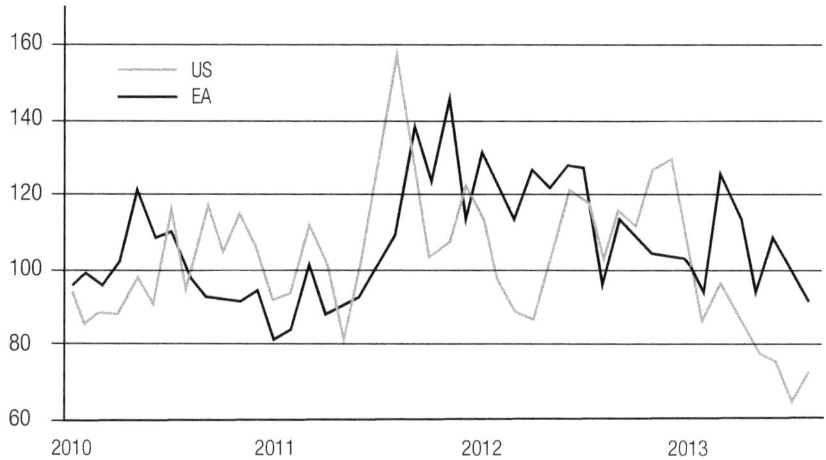

Source: Baker, Bloom, and Davies at www.policyuncertainty.com.

4 Do structural reforms boost growth in a low-growth environment?

In chapter 26, we provided evidence that structural reforms in product and labour markets boost growth. Here we provide additional evidence of the impact of structural reforms, taking into account the macroeconomic environment. We make the following points.

First, a restrictive macroeconomic environment is not necessarily an obstacle to reforms. Eurozone countries that have been among the most active in reforming, have also undertaken substantial budgetary consolidation, and this has been particularly the case for countries that have been under market pressures or financial-assistance programmes (Figure 3).

This can well raise legitimate concerns about the impact of reforms that are implemented in a context of budgetary retrenchment and overall weak demand. If monetary policy is unable to respond, any negative short-run demand effects of reforms cannot be mitigated. Clearly, the payoff from reforms may take more time to materialise in such a case. Recent OECD work has shown for instance that some reforms of unem-

Figure 3 Countries most active at reforming have also consolidated their budget

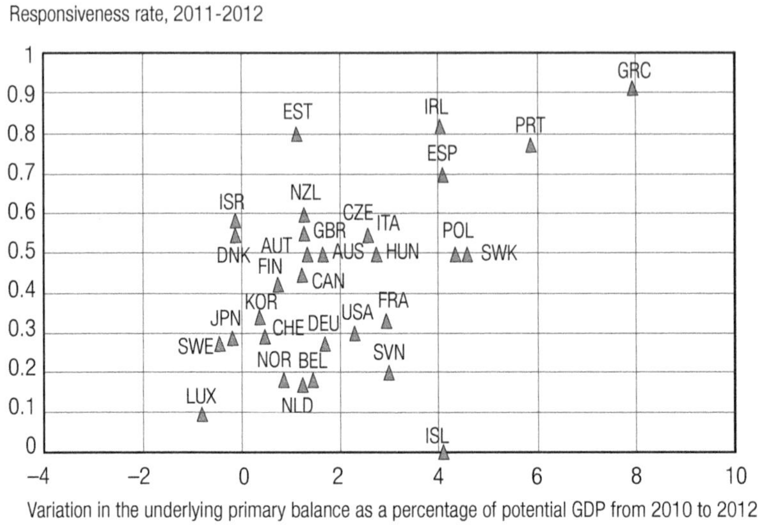

Note: The responsiveness rate indicates the extent to which OECD countries have followed-up on "Going for Growth" policy recommendations. It is measured as the ratio of actions taken in response to specific recommendation over the total set of recommendations.

Source: OECD (2013a) and OECD Economic Outlook Database.

ployment benefit or employment protection legislation can reduce employment in the first few years after the change if introduced in a weak conjuncture (OECD 2012).

Second, in spite of this many structural reforms can support demand either directly, such as in the case of reforms that stimulate investment (e.g. improvements in framework or regulatory conditions), or indirectly by boosting confidence and thereby bringing market relief.

A key condition for these effects is availability of credit for firms to invest and for households to support spending, underlining the necessity of banking repair in the Eurozone to support the reform process. Reform of pension systems shows how policy actions now can raise confidence and have fairly immediate direct impacts. For instance, delaying effective retirement age to reflect increases in life expectancy, delivers a strong signal that one of the main sources of long-term budgetary pressures is being addressed through reform. This can have short-term benefits through confidence and lower market pressures – allowing for the pace of consolation in the short-term – and through higher employment rates, in this case of older workers. Indeed, one notable feature of the Great Recession, especially as compared to earlier severe downturns, has been the increase in the participation rate of workers aged between 55 and 64 in the labour force (Figure 4 and OECD 2013c). This was particularly the case in Eurozone countries that had very low participation rates a decade ago, and that have implemented substantial reforms in pension systems and pre-retirement schemes in the years preceding the crisis. Reforms in countries such as France, Germany and Spain have included a phasing out of job search exemptions for workers over 55, an extension of the minimum contributory period for full-pension entitlement and stronger financial incentives for remaining active at or close to retirement age. In line with these reforms, these countries and others have refrained from encouraging premature exit of older workers from the labour force, a practice often observed in the past.

Figure 4 Labour-force participation of older workers since the crisis

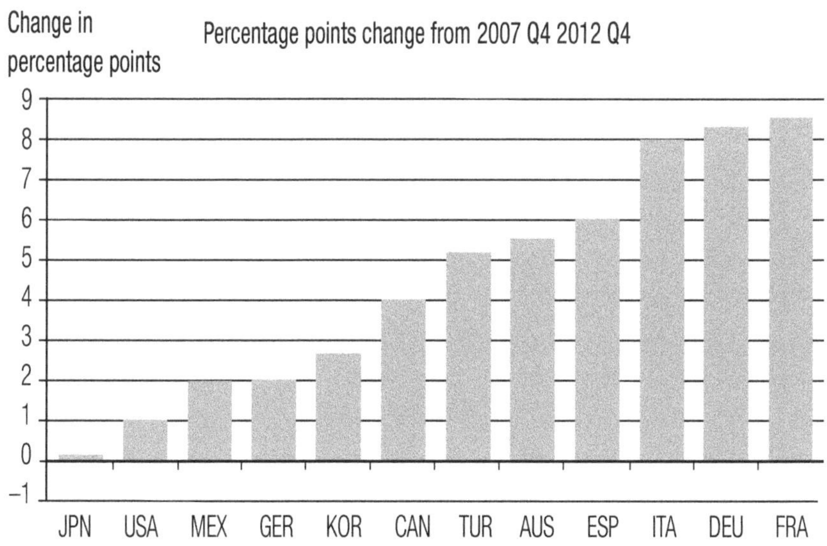

Source: OECD, Labour-force statistics database.

Third, reforms aimed at reducing regulatory barriers to firm entry and at exposing sheltered sectors to stronger domestic and foreign competition can boost both growth and employment, while involving little or no budgetary cost in the short-term (Bourlès et al. 2010, Conway et al. 2006).

While there is no question that typical reforms in this area can take some time to materialise (Figure 5), fairly rapid employment gains can nonetheless be expected in sectors such as retail trade and services. It is important to bear in mind that in the longer term, reforms that boost growth through employment gains in the private sector will greatly facilitate fiscal consolidation, adding to fiscal space. Furthermore, recent work (Andrews and Criscuolo 2013) has shown that more competition-friendly regulation tends to be associated with higher levels of investment in knowledge-based capital, a fundamental source of growth for advanced economies.

Figure 5 Changes in labour-force participation following a "typical" product-market reform

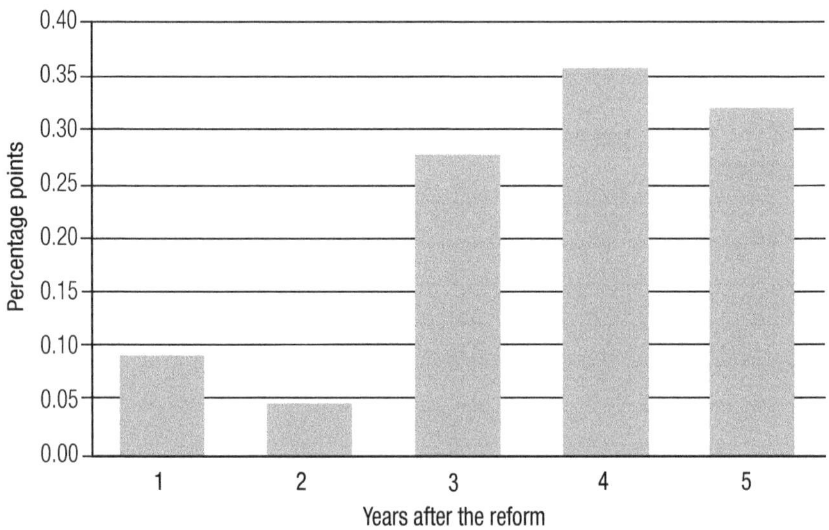

Note: The bars measure the estimated increase in the labour force participation each of the first five years after a reform is implemented where the reform is equivalent to the average size of reform across OECD countries observed in the past 30 years.

Source: OECD (2012), Chapter 4.

Fourth, labour and product-market reforms can boost growth through improved competitiveness, provided they complement each other.

Southern Eurozone countries have been quite active in reforming labour-market policies (especially Greece, Portugal and Spain), including in areas where reform has proved difficult in the past (wage bargaining and employment protection). For instance, both Portugal and Spain have implemented changes to collective bargaining arrangements to give firms more leeway in the application of agreements and make wages more responsive to local economic conditions. These countries are making some progress in regaining competitiveness as measured in terms of unit labour costs and, to a lesser extent, when measured in terms of relative prices (Figure 6). Labour-market reforms are contributing to wage moderation and will over time help to raise productivity. However, the adverse impact on real wages and domestic demand would be mitigated – and the favourable impact on exports be boosted – by more effective product-market reforms to reduce prices.

Figure 6 Unit labour costs and price-competitiveness developments

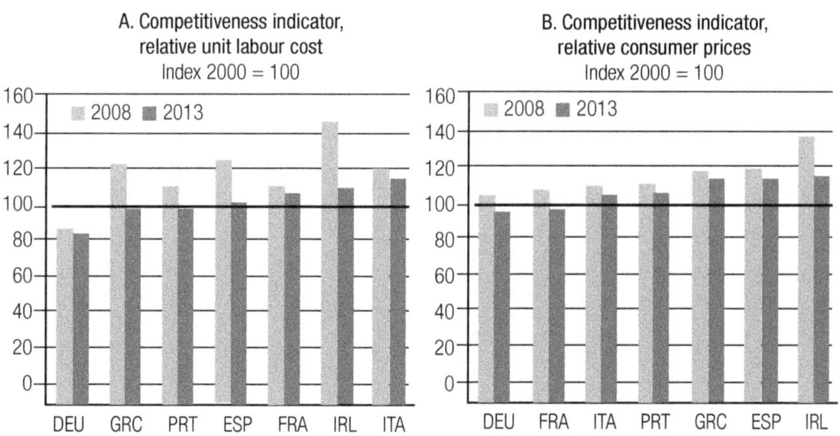

Source: OECD Economic Outlook Database.

Fifth, restoring fiscal sustainability and improving competitiveness are necessary conditions for these countries to reduce current-account deficits and return to healthy growth.

Clearly, such an adjustment would be facilitated by stronger external demand. In this regard, the uneven pace of structural reforms across Eurozone countries is not helpful (See Figure 5 above). More active reforms and relatively higher inflation in Eurozone surplus countries would help achieve intra-Eurozone rebalancing and hence overall growth, and would ensure that as deficit countries take measures to restore competitiveness and fiscal sustainability, surplus countries implement their own reforms to support global demand. Desirable reforms in surplus countries include reduced barriers to entry in the services sector to reorient activity towards domestic consumption and boost investment in such a sector.

5 To conclude

Overall, while fiscal consolidation in the Eurozone will be less of a drag on growth in the years to come than in 2011-12, the ongoing recovery will remain fragile and sluggish unless targeted measures are taken to support the economy and, in particular, investment spending. Such measures should aim to restore a fully functional financial sector, reducing policy uncertainty and opening up investment opportunities in both surplus and deficit countries through structural reforms.

28 Lacklustre Investment in the Eurozone: Is There a Puzzle?*

June 2014

1 On the importance of investment for the Eurozone economy

According to the European Commission, real economic activity in the Eurozone is expected to recover at a moderate pace until 2015, and to remain significantly weaker than in the US (European Commission 2014d).

One driving factor behind the differences in the growth outlook for the Eurozone and the US is investment. Investment constitutes an important component of aggregate demand, accounting for around 20% of real GDP in the Eurozone (21% of GDP in the US). So it comes as no surprise that the sharp fall in investment following the financial turmoil in 2008 contributed substantially to the severe economic downturn in the Eurozone. Investment is now picking up, but only slowly. While the investment to GDP ratio is projected to go back to its long-term average in the US, it is set to remain below it in most Eurozone Member States until 2015, with the shortfall particularly large in the more peripheral countries (see Figure 1).

Weak investment spending has important consequences for the short-term outlook via its impact on aggregate demand. But it also has important consequences for medium-term growth via its impact on the capital stock, thus affecting medium-term productivity prospects through the diffusion of new technologies and innovation. We estimate that a 5 percentage-point reduction in the investment rate leads to a reduction in potential growth of nearly 0.5%.[1]

* Co-author: Philipp Mohl (European Commission), Vox CEPR, 4 June 2014.

Figure 1 Developments of real gross fixed capital formation to GDP ratios

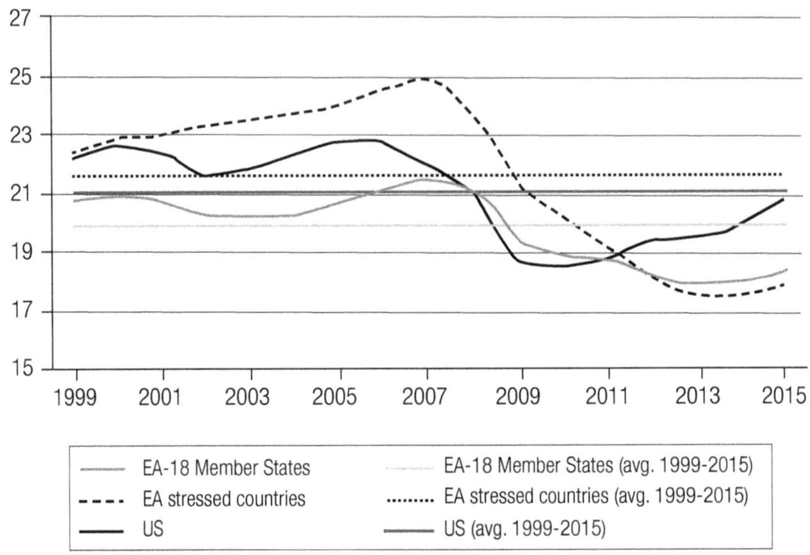

Note: The group of stressed countries consists of Greece, Ireland, Italy, Portugal, and Spain.

Source: European Commission.

2 It's the accelerator, stupid! Or is it?

The sluggish growth outlook is clearly hampering investment through the traditional accelerator effect (Chirinko 1993). Accelerator models relating investment to GDP usually show a reasonably good fit for the Eurozone (see Figure 2). Of course, the accelerator model should not necessarily be interpreted as showing causality running from GDP growth to investment. But overall, it is clear that lower GDP growth compared with previous cycles has reduced the need for businesses to expand capacity.

One might argue that the weakness of investment is related to the restructuring process of Eurozone economies due to the necessary reduction of overcapacities. In Spain, for instance, it is well known that the crisis has led to a sharp adjustment in the construction sector, resulting in a substantial fall in residential investment. However, lacklustre investment is not limited to the housing sector.

Figure 2 Investment regressions using the accelerator model for the Eurozone

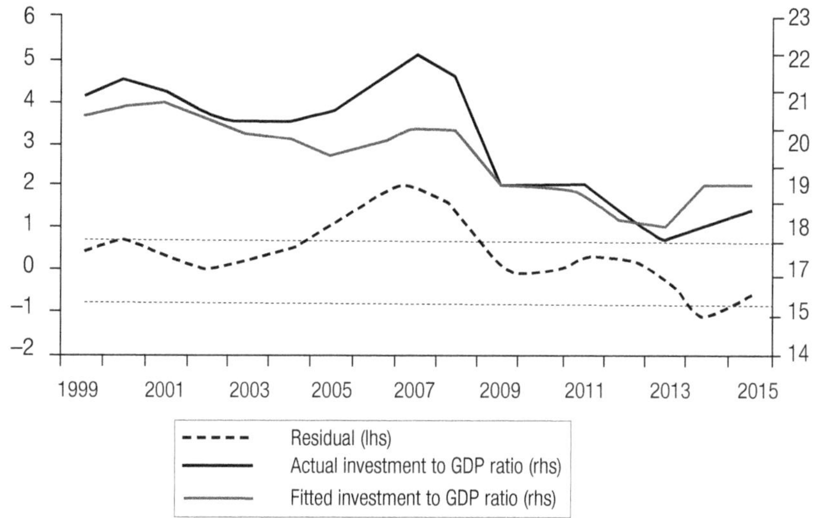

Note: Estimations based on an EA-12 sample using real gross fixed capital formation to GDP ratios.

Source: European Commission.

The need to deleverage and reduce overcapacity has weighed on investment in many advanced economies. Commission studies show that deleveraging by households and non-financial corporations can have strong short- and medium-term impacts on the investment rate, as private agents cut investment and other forms of spending to fund the repair of their balance sheets (Cuerpo *et al.* 2013, Ruscher and Wolff 2012). This is illustrated by the strong negative correlation between the change in corporate investment since the crisis and the accumulation of debt by non-financial corporations in pre-crisis years (see Figure 3).

In the Eurozone, three additional factors in particular continue to weigh on investment: a) the decline in public investment, b) financial fragmentation, and c) high levels of economic uncertainty.

Capital formation in the Eurozone is being affected by the decline in public investment, which accounts for about 12% of total investment in the Eurozone. The decrease is largely the result of the sovereign debt crisis, which triggered significant fiscal adjustment across the Eurozone.

Figure 3 Non-residential investment and non-financial corporations' debt

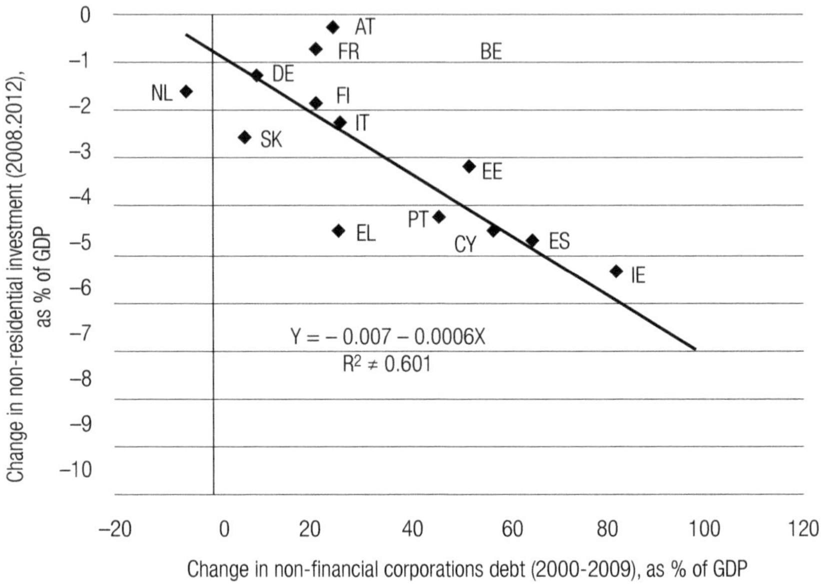

Source: European Commission.

To some extent, it also reflects the continuation of the trend towards shifting parts of public sector investment to the private sector – in areas such as health, education, and transport infrastructure – which began before the crisis.

While the cut in public investment is therefore partly a response to previously excessive spending, short-term budgetary pressures have in many cases led to myopic policymaking in which governments slash public investment in order to achieve savings. Today, there is a clear need to re-prioritise public spending towards more growth-friendly areas and to maximise its efficiency. That, together with a more neutral fiscal stance, should contribute directly and indirectly (via the accelerator) to strengthen investment.

The sluggish rebound of investment can also be explained by the financial fragmentation in several Eurozone Member States. Fragmentation restricts the supply of credit to the real economy, starving investment of its oxygen. Financial markets in the EU – most notably sovereign and equity markets – have strengthened in recent months, but bank lending rates have so far not improved to the same extent. In peripheral Member States, such as Spain and Italy, there is hardly any evidence of bank lending rates falling, and the financing conditions of the private sector remain much less supportive in these countries than in Germany or France.

Finally, investment activity is probably also being impeded by high levels of economic uncertainty (Bernanke 1983, Dixit and Pindyck 1994). High uncertainty weighs negatively on private spending and economic growth by offering agents an incentive to postpone investment, consumption, and employment decisions (European Commission 2013c). Elevated uncertainty becomes all the more damaging for growth and investment because it magnifies the effects of credit constraints and weak balance sheets by forcing banks to reign in credit further and deterring companies from investing, so as to minimise the risks of irreversible decisions.

Standard indicators of policy uncertainty and financial market volatility have come down significantly since the acute phase of the sovereign debt crisis – a development which should support investment spending in the coming quarters. Nevertheless, uncertainty in the Eurozone has not yet returned to its standard cyclical level. Downside risks to the growth outlook remain significant not only because of the external environment, but also because of the possibility that the structural, fiscal, and institutional reforms that are necessary to ensure a sustainable recovery could stall.

3 How to unleash investment spending?

The policy agendas for investment and growth are closely linked. The strengthening of world demand and the gradual rise in consumption projected in the Eurozone should support investment spending over the next few quarters. However, without further policy action, investment growth will continue to disappoint.

Additional structural reforms are therefore needed in all Eurozone Member States to support the investment outlook, despite the achievements reached in some – particularly the more vulnerable – Member States. This would boost investment not only via the accelerator effect, but also via contributing to a faster re-allocation of labour and capital from the slow-growing (deleveraging-constrained) sectors to those which benefit from better demand conditions. We have conducted model simulations that show that Eurozone GDP could be up to 3.6% higher after 10 years if Member States adopted measures to halve the gap vis-à-vis the average of the three best-performing EU Member States in different labour and product market reform areas (European Commission 2013e).

The economic literature shows that reforms to foster a pro-competitive environment in Europe and increase the efficiency and supply of product and service markets are of particular importance for investment. In this context, a further deepening of the Single Market – not only in manufacturing, but also in financing and network industries (such as energy, transport, and digital markets) – would be highly welcome.

The Eurozone economy would also benefit from measures to further reduce policy uncertainty. A credible implementation of the enhanced fiscal framework is imperative to bring debt ratios in a number of countries to sustainable levels and thereby remove any uncertainty surrounding the necessary consolidation process. The focus on a growth-friendly consolidation strategy should minimise the short-term costs. To reduce uncertainty regarding the robustness of the recovery, policymakers also need to stick to the reform commitments made in the context of the European Semester, the EU's annual cycle of policy coordination.

Financial sector reforms, including the completion of the Banking Union, also rank at the top of the policy agenda to boost investment. Important and necessary steps have already been taken at EU level to set adequate framework conditions and restore lending to the economy. The completion of a fully-fledged Banking Union is a key building block of the EU's efforts to improve its financial sector. However, further measures are needed to make our financial sector more efficient and less dominated by banks. In this context, the latest Commission initiatives to support long-term investment – for instance by improving the access of funding of Small and Medium-sized Enterprises (SMEs) – are central (see European Commission 2014c).

The deleveraging process in the household and corporate sectors is painful but necessary, and needs to be properly managed. It could be supported by reforming inefficient bankruptcy frameworks so as to facilitate the necessary consolidation and significantly reduce costs. The recent Commission Recommendation on a new approach to business failure and insolvency (European Commission 2014b) provides minimum standards to encourage Member States to put in place frameworks that enable an efficient restructuring of viable enterprises in financial difficulty.

It is even more important to tackle these issues given the size of the investment gap in the EU in a number of areas. There is a clear need for infrastructure investment – estimated to be on the order of €1 trillion for trans-European networks for transport, energy, and telecoms up to 2020 only. The EU budget has increased the availability of financial instruments for such a purpose. An investment partnership at the EU level would be an important catalyst at the current juncture.

In brief, there is no place for complacency. Tackling the remaining challenges, keeping the reform momentum alive in all Member States, and using the synergies through an investment partnership at the EU level remain crucial – not only for the Eurozone's investment, but also for its medium-term growth performance.

Note

[1] The estimations are based on an EA-12 sample. They reflect a lower bound estimate, assuming that lower investment goes along with unchanged employment and only incorporates the productivity effects stemming from lower capital intensity. The Commission currently uses an output elasticity of capital of around 0.35 (D'Auria *et al.* 2010).

29 Lacklustre Investment in the Eurozone: The Policy Response*

December 2014

1 Explaining investment weakness

Weak investment has been the main source of weakness in the Eurozone recovery (European Commission 2014e, Claeys et al. 2014a). While private consumption in the Eurozone in 2014 was at roughly the same level as it was in 2007, total investment was about 15% below its pre-crisis peak (see Figure 1).

The weakness in investment is not confined to the construction and real estate sectors of countries that are grappling with imploding real estate bubbles. It is broad-based and affects the vast majority of the Eurozone economies and most of their sectors, with corporations withholding investment spending more than households or governments. The macroeconomic costs are high: not only does investment weakness affect the short-term outlook via its impact on aggregate demand, it also reduces the economy's potential. The European Commission's estimates show that a 5 percentage point reduction in the investment rate leads to a reduction in potential growth of nearly 0.5%.

As I have argued, the weakness of investment can be explained by a range of both cyclical and structural factors:[1] a) the need to deleverage and reduce overcapacity, especially in the construction sector; b) regulatory bottlenecks in, for example, network sectors; c) sluggish economic growth via the accelerator channel; d) the decline in public investment; e) financial fragmentation; and f) high levels of economic uncertainty.

---

* Vox, CEPR, 22 December 2014.

Figure 1 Developments in real gross fixed capital and private consumption (index 2007 = 100)

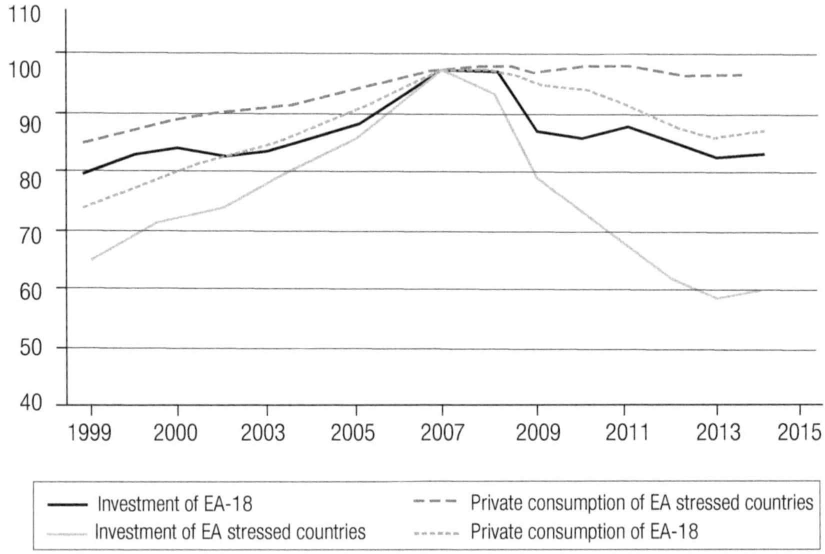

Note: Investment is measured as real gross fixed capital formation. The group of stressed countries consists of Cyprus, Greece, Ireland, Italy, Portugal and Spain.

Source: European Commission.

2 The need of a comprehensive policy strategy

A comprehensive set of policies is needed to address this mix of factors. Indeed, a number of policy initiatives have been implemented and more are in the pipeline.

Well-designed and properly implemented structural reforms in labour and product markets are the appropriate response to the structural factors. In the standard textbook growth model, the steady-state investment rate is determined by the rate of growth of employment and total factor productivity (TFP). Weak TFP and employment growth are most likely weighing on capital formation, hence the need for structural policies to address these growth factors. In some EU countries, investment demand is still held back by the need to adjust to the macroeconomic imbalances accumulated before the crisis. Far-reaching reforms have taken place in countries such as Spain or Ireland, although the correction of accumulated imbalances will still take time. Furthermore, most EU members face depressed medium-term growth prospects due to population ageing, weak TFP and the impact of the crisis on supply. Also, regulatory bottlenecks in network industries continue to keep private investment levels low. Reforms to restore the sustainability of public finances, complete the single market, cut red tape, support job creation and promote growth in general are at the core of the EU's policy agenda, and will provide a key pillar of support to investment.

Other measures that aim to create an appropriate policy mix have the capacity to affect more cyclical factors, such as widespread economic uncertainty and the persistent weakness of domestic demand. As highlighted by Mario Draghi in his Jackson Hole speech in August 2014 (Draghi 2014), tackling such problems requires a comprehensive policy strategy that addresses both demand and supply. The ECB has announced non-conventional monetary policy tools to prevent the dis-anchoring of inflation expectations. On the fiscal side, as the recent assessment of Eurozone members' draft budgetary plans indicates a broadly neutral fiscal stance in the Eurozone in 2015, the balance between fiscal sustainability requirements and cyclical stabilisation concerns appears to be appropriate. The big picture, however, looks rather different under the microscope. While some Eurozone countries still need to do more in order to comply with the EU's fiscal rules, other countries have the space to provide fiscal support. Importantly, more efforts should be made to prioritise productive investment, raise the quality of public expenditure and make tax systems fairer and more efficient. The progressive phasing in of the Banking Union – including the recent results of the comprehensive assessment of banks' balance sheets – is contributing to the diminution of policy uncertainty and financial fragmentation.

3 The Investment Plan for Europe: the €300 billion question and more

In November 2014, the Commission under President Jean-Claude Juncker, put forward an Investment Plan for Europe, which aims to mobilise over €315 billion of additional public and private funds over the period 2015-2017 through targeted actions to remove uncertainty and improve the overall investment environment (European Commission 2014f). This plan needs to be seen as an integral part of the broader policy agenda and it complements the numerous policy actions aimed at addressing different factors hindering investment and ensuring an appropriate short-term policy mix.

The focus of the plan is predicated on two main considerations: first, there are investment needs in some sectors that are not easily met by the private sector due to their risk profile; and second, although there is no real shortage of liquidity at present, this is not translating into real investment.

To achieve this, the plan proposes action on three fronts: (i) catalysing investment finance by expanding the pool of risk bearing capacity; (ii) actions to create a transparent pipeline of investable projects to bring certainty to private investors and provide technical assistance to public investors to better construct their investment projects; (iii) improving the overall investment climate by eliminating barriers to investment at both European and national level. Not surprisingly, the €315 billion financing

Figure 2 The Investment Plan for Europe

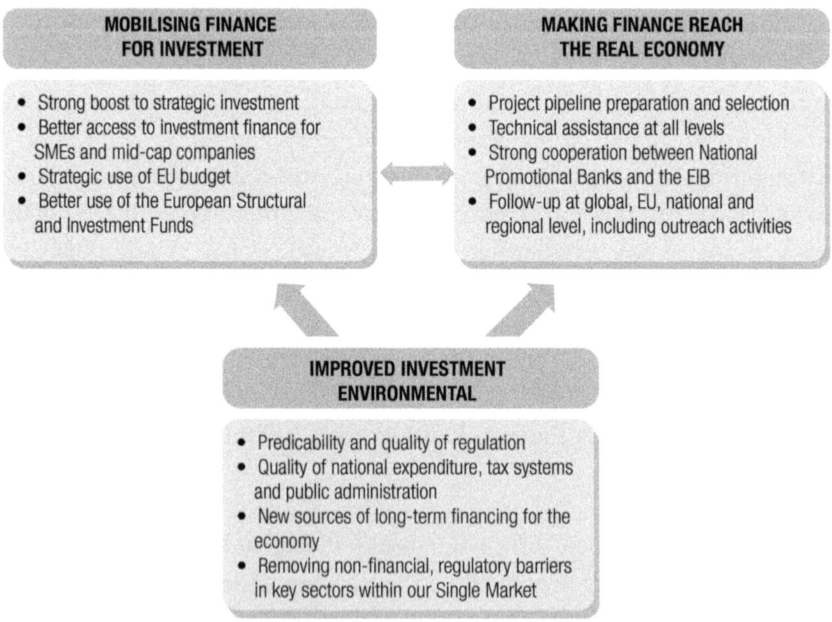

Source: European Commission (2014f).

part of the plan attracted most of the headlines. It is clear though that the additional funding will not deliver all of its potential unless other strands of the plan are properly implemented.

How will the plan mobilise extra investment?

The objective is to support (i) long-term investment in areas that are essential for growth in Europe, and (ii) SMEs and mid-cap firms. For this purpose, a new European Fund for Strategic Investment (EFSI) will be created. Its risk-bearing capacity consists of €16 billion of guarantees from the EU budget and €5 billion of commitments from the European Investment Bank (EIB). The EIB will be able to use this €21 billion in risk-absorbing capacity to provide around €60 billion in finance to selected projects. EFSI-supported products will typically target the more complex and riskier parts of a project's financing, reducing the risks for private investors. Lowering the financial riskiness will make it easier for a project/firm to attract additional financing from private sources. In this way, it is expected to catalyse up to €315 billion of investment in projects over 2015-17. This estimate, which assumes that every Euro invested by the EFSI will attract four Euros from the private sector, is in line with the historical experience of EU programmes and the EIB, and not overly optimistic.

Some commentators argue that the amount of public spending envisaged is too small to have a meaningful effect (Mazzucato and Caetano 2014, Zuleeg 2014). This criticism overlooks two important facts. First, there is at present no lack of investable funds. Institutional investors command very sizeable funds that are looking for deployment under the right conditions. The Plan has been designed to mobilise this private capital. The ratios of public to private capital envisaged in this context are estimates based on past EIB experience. Moreover, the governments and national promotional banks are invited to join the fund or to co-invest alongside it. EU Structural Funds could also be used more efficiently to catalyse more investment and EU countries could reprioritise investment in their budgets.

Another criticism has been that the envisaged contribution of the EU to the EFSI is taken from other EU funds with no net increase in public spending and therefore no possible macroeconomic effect (Gros 2014, Maystadt 2014, Münchau 2014). The guarantee provided by the Commission to the EFSI will indeed be diverted from other EU spending (notably the Connecting Europe Facility and Horizon 2020). However, support to investment will increase, as EU funds previously allocated as grants will leverage considerably more private capital under the EFSI.

How should the additional investment be allocated?

The objective of the ESFI is to support long-term investment of European significance in infrastructure, education, transport, research, innovation, and renewable energy. A key operational challenge is to identify and fund projects that are viable and have a significant impact on growth. An Investment Task Force made up of the Commission, the EIB and the Member States has completed a first screening exercise to identify a pool of investable projects. An independent Investment Committee will select the projects[2] covered by the EFSI guarantee based on their viability and making sure that public support does not crowd out private investment. The projects will be chosen solely on their merits, irrespective of their geographic location. As regards the support of investment for SMEs and mid-cap companies, the core objective is to help overcome capital shortages by providing higher amounts of direct equity and additional guarantees for high-quality securitisation of SME loans.

The proper selection of projects will be key to minimising the deadweight losses due to financing projects that would have taken place in any case. Some commentators (e.g. Claeys et al. 2014b, Veugelers 2014) have suggested that this could significantly reduce the net macroeconomic effects of the plan. To minimise this risk, the EFSI will target the more difficult segments of the markets, while leaving the plain vanilla products for others to offer. Moreover, all projects will be subject to the EU's state aid rules, under which the requirements of addressing unmet needs and avoiding private sector crowding out are central.

4 A key complement: removing sectoral and other financial and non-financial barriers

A business environment more conducive to investment is still needed in many parts of Europe. This requires further efforts to reduce the administrative burden and simplify the regulatory environment for business.

More also needs to be done to remove barriers to investment in the Single Market, with the European Energy Union and the Digital Single Market playing an instrumental role in this respect. The re-launch of transparent securitisation will help convey new financing, particularly to SMEs. Over time, the creation of the Capital Markets Union should also support investment by reducing financial fragmentation and helping European firms to diversify their funding sources away from banks.

Given its persistent weakness, investment must be at the core of any strategy to revive growth in Europe. At the global scale, this chimes with the G20's focus on investment as a key policy challenge. The Investment Plan presented by the Commission has the potential to stimulate capital spending and kick-start a sorely needed investment recovery. However, it is no silver bullet and will only be effective if implemented properly and accompanied by ambitious structural policies and an appropriate policy mix.

Notes

[1] See chapter 28 and also Barkbu et al. (2014), Bach et al. (2013), and European Commission (2014e) for analyses of factors behind weak investment.

[2] There is no automatic link between the list of investable projects prepared by the Task Force and the selection of projects by the EFSI Investment Committee.

30 Three Waves of Convergence: Can Eurozone Countries Start Growing Together Again?*

April 2015

1 Introduction

There is a widespread view that the monetary union is now acting as a straitjacket on countries in the periphery, that it is no longer delivering convergence in living standards. In this vein, the Euro Summit of 24 October 2014 called for work to continue to "develop concrete mechanisms for stronger economic policy coordination, convergence, and solidarity," and invited the President of the European Commission, in close cooperation with the President of the Euro Summit, the President of the Eurogroup, and the President of the European central Bank, "to prepare next steps on better economic governance in the Euro area."[1]
This chapter argues that convergence in the Eurozone has never stopped – what changed over the main phases of the monetary union was the type of convergence.

The type of convergence currently at work is neither nominal convergence (i.e., convergence in nominal variables like inflation and interest rates) nor real convergence as commonly understood (i.e., convergence in per capita incomes), but a convergence that concerns the structure of the economy. Structural convergence is posing the basis for renewed real convergence. However, for this to happen, the right institutions and policies need to be in place at the EU/EZ level and the national level.

---

* Co-author: Alessandro Turrini (European Commission), Vox CEPR, 17 April 2015.

2 The faces of economic convergence

Different meanings have been given to the term "economic convergence." In growth literature, convergence refers to the expected tendency for countries to grow faster the lower their GDP per capita level. Real convergence (i.e., narrowing differences in terms of per-capita GDP, relative endowments of productive factors and relative factor prices) is what neo-classical growth theory predicts.

The debate at the start of the Economic and Monetary Union (EMU) was also centred around convergence. In particular, the Maastricht criteria emphasised nominal convergence (defined in terms of nominal variables such as interest rates, inflation, exchange rates, government deficits and debt): the objective was not only to create a single currency, but also a stable currency (e.g., Buti and Sapir 1998). It was expected that the adoption of a single currency would give strong incentives to carry out structural reforms to compensate for the loss of monetary policy as a stabilisation tool.

The academic debate put the emphasis instead on Optimal Currency Area (OCA) theory and the extent to which real convergence was sufficiently advanced to make the economies of the countries participating in EMU synchronised, so as to reduce the risk of unaddressed asymmetric shocks in a monetary union. The debate on the possible tension between nominal and real convergence surrounded also EU enlargement, with emphasis on the possible difficulties encountered by accession countries in respecting Maastricht criteria on inflation, interest and exchange rates in light of the operation of Balassa-Samuelson effects (e.g., Grauwe and Schnable 2005).

Real convergence was implicitly assumed to work in the direction of making the economies participating in the monetary union more similar in terms of economic structures, thereby approaching EMU to the OCA requirements and easing the respect of the Maastricht nominal criteria. However, the facts proved this expectation wrong. The first decade of EMU showed that structural convergence is not necessary a by-product of nominal and real convergence.

3 The three waves of convergence in EMU

The run up to EMU coincided with nominal convergence: differences in inflation rates among the countries participating in the monetary union narrowed. The average level of nominal interest rates and their dispersion across "EMU-ins" dropped dramatically, in light of converging inflation differentials, reduced exchange rate risk, and reduced government deficits (see Figure 1).

Figure 1 Interest rates: Mean and variance across EA-12 countries

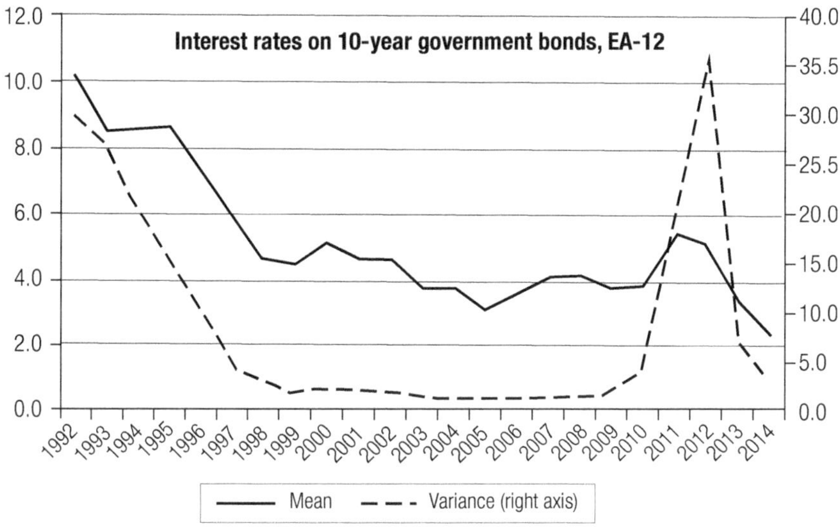

Source: Elaborations on AMECO data.

The years preceding the completion of EMU were also characterised by a strong record of real convergence, with higher growth rates registered in countries with lower income per capita.

After EMU completion, nominal convergence was virtually achieved, with the notable exception of government debts. The fall in interest rates was accompanied by a major process of integration of financial markets, notably bond markets. The statistics also showed that real convergence was still working as expected (see Figure 2). The belief that the OCA criteria were "endogenous" became popular, namely that these criteria, although not satisfied *ex-ante*, would have been satisfied *ex-post*, thanks to the fact that EMU participation would have implied increased trade integration and a stronger degree of co-movement of economic cycles (Frenkel and Rose 1998).

Real convergence during the first ten years of EMU was made even more visible by the massive capital flows running from the "center" to the "periphery" of the Eurozone, in light of vanishing exchange rate risk and reduced default risk perceptions. This process was paralleled/accompanied by widening current account deficits in the periphery and growing surpluses in the core (see Figure 3). Capital inflows coincided with accelerated growth rates. As shown in Figure 2, countries in the periphery, while receiving capital inflows and recording current account deficits, were also registering sustained domestic demand and reducing unemployment at a fast rate (see Figure 4).

Figure 2 Scatterplot across EZ countries of per capita GDP growth (1999-2007), GDP per capita level in PPP (1999)

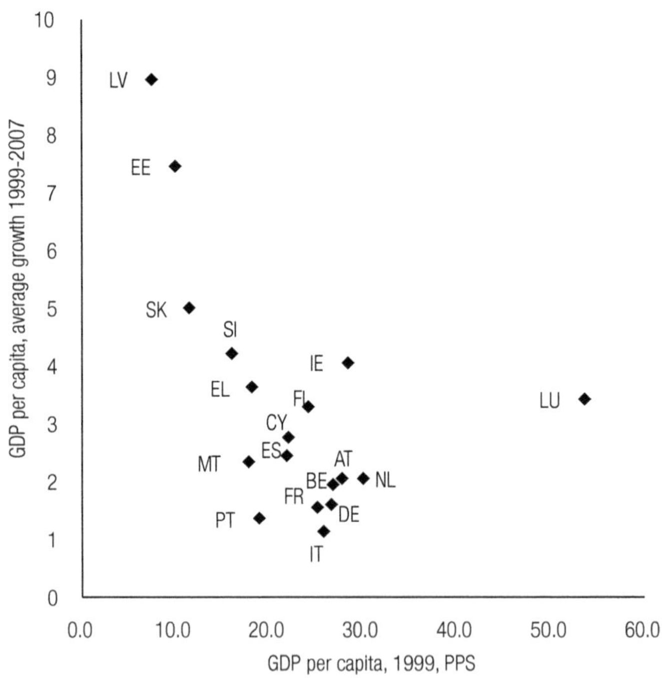

Source: Elaborations on AMECO data.

Figure 3 Current account and unemployment developments, average for core versus periphery EZ (weighted average)[2]

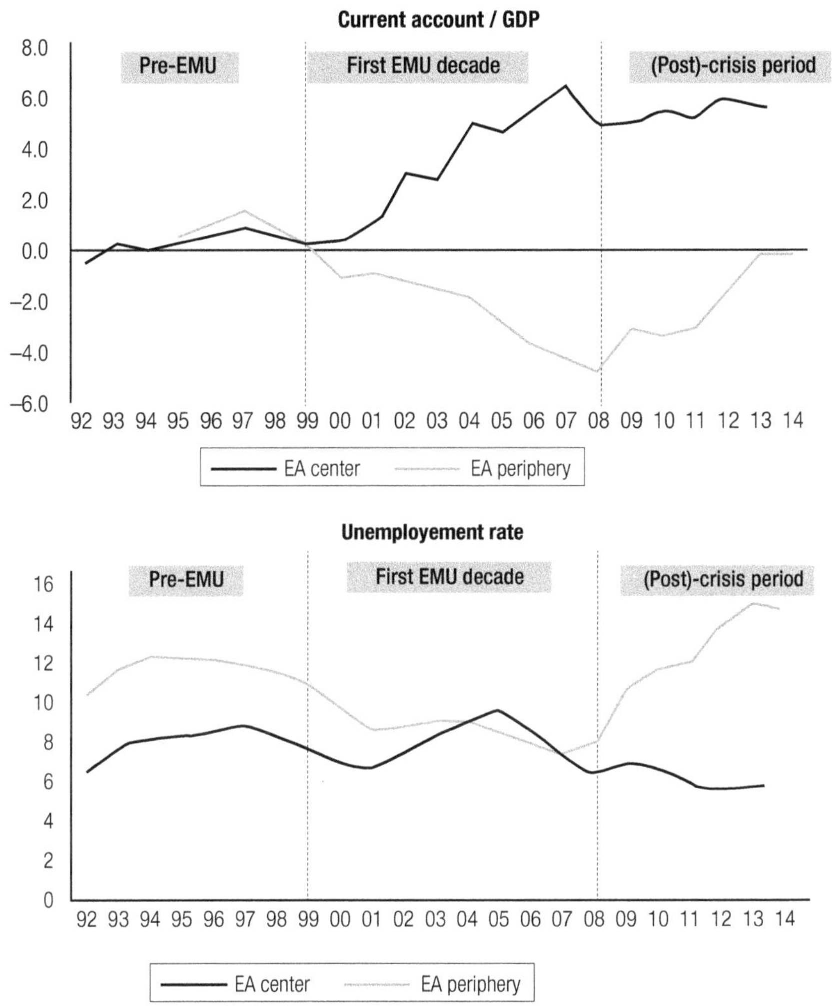

Source: Elaborations on AMECO data.

The sustainability of the additional growth accruing in the periphery was however dependent on the quality of the investments made possible by cheaper capital. In this respect, it did not help that buoyant capital inflows were matched by persisting inflation differentials and competitiveness losses in the periphery. Investment in the periphery became increasingly profitable in non-tradable activities. Large-scale bubbles in the housing sector were fuelled in countries like Spain and Ireland. Symmetrically, countries in the centre started growing increasingly out of exports, also thanks to improvements in price competitiveness, while relatively high real interest rates prevented the overheating of asset markets, notably housing. Moreover, the satisfactory growth performance registered in the EZ periphery led to a situation of "reform anaesthesia" – important reforms to facilitate an effective adjustment in the monetary union were delayed because they were not seen as urgent (European Commission 2008).

In a nutshell, real convergence during the first EMU decade largely coincided with structural divergence.[3] The structure of the economies at the centre and those at the periphery became increasingly different. As shown in Figure 4, the economies of the centre were relying more and more on exports and tradable activities, while those of the periphery were increasingly dominated by non-tradable sectors and construction.

Figure 4 Cumulative growth rate of non-tradable/tradable value added, and construction / total value added (Weighted average for EZ core versus EZ periphery, averages for sub-periods: run up to EMU, first EMU decade, post-crisis)

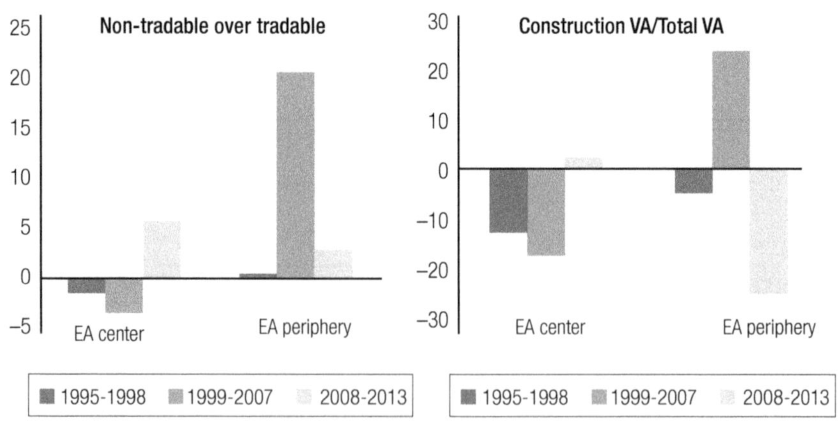

Source: elaborations on AMECO data.

In a sense, the well-known "Walters effect" (i.e., the destabilising effect of real interest rate differences between a low-inflation centre and a high-inflation periphery: see Walters 1986) had implications that went beyond cyclical stabilisation. One could argue that a "super Walters effect" operated during the first EMU decade, whereby not only cyclical positions, but also economic structures were driven by persistent real interest rate differences.

The financial crisis acted as a detonator of the imbalances accumulated during the first decade of EMU. Capitals started flowing in opposite direction, amid a general reappraisal of risk. The developments taking place since the run up to EMU were partly reversed – nominal divergence in interest rates linked to growing spreads between the centre and the periphery took place together with real divergence in growth and unemployment rates (see Figure 3). The correction of current account imbalances was accompanied not only by a compression of domestic demand in the periphery, but also by competitiveness gains and a re-composition of output towards tradable activities.

4 Can Eurozone countries start growing together again?

After years of protracted divergence, the most recent data points to an acceleration of growth and employment in most EZ countries in the periphery. The easing of bond market tensions, the reduced fragmentation of financial markets, and the reduced pace of the necessary fiscal consolidation in distressed countries are all contributing factors. Will this be enough? Will it last?

The current process of structural convergence is a necessary requisite for more real convergence going forward. As the economies in the periphery cannot rely again on growth patterns mainly driven by external borrowing, there is no alternative – the conditions for stronger non-tradable and export growth need to be in place. Though this process is necessary for renewed convergence in living conditions across EMU, what has been achieved so far will by no means be sufficient.

The first reason is that much of the structural convergence observed is linked especially to the contraction in the non-tradable sector in periphery countries. A protracted expansion of the export sector requires ambitious reforms, supportive policy frameworks, and a sustained recovery in export markets. In this respect, the Commission has launched a three-pronged agenda to strengthen the recovery in Europe based on a renewed commitment to structural reforms, a commitment to fiscal responsibility that also takes into account growth objectives within the available fiscal space, and boosting investment via additional resources and the removal of bottlenecks.

Second, as discussed in chapter 20, the need for an export-driven growth strategy in the periphery may clash with the need to ensure sound public finances since price competitiveness gains in the periphery may imply debt deflation. A successful anti-deflationary stance by monetary authorities will play a key role in easing such a trade-off.

Last but not least, sustainable convergence will require a credible institutional framework underpinning EMU and the preservation of a climate of trust. The financial crisis helped realign the market assessment of country risk with fundamentals. The market reaction proved, as so often, too strong and too late, but it did provide the basis for adjustment and structural convergence, including by means of much-needed reforms. Looking forward, the extent and sustainability of restored convergence will depend crucially on whether markets will maintain confidence in the economies of the EZ periphery. Recent EU level initiatives will help in this respect – strengthened financial market regulation and the establishment of a single supervisory mechanism for the banking sector will help ensure the compatibility between restored convergence and macro-financial stability. By taking an EZ wide view on supervision it will help lessen macro-financial risks. The establishment of a Capital Markets Union will contribute to the integration of equity markets across the EU, thus reducing the volatility of cross-border investment, enhancing risk-sharing, and most importantly helping to reallocate excess savings within the EZ via equity rather than debt. Both developments should help tackle the super-Walters effect that hampered structural divergence in the pre-crisis period.

Notes

[1] The issue of convergence in the Eurozone is discussed also in the Four Presidents' Analytical Note "Preparing for Next Steps on Better Economic Governance in the Euro Area", Informal European Council, 12 February 2015.

[2] Centre: BE DE LU NL AT FI. Periphery: EE IE EL ES FR IT CY LV LT MT PT SI SK. Centre and periphery EZ countries grouped according to their external position, as in chapter 24. With few exceptions, countries in the centre recorded a surplus over the 1999-2009 period, while periphery countries recorded a deficit.

[3] Similar conclusions are reached in existing papers, e.g., Marelli and Signorelli (2005).

31 Overcoming Eurozone Wage Inertia*

October 2017

1 Can we have price stability, Eurozone rebalancing, and uncoordinated competitiveness developments?

Pessimistic views on Eurozone rebalancing are not uncommon (e.g. Darvas 2012). However, in chapter 24, at the end of 2012, we had an optimistic take on the issue overall, noting the rapid reduction of large current account deficits and a turnaround in unit labour cost dynamics, supporting adjustment going forward. With hindsight, Eurozone rebalancing has indeed made some progress but the optimism of on rebalancing prospects has not fully materialised.

First, the substantial reduction of most current account deficits has not been matched by progress in terms of reducing large surpluses. Quite the opposite: the combined surplus of Germany and the Netherlands, which explained more than 90% of the Eurozone surplus in 2016, has been growing continuously since 2001 and is projected to start falling in nominal terms only in 2017. As a result of the simultaneous reduction of large deficits and the lack of correction in large surpluses, the Eurozone as a whole has gradually moved to a surplus position exceeding 3% of GDP, reflecting a growing gap between aggregate domestic demand and income which underpins exceptionally low inflation rates. The current account surplus of the Eurozone is estimated above the level that can be justified on the basis of fundamentals according to European Com-

* Co-author: Alessandro Turrini (European Commission), Vox CEPR, 6 October 2017.

mission estimates (European Commission 2016g, h), and slightly above according to IMF estimates (IMF 2017c). From a global perspective, the Eurozone surplus almost corresponds to the combined surplus of China and Japan.

Second, the gap in terms of unit labour cost dynamics between surplus and deficit countries peaked around 2012 and has eroded somewhat since then (Figure 1). A recovery of wage growth from exceptionally low rates in net debtor countries, coupled with missing productivity gains, has played a role, but the lost advantage of net debtor countries in terms of labour cost dynamics is also related to persistent moderate wage dynamics in surplus countries. The persistence of relatively subdued wage growth in surplus countries is to some extend at odds with what could be predicted on the basis of the working of Phillips curves – a tighter labour market in low-unemployment surplus countries should be accompanied by stronger wage dynamics.

Figure 1 Nominal compensation per employees in the Eurozone: Surplus versus deficit countries

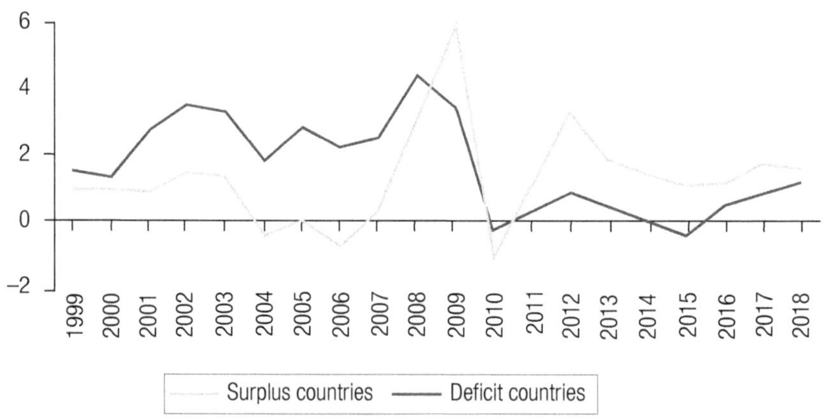

Notes: Surplus countries: BE, DE, LU, NL, AT, FI. Deficit countries: remaining EZ19 countries. All surplus countries recorded a current account position balanced or in surplus over the 1999-2012 period (the only exceptions being DE and AT before 2002 and FI after 2010, while all deficit countries recorded a deficit between 2000 and 2012.

Source: European Commission.

Instead, since 2014, a flattening of the Eurozone Phillips curve has been observed, with considerable reductions in Eurozone unemployment having taken place with virtually no change in nominal growth rates (Figure 2).[1] Such a persistent moderate growth in nominal wages is another factor that hinders the achievement of monetary policy objectives with regards to inflation and that, as pointed out in chapter 20, would make the two objectives of Eurozone rebalancing and debt sustainability incompatible (see chapter 20). A multitude of possible explanations have been advanced for the muted upward cyclical reaction of wages, including the role of long lags in revising collective wage contracts, low inflation expectations playing a role in wage contract renewals, reduced labour productivity growth, labour market slack being more serious than revealed by unemployment figures, and a reduction in the wage share due to changing bargaining power of wage setters linked to, among other things, technological change (e.g. European Commission 2016d, ECB 2017a, IMF 2017a).

On the basis of the above arguments, one can formulate an impossible trinity as follows: can we have at the same time price stability as defined by the ECB, Eurozone rebalancing, and uncoordinated competitiveness developments?

Figure 2 The Eurozone: Phillips curve relation, 2000-2016

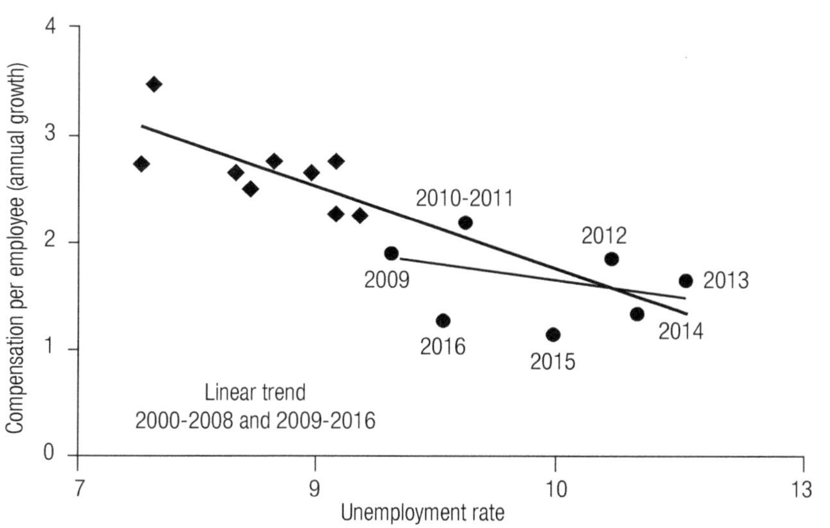

Source: Elaborations on AMECO, EZ19.

2 The current coordination framework and its rationale

After the start of EMU, in view of growing competitiveness divergences and widening external imbalances, there was awareness of the need to strengthen the coordination of policies affecting competitiveness (e.g. Allsopp and Artis 2003, European Commission 2008). It was acknowledged that purely market-driven competitiveness dynamics may not guarantee a sufficiently swift operation of the automatic adjustment mechanism in the face of asymmetric shocks, and that tensions may emerge between the two objectives of internal (output close to potential) and external equilibrium (a balanced current account position, taking into account fundamentals). The current position of the Eurozone and the large members in terms of internal and external equilibrium can be depicted as in Figure 3 using the well-known Swan's graphical representation in the real exchange rate-output space. While for Germany and the Netherlands a roughly balanced internal position coexists with a large current account surplus, for Italy a current account surplus is matched by output below potential, while France is characterised by a negative output gap and a current account deficit. To achieve both internal and external equilibrium, one instrument is not enough – policies affecting both domestic demand and competitiveness are needed, with combinations that depend on the specific country situations.

In principle, a case for coordination of competitiveness developments builds from two basic considerations. First, while output gap divergences tend to be automatically re-absorbed via the market mechanism – since countries with tighter labour markets tend to exhibit higher wage growth – the market mechanism does not necessarily help external adjustment, and policy intervention may become necessary. Second, since competitiveness is a relative concept and Eurozone countries are highly integrated, the effectiveness of policies to affect competitiveness depends also on policies in partner countries.[2]

The fact that market-driven competitiveness developments may not necessarily be helpful for external equilibrium is exactly what was observed after the start of EMU, when output above potential in the Eurozone periphery justified relatively buoyant wage growth. Competitiveness losses helped curbing overheating in the periphery but, over time this process led to growing external imbalances, and the crisis acted as a catalyst for their correction. The crisis also made clear that disruptive current account reversals may also take place inside an incomplete monetary union like the Eurozone. Consistently, more recently, ideas have also been floated suggesting a structured framework to coordinate policies affecting competitiveness to prevent the building up of large external imbalances (e.g. Sapir and Wolff 2015).

In light of the experience with the first EMU decade, surveillance procedures aimed at enhancing coordination of policies to prevent and correct macroeconomic imbalances were introduced, with the Macroeconomic Imbalance Procedure becoming operational in 2012.

Policy recommendations to adjust current account deficits have focused on the need to improve competitiveness primarily via productivity gains, but also by means of appropriate wage dynamics.

The focus of policy recommendations aimed at fostering adjustment in surplus countries was instead mainly centred on the need to stimulate investment. The recommendation to use fiscal space in surplus countries has been met with resistance and given rise to a politically charged debate within the Council. Recently, a growing number of commentators (e.g. Bofinger 2015) and policy institutions (e.g. IMF 2017b) have shifted, raising the question whether surplus countries should start focusing more on the role that wage dynamics can play in the rebalancing process.

Figure 3 Internal and external (dis)equilibria in the Eurozone

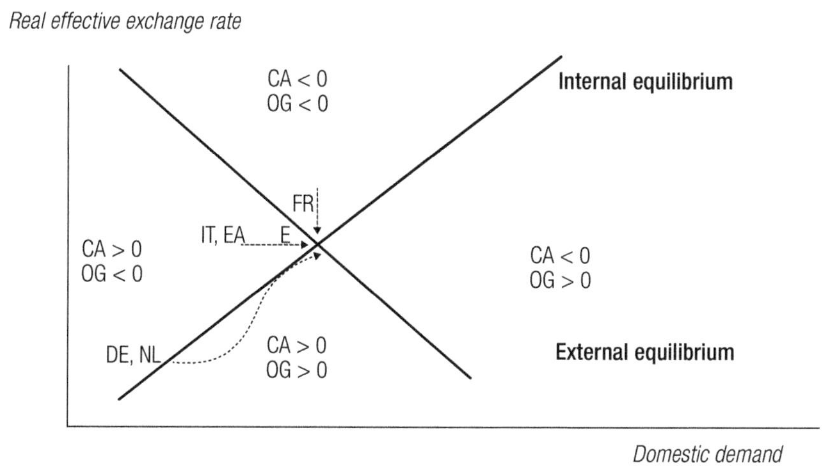

Source: Own elaboration.

Consistently, in 2017 the EU Council recommended that Germany and the Netherlands create "conditions to promote higher real wage growth, respecting the role of the social partners."

3 Why coordination helps

The need for coordination to steer competitiveness developments across Eurozone countries is becoming particularly evident in the current context for a number of reasons.

First, wage dynamism in surplus countries would help monetary policy achieve inflation objectives while at the same time supporting Eurozone rebalancing. Wage growth in crisis-hit countries is curbed by persistent labour market slack, impaired profit margins, and moderate inflation expectations of wage setters. The pick-up in Eurozone-level wage growth which is necessary to lift core inflation on a sustainable basis will therefore more likely come from countries with tighter labour markets, such as Germany and the Netherlands.

Second, overcoming wage inertia in surplus countries would help tackle more decisively Eurozone rebalancing by supporting demand. Wage growth in Germany is below what would be predicted on the basis of fundamentals (European Commission 2016b), while consumption as a share of total income is falling. Currently, the difference between the consumption share in GDP in large surplus countries like Germany and the Netherlands and other Eurozone countries has reached record high levels and does not show any tendency to narrow (Figure 4). In net debtor countries and countries with current account deficits, reforms aimed at fostering productivity growth and therefore improving competitiveness will be necessary.

Third, as opposed to what happened during the first EMU decade, stronger wage growth differentiation would contribute in the present context to both internal and external equilibrium, as labour markets in countries with large current account surpluses are comparatively tighter. Hence, desirable policies would not go against market dynamics, but rather should ensure that such dynamics operate unhindered.

Figure 4 Consumption and investment share in GDP, Germany andthe Netherlands versus rest of the Eurozone

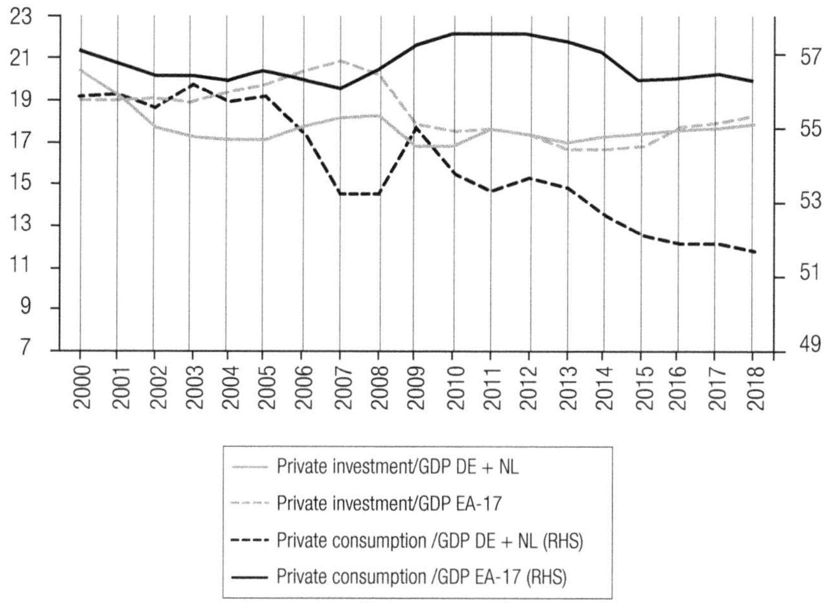

Source: Elaborations on AMECO, EZ19.

4 Conclusion

Although wage developments are mainly the result of the interaction between market forces and the institutions underpinning collective bargaining, governments can play a role in affecting relative unit labour costs and competitiveness in a number of ways, including the tax and benefit system ("fiscal devaluations"), the setting of minimum wages and government wages, the steering of collective bargaining in the private sector via tripartite agreements and social pacts, or, where collective bargaining is regulated by law, the review in consultation with social partners of the legislated frameworks regulating wage setting. In this latter respect, recent reforms have generally focused on reducing obstacles to the decentralisation and articulation of wage bargaining, but, in line with positions echoed in the EMU debate (Calmfors 2001, Blanchard, Jaumotte and Loungani 2013), developments in the direction of strengthened national-level coordination would also help an aligned reaction of wages to cyclical conditions across sectors and firms, which in the current context would also contribute to Eurozone rebalancing.[3] Since the above instruments interact in different ways with the rest of the economy, their effectiveness in steering competitiveness developments would differ, as well as their overall impact, and a shared understanding of these effects is a pre-requisite for fruitful policy discussions.[4]

Although a formal and structured coordination process aiming at a definition of quantitative targets is hardly realistic – and possibly not desirable in light of information gaps, uncertain policy effects, and implementation gaps – an enhanced dialogue at the Eurozone level may ease the achievement of shared objectives and help leverage existing surveillance instruments.

Notes

[1] Country-level estimates of Phillips curves however show substantially stable reaction of wage inflation to unemployment over the past decade once the role of past inflation and inflation expectations is taken into account (e.g. Blanchard et al. 2015).

[2] The introduction of Article 136 TFEU has strengthened the basis for economic policy coordination among Euro-area countries on top of the provisions on economic policy coordination already contained in Article 121 that concerns all EU countries, according to which, "Member States shall regard their economic policies as a matter of common concern and shall coordinate them within the Council…."

[3] Bargaining decentralisation helps adjustment in EMU if monetary unification increases the frequency of shocks hitting specific sectors and firms compared with that of shocks hitting the overall national economy (Buti et al. 1999).

[4] In particular, policies that help raise labour demand and end employment are more likely to stimulate output in a member state's economy and in the rest of the Eurozone (e.g. IMF 2015b).

Part E.
Eastern Enlargement, Global Governance and the Euro

Over the past fifteen years, the EU has changed in a dramatic fashion. It has enlarged to Eastern Europe, and it has been increasingly involved in global governance. The chapters in this section focus on this double shift.

The impact of the enlargement of the EU from 15 to the current 27 members has been much debated. Based on the experience of the first five years, enlargement made the EU more competitive and allowed both old and new Member States to enjoy major benefits from eliminating trade barriers, gradually allowing higher cross-border labour mobility, promoting financial integration and strengthening institutions.

The countries who joined the EU in the mid-2000s (EU11) are among the most open economies globally. The process of trade integration and the creation of global value chains have driven a significant inflow of foreign direct investment (FDI) into these countries. While integration in the EU and FDI have enhanced the growth potential of the EU11, these developments have also made them more vulnerable to external shocks. To make these gains permanent, reforms should focus on increasing economic and social resilience.

International economic cooperation is under stress. The global economy faces fragmentation across institutional, economic, and social dimensions. The actions taken in 2008-2009 by the G20 avoided an outright depression, but questions remain over the ability of the G20 to evolve from a short-term crisis response forum to effectively addressing longer-term challenges. To "win the peace," the G20 has to redesign international economic policy coordination, and ensure that the focus is kept on a limited number of strategic deliverables addressing the key concerns of our citizens, starting with greater inclusiveness and fairness. Europe can play a leading role in a world in search of a new anchor.

Although the Euro instantly became the second-most important global currency upon its creation, its international role was not a primary concern for policymakers at the time. The Eurozone enjoys full "monetary independence," but not yet "monetary sovereignty." However, there is no silver bullet to rapidly increase the use of the Euro abroad. This requires a comprehensive package of reforms, starting with decisive progress on completing EMU's architecture, as well as unifing and deepening its financial markets. It also needs time to break inertia in international public and private portfolio allocations and invoicing practices.

32 Five Years after the Enlargement of the EU*

June 2009

1 New members and old members

The biggest enlargement in the history of the EU took place in 2004. While it may be too soon to draw final conclusions, the findings of a comprehensive report by the European Commission (2009) suggest that the first five years of the enlargement were a major success. The present severe downturn does not put this assessment into doubt, but it certainly highlights many of the future challenges.

In particular, the new Member States benefited from faster growth that enabled them to move from a GDP per capita equal to 40% of the EU-15 average prior to enlargement to 52% in 2008. The EU made a difference. Based on growth regression analysis, it is estimated that each year during the period 2000-2008 accession new Member States' economies grew by 1.75% on average. This compares favourably with the Commission services' *ex ante* estimate in 2001 of 1.3% additional growth in a central scenario. Explanatory factors for this growth premium include the productivity improvements due to FDI and the associated transfer of technology. Model simulations suggest that the narrowing of the interest rate spread was also of particular importance. Estimations suggest that the new Member States enjoyed a 50-100 basis point advantage relative to other emerging countries with comparable fundamentals prior to accession. This contributed 0.3% of additional growth. With the outbreak

* Co-authors: István Székely and Filip Keereman (European Commission), Vox CEPR, 20 June 2009.

of the financial crisis in 2007, risk premia have risen, but it seems the new Member States continue to benefit in this regard, certainly those under the protective umbrella of the Euro.

Old Member States gained from enlargement as well. Firstly, they benefited from a larger export market. It is estimated that exports to the new Member States in the 5 years after enlargement contributed 1 percentage point on average per year to an overall annual export growth of 6% in old Member States. Partly as a result, most of them realised a comfortable trade surplus with the new Member States.

Secondly, the private sector responded to the challenges of enlargement by restructuring production networks and locating plants to maximise efficiency. This helped maintain global competitiveness, boost growth across the EU and ultimately safeguard jobs in the old Member States. Sizable short-term adjustment costs arose in some sectors (e.g. food, clothing, publishing, communication equipment, office machinery, motor vehicles) as employment in old Member States was negatively correlated with the rise in employment in new Member States. However, as the report points out, in several sectors (machinery, furniture, medical instruments, chemicals, wood) investment in new Member States went hand-in-hand with employment creation in the old.

Finally, enlargement did not lead to a flood of migrant workers "stealing" jobs in the old Member States. Since 2004, about 1.6 million people migrated from new to old Member States, bringing the total to 3.6 million. This is less than 1% of the working age population in the old Member States, except in Ireland where it reached a much higher level (about 5 %). According to simulations with ECFIN's QUEST model, this migration adds around 0.4% to GDP in the medium-term as bottlenecks in labour markets ease and the skill composition of the migrants is favourable, albeit not optimally used in the short-term.

In short, global competitiveness, and thus the growth potential, of the EU economy as a whole strengthened through deepening financial intermediation and integration, accelerated knowledge transfer, and increasing cross-border employment. Increased FDI, cross-border holding of financial assets, and remittances of migrant workers improved allocative efficiency and risk-sharing, promoting a higher degree of specialisation and raising productivity across the enlarged EU.

2 The EU made a difference, but not every country took full advantage

EU policies and institutions, including the Stability and Growth Pact, the Lisbon agenda, the Single Market rules and the EU transfer system, played an important role in explaining why benefits of EU enlargement went beyond the classical benefits of economic integration. Structural and cohesion funds provided sizable new resources to lower-income Member States, focused efforts on growth-enhancing investments in infrastructure and human capital, and increased the quality of public spending in general. Model-based calculations suggest that the transfers new Member States will receive through 2013 from structural and cohesion funds will increase their income level by about 4% permanently.

However, not every country has fully exploited the potential benefits of EU enlargement, and some of the processes involved in economic and financial integration have also created vulnerabilities, mostly because of poor domestic policies. History shows that catching-up cannot be taken for granted, and that it is not a linear process (see Figure 1), pointing at the responsibility of policy makers in this regard. Moreover, the current

Figure 1 Catching up, then and now

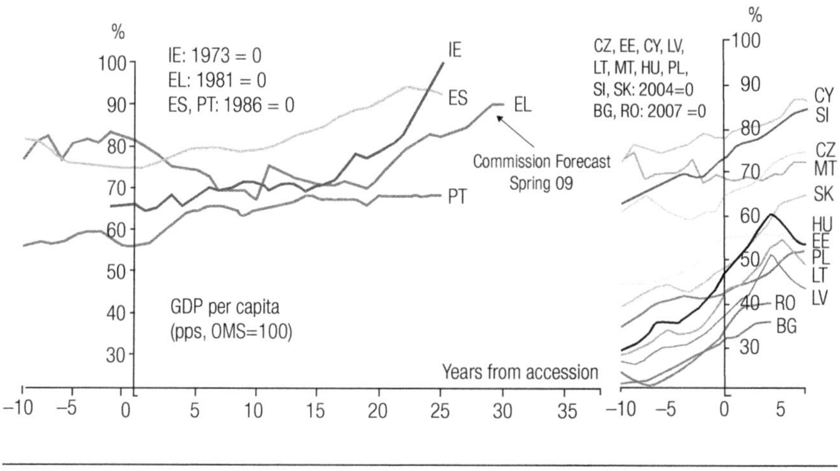

Source: European Commission.

crisis will no doubt stress test the development model the new members have followed so far. This model was based on easy access to relatively cheap foreign capital (made possible by rapid financial integration) and led to rapid financial deepening in these countries. Thus, these countries could not only exploit investment opportunities in productive sectors but also significantly raise consumption and increase housing investment.

3 A three-pronged strategy to safeguard achievements

In 2009, the EU faced the most severe global economic crisis since its creation. This crisis may have strong longer-term effects on potential growth, as the relative price of risk is likely to have increased significantly and the pace of financial integration and deepening could slow down as a result of the necessary re-regulation of the financial system. As the new Member States were particularly affected, real convergence may be hindered in the longer run. To preserve cohesion in the EU, it is essential to ensure that the setback is only temporary.

The new Member States are not left on their own. The European Commission is working on a three-pronged strategy to respond to the crisis. First, it is crucial to enhance multilateral surveillance with a view to reducing external vulnerabilities. A significant part of foreign capital has been allocated to non-productive uses and foreign exchange risk has not been allocated optimally in the system, leaving households and firms in the non-tradable sector with too much currency risk. Private markets have also created sizable maturity mismatches, mostly in the financial system and in foreign exchange. Maintaining fiscal sustainability will be critical to keep interest rates low and avoid the crowding out of private business. While the Stability and Growth Pact will most certainly play a central role in this regard, strong national fiscal frameworks are equally important. The Lisbon agenda is more relevant than ever, as the reforms identified in this process are crucial to counterbalance the negative impact of the crisis on potential growth and to increase the resilience of European economies.

Second, more financial resources have been made available based on a case-by-case basis reflecting the fact that new Member States differ (as illustrated, for example, by their interest rate differentials). The EU Balance of Payments facility was increased in two steps from €12 to €50 billion. As part of a multilateral rescue effort, also involving the IMF and the World Bank and based on a programme including strong conditionality, three countries (Hungary, Latvia and Romania) have tapped this facility so far for a total amount of €14.6 billion. Other international financial institutions (such as the European Investment Bank and the European Bank for Reconstruction and Development) have also stepped up their lending targets for 2009-10 to provide co-ordinated financial assistance mainly through equity and debt finance for private firms and credit lines for banks. The EU also contributed significantly to the increase of financial resources of the IMF in the form of a €75 billion loan. Finally, through advance payments amounting to €2.3 billion, on top of the €4.7 billion normally envisaged in 2009, EU transfers to the new Member States were front-loaded.

Given the importance of strengthening financial markets, the third element of the strategy is to foster co-operation between home and host supervisors and to get parent banks from the old Member States on board in the multilateral support programmes. Home supervisors should assume primary responsibility for ensuring proper recapitalisation, guarantees, and external liquidity for the banking groups as a whole, while host supervisors and macroeconomic policy makers need to focus on macroeconomic stability, adequate oversight of portfolio quality and risk management, and preserving appropriate liquidity and capital buffers. The assistance packages should be flanked by a commitment of parent banks to maintain their exposure to the countries concerned and to recapitalise foreign-based subsidiaries if the results of stress-tests indicate the need for such action. Romania and Hungary were the first EU Member States where this new approach was applied.[1] Enhanced monitoring of parent banks' commitments is undertaken in the context of the reporting requirements under the balance-of-payments assistance. BIS data through the last quarter of 2008 indicates worldwide deleveraging by banks, but this process is least pronounced in new Member States, most likely because of their EU membership.

4 Conclusion

Summing up, the 2004/07 enlargement made the EU more competitive, and it is therefore better positioned to face the new challenges that the current crisis has created. By eliminating trade barriers, gradually allowing higher cross-border labour mobility, promoting financial integration, strengthening institutions, and significantly reducing political risk in the new Member States, enlargement brought about major benefits for both old and new Member States. Notwithstanding these achievements, the financial crisis has revealed major vulnerabilities that are not limited to the new Member States because of the increased interdependencies within the enlarged EU. These vulnerabilities need to be addressed and adequate measures should be taken to limit the setback to real convergence within the EU

Note

[1] See joint EC/IMF press releases of 19 May 2009 on Romania and of 20 May 2009 on Hungary (European Commission and IMF 2009a, b).

33 Trade Shocks, Growth, and Resilience: Eastern Europe's Adjustment Tale*

June 2019

1 The unusual nature of the EU11

Eastern European countries (hereafter, EU11[1])are among the most open economies globally (Figure 1). Their degree of trade openness has increased and the nature of their trade flows has changed rapidly in this millennium in large part because they joined the EU.

Other factors also contributed, such as the reform driven by their transition from central planning to market economies and their preparation for EU membership, as well as global trends that led to the emergence of global value chains (GVCs) in this period.

However, important characteristics of EU11 countries differ from those of other countries with similar degrees of trade openness. Their institutions and their social support systems are less developed than those of small open EU15 countries, and their households have less financial savings to smooth their consumption. As the capacity of an economy to absorb shocks and manage structural changes depends greatly on the quality of its institutions and social support system, this is an important difference within the EU.

On the other hand, similarly open lower-middle income countries in other parts of the world are not part of a supra-national organisation like the EU. They have not adopted the institutional and legal systems of highly developed countries, and they are not part of a single market with free movement of capital and labour. As trade flows are significant-

* Co-author: István Székely (European Commission), Vox CEPR, 28 June 2019.

Figure 1 Export openness

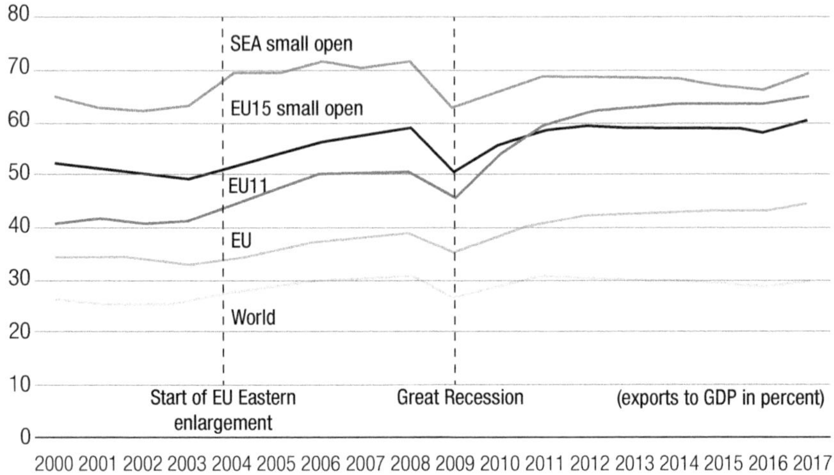

Note: EU15 small open includes Austria, Belgium, Denmark, Finland, the Netherlands and Sweden. SEA small open includes Cambodia, Korea, Malaysia and Vietnam. EU11 includes Bulgaria, Croatia, Czech Republic, Estonia, Hungary, Latvia, Lithuania, Poland, Romania, Slovakia and Slovenia.

Source: Own elaboration from World Bank.

ly influenced by the decisions of firms in the location of their production and labour migration, these characteristics of EU11 countries are highly relevant if we want to understand the impact of trade and other shocks on them.

EU11 countries show many important similarities when it comes to trade integration, most importantly the large share of intra-EU trade and its implications for growth and development. Nevertheless, there are also important differences among these countries regarding their level of development: the composition and quality of their exports, and the degree to which they participate in GVCs.

While most economist would agree on the positive economic effects of closer trade integration at the aggregate level, there is an increasing awareness of the importance of other aspects, such as: a) income distribution and more broadly equal chances and fairness (Milanović 2016, OECD 2019a); b) agglomeration effects and the resulting regional disparities and the increasing prices of housing and regional labour market mismatch (EBRD 2018, Ossa 2019); c) labour migration and the resulting fiscal and social implications (Andor 2019), and d) more lasting impact on societies than previously experienced (Buti 2019).

The recent crisis in Europe demonstrated that the focus on narrowly defined aggregate economic growth and economic resilience is not sufficient to understand the longer-term impact of economic shocks. These shocks stimulate growth but can also trigger a crisis. A broader focus that entails social and political aspects is necessary to understand current developments and to formulate adequate polices (Székely 2019). Put differently, it also matters who benefits and who loses out from rapid trade integration and convergence, who absorbs the hits during a crisis and how, as well as how different groups in society – winners and losers – and society as a whole react to the challenges trade integration brings about.

If left unaddressed, negative social trends created by market forces can reverse reforms, and ultimately lead to an erosion of growth potential and economic resilience (Székely and Ward-Warmedinger 2018). They can also have major implications for political developments at the national and the European level. These may prevent the deepening of European integration.

2 Global value chains and FDI inflows

The emergence of GVCs (Baldwin 2012, Baldwin and Obuko 2019) changed the nature and impact of trade integration. Intra-regional value chains currently predominate (Antras and De Gortari 2017). But as trade costs fall, the global (including European but extra-EU) component of value chains is likely to increase. Similarly, as the service component of GVC increases rapidly, competitive pressure from global markets increases.

GVCs, particularly their service component, are strongly impacted by disruptive technological innovation, with major impact on the skill structure of labour demand. This leads to a constant relocation of the different elements of GVCs. This possibly means reshoring certain parts to EU15, but also the offshoring of core elements from EU15 to EU11 or to countries outside the EU (Mayer and Head 2019). This trend is likely to strengthen in the future.

Trade integration and the creation of GVCs also drove the inflow of FDI into EU11 countries. Imports of modern technology and capital deepening, as well as a rapid modernisation of the product structure, had a positive impact on productivity of local suppliers (Harding and Smarzynska Javorcik 2011, Hagemejer and Muck 2019). This confirms the empirical analysis in Alfaro and Chen (2012), which shows that multinational production causes both knowledge spillovers and factor reallocation in domestic markets. Policies that make this more likely include improving credit access and labour supply (particularly skilled labour) while eliminating regulatory barriers. These are typical of reforms in EU11 countries.

As with trade, many of the underlying forces that promoted FDI were global. Geographical proximity helped, but EU accession provided fertile ground for these forces to work, as it helped improve institutions and create a higher degree of legal certainty for investors (Buiter and Lubin 2019). EU11 countries benefited significantly from the reduction of barriers to trade. Merlevede and Purice (2019) have estimated that supplying inputs to a multinational just across the border enhances productivity only when countries share an EU border. These spillover effects become even stronger when borders become seamless, as is the case in the Schengen Area.

As a result, inward FDI (excluding special purpose entities, or SPEs) relative to GDP in EU11 countries has caught up with the trend observed in the most developed small open economies in the EU and the world (Figure 2). The same however has not been true for outward FDI.

As the overall capital stock relative to GDP is smaller in EU11 than in EU 15 countries, the share of FDI in total stock of capital is higher (Figure 3). Put differently, foreign capital, and thus foreign influence in the corporate sector, is more important in these countries – particularly in their export (tradable) sector. The technological sophistication of FDI is also significantly above the rest of the economy. A large part of R&D takes place in these companies, and they employ a higher share of skilled labour than their share in the private economy.

Proximity to Germany, where companies were among the first in the EU to create GVCs, and to other main European markets, and their abundance of low-cost but relatively skilled labour, made EU11 countries perfect targets for integration into European (mostly German) GVCs.

Figure 2 Stocks of Inward and outward FDI in small open EU15 and EU11 countries

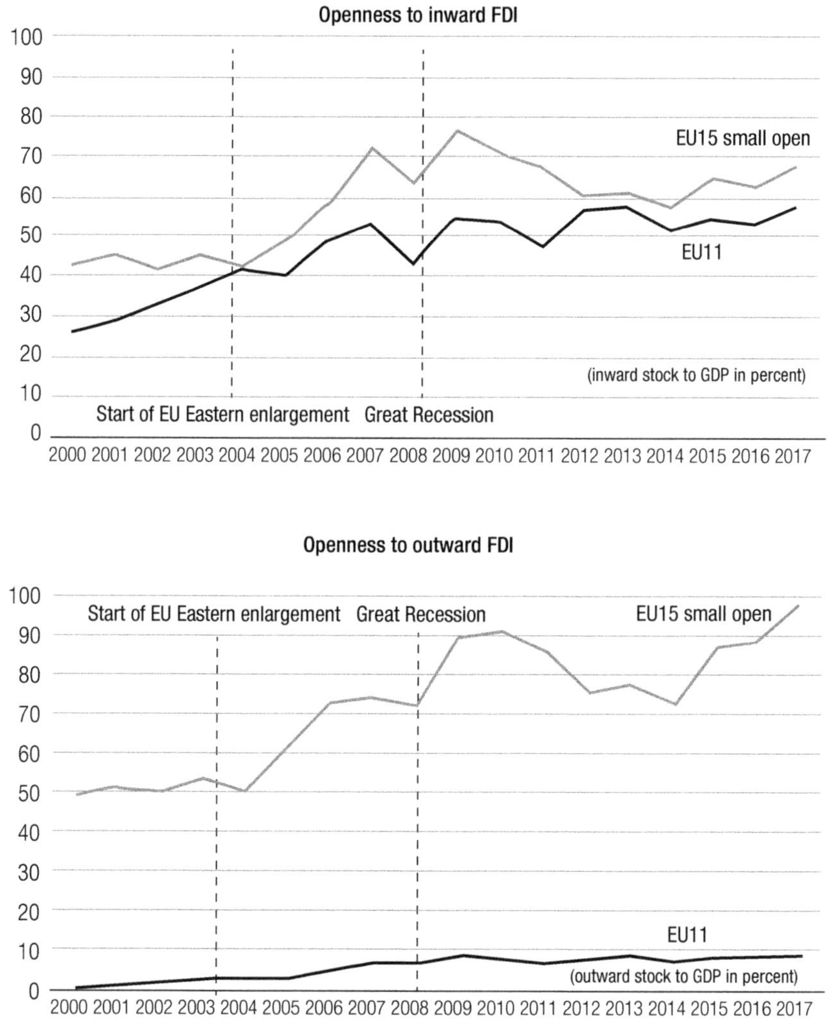

Note: EU15 small open includes Austria, Belgium, Denmark, Finland, the Netherlands and Sweden; EU11 includes Bulgaria, Croatia, Czech Republic, Estonia, Hungary, Latvia, Lithuania, Poland, Romania, Slovakia and Slovenia. Unweighted group averages.

Source: Own elaboration based on data from UNCTAD.

Figure 3 Value added produced by foreign-controlled enterprises

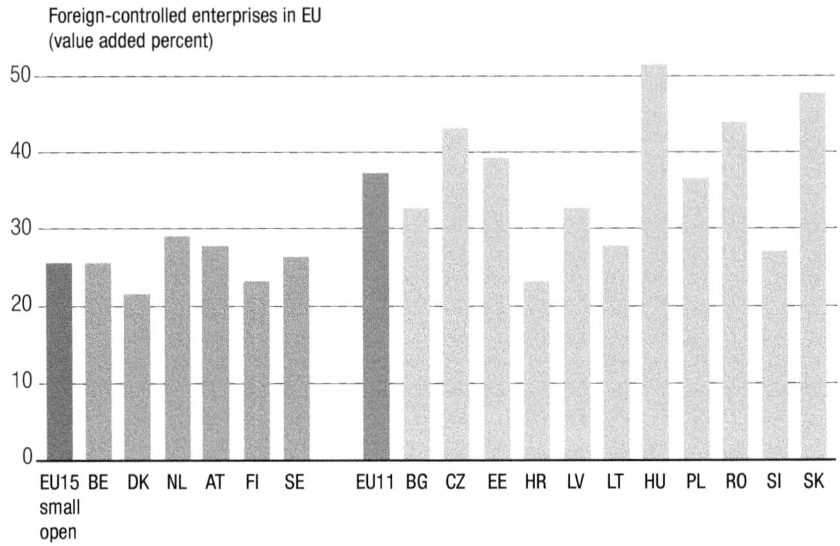

Note: EU15 small open includes Austria, Belgium, Denmark, Finland, the Netherlands, and Sweden; EU11 inlcudes Bulgaria, Croatia, Czech Republic, Estonia, Hungary, Latvia, Lithuania, Poland, Romania, Slovakia and Slovenia. Unweighted group averages.

Source: Eurostat.

They were in the right place, at the right time, and in the right condition to benefit from this global process. Companies benefited increased the closer to the centre of gravity and the better the transport infrastructure. Export-oriented companies, particularly those that are part of a GVC, are predominantly foreign-owned and highly concentrated in certain regions.

Increasing FDI has further accelerated the already strong agglomeration effects and increased the demand for higher skills, and the wage premium they command. FDI is highly concentrated in important urban areas, particularly in capitals and in areas that are close to the main west European manufacturing firms creating GVCs (Szabo 2019).

Figure 4 Regional differences in inward FDI in EU11 countries

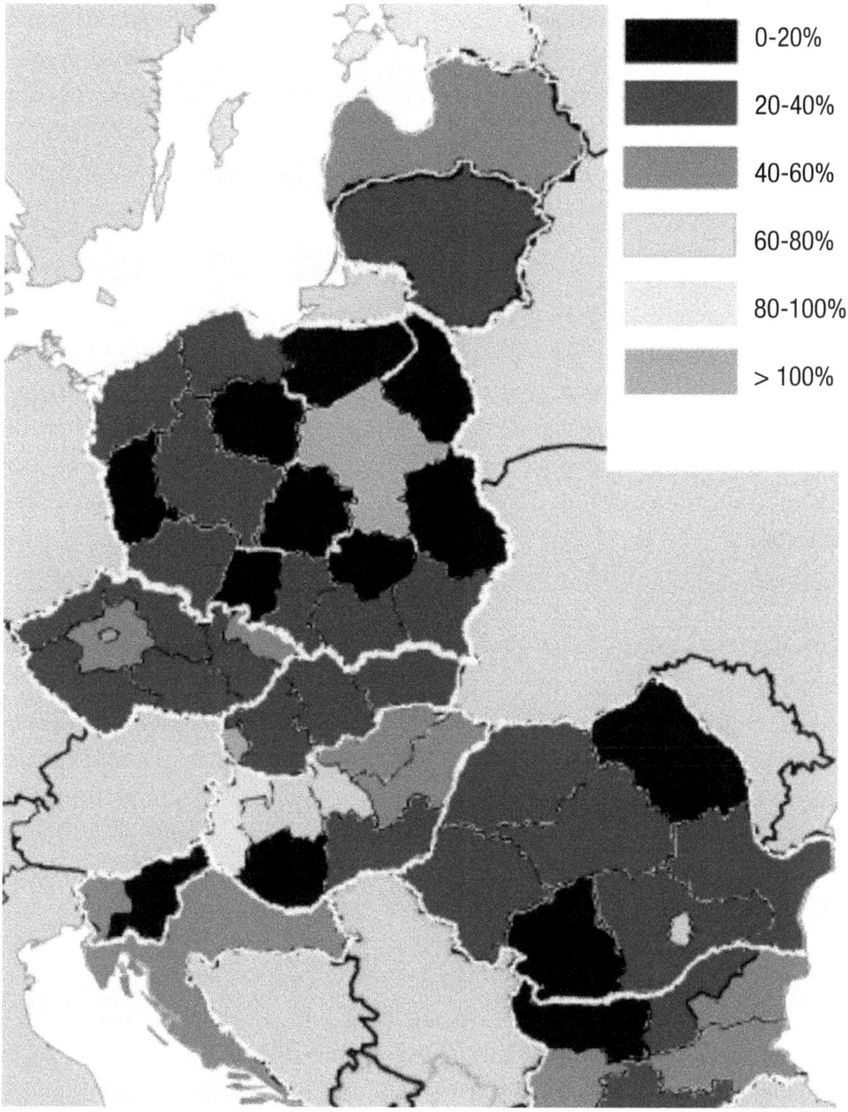

Source: Statistics of national central banks and/or national statistical institutes.

3 Economic responses during the crisis: a model-based simulation

One of the salient characteristics of the crisis experience of EU11 countries was that, in many of these countries, the decline in domestic demand has been much bigger relative to the decline in GDP than in core EU countries. Reasons include credit-driven consumption, and a real estate boom in the run-up to the crisis. At this stage, the real estate boom seems unlikely to be repeated, though in some countries household credit and house prices have picked up sharply.

With the help of calibrated DSGE models, we can pinpoint two important characteristics of EU11 countries that can explain a large part of this phenomenon, and will remain relevant moving forward:a) a large share of foreign ownership of productive capacities, without a comparable magnitude of outward FDI, and b) a large share of hand-to-mouth consumers – that is, people who have little savings and thus have to live on their current income. This is partly a consequence of the first characteristic.

As the charts in Figure 5 show, these characteristics have important implications for how the economy reacts to a global recessionary shock in an EU11 country with high foreign ownership of productive assets relative to an EU15 country, and relative to the hypothetical case of an EU11 country without sizable foreign ownership. Regarding the former comparison, which is more relevant to understanding recent and future economic developments in EU11 countries, domestic demand – particularly consumption – declines more sharply. The decline in investment is bigger, reflecting the accelerator effect of higher consumption decline. Since exports follow similar paths, trade balance paths are very different.

Given the high share of non-tradables in consumptions, a much larger decline in consumption, which is not fully passed on to imports, implies that non-tradable sectors decline much more in an EU11 economy with sizable foreign ownership. Moreover, despite relatively flexible labour markets, hysteresis is still significant. Equally importantly, investments recover more gradually.

In short, growth potential may be further reduced. Thus, not only actual production but also potential output can be more volatile than in more mature economies. As Figure 6 shows, this matches real life.

Figure 5 Response to a recessionary shock in EU11 countries, with and without major foreign-ownership of productive capital

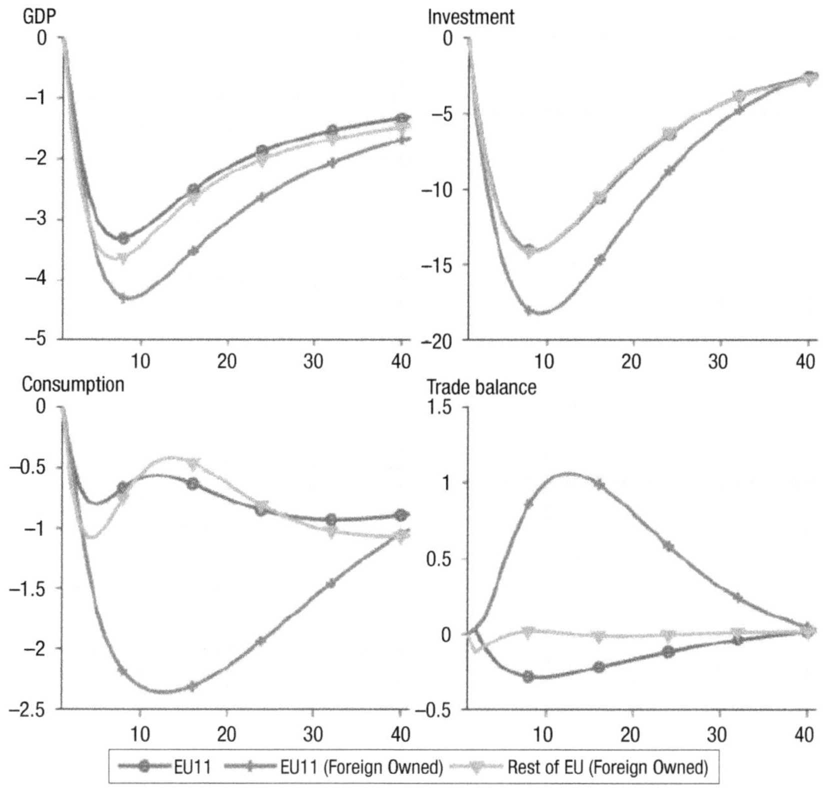

Note: QUEST models calibrated to EU11 and rest of EU countries. The model used for EU11 (Foreign Owned.) assumes a high share of foreign ownership of productive capacities in EU11 countries. Models assume flexible exchange rate regimes.

Source: European Commission, DG ECFIN staff calculations using Quest model.

Figure 6 Potential output growth, 2001-2018

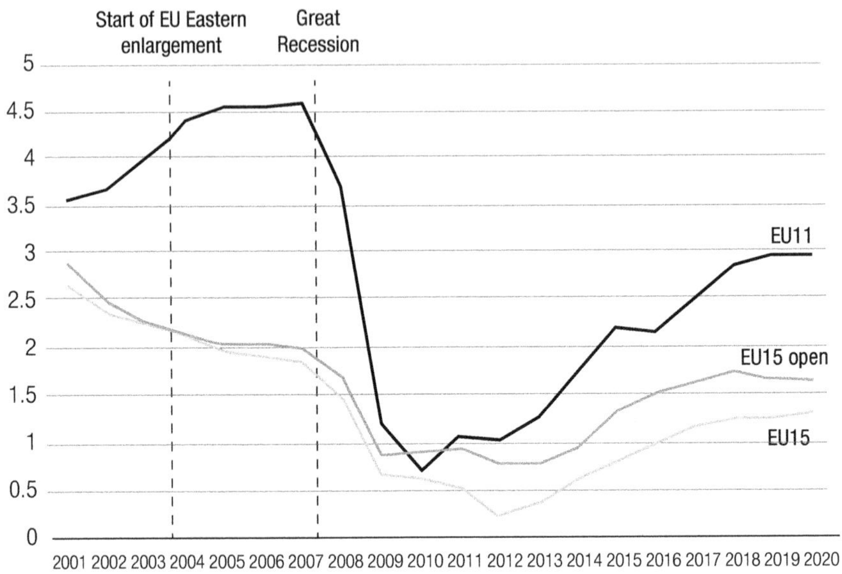

Note: EU15 small open includes Austria, Belgium, Denmark, Finland, the Netherlands and Sweden. EU11 inlcudes Bulgaria, Croatia, Czech Republic, Estonia, Hungary, Latvia, Lithuania, Poland, Romania, Slovakia and Slovenia.

Source: AMECO, European Commission.

4 Adjustment to shocks

A crisis tends to accelerate the relocation of production and reorganisation of GVCs as it puts renewed pressure on multinational firms to reduce costs (Zlate 2016). As Figure 1 showed, after the initial shock, EU11 countries benefited from the relocation effect in the recent crisis because their export openness increased significantly after a temporary crisis-related decline.

Summing these two effects (a bigger shock to the non-tradable sector and a renewed reallocation of modern export-oriented production to EU11 countries), winners win more and losers lose more. The growth potential at the aggregate level may have been largely restored, but the vulnerabilities have increased. In the absence of an efficient state with high-quality public expenditure and social support system, this may destabilise societies and domestic politics. Reversals in reforms in the region are a likely manifestation of this impact (Székely and Ward-Warmedinger 2018).

In Figure 5, the models incorporated exchange-rate flexibility. Flexible exchange rate regimes, especially when they are allowed to work, help absorb external shocks, and can be particularly helpful when external shocks are asymmetric. Model simulations confirm this. Without this, volatility in output increases.

Joining the Eurozone takes away the exchange rate as an adjustment tool, but EU11 countries that have joined the Eurozone had given up this tool beforehand. A major part of the excess output volatility in these countries during the recent crisis was related to the excessive macroeconomic imbalances that had been accumulated in the boom years prior to the crisis.

The focus should be on avoiding this in the future. In fact, the Macroeconomic Imbalances Procedure, and more broadly surveillance under the European Semester process, should help.

Some EU11 countries have not yet joined the Eurozone or expressed interest in doing so. They have floating rates as an adjustment tool at their disposal. It served them well during the crisis (IMF 2016c), though of course could not eliminate the consequences of poor policies.

With foreign exchange-denominated loans greatly reduced, they can use exchange rate flexibility more than before the crisis. But, as in the crisis, exchange rate flexibility will not be a panacea for poor macroeconomic policies and lack of structural reforms. Just the opposite – with poor polices, the volatility of the exchange rate could aggravate the situation.

5 Policy options

Policy options to react to trade shocks can range from the short-termism of protecting rents tied to vested interests, to longer-term strategies of adopting appropriate structural reforms and enhancing the quality of institutions. Structural reforms may help the economy to remain an attractive investment destination, or move up the value chain, leap-frogging others. Currently we see both these responses.

Trade protectionism of any form would be particularly detrimental for EU11 countries (Vandenbussche et al. 2017), and their policymakers understand this well. Less well understood by them is that restrictions on FDI in their non-tradable sectors (such as retail trade) and sectors that are less exposed to competition from the outside (certain service sectors) also reduce their competitiveness and capacity to attract FDI in the tradable sector (Blanchard 2007).

We know the reforms – accelerate human capital accumulation, improve the business environment, strengthen institutions, reduce corruption – that would make a lower-middle income country a more desirable destination for FDI and domestic private investment to enhance their growth potential (EBRD 2019, Berglof et al. 2019). These standard reforms help improve allocative efficiency and innovation. The country-specific recommendations issued to these countries as part of the European Semester process reflect this well (European Commission 2018c), and similar recommendations are given to these countries by other international organisations, such as the IMF, the World Bank, the EBRD, or the OECD.

Less emphasised is the need to strengthen local firms, to help them to become European or global firms, invest abroad, and thus create more symmetry between inward and outward FDI in EU11 countries.

But success on this front may also make EU11 countries more vulnerable to external shocks (Deltuvaitė 2017). Therefore, the right balance and sequencing of reforms is needed to make their convergence not only fast but also sustainable – economically, socially and politically. Given their strong exposure to global shocks, social policy reforms should address all three dimensions – pre-, in- and post-market – to make EU11 countries more socially, and thus politically, more resilient. Institutional reforms are key on all fronts, and can also help to build capacity and use EU funds more efficiently.

Reforms at the EU level that can mitigate the negative impact of outward labour migration on national social security systems, and reforms that can help EU11 countries to strengthen their unemployment systems and diversify away risk related to labour income, are very important areas (Andor 2015, Andor and Pasimeni 2016).

Continued capital imports will remain a necessary element of a development strategy, and risk diversification is essential for such small and highly specialised open economies. The crisis clearly demonstrated the vulnerabilities of debt financing. Thus, reforms that can reduce these vulnerabilities, such as the completion of the Banking Union (which is important also for EU11 countries outside the Eurozone as their banking sectors are dominantly owned by banking groups in the Eurozone). Reforms that can make alternative sources of finance more easily available, such as the completion of the Capital Market Union, are also an essential part of such a strategy.

Note

[1] EU11 are the countries from the Baltics, Central and Eastern Europe, and the Western Balkans that joined the EU since 2004: Bulgaria, Croatia, Czech Republic, Estonia, Hungary, Latvia, Lithuania, Poland, Romania, Slovakia and Slovenia.

34 "Winning the Peace": The Challenge for the G20*

November 2016

1 Introduction

The G20 has emerged as the premier forum for international economic cooperation. The actions taken in 2008-09 by the G20 avoided an outright depression during the financial crisis. But while there was widespread agreement on what to do when the crisis broke out, this has not been the case since 2010, when the economic situation and outlook became increasingly divergent and governments started to have different interpretations of the challenges ahead and of the policy mix to adopt. Going forward, this raises the question of the G20's ability to evolve from a short-term crisis response forum to effectively addressing more long-term challenges. In other words, the G20 should shift its focus from "winning the war" – i.e. responding to the 2008 crisis to avoid the meltdown of the global financial system – to "winning the peace," i.e. overcoming the legacy of the crisis and creating conditions for strong, sustainable, balanced, and, not least, more inclusive growth (Bertoldi et al. 2013, Buti 2016).

Making the case for global cooperation is all the more critical in the context of growing populism and protectionism. This should also be seen in light of the 2016 US election and the incoming administration of President-elect Donald Trump being potentially less internationally engaged.

* Co-author: Helene Bohn-Jespersen (European Commission), Vox CEPR, 25 November 2016.

2 The G20 is lagging behind on its growth ambition

G20 Leaders at the Brisbane Summit in 2014 set out the goal to increase G20 GDP by 2% in five years as a way of getting medium- and long-term growth back on track after the financial crisis. So far G20 members have made important progress but the goal might not be reached by the deadline of 2018. This is to be done by implementing reforms set forward in G20 members' individual growth strategies. Notwithstanding the efforts made, progress differs across sectors and countries, and the G20 is only about halfway there so far – with the impact of reforms set to collectively raise GDP by 1% by 2018. In addition, global growth has been repeatedly revised down. When we apply the 2% growth ambition to the current baseline (see Figure 1) we can see the importance of an integrated approach that combines short-term, medium-term, and long-

Figure 1 Potential impact of structural reforms, and reform gaps

a) Potential impact of structural reforms

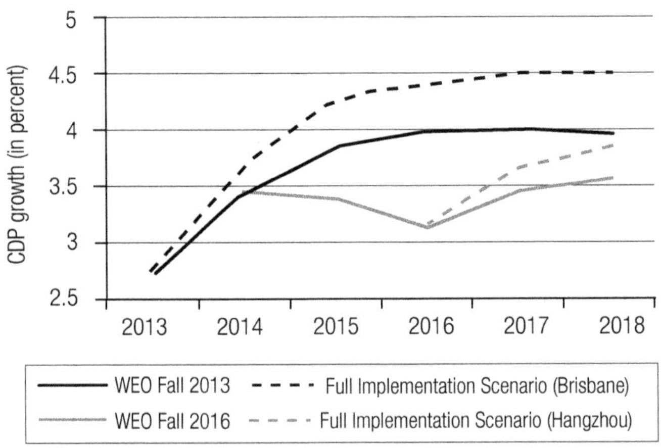

Note: At the Brisbane Summit, the potential impact of the G20 growth strategies was ambitious (the dashed blue line adding 2% of GDP by 2018). Today, due to a number of downward revisions to the baseline and slower than expected implementation of the agreed structural reforms, the full implementation scenario results in a lower impact (the purple lines) implying a significantly lower level of GDP by 2018 taken together.

Source: Calculations by the European Commission based on OECD and IMF assessments.

b) Reform gap

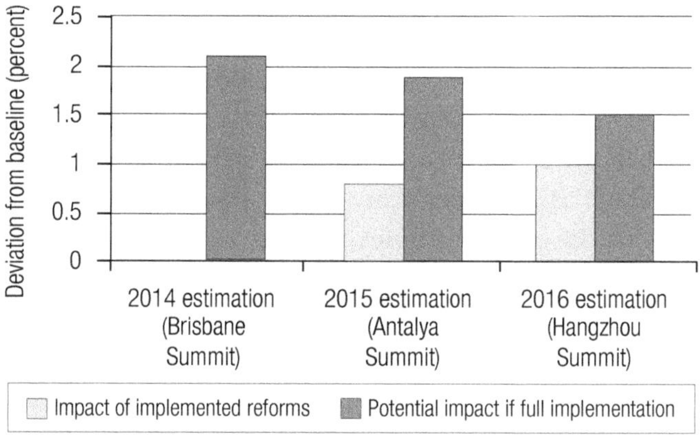

Note: The potential impact of full implementation of the G20 growth strategies by 2018 has diminished over time (from 2.1 to 1.5%) as the pace of implementation has been slower than expected. To deliver the full GDP impact by 2018 as proposed in Brisbane, the G20 growth strategies would have to be fully implemented by end 2016 and additional measures would have to be taken. Currently, implementation is half way and if all outstanding measures are put in place by the end of 2017, GDP could be 0.5% higher.

Source: Calculations by the European Commission based on OECD and IMF assessments.

term measures by using all policy tools – monetary, fiscal, and structural – to ensure the global recovery. At this stage, a complete implementation of all outstanding policy commitments, which is far from given, is estimated to have a collective GDP impact of 1.5% by 2018. It is clear that the lack of reform comes at a cost – while in view of the repeated downward revisions of growth, we would need the opposite, i.e. stepping up the pace of reform.

3 Necessary conditions for G20 to deliver growth

What do we need for a better outcome when discussing the economic policy mix in the G20? When looking at when international policy coordination has been successful in the G20, several shared factors seem to be present. Can we draw some lessons from successful policy coordination, e.g. on ensuring sufficient resources for the IMF, international tax issues, financial regulatory reform, and anti-money laundering? We see four conditions on why the G20 has been able to continue to deliver on tax and financial regulation, but less so on macroeconomic policy.

A first precondition is having an aligned diagnosis of the problem. The IMF in their latest World Economic Outlook projected global GDP growth at 3.1% in 2016 and 3.4% for 2017, which is well below the pre-crisis average of 3.8% per year. At the same time, the OECD has pointed out that the global economy remains in a "low growth trap" with weak global demand, trade, investment, and productivity. This diagnosis of a subpar global recovery, and the reasons behind it, are shared among many G20 members. However, other G20 members view global economic growth in line with the long-term trend, while also taking into account the developments of ageing populations. These diverting views may also reflect that some countries are operating close to potential, while others show slack. In the Eurozone, for example, the economic slack is still significant with weak domestic demand, primarily held back by investment (European Commission 2016e). This leads to different interpretations of the policy actions needed – depending also on whether it relates to an advanced economy, emerging market, commodity exporter, and so on. The diagnosis in other policy areas is more broadly shared, which has led to a greater reform momentum in the areas of international tax transparency or financial sector regulation.

Second, there is a need to be able to show success in implementing commitments. G20 commitments should be sufficiently tractable, controllable, and measurable, allowing members to directly link their commitments to the deliverables/outcomes. In areas such as financial regulation or tax transparency, it is easier to monitor implementation as members are expected to implement the same or similar types of measures – such as specific technical frameworks for enforcement or oversight. This is not as straightforward as when "one-size-fits all" measures are not an appropriate approach. Economic policies are by default country-specific and, as such, conditional on the income level, cyclical position, fiscal space, and societal preferences of the country in question (IMF 2016b). That being said, it is welcome that in 2016 the G20 agreed on an indicator system that helps to assess and monitor the progress of structural reforms, as well as their adequacy in addressing structural challenges, e.g. public investment as a share of GDP, trading across borders, etc. (G20 FWG 2016).

Third, policy coordination needs to be inclusive and relevant for citizens. An example of this kind of coordination by the G20 can be seen on the tax agenda where citizens clearly support fair tax policies, as the profits are used to improve inclusiveness as well as providing much-needed public goods and services. In policy areas such as financial regulation and taxation, the actions taken by the G20 respond to visible economic and political challenges, for example the problems exposed by the Panama leak and the financial crisis. Tackling shared problems brings increased ownership across society.

Finally, the benefits of international coordination need to be visible. Positive spillovers from coordination are a major reason for the existence of the G20 in the first place. In a recent paper, the IMF has underlined again that coordinated policies across major economies amplify the helpful effects of individual policy actions, through positive cross-border spillovers (Gaspar et al. 2016). At the same time, minimising negative spillovers is also a very important objective. In fact, building a climate of trust in regular meetings is already a first step in reaping the benefits of positive spillovers, and could be seen as a welcome insurance policy in addressing sudden global disruptions. A very obvious example of visible positive benefits from coordination is the G20 Leaders' agreement in Brisbane on the new global Common Reporting Standard for Automatic Exchange of Information (AEoI), to be implemented by 2018. Even before its actual implementation, the impacts of AEoI are already being realised. A total of €48 billion in additional revenues were collected by governments through voluntary disclosure in 2014. More will come by progressing with implementation (Gurría 2015). Therefore, benefits of international cooperation and coordination should be clearly communicated to the public, so as to be easily understood and accounted for. This in turn would raise the credibility of the G20, for example by recognising how the G20 managed to avoid a global depression similar to that of the 1930s by agreeing on a coordinated macroeconomic stimulus response. At the same time, it is easier to identify clear economic and financial spillovers than the more indirect ones stemming from the political economy of working together. There, the perceived benefits appear less pronounced more recently.

4 Reformulating international economic policy coordination

Now the question is how to get better traction for the G20 Growth Strategies, which is the main instrument of economic policy coordination. How can the G20 operationalise the four conditions set forward above to ensure more successful economic policy coordination? We outline four suggestions.

First, the diagnosis of the problems facing the global economy should be strengthened at the political level (Bertoldi et al. 2016). G20 Leaders committed to using all policy tools – monetary, structural, and fiscal – to ensure the global recovery. Building on the increased common understanding that monetary policy is overstretched, there is a need to activate structural and fiscal policies. Structural reforms must be pursued more forcefully to close the gap on outstanding commitments at least. G20 members have already committed to structural reforms in their growth strategies – now it is an issue of implementation. Fiscal strategies are equally important to support the common G20 growth objective and address inclusiveness. In this respect, an area for progress could be to integrate concrete steps on fostering the quality and composition of public finances into the growth strategies – as this is as an important consideration as the fiscal stance, especially for countries with fiscal constraints. Overall, stepping-up the quality of public finances fits well within the conditions set forward above for G20 reform delivery, and could be a constructive way forward to improve the global economic policy mix. This could complement the upcoming German G20 Presidency's focus on fiscal resilience by fostering growth and inclusiveness.

Second, tractability could be improved by a better identification of measures and deadlines for delivering on economic policy commitments agreed by G20 members. This could be done by streamlining and focusing the growth strategies while strengthening peer review. Instead of having broad key commitments, each G20 member's growth strategy could be focused on a few measurable, specific and high impact headline policy measures. Tractability could be further underpinned by a different type of peer review, e.g. focusing on policy themes by sharing best practices on key policy actions and the conditions for their effective implementation. Furthermore, a greater transparency about the economic impact of different measures could foster a better understanding of what type of reforms worked, where, and why.

Third, to increase ownership and ensure that the reforms and policies brought forward respond to the real needs of citizens, each G20 member should identify a limited number of reforms themselves (as opposed to the broad number of reform commitments that are contained in the G20 growth strategies at the moment) that have the most substantial growth and/or equity impact. Further, there is room for improving communication to the public regarding the concrete outcomes and benefits of the policy action taken by the G20.

Lastly, we need to show the positive spillovers from international coordination. Areas with clear benefits from international cooperation are, for example, infrastructure investment, investment into the digital economy, or lower or less distortive taxation. Increased cooperation on these issues would have a positive effect on inclusiveness both directly and indirectly as such reforms can target growth, productivity and equity. Simulation results from international policy coordination always depend on the selected model framework and assumptions. That being said, the IMF has also weighed in on the benefits of policy coordination and cooperation to improve outcomes. The IMF found that: "Complementary and mutually reinforcing action in all members would help secure stronger and healthier global growth. The upside scenario shows that tangible benefits for the entire membership in terms of jobs and growth are within reach – global output would be higher by about 2½% in five years and global imbalances would be lowered further by ¾% of GDP. Cumulative gains would be larger. Collective and comprehensive policy action also helps insure against possible welfare losses associated with downside risks" (IMF 2012a). Analyses by the European Commission and other institutions show that there can be positive spillover effects from simultaneous reform implementation and from higher public investment in countries with low debt and deficit levels under the current monetary policy constraints (Varga and Int'Veld 2014, In't Veld 2016, Blanchard et al. 2016).

In conclusion, to win the peace, G20 members as well as G20 Presidencies have to recognise the need for integrating prior policy commitments with new priorities, and ensure that the focus is kept on a limited number of deliverables to which all G20 members can agree. For the upcoming German G20 Presidency, this means linking the Hangzhou commitments to their overarching priority of resilience. Broadening the discussion to also include elements on the composition and quality of public finances would help build greater support for debt sustainability, as well as address growth and equity challenges. The G20 needs to walk the talk with regards to the three-pronged approach to shift the burden away from monetary policy and use all policy tools to ensure a strong, more sustainable and better balanced recovery, in a way that fosters inclusiveness to a much greater extent. Only by addressing protectionism and populism head-on can the G20 win the peace. That requires that all members remain fully engaged.

35 Governing a Fragmented World Economy: Towards Inclusive Multilateralism*

July 2018

1 Clouds are gathering on the outlook

In November 2008 the international community came together in Washington to react to the global economic and financial crisis. In the aftermath of the G20 summit, the concerted actions of the G20 members to stimulate their economies and refrain from protectionist measures were crucial in avoiding another Great Depression (Summers and Schoenfeld 2012). The global economy returned to positive growth again by 2010. But that consensus did not last. Since 2010 governments started to differ in their readings of the origins of the crisis, the challenges ahead, and the policies to adopt, which in turn led to a suboptimal global policy mix. Global growth was slow in picking up afterwards, and while it accelerated in 2017, it is now under the threat of increased downside risks (IMF 2018).

2017 marked a positive turning point for the global economy, with global output expanding by 3.9%. Growth has been broad-based and synchronised across the world. The EU economy grew at its fastest rate in ten years at 2.4%, the US and Japan also grew strongly. Emerging economies did well: China and India grew by 6.9% and 6.4% respectively. In the 2018 Commission Summer Forecast (European Commission 2018g), we project a further acceleration in global growth to 4.2% in 2018 and 4.1% in 2019. While the headline figures are still positive, much has

---

* Co-author: Mirco Tomasi (European Commission), Vox CEPR, 20 July 2018.

changed recently. The US policy mix has become pro-cyclical due to a significant fiscal expansion. Trade tensions are escalating on the back of China's over-capacity, which prompted the US decision to impose import tariffs on steel and aluminium. These developments have added to the already existing uncertainties related to geopolitical risks and have greatly increased the possibility of a slowdown in global growth.

Such developments build on growing institutional, economic and social fragmentation across the world which set in during the financial crisis.

2 Institutional, economic and social fragmentation remain pervasive

In the wake of the crisis, the G20 emerged as the premier forum for international economic and financial cooperation around the world. In parallel, a host of new institutions have been created often with overlapping mandates and no clear roadmap for cooperation. For example, new multilateral development banks (MDBs) were created in Asia (the Asia Infrastructure Investment Bank) and by the BRICS countries (New Development Bank), and regional financing arrangements became more prominent in providing emergency liquidity alongside the IMF - this has increased the financial firepower but also the complexity of the system. The WTO effectiveness has been weakened by the adoption of unilateral trade measures in some countries and by the failure to agree on new nominations to the Appellate Body. Global efforts to tackle climate change have been compromised by the US decision to abandon the UN Paris Agreement on Climate Change. Tensions among world leaders were also manifest at the last G7 Summit in Canada in June 2018. There is now the risk that the G20 might fail to "win the peace," i.e. to deliver the necessary public good of global economic policy cooperation in the post-crisis world (see chapter 34).

Since the outbreak of the financial crisis, global imbalances have been reduced but they remain considerable. Two developments stand out. First of all, emerging countries now have, on aggregate, current account deficits (Figure 1). Large current account surpluses can now be found among advanced economies. The US records a persistent current account deficit which may now further increase due to pro-cyclical fiscal policies. Second, the single largest source of external surpluses is now the Eurozone.

Figure 1 Global imbalances: Current accounts as a percentage of world GDP

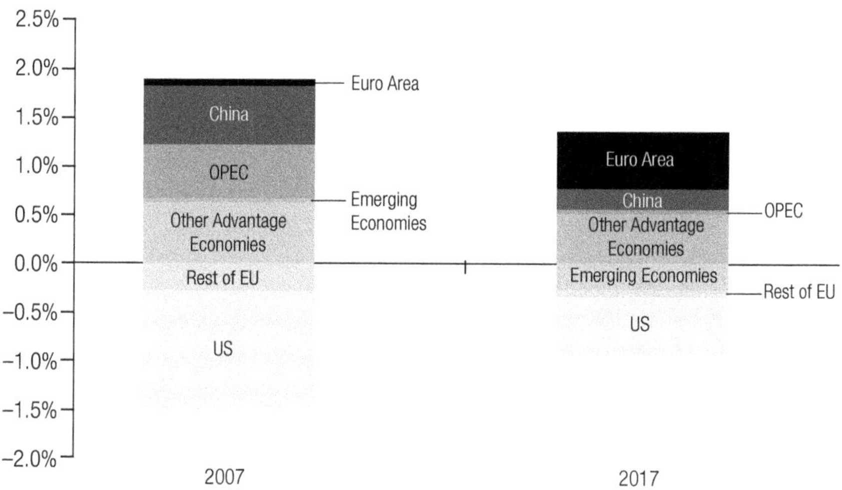

Source: Own calculations based on IMF WEO Database and World Bank Database.

This is due in part to an asymmetric rebalancing within the monetary union, where countries that used to have current account deficits prior to the crisis have turned them into surpluses, but pre-crisis surplus countries have remained in surplus and in some case it has increased. These developments imply potential fragilities for emerging economies and rising trade tensions among advanced countries.

Social fragmentation has started to receive more attention recently (Figure 2). While inequality between emerging and advanced countries has been reduced, inequalities within countries have surged since the 1980s. The increase in income inequality at global level hides important differences across countries. In emerging economies inequalities are higher but they have slowly been reduced over the past 30 years. Conversely, advanced countries such as the old Member States of the EU and the US have seen income inequality increasing. Globalisation and trade integration have contributed to the increase in income inequality through skill-based and geographical distributional impacts. Nation states and multilateral institutions failed to adequately counter these trends so far. Socioeconomic and regional inequalities fuel popular discontent and opposition to economic openness and international cooperation, leading governments to revert to inward-looking policies and protectionism.

Figure 2 Social fragmentation: the "Whale Graph" of global inequality

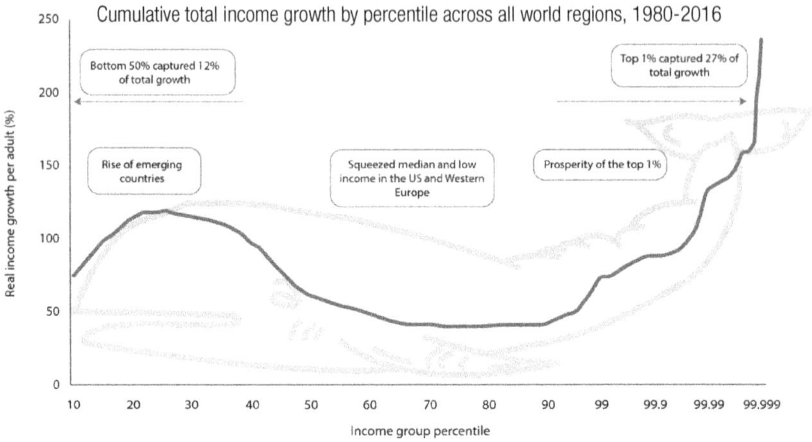

Source: Own calculations based on World Inequality Database.

3 What kind of multilateralism?

Multilateralism should be seen as a means to an end, a vehicle to achieve certain goals, not as a goal in itself. Economic integration is making spillovers across countries more and more relevant. In addition, there are a number of common policy challenges that require international cooperation and that cannot be dealt with by individual countries working in isolation, such as demographics, migration, climate change, and the widening inequalities that feed citizens' disenchantment with international economic integration. A multilateral approach to tackle these challenges is more effective than a proliferation of bilateral deals since it creates synergies and solves coordination problems, achieving positive-sum results.

The starting point is to prioritise greater inclusiveness. Economic integration has helped the world to grow more quickly, but not enough attention was paid to the geographical and distributional impacts that occurred in parallel (Rodríguez-Pose 2018). While domestic policies play an important role in reducing inequalities, distributional impacts have not been sufficiently integrated into global policy strategies. For example, fair and clear rules in trade, taxation and foreign investments have not been consistently applied. This led to blatant cases of tax avoidance as well as distortions to international competition that have direct impacts on citizens in terms of employment and dislocation. This is also one of the triggers of protectionist tendencies; economic openness can only be sustained if it is underpinned by fairness (Dervis 2016).

A growth-friendly correction of macroeconomic imbalances remains a necessary precondition for a sustainable global expansion. Excessive global imbalances are a recurrent threat to global economic stability and their resolution is consistently asymmetric due to different incentives to adjust in current account deficit and current account surplus countries. In the absence of a self-correcting mechanism, global economic policy coordination needs to be stepped up. This is not just a question of trade policies but also, and most importantly, of capital flows which today determine the direction of current accounts. Therefore, global imbalances should continue to be a concern of finance ministers as they relate closely to saving and investment decisions (Pettis 2018). The G20 is the right platform to develop an agreed diagnosis of the problems and devise globally consistent policy responses. Reducing global imbalances will take away another of the root causes of today's trade tensions. At the same time, the Global Financial Safety Net needs be further strengthened (IMF 2016a), ensuring a central role for the IMF – with adequate resources – in close collaboration with the various regional financing arrangements that have been set up in recent years.

The implementation of a global policy agenda requires strong multilateral development banks in order to deliver global public goods and put into practice internationally agreed priorities. Their fragmentation since the crisis offers opportunities as more sources of finance become available but also challenges as different mandates may be competing or overlapping (Bhattacharya et al. 2018). For this reason, the G7 in 2017 agreed on principles for effective coordination which call on Multilateral Development Banks (MDBs) to harmonise to the highest standards their environmental, social and fiduciary safeguards, as well as their standards on tax compliance, money laundering and the financing of terrorism. The G20 could now take the lead in rolling out these principles by becoming the "steering committee" for MDBs, ensuring their full implementation.

4 What should be the role of Europe?

The EU can play a leading role on the global stage to uphold commitments towards an open and fair global international order with a rules-based trading system, the protection of environmental and social standards and efforts to reduce income and geographical inequalities (European Commission 2017b).

In order to play such a role, the EU should however first of all strengthen its internal cohesiveness (Cœuré 2018b). Europe can only be strong if all its Member States share the same values and pursue common interests. In particular, EU countries need to overcome the "reverse creditor paradox": external surpluses should be seen as a source of fragility rather than a source of strength since they amplify the exposure of the region to external shocks and exacerbate global imbalances. Given its size and importance, the internal policies of the EU in fact have a global dimension. In this vein, policies in areas such as research and development, digitalisation, the Capital Markets Union, defence and security are clearly indispensable to address challenges and counter threats that are too important to be tackled at the country level. Similarly, the completion of the EMU is also fundamental to enhance the unity, resilience, efficiency, and democratic accountability of the Eurozone. By strengthening the EMU, Europe would become more resilient and a stronger global player

Second, the EU should leverage its existing strengths. The EU has the capacity to lead by example on many fronts such as climate change, social and environmental standards, data privacy rules and so on. For example, the new EU General Data Protection Regulation has recently been implemented with the aim of protecting all EU citizens from privacy and data breaches. Another example would be a more strategic use of the Multiannual Financial Framework (MFF) of the EU budget in particular to tackle pressing challenges such as migration. The Commission proposal for the next MFF 2021-27 is a step in the right direction. The proposed allocation for "migration and border management" more than doubles compared to the previous MFF, reaching nearly €35 billion. (European Commission 2018b).

Third, the EU should proactively seek global solutions to global challenges. Tax avoidance, for example, has become much easier in a globalised world and the international community needs to tackle this by fully implementing its commitments on base erosion and profit shifting. A global solution should be found to the issue of taxation of the digital economy. As a first step, in March 2018, the European Commission presented two proposals for the fair and effective taxation of the digital economy. The first proposal is a comprehensive solution to adapt corporate tax rules to digital economy, notably by allowing Member States to tax businesses with a significant digital presence in their jurisdictions. The second proposal is an interim tax on revenue generated by particular digital activities. These proposals should be seen as steps towards finding a global solution as the OECD work on the topic is expected to be finalised by 2020.

Finally, the EU should contribute to avoiding a protectionist race to the bottom (Rodrik 2018) similar to the one that occurred in the 1930s which gave rise to the Great Depression (see Figure 3). This can be done, for example, by focusing on modern trade agreements – such as those that the EU has concluded with Canada, Mexico and Japan – that reflect an inclusive economic agenda making provision for workers' rights, environmental protection, responsible investments, food security, consumer protection, and management of natural resources. Going forward, a reform of the WTO could also be useful in order to update this insti-

Figure 3 World trade as a share of global GDP, comparing Great Depression and Great Recession

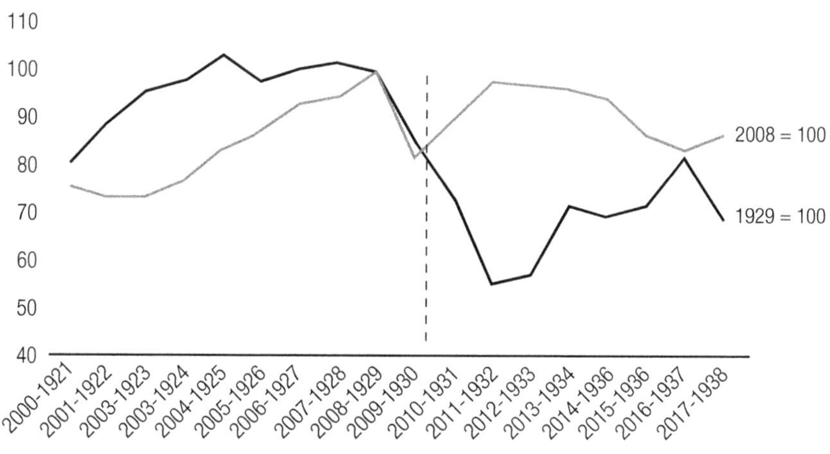

Source: 1921-1938: own calculations based on dataset from Klasing and Milionis (2014); 2000-2017: own calculations based on WTO and IMF WEO.

tution and to ensure an internal level playing field continues. Following the conclusions of the European Council (European Council 2018), the European Commission will now work on a comprehensive approach to improving, together with like-minded partners, the functioning of the WTO in crucial areas such as (i) more flexible negotiations; (ii) new rules that address current challenges, including in the field of industrial subsidies, intellectual property and forced technology transfers; (iii) reduction of trade costs; (iv) a new approach to development; (v) more effective and transparent dispute settlement, including the Appellate Body, with a view to ensuring a level playing field; and (vi) strengthening the WTO as an institution, including in its transparency and surveillance function.

5 Conclusions

The world is more interconnected than it has ever been – it is neither possible to address important global challenges in an isolated manner nor to rely on the status quo of international economic governance. Multilateralism should be seen as a tool to deliver global public goods and internalise spillovers. The growing discontent with globalisation should therefore be reflected in the policy content of our multilateral efforts, while greater attention will have to be paid to the issue of inclusiveness and a better sharing of the benefits of economic growth. Europe can and should play a leading role in revamping international economic cooperation, overcoming institutional, social and economic fragmentations and keeping the global economy open, in the knowledge that we all benefit from it.

36 The International Role of the Euro: From Monetary Independence to Monetary Sovereignty*

February 2019

1 The international role of the euro: time to revisit the benign neglect

Twenty years ago, the creation of the euro brought a major change to the international monetary system (Bénassy-Quéré et al. 1998). At the beginning, the ECB and the European Commission focused on building the necessary structures to ensure the smooth functioning of the "new born" currency in the Eurozone. Although Europe's common currency instantly became the second-most important global currency upon its creation, the internationalisation of the euro was not a primary concern for policymakers at the time. The ECB and the Commission were therefore content to follow a policy to "neither hinder nor promote" the internationalisation of the euro.

Twenty years later, however, much has changed and it is time to revisit Europe's traditional "benign neglect" towards the international use of the euro. We argue that the balance between the benefits of having a widely used international currency and the costs that arise from the responsibilities involved has shifted in the direction of the former.

On the cost side, some originally feared that a greater internationalisation of the euro would weaken Europe's "monetary independence." Two arguments supported this position: the first is a variant of the so-called "Triffin dilemma," which posits that a dominant global currency neces-

* Co-Author: Lourdes Acedo Montoya (European Commission), Vox CEPR, 1 February 2019.

sarily entails a large current account deficit; the second is based on the loss of control of monetary aggregates when a currency is widely used by non-residents.

If the validity of the Triffin dilemma is today a subject of debate, the tension between short-term domestic priorities and longer-term global interests remains valid, and so is the risk that global demand for safe assets remains dangerously unsatisfied or forces excessive US external debt. Independent monetary policy is about controlling the path of short-term interest rates, which in turn affects the domestic savings and investment balance as well as monetary developments. Higher foreign demand for euro-denominated assets would likely render monetary policy transmission more difficult as domestic investments would become easier to finance by foreign savings.[1] Monetary aggregates would also increasingly reflect foreign demand for euro bills and bank deposits. The argument about monetary aggregates is, however, less relevant today than at the time of the launch of the euro. The ECB has, by now, accumulated longer-term experience with monetary analysis and has developed a broad set of tools and instruments to conduct such analysis. These should allow it to extract from the monetary data relevant signals for longer-term inflation developments in the Eurozone even in the context of an expanded international role for the euro.

Moreover, the way in which the international monetary system works has changed and thus the modalities through which the Triffin dilemma operates, with the evolution of global governance towards a more multipolar system (Buti 2017). Bordo and McCauley (2017) consider, in particular, that the view that a currency's reserve role requires current account deficits is flawed. This is because it assumes that "only US liabilities can provide US dollar reserves," while in fact, "borrowers resident outside the United States widely use the dollar to denominate debts that are in turn largely held by non-resident creditors." Moreover, this argument is empirically questionable. In fact, the current account position reflects other factors beyond the exchange rate, such as the fiscal position, demographics, net external liabilities, GDP per capita, financial development, or current account openness.

In terms of benefits, greater international use of the euro would be positive for the Eurozone in two mutually reinforcing ways. First of all, it would strengthen "monetary sovereignty" by making it possible for European companies to trade around the world without the threat of extraterritorial actions by third-party jurisdictions to disrupt payments. Another valuable benefit would come from "scale effects." Wider global use of the euro by, and between, third countries would improve the liquidity of, and preference for, euro assets. It would thus improve funding and trading costs for the Eurozone and enhance the Eurozone's resilience to financial shocks. A more liquid monetary system improves market efficiency and reduces transaction costs and risks of disruptions (Krugman 1984, ECB 2017b). A larger and more robust monetary system should also be less vulnerable to country- or institution-specific shocks, as it reduces their relative significance. In addition, private agents also stand to benefit from lower exchange rate risk and lower hedging requirements, as they would be able to invoice and settle more trade-related payments in euros. Wider use of the euro would also imply lower funding costs in euros ("exorbitant privilege") for domestic private and public debt issuers (Gourinchas and Rey 2007). Moreover, domestic financing conditions in euros could become less dependent on global swings in risk sentiment. Fiscal revenues for the public sector (national central banks) would also arise from a broader use of Euronotes internationally (i.e. seigniorage).

If there is an extensive economic literature on the benefits of scale effects, the importance of monetary sovereignty has only recently come to the forefront. This is because the economic and financial crisis has brought important changes to the global economy and governance. New technologies and economic powers have emerged. The world is more diversified, with some pointing to the emergence of a multipolar system of several currencies (Eichengreen et al. 2017). The dominance of the US dollar remains unchallenged, but China in particular has been very active in promoting the internationalisation of its currency.[2] More recently, the US' withdrawal from the Iran nuclear deal and its subsequent reinstatement of sanctions, together with increased strains in global governance and trade, have exposed global vulnerability to the US dollar's international dominance. Thus, greater international use of the euro would also have benefits for the global economic system. In the first place, a credible alternative to the US dollar system would defeat the purpose of unilateral actions via dollar payment systems, as market operators would have other choices. On the economic side, the presence of a competitor currency would reduce monopolistic rents from global users of dollar-based payment systems, such as by correspondent banks, card payment providers, or reserve asset issuers.

In sum, the first two decades of the euro have shown that there remains an untapped potential for the euro to play a stronger international role. The benefits of such a role are becoming clearer, while the original fears of losing control over monetary aggregates today appear overstated. The figures on the international use of the euro show that despite its young age, the currency is already an important international player. However, in a changing global context, policymakers can help strengthen Europe's monetary sovereignty by giving the euro the means to play a larger role in the international arena with the support of market participants.

2 The international role of the euro in figures: untapped potential?

The euro has been the second-most important world currency since its creation, despite the economic and financial crisis somewhat stalling its international progression. It is a currency that matters to the international monetary system and plays a crucial role in our neighbourhood. The robustness of the Eurozone together with trade and geo-political linkages has led about 60 countries to tie their currencies in one way or the other to the euro.

The euro is used as a global means of exchange and a store of value. The role of the euro as a global reserve currency has been broadly stable over the past 20 years at about 20%. This is one third of the US dollar's rate, which has been losing ground since the 9/11 terrorist attacks. Other currencies, like the Japanese yen, the pound sterling or the Chinese renminbi, are very distant followers to the US dollar and the euro, with only a marginal use as reserve currencies. However, the role of other currencies, notably the Chinese renminbi, is rising as reserve holders diversify their portfolios to reflect, for example, China's growing share of global GDP. Regarding debt issuance, by end 2017 about 20% of international debt issuance was denominated in euros, well below pre-crisis rates. Debt issuance in US dollars has followed the opposite path over the same period (Figure 1).

Over recent years, the ECB established a number of currency swap lines with major central banks as a liquidity backstop to reassure banks in case of market impairments.[3] Thus, the euro also plays an important role in safeguarding global financial stability.

Figure 1 Currency composition: US dollar and euro shares in foreign currency reserves and outstanding international debt securities

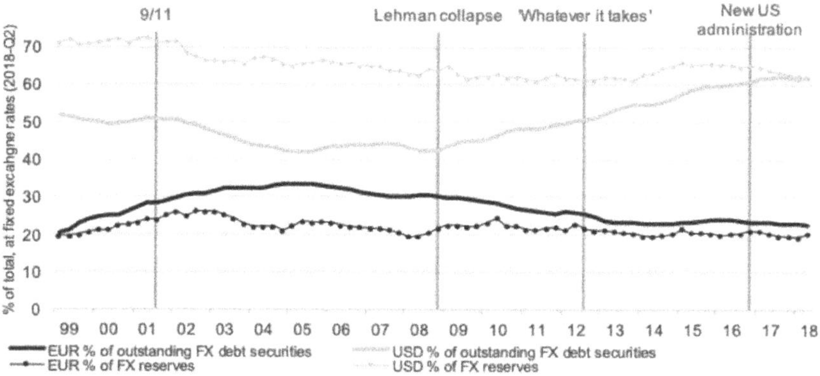

Source: Own elaboration from IMF COFER and BIS international debt securities (all issuers, currencies and sectors, international markets).

Although the euro's role in international payments would seem on a par with the US dollar (Figure 2), the data is influenced by intra-EU payments. Moreover, despite its relatively wide use in international payments, less than 60% of the Eurozone's exports outside the EU are actually invoiced in euros, in contrast with the US where about 90% of exports are invoiced in US dollars.

Figure 2 Currency composition of global payments

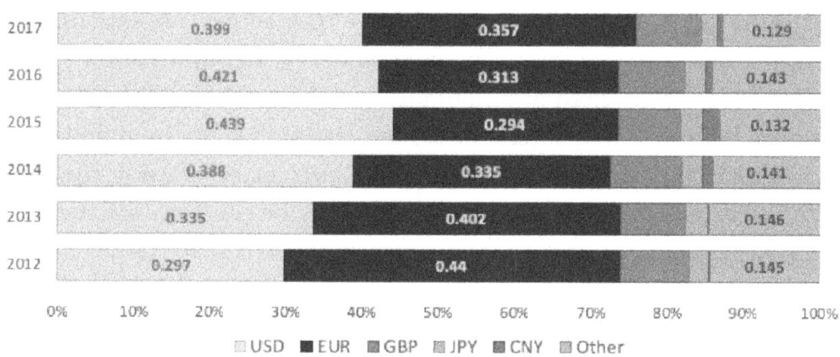

Source: Own elaboration from SWIFT.

3 Determinants of the global use of a currency: where does the euro stand?

The decision to use a particular currency is made by market participants, in the financial markets, by central banks and by exporters and importers of goods and services. The relative attractiveness of a currency depends on factors such as the size of its domestic economy; the credibility of its institutions; the presence of deep, liquid and free financial markets; well-functioning infrastructures for clearing and settling payments; as well as an established track record of economic and financial stability. The euro scores quite well on many of these criteria, a fact which is reflected in its relatively wide use abroad. However, there are factors that hinder its wider internationalisation.

In particular, there is less liquidity in euros due to macroeconomic, institutional, and market-related factors. The euro is a young currency, the architecture of the EMU is still incomplete, and there is only a limited pool of safe assets denominated in euros. Market factors relate to the dominance of US- and UK-based banks and exchanges, as well as underdeveloped payments systems that constrain the Eurozone's monetary sovereignty. Thus, policymakers can influence the international appeal of the euro by strengthening its underlying economic fundamentals as well as its institutional framework and financial infrastructures.

When market participants choose one currency over another, network effects play a crucial role. The more a currency is used, the more likely it is to be chosen by other market participants. Today the prevailing network effects still favour the US dollar in many cases.

For example, in foreign exchange market transactions the euro plays a strong role on the continent but minor one in other world regions. Outside of the EEA, almost all cross-currency transactions are settled in US dollars (Figure 3). For virtually every currency, bid-ask market spreads vis-à-vis the dollar are tighter than for the euro, reflecting liquidity. This is especially true in non-interbank trades, leading to persistent dollar "triangulations" (i.e. conversion between two currencies by using the dollar as an intermediary). One practical reason may be the dominance of US- and UK-based banks in the foreign exchange market, as market-makers, they tend to favour the US dollar. These actors also dominate foreign loans in developing countries (in Africa, for example). Therefore, in some cases, loans granted in local currencies are followed by large forex activity with the US dollar or the British pound.

Figure 3 Currency pairs (volume as % of total FX volume, net-net basis 2016)

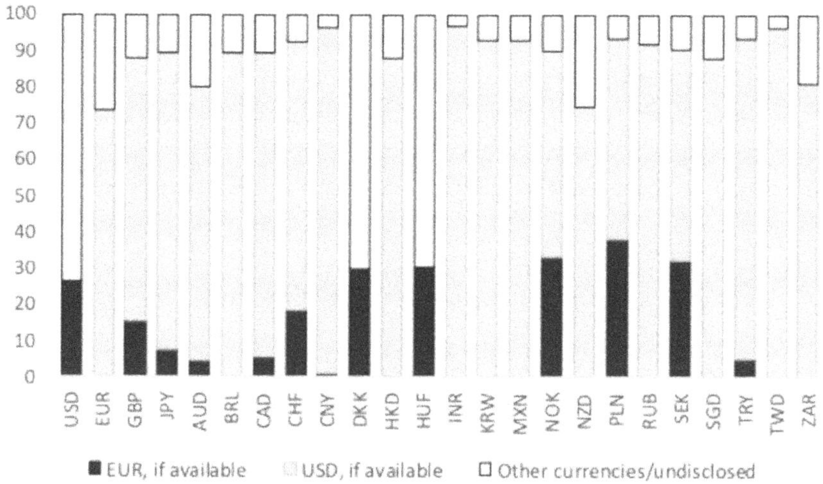

Source: Own elaboration from BIS OTC derivatives statistics.

Another example concerns exports (Goldberg and Tille 2016, Gopinath and Stein 2018). A company in the Eurozone may decide to invoice in a currency other than the euro based on macro considerations, which are linked to the possibility of insuring and hedging against exchange rate movements. These financial products tend to be more easily available in US dollars, given the liquidity and depth of dollar-denominated financial instruments. Micro and strategic determinants relate to the demand elasticity and the competitive structure of the market, the size of the importers and the competitors, which may push European companies to use their currency instead of the euro.

With no Eurozone-wide safe asset, the safe-haven status of US treasuries is a permanent feature that raises demand for the dollar, particularly during downturns when there are flight-to-safety capital flows. A temporary factor at present is related to the fact that today's US monetary policy implies that dollar-denominated financial assets provide better returns.

Finally, history/inertia also plays a significant role both at global and sectoral level (Krugman 1984). The prominence of the dollar is sustained by the central role that the US has played over decades in the global financial, trade and monetary system. At the sectoral level, trade in commodities is dominated by the US dollar despite the EU being the largest energy importer, with an annual energy import bill that averaged €300 billion in the last five years, around 85% paid in US dollars. But history is not static, Eichengreen et al. (2017) argue that changes in technology, trade and finance structures have a bearing on the international monetary system and that several international reserve currencies can coexist.

4 Towards a stronger international use of the euro

The first 20 years of the euro has been a remarkable success story. Europe's single currency has brought stable prices, lower transaction costs, more economic integration and competition to all its members. The institutional set-up of the Eurozone is unique compared to other currency unions, with a centralised monetary policy and decentralised economic and budgetary policies. This makes coordination of its Member States' fiscal and economic policies crucial to ensuring the proper functioning of its monetary union. At the height of the economic and financial crisis, policymakers took decisive actions to strengthen the Eurozone's architecture and policy coordination. Moreover, the ECB has acquired global renown for its conduct of monetary policy. The euro may be a young currency but it is mature enough to take a more decisive international stand to buttress monetary sovereignty.

There is no silver bullet that would rapidly increase use of the euro abroad. This requires a comprehensive package of measures and time. The Commission proposed on 5 December 2018 a number of avenues to explore and develop together with market participants (European Commission 2018i).

Starting at the foundations, completing the EMU should be a priority as it would cement the credibility of the Eurozone. The Banking Union, in particular finalising the backstop to the Single Resolution fund and the European Deposit Insurance Scheme (EDIS), would reinforce financial stability by further reducing the exposure of banks to their national sovereigns. A deepened Capital Markets Union would provide more diversified and liquid financial markets allowing for more private sector risk-sharing.

The euro would be more attractive internationally if there were a sufficient supply of euro-denominated safe assets, an important disadvantage today compared to the US. Safe assets allow an efficient functioning of financial systems and the development of capital markets, reducing financing costs for the economy. Euro-denominated safe assets would contribute towards the development of the European financial sector in general and the global relevance of European financial regulation, as well as EU-based payment systems. Several options for a Eurozone safe asset have been put forward with different design features (European Commission 2011c), ranging from full to partial common issuance, some based on mutualisation and others entailing no joint liabilities, but there has been very limited political traction to date.

Other measures aim to make it easier for market participants to use the euro by insulating against extraterritorial unilateral actions by third country jurisdictions. For instance, the Commission's December Communication proposes to strengthen the liquidity and resilience of European market infrastructures, create a fully integrated instant payment system in the EU, and increase market liquidity for euro currency pairs other than euro/dollar.

Other actions may have a smaller quantitative impact but are qualitatively important, such as encouraging European bodies to increase their share of debt denominated in euros or further developing Europe's economic diplomacy to promote the use of the euro in payments and as a reserve currency. Moreover, the Commission also proposes to provide technical assistance to facilitate developing countries' access to the Eurozone payments system and, hence, support trade.

Finally, in spite of their position as large buyers or major producers, European businesses still trade in US dollars in key strategic markets (energy, commodities, transport), often even between themselves. This exposes businesses to currency and political risks. Working with market operators is, in this case, essential to identify concrete actions that could be taken to encourage the use of the euro.

5 Conclusion

The Eurozone has full "monetary independence," but "monetary sovereignty" needs to be built on the basis of a reassessment of the benefits and costs attached to the international role of the euro. The world that we have known, characterised by the economic and technological superiority of western countries and the construction of a law-based multilateral order, is changing with the global relevance of China and competing approaches towards multilateralism. Europe cannot afford to remain on the side-lines if it wants to continue to shape the world according to its values and visions. This implies a larger role for Europe on the international scene, and the euro has a role to play too. The economic costs attached to an international role of the currency should be reassessed. On the one hand, fears about an outright appreciation of the euro with the corresponding deterioration of the current account should be evaluated against a broader assessment of the balance of payments. On the other hand, fears about losing control over monetary aggregates maybe overstated given the availability of new monetary policy tools.

A greater global role for the euro implies greater global responsibilities. The ECB, for example, would need to consider the impact that its monetary policies could have on countries outside the Eurozone as well as within, as funding costs in these markets could become more dependent on financing conditions in the Eurozone (Gourinchas and Rey 2013, Farhi and Maggiori 2016). Moreover, Europe would have to be ready to provide insurance to the world during crises by ensuring a sufficient supply of its currency to the rest of the world. This "exorbitant duty" is the corollary of the "exorbitant privilege" of lower domestic funding costs that comes from having a domineering global currency (Gourinchas et al. 2010).

Boosting the international role of the euro will take time and require a combination of measures, of different size and importance. One has to start with the foundations, by reinforcing the monetary union as well as by completing its construction. In this sense, some reforms are already under discussion, while others have been proposed by the Commission and are being discussed by Member States. The latter have to be accompanied by more micro, specific reforms. These are necessary, as the use of the euro has many dimensions including diplomacy, improvements in payment systems and favouring the use of the euro in energy and commodities trades. Looking ahead, increasing market liquidity also through the provision of euro-denominated safe assets would be important.

It is true that market participants choose the favoured currency for their trades. However, policymakers can influence the appeal of the euro through concrete actions to reinforce the Eurozone's architecture and the depth and efficiency of the Eurozone's financial markets.

Notes

[1] In February 2005, the US Fed Chairman Alan Greenspan pointed out that long-term interest rates had trended lower despite a 150 basis point increase in the federal funds rate and referred to this phenomenon as a "conundrum."

[2] Allowing the use of the Renmimbi for foreign trade settlement for Chinese firms, establishing a fully convertible offshore market, concluding more than 30 swap agreements between the People's Bank of China and other central banks including the ECB and, allowing authorised offshore institutional investors to access to the Chinese inter-bank bond market.

[3] In 2011 the ECB established currency swap lines with the Bank of England, the Bank of Canada, the Bank of Japan, the Federal Reserve and the Swiss National Bank, and in 2013 with China.

Part F.
Between Two Crises

As it was leaving behind the legacy of the Great Recession, a new, even bigger shock hit the European economy and society. The pandemic has stricken Europe in its very foundations, triggering a fundamental rethinking of its macroeconomic framework and growth model. Europe's soul searching and the lessons from the financial crisis are the focus of the chapters in this section.

Even before the pandemic, the issue of the appropriate policy mix had come to the fore. As monetary policy is widely recognised as facing increasing constraints, fiscal policy and structural reforms need to play a stronger role. In particular, fiscal policy must become more supportive, notably in the Eurozone. Undertaking the right type of public investment – in infrastructure, education or to mitigate climate change – would both stimulate our economies and contribute to making them stronger and more sustainable.

Both the severity of the recession in Europe following the COVID-19 crisis and the subsequent bounce back differ markedly across Member States. Avoiding what could be remembered as the "Great Fragmentation" is a key goal of the EU strategy – Next Generation EU – with the Recovery and Resilience Facility at its heart. As learned during the financial crisis, an ambitious policy response must boost Europe's "indigenous" growth drivers. Whether such strategy will also lead to deeper political integration, will depend on finalising long-lasting institutional "chantiers" such as Banking Union and Capital Markets Union.

To make a success of Next Generation EU, a robust implementation of the Recovery and Resilience Programmes (RRPs), especially in countries benefitting most from the EU transfers, is needed. These plans include the investment and reform projects as well as their implementation mechanisms. Veto play-

ers' theory help explain and predict the governance arrangements chosen by EU countries. Member States' institutional features and the internal cohesion of governments and parties are important determinants of the governance of RRPs.

The economic policy response to the pandemic broke new ground, in terms of its ambition, the tools used, and its institutional characteristics. Three sets of factors explain this: our evolving understanding of macroeconomics, the nature of the current crisis, and the policy learning from the financial crisis. As national governments embark on the implementation of the RRPs, four sets of issues will be important in shaping the legacy of the pandemic for European integration: first, redefining the new boundaries between the state and the markets; second, revisiting the nature of subsidiarity; third, reconnecting the EU domestic and external agenda; and, finally, learning to respond to longer term structural shifts.

37 Right Here, Right Now: The Quest for a More Balanced Policy Mix*

October 2019

1 Introduction

Over the past few years, economies in the OECD and in particular in the EU had been growing at cruising speed, after having seemingly shrugged off the remains of the global financial crisis. The US is experiencing its longest bout of uninterrupted positive GDP growth on record. Similarly, despite lower growth performance, the EU has been growing for 25 consecutive quarters and its unemployment rate is now at its lowest since 2000.

Yet, worldwide growth has decelerated sharply in 2019, hampered by a global trade and investment slump along with a steep drop in manufacturing activity in Europe and most notably in Germany. Recent indicators suggest that growth could weaken further (IMF 2019). Rising uncertainty has been driving this slowdown, as a result of increasing economic tensions between China and the US, geopolitical developments in the Middle East (with the associated risk of a sharp rise in oil prices) and the political deadlock over Brexit. The materialisation of these risks could put the world economy on a collision course. Even if they remain only looming threats, high and increasingly entrenched uncertainty is sufficient to put a brake on investment and growth.

The impact of these tensions is exacerbated by a number of structural developments, particularly in Europe. The drop in potential growth, evident since the 2000s, has prompted concerns of "secular stagnation"

---

* Co-author: Laurence Boone (OECD), Vox CEPR, 18 October 2019.

Figure 1 Global trade growth and policy uncertainty

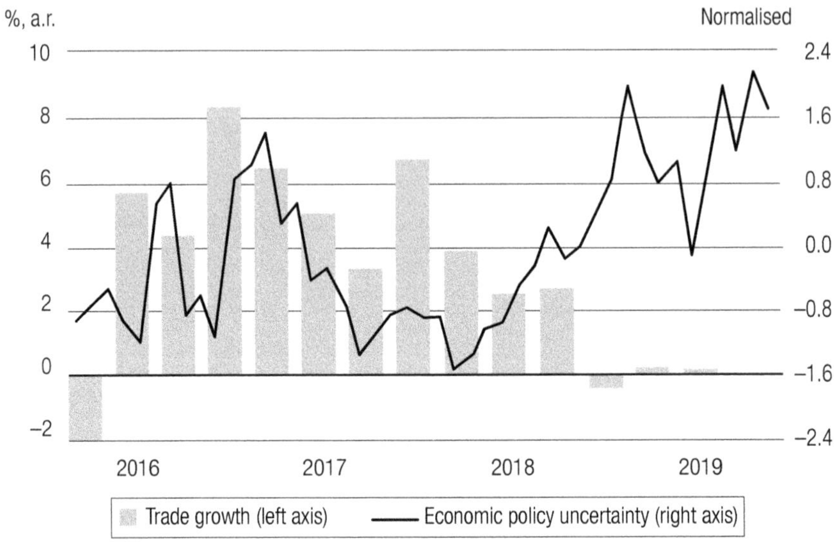

Note: Global uncertainty index normalised to 0 over the period.

Source: Own elaboration from www.policyuncertainty.com and OECD Economic Outlook database.

affecting the US and Europe. An important driver could be the slow diffusion of technologies: as Anzoategui et al. (2019) argue, much of the slowdown in productivity after the recession can be attributed to lower technology adoption. In addition, demographic change is taking a toll on growth potential while the appetite for reforms has slowed.

2 A better policy set-up is needed to lift economies back to growth

The conjunction of cyclical and structural impediments to growth calls for a review of the customary economic policy response to a deteriorating economic climate. Current inflation and policy rates, which are expected to remain at their low levels, suggest that ever more accommodative monetary policy will not be enough to revive GDP growth. At the same time, nominal GDP growth rates being above interest rates paid on pub-

Figure 2 Three-month interbank interest rates (%)

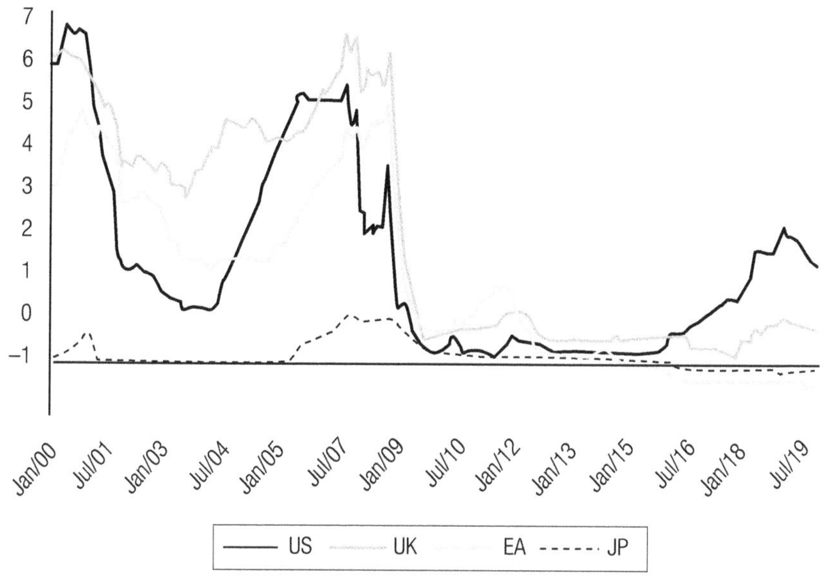

Source: Own elaboration from Bloomberg.

lic debt for most countries, and set to remain there for long term, increase the space for public investment.

Since the outset of the financial crisis, monetary policy has remained exceptionally accommodative, bringing interest rates close to zero (see Figure 2). In particular, the Fed continues to take expansionary measures, while the Bank of Japan maintains an extraordinary degree of monetary accommodation. Zooming in on the Eurozone, the ECB announced a stimulus package in September 2019 as it cut the deposit rate further by 10 basis points and relaunched its quantitative easing (QE) programme, together with expanded forward guidance. However, monetary policy faces increasing constraints.

The other policy instruments in the toolbox – both fiscal and structural – thus need to help. Together with the structural reforms needed to lift productivity durably, public investment could be put to use to halt the ongoing slowdown and prepare the ground for stronger and more sustainable economies. In fact, the same factors that constrain monetary policy are a bonanza for fiscal policy, which jointly with structural reforms can lift growth in a sustainable way.

Fiscal interventions are more powerful when inflationary pressures are low and monetary policy is likely to accommodate fiscal expansions as long as inflation remains below target. The Eurozone as a whole has fiscal room to manoeuvre, even though the situation differs markedly across countries. But while the slowdown is becoming entrenched, under current plans, fiscal levers are not being activated: on average in the Eurozone, the fiscal stance is expected to be broadly neutral in the next two years.

At the same time, the appetite for reforms with potential to lift growth and employment in the longer term – such as easing barriers to entrepreneurship, improving and expanding training, and supporting R&D and technology adoption – has waned, as shown by the implementation of the Going for Growth recommendations (OECD 2019c) or EU country-specific recommendations. Yet, such reforms are needed to reverse the slowdown in productivity that started even before the crisis but was exacerbated by the hysteresis effects of the Great Recession on investment and skills. Structural reforms are also needed to make growth more environmentally sustainable, by aligning policies and regulation with the goal of transition to a low-carbon economy (OECD 2015).

In addition, reforms are easier to implement when accompanied by a supportive policy mix, while in times of faltering demand, structural reforms alone may weigh on inflation and already weak demand (Eggertsson et al. 2014). In effect, reforms introduced when the economy is weak have a better chance of succeeding when undertaken together with supportive macroeconomic policies and renewed public investment, and when they put more weight on measures that also boost demand in the short-term, such as strengthening job search assistance and training and improving the tax structure (Caldera Sanchez et al. 2016). Simulations on the Eurozone run by the OECD for its Economic Outlook illustrate how combining a temporary public investment push with productivity-enhancing reforms can help bring forward the long-term benefits of reforms (OECD 2019b, d).

3 There is a strong case for a more supportive fiscal policy in the Eurozone

In the Eurozone, the inadequacy of a policy mix that relies heavily on the monetary policy pillar is becoming particularly obvious, as notably emphasised by the institution itself (Draghi 2019b). Meanwhile, the "reflationary" efforts conducted by the ECB are meeting increasing resistance both within and outside the institution.

Consequently, the usual arguments for relying mainly on automatic budgetary stabilisers and monetary policy when dealing with adverse shocks to the Eurozone may have to be reconsidered. In particular, modelling work done by the European Commission (In't Veld 2019) shows that when monetary policy is constrained by the zero-rate floor, fiscal stimulus has a stronger impact on growth in the short-term and a more benign effect on the debt ratio in the long-term.

While the benefits of a more supportive fiscal policy already appear sizeable at the current juncture, depending on how events unfold, the failure to act could result in snowballing negative effects going much beyond those captured in the usual simulations. In particular, the lack of action may increase the risk of the economy moving to inferior equilibria where deteriorating expectations of growth, employment and price developments, as well as private sector balance sheet effects, may further add to the current downward spiral. In these circumstances, the costs of too little stimulus in a worsening economy are likely to outweigh the costs of too much stimulus should a more favourable scenario materialise. The large compounded downward risks call for a risk-based approach to fiscal policy, with more pre-emptive rather than reactive policy action.

In absence of a common Eurozone budget, the current situation offers an opportunity for a truly coordinated approach to a supportive but differentiated fiscal stance in the 2020 budget plans. A more active role for fiscal policy in the policy mix would require differentiation between Member States with fiscal space and Member States with high debt, taking into account the divergent sustainability challenges. Furthermore, it is also important to improve the quality and composition of public finances, in particular boosting investment to ease the climate transition, and step up structural reforms.

Figure 3 Effects of differentiated fiscal expansion: Germany and the Netherlands

a) GDP

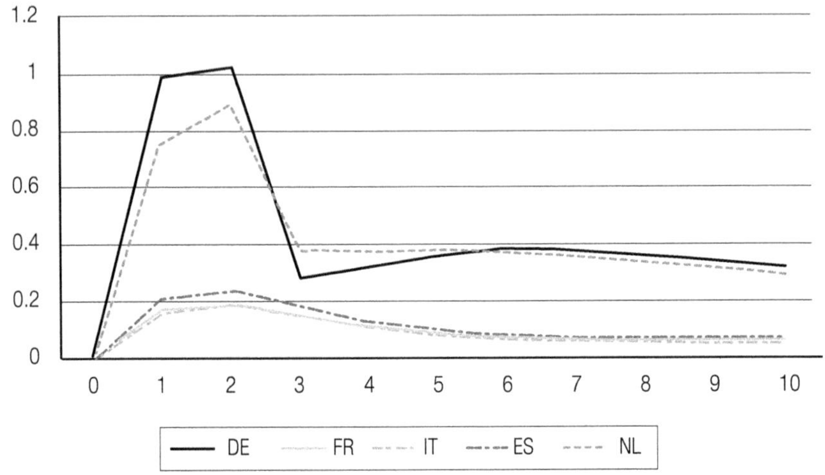

b) Debt-GDP ratio

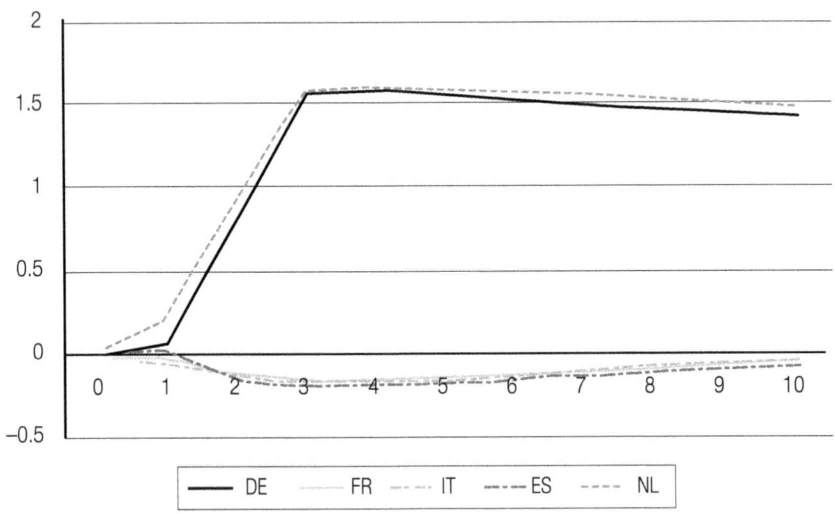

Note: GDP effects as percentage difference and debt-GDP ratios as percentage-point difference from baseline for a 1% of GDP increase in public investment for two years in DE and NL. Default assumptions for debt profile: rg =0 (ig=2, π=2, g=1.7).

Source: In't Veld (2019).

Illustrative simulations with the Commission's QUEST model suggest that an increase in public investment of 1% of GDP for two years in Member States with fiscal space, with monetary policy at the zero lower bound, leads to GDP increases of around 1% during that period in the concerned Member States and slightly less for more open economies (Figure 3). In the medium run, even after the stimulus has been removed, output remains above the baseline due to productivity gains from higher investment. Spillovers to other Eurozone Member States are modest at around 0.1-0.2% of GDP. The resulting effects of a temporary fiscal stimulus on debt to GDP ratios are benign, thanks to higher growth. In the Member States with fiscal space, the debt-to-GDP ratio would increase around by 1½ percentage points in the short-run, fading out in the long-run. A more persistent expansion in public investment in surplus countries, which would correct past cutbacks, would give a bigger boost to the Eurozone economy, with larger spillovers to other countries and a still manageable increase in debt ratios compared to the baseline scenario (In't Veld 2016). Where interest rates are negative, as is presently the case for most countries, the debt dynamics are even more favourable.

High fiscal multipliers and benign effects on debt developments rely on the nature of the fiscal impulse. Investment spending, which supports the economy's productive capacity and is time-limited in nature, has a stronger impact. A differentiated investment stimulus in line with the spirit of the EU fiscal framework would be most effective.

4 Now is the time to invest in stronger and more sustainable economies for the future

The case for a more active use of fiscal policy is not only rooted in the critical role it must play to drag weak economies out of the risk zone. The current situation also offers an opportunity not to be missed to address deep economic challenges and invest in the future. The low interest rates at which governments are borrowing, even at long maturities, mean that many of them can more easily undertake investments to raise long-term growth, sustainability and wellbeing without putting strain on public finances.

In the aftermath of the global financial crisis, governments often resorted to cuts in public investment to achieve fiscal consolidation in a way deemed less painful than raising taxes or cutting social spending or the public sector wage bill. Throughout the post-crisis period, this shortfall in public investment has not been made up for. A decade of infrastructures that were not built or were not properly maintained has been taking its toll on productivity and growth potential. It risks turning into persistently missed chances to better connect people, firms and regions to opportunities.

Some countries, such as Germany, are in dire need of stronger investment. Across the EU, almost half of firms are held back in their investment decisions by the inadequacy of transport infrastructure, and the same number by the lack of access to digital infrastructure (Figure 4). High-speed networks are the backbone of a knowledge economy and a pre-condition for firms to innovate and thrive in the near future. Bridging the rural digital divide is also key to reduce regional disparities and

Figure 4 Firms reporting that infrastructure is an obstacle to their investments (%)

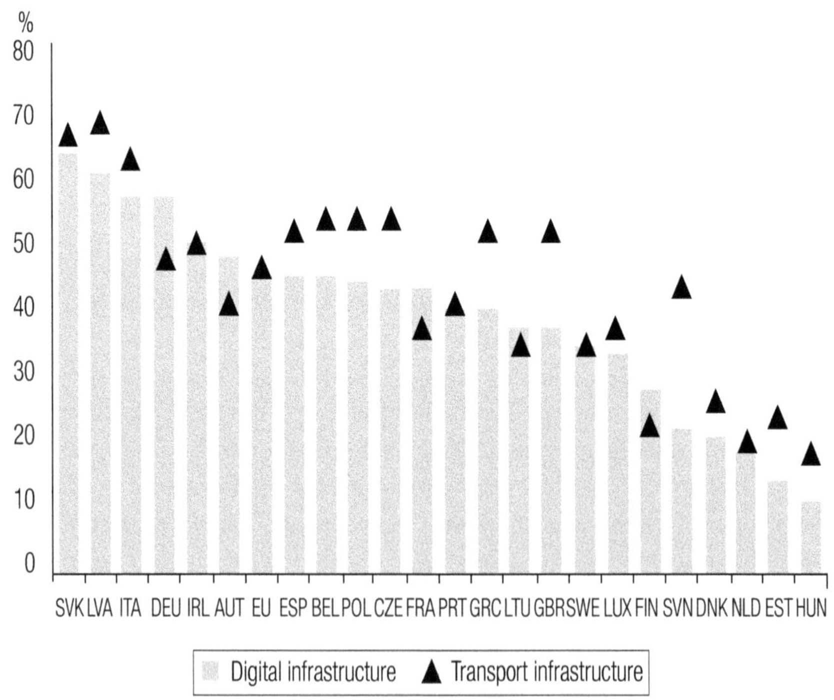

Source: Own elaboration from European Investment Bank Investment Survey (2018).

improve social cohesion. Further investment in health, education and skills would also support a more durable and more inclusive growth.

At the same time, the need to invest in makingout economies more "green" is becoming ever more pressing, as delaying action will entail steeply rising costs of climate change mitigation (IPCC 2018). The growing scale and reach of climate-motivated demonstrations and civil disobedience actions in recent months have given a political urgency to the issue. The energy transition will require more investments – and different investments than under the current trajectory – to decarbonise entire sectors starting with energy, industry and transport. In the EU, President-elect von der Leyen has announced a "Green Deal" to accelerate the transition towards achieving carbon neutrality by 2050 (von der Leyen 2019). Such an initiative could mobilise public and private resources to lift innovation and investment in low-carbon technologies and build more sustainable economies.

38 Economic Policy in the Rough: A European Journey[*]

January 2020

"I've seen things you people wouldn't believe [...] All those moments will be lost in time, like tears in rain."
– *Blade Runner*, directed by Ridley Scott (1982)

1 Introduction

In this chapter, I attempt to give a sense of my long-lasting experience – between 2008 and 2019 – as Director General for Economic and Financial Affairs (ECFIN) at the European Commission. As this journey has revolved around the economic and financial crisis in Europe, I chose the title "Economic policy in the rough" and the above quote from Ridley Scott came to mind.

This encapsulates both a sense of my journey through the Euro crisis, as well as my policy conclusions. Out of these 11 years at ECFIN, I selected "moments of the Ridley Scott type" for this article – past episodes that I think are relevant to interpreting the policy predicament today and in the future. Some of these moments are known to have been pivotal – others are less prominent, but in my interpretation were crucial nonetheless.

The moments I have chosen are Latvia asking for financial assistance in 2008, the G20 meeting in Toronto in 2010, the Deauville meeting later that year, Mario Draghi's speech at Jackson Hole in 2014, and – as an extended moment – the developments in Greece, starting in 2010

[*] CEPR Policy Insights, 7 January 2020.

with a recognition of the fiscal problem, the "Grexit" debate in 2015, and Greece successfully exiting the programme in August 2018.

I will give a brief snapshot of what happened at each moment, and then focus on the lessons to be drawn from them. At the end, I will attempt to tie everything together to derive insights for the future of Economic and Monetary Union (EMU) and the desirable policy mix.

2 Moment one: Latvia and the other Baltics – a prequel to the crisis

The first moment occurred prior to the Eurozone crisis, and can be seen as its prequel. In the mid 2000s, Eastern Europe, and the Baltics in particular, exhibited strong economic performance (leading to the term "Baltic tigers") which was fuelled by a "catching-up effect" as well as capital pouring into the countries, a credit expansion and housing bubbles. The reckoning came towards the end of 2008, in the form of sudden capital flow reversals and the need to enact drastic adjustment programmes. I single out Latvia (see Figure 1) since it was the most affected: a slowdown had already begun in 2007 due to rising inflation and loss of competitiveness, as well as tightening credit that reflected banks' increasing concerns regarding their loan portfolios (Blanchard, Griffiths and Gruss 2013). In 2008, as the world was hit by the financial crisis, there was

Figure 1 GDP growth in Latvia and the Eurozone (%)

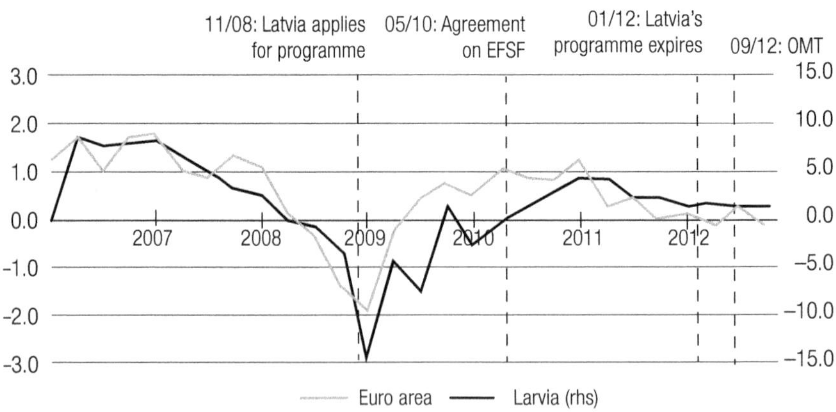

Source: European Commission.

a sudden capital reversal, a credit crunch and a sharp drop in exports. On 8 November, the Latvian government announced it was buying 51% of Parex Bank, the largest domestically owned bank. The country was forced to apply for an IMF–EU Balance of Payments (BOP) assistance programme a few weeks later. As part of the programme, Latvia implemented an unprecedented fiscal adjustment and a wide-ranging set of reforms while retaining the exchange rate peg to the euro, which allowed it to exit the programme in the beginning of 2012. The deep structural adjustment proved very painful, but allowed the country to correct the large imbalances and laid the foundation for the subsequent strong growth.

I think four lessons can be crystallised from the developments in Latvia and the Baltics:

1. Financial crises even in small countries can have pervasive effects and a high potential for contagion. This contagion risk was not perceived at the time. I vividly remember a conference call with Member States and the IMF on Latvia in which I raised the issue of contagion to the rest of the Baltics and Eastern European countries. The reply at the time was that any risk of contagion could be tackled via individual IMF BOP programmes for all countries concerned. But this country-by-country approach is clearly not suited to preventing contagion. At the time, the risk of contagion was not fully embodied in the IMF's reasoning, which has since changed substantially.
2. The Baltics' story could have been used to inform programmes for struggling Eurozone countries and prioritising Eurozone actions. At the time, we did not recognise that the events in the Baltics were relevant for the Eurozone, and hence they did not lead to deeper financial market integration and recapitalisation of banks. The proposal for creating a Banking Union had to wait for the sovereign debt crisis and was only adopted in June 2012.
3. Sustained capital inflows embellish fiscal accounts, and bad fiscal accounts are often the effect, not the cause, of a crisis. At the outset of the crisis, the Baltics generally had low debt and deficits. However, the fiscal accounts deteriorated immediately and dramatically following the sudden stop. We also witnessed this in southern Eurozone countries, where the focus was often on the effects, not on the causes, of the fiscal imbalances.
4. The exchange rate regime is more than a monetary arrangement.

At the outset of the crisis, the Baltic countries had various forms of fixed exchange rate regimes. When the events unfolded in 2008, we undertook wide-ranging economic analyses to determine whether the exchange rate regime should be changed or not, since the rationale for heavily "euroised" countries to devalue the exchange rate, or move to a form of floating exchange rates, was not clear-cut. Even with our findings from investigating balance sheet effects, competitive implications, econometric simulations, and so on, in the specific case of Latvia, both the case for keeping and the case for changing the exchange rate could be made. When we approached Commissioner Joaquin Almunia, who was in charge of economic and financial affairs, with these findings, he countered our exposition with "I appreciate your empirical results. Interesting, but irrelevant. I do not want to have a midsized Russian oligarch buying the country." Hence, Latvia's currency was not devalued, and we learned that the exchange rate regime has a deep (geo)political dimension. Eventually, the deep structural reforms underpinned the rapid growth when the countries exited the programs and the recovery set it.

3 Moment two: the Deauville meeting on 18 October 2010

The second moment I selected is well known: the compromise struck in October 2010 between the French President, Nicolas Sarkozy, and the German Chancellor, Angela Merkel, in a meeting in the French city of Deauville, which is widely accepted as having been pivotal for the Euro crisis.[1] Sarkozy and Merkel were hosting Russian President Dmitry Medvedev to discuss foreign policy cooperation, notably in the Middle East. But in fact, the main topic of discussion was the Eurozone crisis, and Merkel and Sarkozy reached a Franco-German compromise that was heavily catered to their domestic audiences (Brunnermeier, James and Landau 2016). France would accept a tightening of the rules in the Stability and Growth Pact but with no automaticity in sanctions (the latter having been a major French demand). Germany, in turn, would accept a change to the EU Treaty to set up, by 2013 at the latest, a permanent rescue mechanism – which would become the European Stability Mechanism (ESM) – to succeed the European Financial Stability Facility (EFSF). But this was not all. Merkel also managed to extract from Sarkozy an agreement

Figure 2 Eurozone 10 years treasury bonds, spreads to German Bunds

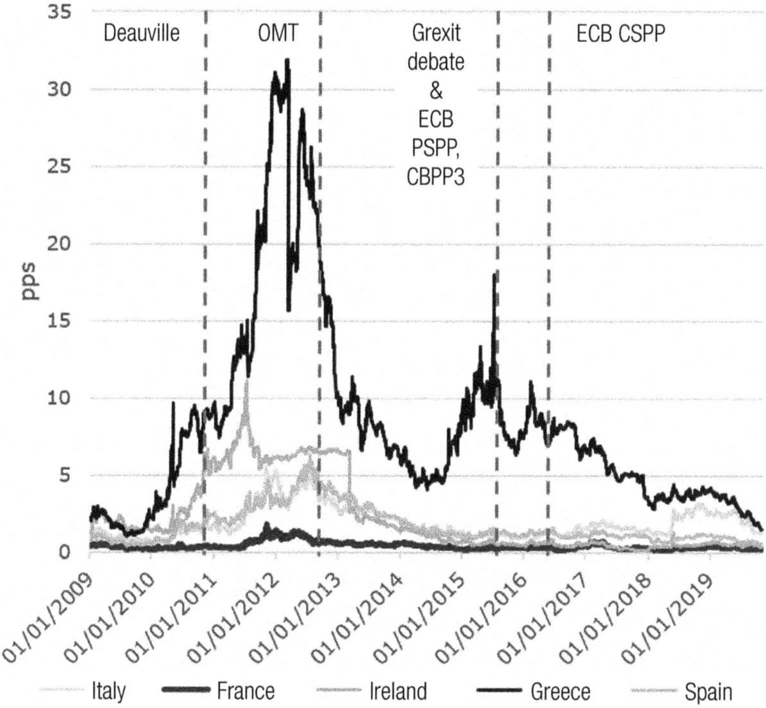

Source: Own elaboration from Bloomberg.

that, as of 2013, any future crisis assistance would be accompanied by the bail-in of creditors – so-called private sector involvement (PSI). There was no prior consultation or coordination with the ECB, the Eurozone partners or the US. The financial markets reacted very strongly following the meeting, with the long-term treasury bond spreads of many countries widening by an unprecedented magnitude, most dramatically in the case of Greece (Figure 2), causing some scholars to describe Deauville as Europe's "Lehman moment" (Tooze 2018).

As with the Baltics, I would like to draw four lessons from Deauville and its aftermath:

1. *Financial markets operate according to "horizontal and vertical lines."* There is no gradual pressure on borrowers, or in other words, the

financial markets change suddenly from benign phases to extremes, like Greece's treasury rate shooting up by more than 30 percentage points after being closely aligned with the Bund's rate for most of the last ten years of EMU. Hence, it is a daring undertaking to rely on markets to discipline countries.

2. *Risk-reduction measures, if they are not coupled with risk-sharing measures, can actually increase risk, instead of reducing it.* Countries who are "pure risk-reducers" are actually their own worst enemy: proposals such as the automatic debt restructuring may trigger "Armageddon" in financial markets, and result in more instead of fewer bailouts. Equally, "pure risk sharers" underestimate the limited political capital for unilateral solidarity. The importance of reducing and sharing risk in parallel is topical today, for instance in the context of the completion of the Banking Union with the creation of a single deposit guarantee. As spelled out in the report by the Commission on completing EMU (European Commission 2017c), a change in regulatory treatment of sovereign exposures would need to go hand in hand with some form of Eurozone safe asset.
3. *EU-level decisions should be insulated as much as possible from domestic political economy considerations.* While it has proven to be highly difficult to make advances on this front, it is of great importance for the good functioning of the EU, especially on matters with potentially high relevance for the financial markets. More generally, processing everything through the "moral hazard lens" does not lead to sound policies. Whilst providing the right incentives for policymaking is essential, moral hazard considerations have to be tempered by the need for urgent policy responses. This is particularly true in times of economic and financial stress, as was the case in Greece for instance, or in the sovereign debt crisis in the Eurozone in 2011-12.[2]
4. *Not coordinating with partners and the ECB can be very dangerous.* For instance, Jean-Claude Trichet, then-president of the ECB, was convening with EU finance ministers in Luxembourg at the time and was taken by surprise by the Deauville agreement, which he immediately opposed fervently. A prior consultation of the ECB, or better encompassing financial markets' psychology in decision making, could have led to different decisions and potentially prevented the negative fallout from Deauville.

4 Moment three: the Toronto G20 Summit in June 2010

The third – and less well-known – moment is the G20 summit in Toronto in June 2010. Toronto was preceded by important summits in Washington (November 2008) at the beginning of the crisis as well as in London and Pittsburgh (April and September 2009, respectively). At these preceding summits, monetary and fiscal packages that were unprecedented in scale had been agreed to address the crisis. For example, the European Economic Recovery Plan, presented in November 2008 by the Commission, amounted to a fiscal impulse of €200 billion, equivalent to 1.5% of GDP. As a result of the discretionary fiscal stimulus, the sharp drop in GDP and the efforts to shore up the banking system, governments' debts and deficits had ballooned. Many advanced countries had seen their debt-to GDP-ratio rise by 10-20% and deficits (see Figure 3) had significantly increased as well.

In the months before the Toronto Summit, the global economy appeared to be on the mend: growth in emerging economies had returned to pre-crisis levels – China's growth again exceeded 10% – while the

Figure 3 General government balance

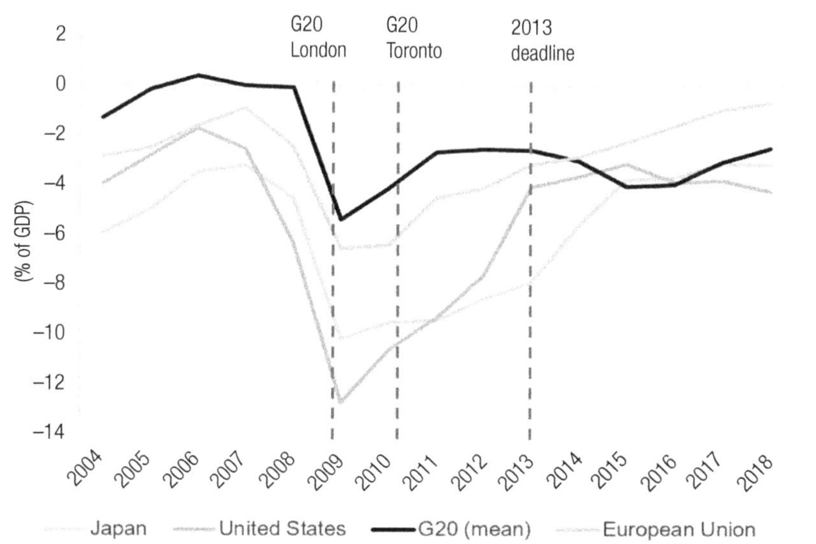

Source: Own elaboration from Eurostat, IMF WEO April 2019.

output gap in almost all advanced economies was slowly shrinking. With this improved economic outlook, domestic considerations took priority over collective endeavours. In June 2010, most of the summit's participants were hence "ready to declare victory"; it looked as if recovery was underway, which would allow the fiscal stimulus to be withdrawn. In particular, countries committed at Toronto to at least halving their deficit by 2013 and to stabilising debt-to-GDP ratios. The commitment to a standstill on trade measures was restated.

As shown in Figure 3, the US and Europe roughly followed through on this commitment, albeit in the context of very different GDP growth rates: in the period between 2010 and 2013, the US grew on average by roughly 2% annually, while Europe experienced a "double dip," with growth of only about half a percentage point for the entire period 2010-2013. *Ex post*, it is evident that it was premature to withdraw the fiscal stimulus by committing to quantitative deficit and debt targets within a strict deadline, given that the global recovery was still too fragile and growth not self-sustainable.

The key lessons we learned from the G20 in Toronto are relatively straightforward:

1. *The "spirit of London" (i.e., a coordinated and cooperative response) was largely lost.* Instead, the efforts at the Toronto and subsequent summits were directed at bridging differences between those countries that were more "hawkish" and those that were more "dovish" regarding fiscal policy, but the divisions held up (see chapter 34).
2. *In the aftermath of crises, early withdrawal of fiscal support can be very damaging and lead to an unbalanced policy mix.* At the time, we did not see the increasing burden that was put on monetary policy. In particular, we did not appropriately weigh risks and costs in the trade-off between sustainability and stabilisation. This is especially true in the current low interest rate environment (see chapter 15), since it decreases the risk associated with new debt and makes it possible to step up public investment. I will elaborate more on this when discussing the fifth moment.
3. *Choosing the composition of fiscal support matters; not all measures are alike in their effects.* Previously, the focus was solely on the size of the adjustment, whereas today we recognise the importance of the quality of fiscal stimuli or retrenchments. Whenever expansionary

fiscal policies are called for, we should give priority to a set of credible policy measures which, besides stimulating domestic demand, tackle longer-term structural challenges and raise our growth potential, for example by supporting the necessary climate transition.

4. *A standstill on trade protection was restated, but protectionism started to creep in.* Measures hampering trade continued to grow over time (Lowe and Luckman 2019), and in Toronto the first signs of the different stances across countries underlying these protectionist developments became evident.

5 Moment four: Greece – a fiscal and a structural crisis

The Greek crisis is a quintessential "extended moment," and given its duration and complexity, I can only give a brief snapshot and offer what I believe were some of the key lessons.

What determined the thrust of Greece's adjustment programme was the country's "original sin": the dramatic revision of the Greek fiscal accounts. The Greek government's deficit, announced in April, was 3.6% for 2009, but *ex post* it was revised to over 15% of GDP (see Figure 4). This revision came as a shock and resulted in Greece losing access to the markets, with the EU needing to intervene in the context of a generalised loss of trust. While for Latvia, as a country outside the Eurozone, a dedicated instrument to intervene (Balance of Payments Assistance) had been available as part of the EU toolbox, there was no such instrument for Greece. Hence, a creative, intergovernmental approach was required to respond swiftly to the acute problems. First, the Greek Loan Facility (GLF) was established in 2010 and disbursed €52.9 billion. This was succeeded by the EFSF in 2012, which disbursed €141.8 billion, and the ESM in 2015, which disbursed €61.9 billion. Overall, between the IMF and the three EU programmes, support in the form of loans amounting to €277.8 billion was provided.

Another key event was the "Grexit" speculation in 2015, when we were but an "inch away" from Greece leaving the Eurozone. Grexit was avoided and three years later, in August 2018, Greece successfully concluded the ESM programme (quite surprisingly, given its previous trajectory). Much was done to assist the country, and while one can rightly criticise the austerity at the onset of the programme as being excessive, the classic criticisms fail to acknowledge that, with all likelihood, Greece would have had to enact much harsher contractionary fiscal measures without the EU-IMF programme, given its loss of market access.

Figure 4 Deficit and GDP growth in Greece

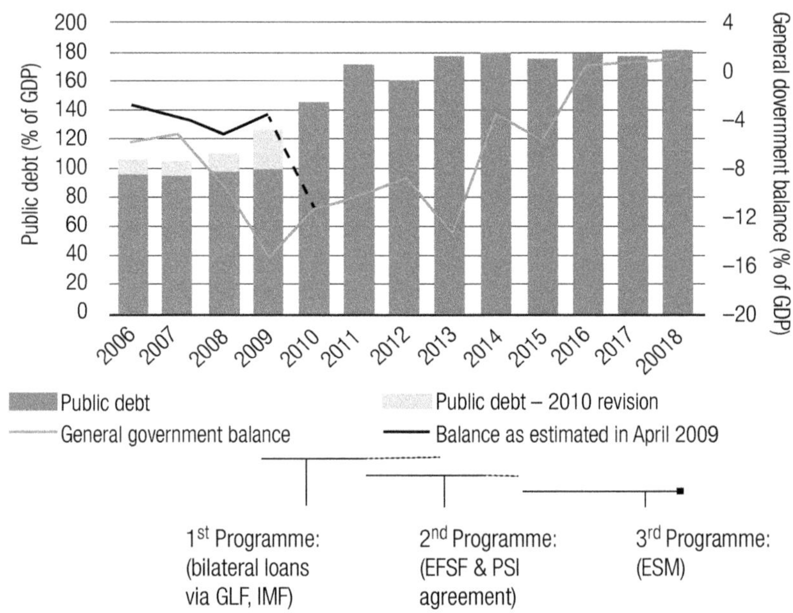

Source: European Commission.

Lessons learned from the Greek crisis:

1. *Greece's fiscal crisis affected the views on other vulnerable countries and the narrative on the Eurozone crisis.* The Greek fiscal woes led to seeing other countries through a "fiscal lens," which I believe to have been a mistake. For instance, if Ireland had come to fall before Greece, perhaps different causes for the crisis would have been diagnosed for other programme countries and events could have unfolded quite differently. Had this been the case we would probably be telling an altogether different story.
2. *Any crisis in a country belonging to the Eurozone is likely to be of a structural nature, and a classic' IMF programme is unlikely to succeed.*

While the grave fiscal problems were both a symptom and a cause of the crisis in Greece, they were not the entire story: Greece faced deep structural problems. Hence, a classic three-year IMF programme was less suited to the task and a longer, more comprehensive "World-Bank-type" programme would have been more appropriate.

3. *Debt sustainability needs to be addressed in a timely, but possibly in a* sui generis, *manner.* When debt relief is discussed, politics and perceptions are to be reckoned with. In the discussions with EU ministers, it was evident that relieving the burden on Greece via haircuts to the principal debt was politically infeasible. Hence, as an imperfect substitute, interest rates were lowered and maturity extended, which is not substantially different in present value terms, but had a starkly different political perception. The ESM estimates that Greece's budgetary savings were 6.5% of GDP and that the implicit interest rates were lower than in Spain, Italy and Portugal since 2012 due to the extension of maturities and the low interest rates (ESM 2019).
4. *Institutional courage is needed to tackle existential crises.* When Grexit came on the table, the Commission faced a stark choice: let Member States sort it out, or get involved. It chose the latter and it was right. Here tribute must be paid to Commission President Juncker, who was repeatedly told at the time by government leaders that the Greek crisis was a question for national governments and not the Commission. Yet Juncker stated that Greece would not exit the Eurozone, and the Commission consistently operated to facilitate such a solution. Hence, similar to Almunia's decision not to abandon Latvia's currency peg, Juncker made a political decision with crucial economic – but also institutional – ramifications.
5. *Democratic accountability is key and the Commission cannot act as an "agent of creditors."* The Commission paid a hefty political price for running the Greek programme, as it was criticised from both sides of the spectrum. On one hand, the Commission was perceived as being an agent of the creditors and the enforcer of austerity – a view that was widespread and persistent among the Greek public, and led to the Commission being seen in an unfavourable light in Athens. On the other hand, the Commission was also unpopular among governments and the public in countries like Germany, since

it was perceived as being too lenient. These perceptions were unfortunate, since the Commission's North Star was always the fundamental common interest of Europe and its citizens, although of course whether we always fully succeeded is up for discussion. The larger responsibilities in crisis management attributed to the ESM will in the future help dispel the perception of the Commission as the "agent" of the Eurogroup.

6 Moment five: Mario Draghi's speech at the Jackson Hole Symposium in August 2014

The last moment I would like to highlight is a speech that Mario Draghi gave at the Federal Reserve Symposium in Jackson Hole[3], Wyoming in August 2014 (Draghi 2014). This speech has received less attention than his famous "whatever it takes" speech in London in July 2012, but its importance was recognised at the time among the community of central bankers, macroeconomic investors and policymakers (Davies 2014). Since then, it helped to change the narrative on EMU's policy mix. At the time, tensions in the Eurozone sovereign debt markets had largely subsided and economic activity had started to recover. But the recovery looked fragile. Moreover, there were deflationary risks, inflation expectations were de-anchoring and, importantly, conventional monetary policy was largely exhausted, with the deposit facility rate having moved into negative territory in June 2014.

In his speech, Draghi advocated for a more balanced policy mix with fiscal policy playing a larger role, and for considering bolder options for monetary policy. He also warned against hysteresis effects in unemployment, as well as a lack of long-term economic cohesion in the Eurozone. His speech was not followed by a meaningful fiscal expansion or a stepping up of structural reform, and the ECB was forced to implement unprecedented monetary policy[4] (Figure 5). However, it helped to change the narrative of the post-crisis policy priorities in EMU.

Lessons learned from Draghi's speech at Jackson Hole:

1. *Monetary policy cannot be left alone; fiscal policy has to do its part in a swift and decisive manner.* Today, with monetary policy facing increasing side effects and diminishing returns, calls for swift and de-

Figure 5 Overburdened central bank

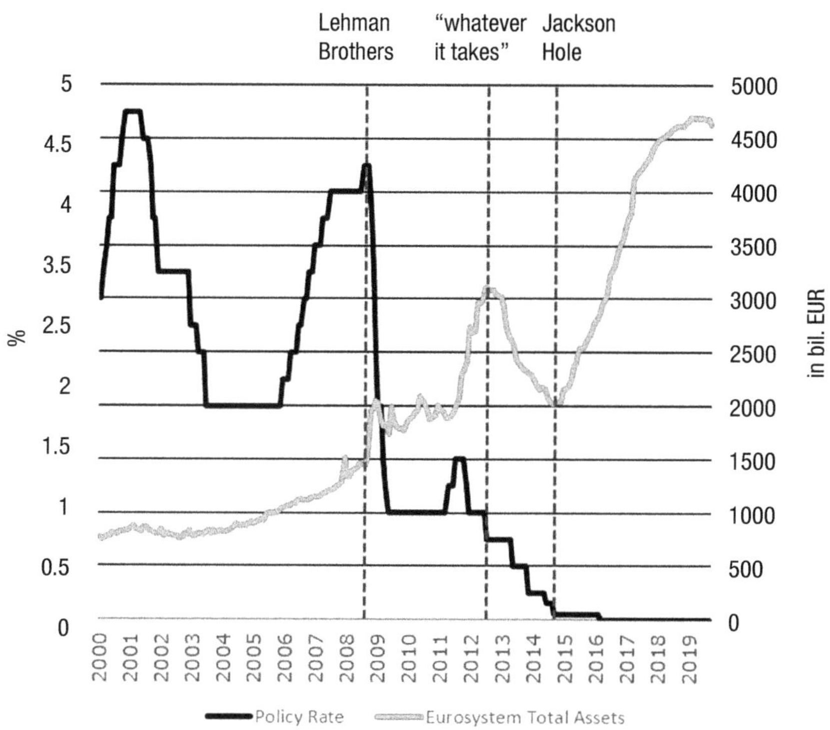

Source: Own elaboration from ECB.

termined fiscal action, in particular by countries with fiscal space, are again being made by the ECB. In his speech, Draghi warned that "the risks of 'doing too little' outweigh those of 'doing too much'." Here, a historical parallel suggests itself in a warning issued by John Maynard Keynes in an open letter to American President F.D. Roosevelt in 1933: "I do not blame Mr. Ickes [US Secretary of the Interior] for being cautious and careful. But the risks of less speed must be weighed against those of more haste. He must get across the crevasses before it is dark" (Keynes 1933).[5]

2. *Achieving a Eurozone fiscal stance only via horizontal coordination of national policies is exceedingly difficult.* In particular, it has not proven politically viable to aim at an adequate fiscal stance for the Eurozone as a whole solely via bottom-up coordination. When a broadly

acceptable overall stance was achieved, that took place via the wrong distribution between countries in violation of the respective fiscal space. This was not fully recognised at the time, and hence Draghi did not explicitly address it in this speech. Since then, this issue has received more attention, and we have argued that a central European fiscal capacity complementing the national budgetary policies is needed to achieve the required fiscal stance for the Eurozone.

3. *Excessive fiscal prudence is also a form of fiscal dominance.* The logic of Sargent and Wallace's (1981) "unpleasant monetary arithmetic" is that unless countries conduct prudent fiscal policy, the independence of monetary policy could be called into question via pressure to monetise the debt. Today, we face the opposite dynamics: in periods during which the central bank is at the effective lower bound, excessive fiscal prudence is a form of fiscal dominance hampering the effort of the central bank to fulfil its mandate. Hence, in today's world, Sargent and Wallace's argument is turned on its head.
4. *A certain amount of risk-sharing is needed in EMU, either via national budgets or via the ECB balance sheet.* In order to function properly, EMU – as any currency union – requires a certain amount of risk-sharing. This can either be accomplished directly via fiscal risk-sharing (via the national budgets and/or a Eurozone central fiscal capacity) or, in a less transparent way, via the balance sheet of the ECB. The Eurozone chose the latter. The limits of this choice, however, are evident today as the ECB is overburdened in fulfilling its mandate.

7 Key lessons for future work on the Economic and Monetary Union

I believe the five moments I have described here bear important lessons for the next steps in the completion of the EMU architecture. They should also lead us to reflect on a better policy mix to ensure balanced and sustainable growth.

As to completing EMU, the key lessons I would draw from the five pivotal moments I have described are the following: we need to (i) complete the Banking Union, (ii) set up a European fiscal stabilisation capacity, (iii) acknowledge the geopolitical relevance of the EMU, and (iv) increase the democratic accountability of European integration. Indeed, these four conclusions are deeply rooted in how the five moments I have described here unfolded.

The crisis in the Baltics revealed the need to address the risks of financial crises and contagion channels, which was a key component of the rationale behind the Banking Union. Another crucial insight guiding the design of the Banking Union has been that risk-reduction requires risk-sharing, which was learned from the events triggered by the Deauville meeting. Deauville moreover also epitomises the risk of "*ultima ratio*" actions stemming from intergovernmental settings and connects to the geopolitical relevance the EMU assumes.

The fiscal stabilisation capacity, which plays a central role in completing EMU's architecture (see chapter 8), is linked to multiple moments. Following Mario Draghi's speech in Jackson Hole, it has become increasingly clear that achieving an EU fiscal stance solely via national coordination is very difficult, underscoring the usefulness of a central fiscal capacity.

There is increasing "demand for Europe" in international economic fora. In order to match this expectation, Europe needs to pull its act together. In particular, the outcome of the meeting in Deauville is a clear demonstration that *de jure* or *de facto* intergovernmental settings increase the risk that decisions are taken too late and in a fragmented way. In order to develop the international role of the euro, progress will also need to be made on completing EMU in terms of governance (see chapter 36).

Finally, the events during the Greek crisis and how EU actions to counter the crisis were perceived by the public revealed strikingly that progress needs to be made on Europe's democratic accountability (Schmidt 2015b). As argued in chapter 10, a move from the intergovernmental method, which gained ground during the crisis, towards the Community method would help in terms of both efficiency (by avoiding the curse of *ultima ratio* thanks to its majority voting) and accountability (by envisaging a role for the European Parliament and not only the national parliaments, which tend to take a "partial equilibrium" view).

In light of the current slowdown and lacklustre medium-term growth prospects, the above moments also indicate that the fiscal, monetary and structural policy mix needs to be changed. As Mario Draghi stated in his speech in Sintra (Draghi 2019a), monetary policy needs to remain patient, persistent and prudent. It needs to be patient since the Eurozone has experienced repeated negative shocks which required it to extend the policy horizon. It needs to be persistent to ensure the sustained convergence of inflation to the target of close to 2%. And it needs to be prudent to be conscious of underlying causes of inflation dynamics and risks, in order to adjust policy if needed.

Fiscal policy needs to fulfil the "three Ts" as first identified by Larry Summers (2008) – it must be timely in order to be effective, targeted by focusing on high multipliers expenditure, and (possibly) temporary. Before the "secular stagnation" debate, it seemed clear that the fiscal stimulus should be temporary, but lately it has been argued that the right fiscal expansion may need to be longer lasting (Furman and Summers 2019). While the jury is still out on the desirable fiscal trajectory in the presence of ultra-low interest rates, there is little doubt that a long-lasting boost of public investment should be undertaken. One such example would be quality investment to ease the environmental transition; here, fiscal policy and investments should be used not only in a temporary manner for stabilisation purposes, but also address a more structural need.

Complementing Draghi's three Ps for monetary policy and Summers' three Ts for fiscal policy, I propose three Fs for structural reforms: they should be feasible in order to be effective instead of aiming for unrealistic targets; forward-looking, for instance regarding environmental issues; and fair, i.e. by incorporating social concerns in a structural reforms 2.0 strategy, thereby moving away from the perception of "blood and tears" reforms.

Together, the letters spell TFP – a fitting acronym to capture today's economic and policy predicament in Europe.

Notes

[1] Note that some scholars disagree that the Deauville meeting played a decisive role in the Euro crisis. For example, Mody (2018, pp. 273-280) attributes the widening spreads to underlying factors. Interpretations along Ashoka's argument, however, remain a minority view.

[2] This aspect has been vividly illustrated by Tim Geithner in his memoir on the crisis management (Geithner 2015).

[3] Since 1978, an Economic Policy symposium sponsored by the Federal Reserve Bank of Kansas has been held in Jackson Hole on a yearly basis. In 2014, the topic of the symposium was "Re-Evaluating Labor Market Dynamics" (see https://www.kansascityfed.org/publications/research/escp/symposiums/escp-2014, Federal Reserve Bank of Kansas City 2014).

[4] For instance, through implementing the Targeted Longer-Term Refinancing Options (TLTRO), Asset-Backed Securities Purchase Program (ABSPP) or the third Covered Bond Purchase Program (CBPP3). Between March 2015 and March 2016, the Eurosystem's net asset purchases averaged €60 billion. This increased to €80 billion in the following 12 months and has since been gradually reduced.

[5] There is at least a slight chance that Mario Draghi had John Maynard Keynes' remarks in mind when drafting the speech, since I had sent Keynes' letter to him in the weeks prior to the symposium in Jackson Hole.

39 A Tale of Two Crises: Lessons from the Financial Crisis to Prevent the Great Fragmentation*

July 2020

1 COVID-19: a tragedy with huge economic costs

The recent forecasts by official institutions and market analysts confirm that the COVID-19 crisis is set to lead to a downturn of historic proportions, much deeper than that witnessed during the financial crisis which followed the bankruptcy of Lehman Brothers in 2008. Figure 1a shows that the current recession is more than twice the size of the one that followed the financial crash and it envisages a partial and much slower return to the pre-crisis growth levels. For 2020 as a whole, in its Winter Forecast the Commission estimates a deep recession with EU and Eurozone GDP declining by 6.3% and 6.8%, respectively (European Commission 2021b).[1]

The crisis has created huge financing needs in terms of equity repair, investment gap and social distress. Figure 1b shows that the additional financing needs of the EU for 2020-21 amount to almost €2 trillion for a baseline scenario and they exceed €2.5 trillion if a stress scenario were to materialise.[2] In Buti and Messori (2020), my co-author and I attempt to apportion such financing needs to the three phases of the crisis developments: emergency, transition, and recovery. We argue that social needs will be particularly present in the initial emergency phase, but partly also during the transition phase. The need to fill the investment gap (public and private) will happen in the transition phase, but only become a key priority in the final phase, whereas the need for recapitalization will characterise both the transition and the recovery phase. Approximately, the

* Vox CEPR, 13 July 2020.

Figure 1 Growth and financing needs

a) GDP downfall and recovery during the COVID-19 crisis and the financial crisis

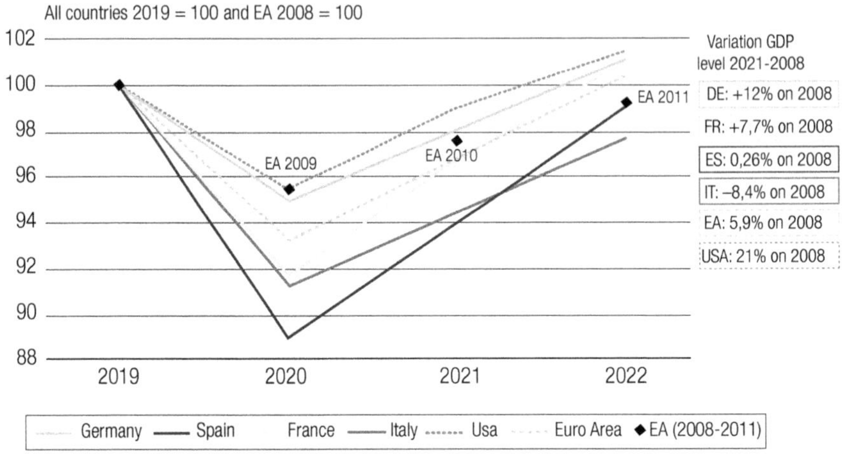

*All countries Winter forecast, except US (Autumn forecast)

Source: European Commission.

b) Financing needs

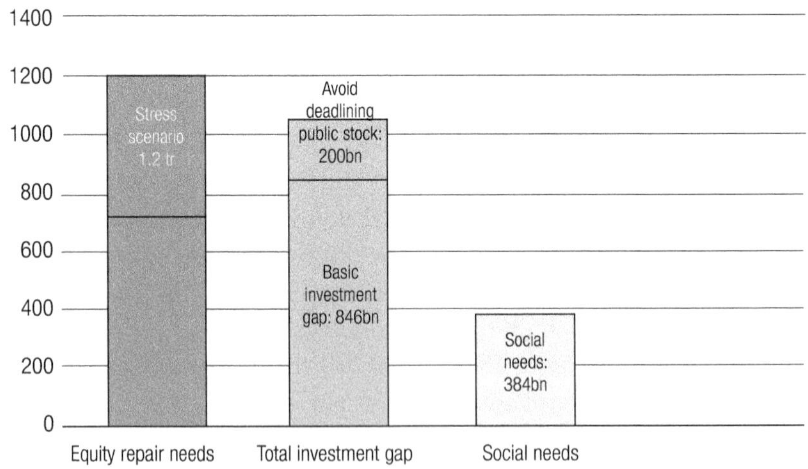

Source: European Commission (2020a).

financing needs in the emergency phase will amount to around €800 billion, the transition phase will need €500 billion while the phase envisaging the recovery will involve financing needs amounting to some €1.2 trillion.

There has been much debate on the dynamics of the crisis and the potentially uneven impact on different countries. Early hopes of a V-shaped recession have faded in spite of recent positive sentiment indicators. In a U-shaped scenario, the recession would last longer and the rebound would be much slower. A W-shaped recession could be possible in case there will be a second wave of infections. The scenario of a "Victorian bathtub" cannot be excluded – here, a period of stagnation would be followed by only a timid recovery due to an increase of private and public debt as well as persistent uncertainty leading to high saving, less investment and constrained consumption. Hysteresis effects would take a toll denting the exit from the crisis and negatively impact potential growth.

According to the European Commission's and most other forecasts, both the severity of the recession in 2020 and the following bounce back of the economies differ markedly among Member States. As shown in Figure 1a, Germany will suffer a much smaller downturn than Italy and Spain in 2020. In a similar vein, the rebound and the level of GDP that these countries will reach in 2021 differ markedly. While Germany will also not return to its 2019 GDP level by 2021, its situation is much less severe than that of Spain and Italy.

Several factors underpin such asymmetric behaviour affecting not only the severity of the recession but also the speed of the recovery. Exogenous reasons pertain essentially to the structure and resilience of the economies, whilst endogenous reasons are related to the interactions between the national policy space and the relaxation of rules at EU level.

Countries relying on services will not recover fully the lost demand given the low consumer confidence and stricter safety protocols. These activities are unlikely to recover fully until an effective medical treatment of the virus is found. The typical case is tourism and leisure that have a sizeable weight in Greece, Spain, Italy, Portugal and Croatia. Moreover, these countries' industrial structure is characterised by a much larger number of SMEs which will suffer more as they have less of a capital buffer to absorb losses and therefore are likely to experience more bankruptcies (McKinsey 2020). In contrast, countries with larger industrial sectors, like Germany and its central European suppliers, are likely to recover more quickly as pent-up industrial demand and order backlogs will restart soon after restrictions are eased.

Besides these exogenous reasons, the asymmetric reaction to the crisis is due to endogenous factors. Given the high public debt levels, countries such as Greece, Italy and Spain do not have as much fiscal space to withstand the shock as Germany and other northern European countries. This means that countries could profit differently from the leeway provided by the Commission's triggering of the General Escape Clause of the SGP and the loosening of the state aid framework.

Taking a long-term perspective, comparing the GDP level in 2021 with that in 2008, the German and the French economies will be 12% and 7.7% larger, respectively. Spain shows a mere 0.2% increase compared to 2008, while Italy would still see a reduction of almost 8.4%. The variation of real GDP in the last 12 years shows the weight that the financial and COVID-19 crisis had on the economies, especially in Southern Europe. Therefore, importantly, the asymmetric impact of the COVID-19 crisis adds to the very divergent behaviour of European economies in the financial crisis and its aftermath.[3]

In all, the present crisis will have a larger impact on the periphery, which had not fully recovered from the financial crisis. However, the shape of the recovery as well as its distributive impact will depend on the ambition and effectiveness of the policy response at national and EU level. An ambitious policy reaction would tame these centrifugal forces and safeguard the integrity of the single market and the economic and political viability of the EU project. A sustained intervention to support the worst-hit countries would avoid seeing the EU move from the Great Recession following the 2008 financial crisis to what may be called the Great Fragmentation where the global and European economies would fracture across countries, regions, sectors and generations.

2 Preventing the Great Fragmentation: lessons from the financial crisis

Preventing the Great Fragmentation is a key goal of the European policy response. To what extent can the lessons learned during the financial crisis be of help in designing such a response? Figure 2 tries to capture in a comparative way the main features of the two crises.[4]

Figure 2 Financial crisis and COVID-19: A comparison

	Financial crisis	Covid-19
Nature and narrative	Policy-induced, asymmetric, no consensual view	Exogenous, common in origin, asymmetric in outcome, consensual view
Solidariety/ responsibility	Risk reduction first, risk sharing later	Common response warranted, no moral hazard concerns
Speed of policy reaction	Slow, under "ultima ratio"	Fast
Policy mix	ECB game in town, harsh structural reforms	More balance, fairness incorporated, focus on investment, green and digital transition
Fiscal coordination	Horizontal: rules-based surveillance of national policies	Vertical: key role of EU budget
Conditionality	Creditors' rule and marked-based	National ownership
Institutional set-up	Intergovenmental	Community method
Institutional innovations	EFSF/ESM, Fiscal Compact, BU	RRF, common borrowing, new Own Resources
International cooperation	G20, close US/EA interactions within G7	Limited

Source: Own elaboration.

1. First, while the financial crisis was a policy-induced shock and there was no agreed narrative between Member States, today's crisis shows a more consensual view regarding its narrative, origin, effects and hence the appropriate policy solutions. There is a much less focus on and traction of moral hazard considerations, which instead characterised the financial crisis. There is also a large consensus that the crisis, as discussed above, while common in the origin, will have an asymmetric impact. The fact that the pandemic hit some countries before others generated a moral duty in those countries less hit to help those where the pandemic hit with more intensity. In economic terms, it also generated a positive externality as the countries down the line could profit from the experience and measures taken by those hit first. However, the most compelling reason for a strong EU response is the need to correct the endogenous fragmen-

tation following the suspension of the fiscal adjustment under the Stability and Growth Pact and the loosening of the state aid rules that gave a large advantage to countries with more fiscal space in helping consumers and enterprises. The ensuing fear of undermining the integrity of the single market and, ultimately, of the Union made redistributive policies politically acceptable.

2. Second, during the financial crisis the policy mix was very unbalanced: for most of the years, monetary policy was the only game in town. With insight, the fiscal stimulus of 2009 was withdrawn too soon, at the first signs of growth. The fact that the sudden stop of capital flows and market run were triggered by the discovery of massive cheating in the fiscal accounts of Greece led to a reading of the financial crisis through "fiscal lenses" in core countries. As a consequence, the surveillance framework was tightened with the adoption of the Fiscal Compact and the strengthening of the SGP. This went hand in hand with reluctance on the part of countries with fiscal space to use it, which implied a very unbalanced policy mix, with fiscal consolidation taking precedence over support to the economy. As a result, too much onus fell on the shoulders of the ECB. This led to a paradoxical overturn of Sargent and Wallace's "unpleasant monetarist arithmetic" which postulates that, in the absence of credible constraints on fiscal policy, fiscal dominance will ensue resulting in pressure to monetise public debt (Sargent and Wallace 1981). In the case at hand, excessive fiscal prudence proved also a form of fiscal dominance: when monetary policy is at the effective lower bound, fiscal inaction hampers the effort of the central bank to fulfil its price stability mandate. During the COVID-19 crisis, the need to react strongly via a decisive fiscal expansion was acknowledge from the start, with the ECB and the Commission being the strongest and most consistent advocates.
3. Third, the experience of the financial crisis shows that achieving an appropriate Eurozone fiscal stance only via horizontal, bottom-up coordination of national policies is exceedingly difficult. When a broadly adequate overall stance was attained in the aftermath of the crisis,it took place via the wrong distribution between countries, in violation of their respective fiscal space. The proposals to set up a Eurozone fiscal capacity, as in the Four Presidents' Report and the Five Presidents' Report (Van Rompuy 2012, Juncker et al. 2015),

did not gain political support. Even the modest proposal by the Commission in 2017 to establish a European Investment Stabilisation Function (EISF) was rejected by a number of countries which saw stabilisation as belonging to the national level in EMU. Today, to help offset the asymmetric outturn of the crisis, a complementary central fiscal intervention is paramount. The strong role for the EU budget in the Commission proposals (see the following section) would complement horizontal surveillance with vertical coordination, as originally proposed by the Sapir Report (Sapir et al. 2003, Buti and Nava 2003).

4. Fourth, political acceptability of a central response has led also to the "resurrection" of the Community method rather than pursuing the intergovernmental approach which dominated the decision making during the financial crisis (see chapter 10). A more consensual view on the adequate policy response and the low political traction of moral hazard views, have helped overcome the "ultima ratio" logic which led to delays in decisions, systematic compensations for any European help, and ultimately to the crystallisation of the divide between creditors and debtors. Given the nature of the shock and its potential ramifications, today European policymakers operate much more under Rawls' "veil of ignorance" as those suffering less today are not necessarily going to be spared tomorrow. For instance, the break-up of value chains and possible protectionist reactions in third countries make economies more reliant on external demand more vulnerable.
5. Finally, there has been a radically different role of international cooperation in shaping and implementing the policy response to the two crises. Whilst the financial crisis saw a strengthening of global governance with the rise of the G20, especially at the outset of the crisis (see chapter 35), international cooperation has taken a back seat in the present crisis. Increasing awareness in Europe that, in a more fragmented world where rules-based multilateralism is called into question, an export-led growth model would be increasingly vulnerable, paving the way to a stronger reliance on the EU single market as "indigenous" growth engine.

In sum, this time it may well be different. Domestic and international conditions appear to be reunited for an effective response to the crisis with a decisive role for the EU level and a renewed boost to policy coordination.

3 The European response: Next Generation EU

The Commission has proposed a package of €750 billion – two-thirds grants and one-third loans – over the period 2021-24 to be financed via issuing common debt. Next Generation EU would complement the measures agreed by the Eurogroup for a total of €540 billion in support of healthcare spending, unemployment and short time work, and credit to the private sector. The centrepiece of the Commission package is the Recovery and Resilience Facility (RRF), which amounts to €560 billion between grants and loans to support investment and reforms, with an emphasis on favouring the green and digital transition.

According to Commission estimates, the recovery package would raise real EU GDP by 1¾% in 2021 and 2022, increasing to 2¼% by 2024. Moreover, given the support of investments to countries productivity, even after ten years GDP levels are estimated to be 1% higher than the baseline scenario. The package is estimated to create two million jobs over the medium-term (European Commission 2020a, Verwey et al. 2020).

Based on the allocation key proposed by the Commission, Member States with below-average GDP per capita levels are expected to see a sizeable boost in economic activity in the medium-term, with GDP levels 4½% above baseline by 2024 for those belonging to the lower debt cluster and 4¼% for those belonging to the higher debt cluster. EU countries with above-average GDP per capita levels would experience smaller but still positive GDP effects of 1¼% compared to baseline by 2024.

Lastly, the Commission package is expected to be self-financing. Overall, the average government debt-to-GDP ratio in the EU27 falls by around three-quarters of a percentage point in the short-run, and falls further below baseline levels over the medium-to-long-term. By 2030, the average debt-to-GDP ratio in the EU is estimated to be almost 3% lower than in the baseline scenario. Specifically, for those Member States with below-average GDP per capital level in the higher debt group, debt to GDP is expected to decline by 5%, and 3¼% for those in the lower-debt group by 2024. According to the simulations, over the long-term,

Figure 3 The European Union response to the COVID-19 crisis

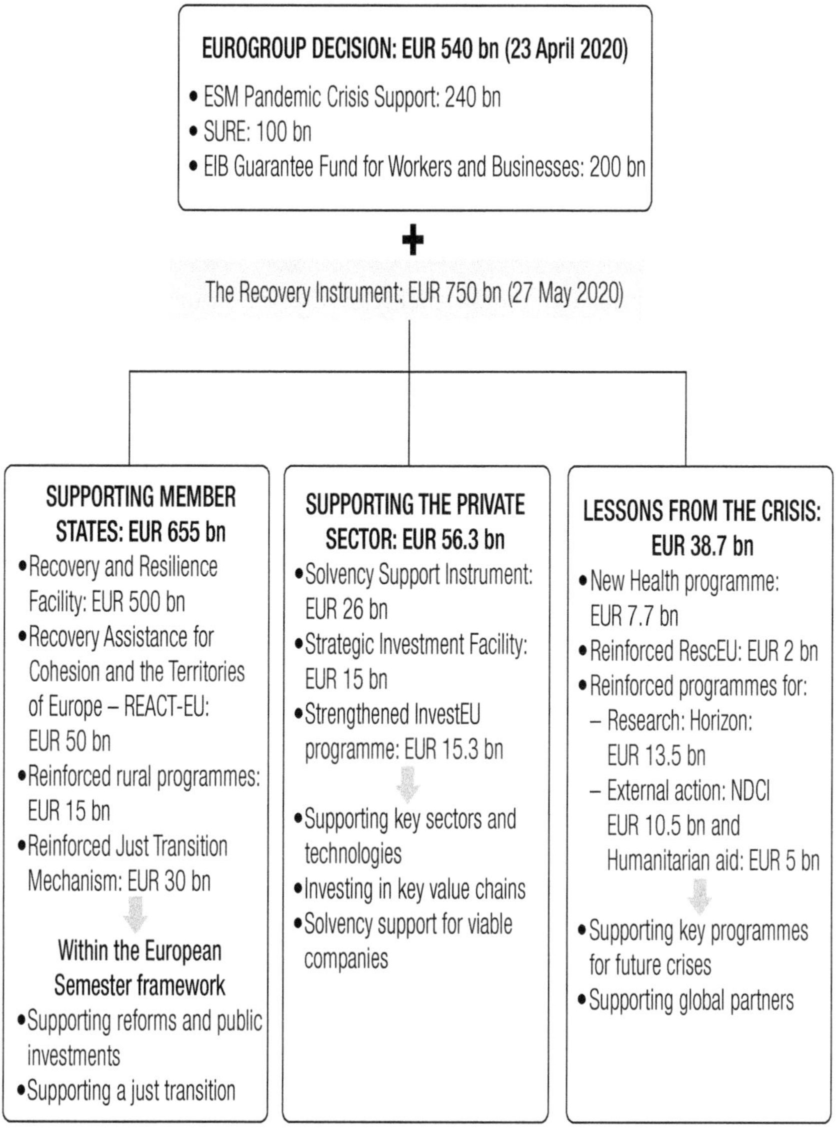

Source: European Commission.

the debt ratio would decline further by 8½% for those in the higher debt group and by 7% for those in the lower debt group by 2030. For the higher income group, the public debt ratio would rise slightly in the medium-term, but by 2030 would fall back to the same level as in the baseline scenario.

4 Stronger political integration ahead?

If adopted, the proposals by the Commission have a chance to strengthen the EU economically. Would that lead also to stronger political integration? Based on Rodrik's globalisation trilemma (Rodrik 2000), Figure 4 illustrates the paths open to Europe in the response to the crisis: Europe cannot achieve deep political integration, strong democratic legitimacy, and decision making essentially based on national institutions at the same time. Options A to C indicate different ways to solve the trilemma.

In the 1980s and 1990s, in response to "Euro-sclerosis," option A was chosen, by establishing the Single Market and EMU: sovereignty was shared at the supranational level by strengthening or creating new European institutions, most notably the ECB. Intergovernmental solutions under option B tended to prevail during the financial crisis: the setting up of the EFSF, later transformed into the ESM, and, on the fiscal front, the adoption of the Fiscal Compact took place in an intergovernmental context where European Council played a leading role rather than Community institutions. Whilst the Single Supervisory Mechanism of the Banking Union was established under Community law, the financial support of the Single Resolution Mechanism and the still-to-be-established common deposit guarantee (EDIS) have been negotiated essentially as intergovernmental tools. Lack of trust and the crystallisation of the division between "creditors" and "debtors" underpinned the intergovernmental approach. Finally, option C prevailed during the immigration crisis of the mid-2010s where, under the impulse of the Commission, some common actions were undertaken, but no common EU immigration policy emerged.

As argued above, the handling of the COVID-19 crisis has so far been characterised by a largely consensual view on the nature and effects of the crisis implying lower concerns of moral hazard and the need to comple-

Figure 4 Trilemma of political integration

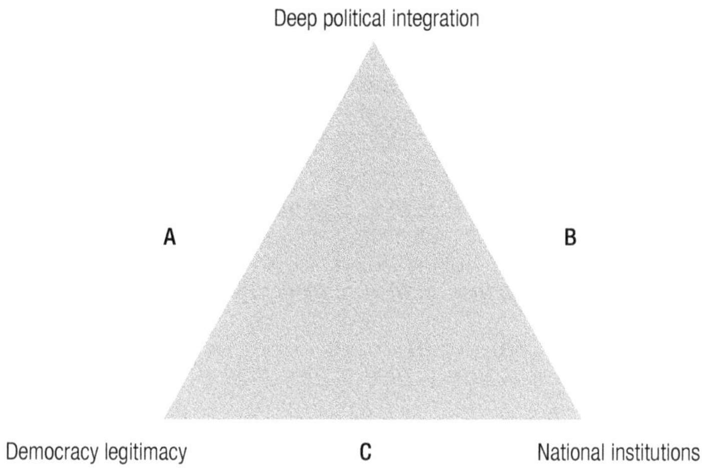

Source: Own elaboration, adapted from Figure 1, chapter 22.

ment the monetary policy response by a centralised fiscal action. The risk of fractured global governance also pushes the EU to devise a response to the crisis that relies more on its inner strengths. As a result, there has been a resurgence of the Community method in comparison to the mainly intergovernmental approach during the financial crisis. Hence, there is chance that option A is chosen with the EU adopting an ambitious response to the COVID-19 crisis, and also finalising long-lasting open institutional proposals such as Banking Union and Capital Markets Union. This would be the best chance to devise an effective response to the crisis and boost European sovereignty domestically and abroad. It would also ensure that the present crisis will not be remembered as the Great Fragmentation.

Notes

[1] The original paper referred to the Commission forecast of Summer 2020 (European Commission 2020b). The present graph is updated to include the 2021 Commission Winter forecast.

[2] The Commission estimates of financing needs are based on the Spring Forecast published in May 2020. Since then the growth outlook for 2020 has deteriorate by about 1 percentage point in both the EU and the Eurozone.

[3] The COVID-19 crisis risks leaving long lasting scars in the social fabric of hardest hit countries. This will concern also intergenerational equity – Cockx (2016) finds that it takes about ten years for young people entering the labour market during a recession to catch up with those that did not.

[4] The analysis in this section draws on chapter 38.

40 Veto Player Theory and the Governance of the Recovery and Resilience Facility*

February 2021

1 The Recovery and Resilience Facility impossible trinity

The Recovery and Resilience Facility is at the heart of Next Generation EU, Europe's plan to tackle the economic fall out of the pandemic crisis. Member States must prepare national plans to receive the EU contributions. These plans include the investment and reform projects as well as their implementation mechanisms. This chapter uses the veto players' theory to explain and predict the governance arrangements chosen by EU countries. It shows that the institutional features of countries and the internal cohesion of governments are important determinants of the governance of Recovery and Resilience Programmes.

With its 672.5 billion euros, the Recovery and Resilience Facility (RRF) represents the biggest component of the Next Generation EU package (750 billion euros). The RRF combines grants and loans with the aim to mitigate the social and economic impact of COVID-19 and create resilient and future-proof economies.

An effective implementation of the RRF via credible and ambitious national Recovery and Resilience Programmes (hereafter, RRPs) is a major challenge. Figure 1 attempts to capture such political challenge via what we call the "RRF impossible trinity"[1]: only solution a) is consistent with the game-changing nature of the RRF, which implies the need to lengthen the time horizon of governments by carrying out investment

---

* Co-Author: Oscar Polli (European Commission), Vox CEPR, 11 February 2021.

projects and reforms which are consistent with the "two Rs" of the RRF. To respond to the need of structural change and enjoy citizens' support, the programmes should help the economies bouncing back after the COVID-19 lockdowns and strengthen their fundamentals by making it more resilient to future shocks.

Figure 1 RRF Impossible Trinity

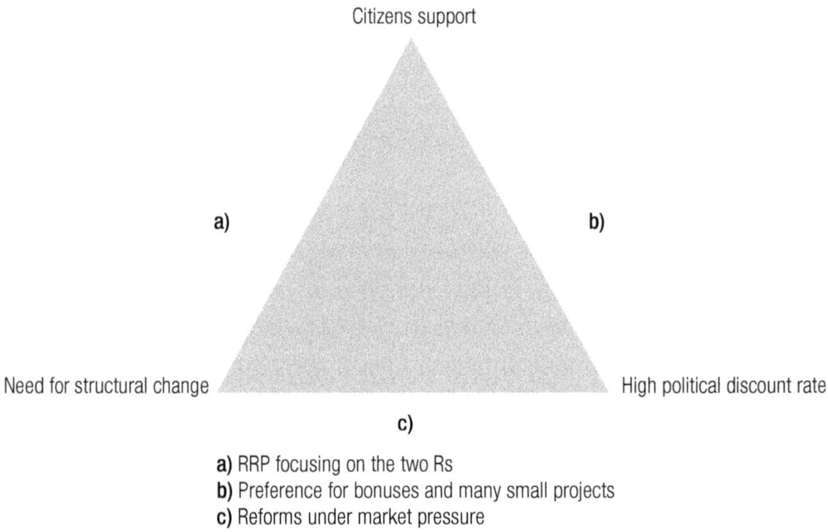

Source: Own elaboration.

2 The governance of the national plans

For solution a) to emerge, an effective governance of the RRPs is needed. The importance of governance was stressed by André Sapir (2020), who demonstrated that it is one of the factors explaining the different intensity of the economic effects of the pandemic in EU countries. Therefore, he underlines that attention should be given to improving governance models. Along these lines, two documents provide concrete guidance to the Member States: the RRF Regulation, which began on 19 February 2021, and the Commission's guidelines published in September 2020 and updated in January 2021 (European Commission 2021a).

RRF Regulation

The structure of the RRF plans is provided by Art. 18 of the RRF Regulation. The RRF plans "*may be submitted in a single integrated document together with the National Reform Programme and shall be officially submitted as a rule by 30 April*" 2021 (Art. 18.3). Those who wish may also submit a draft outline starting from October 2020.

The drafts must include detailed explanations of how they aim to achieve and contribute to the six pillars of the regulation[2], the EU Semester (notably the Country Specific Recommendations for 2019 and 2020) and the green and digital transitions. Thus, they must be coherent with the EU governance, regulatory framework and other EU programmes. They must also include a "*detailed explanation of how the plan strengthens the growth potential*" and other objectives (Art. 18.4).

On the monitoring/reporting side, the plans must envisage milestones (qualitative results), targets (quantitative results) and timetables for the implementation of the reforms and investment projects, the related periods and costs (Art. 18.4). In addition to reporting on these specific phases of their RRPs, Member States should report on common indicators, which are used "*for the purpose of monitoring and evaluation of the Facility towards the achievement of the general and specific objectives*" (Art. 29, 30), namely the RRF pillars or EU priorities and the specificities of milestones and targets.

The Regulation recognises the importance of stakeholders in the implementation and monitoring of the plans, asking that the RRPs include a "*summary of the consultation process of local and regional authorities, social partners and other relevant stakeholders*" for the preparation/implementation of the plans and how their inputs are reflected in them (Art. 18.4). Finally, "*Member States shall report twice a year in the context of the European Semester on the progress made in the achievement of the recovery and resilience plans, including the operational arrangements and on common indicators*" (Art. 27). To achieve this, Member states' biannual reports will be reflected in the National Reform Programmes, which are used for reporting on progress of the plans (Art. 27, 26).

On audit/control, RRPs must explain Member States' "system to prevent, detect and correct corruption, fraud and conflicts of interest, when using the funds provided under the Facility, including arrangements aimed at avoiding double funding" from other EU programmes. Additionally, these explanations of management/control systems and who is responsible should demonstrate how milestones/targets will be achieved to ensure data on these indicators is reliable, including control mechanism, and that sound financial management will be upheld (Art. 18.4, 19.3, 22). Lastly, countries must collect data on the final beneficiaries of funds in order to achieve the milestones/targets and avoid fraud.

European Commission Guidelines[3]

First, the guidelines explain that reforms and investments, with the expected impact, milestones, targets, timelines and costs, should be grouped into homogeneous sets (components). The components should interact with each other and be linked to the green/digital EU flagships[4] of the 2021 Annual Growth Strategy, the European Semester or other priorities. Clarifying the RRF regulation, for each component's projects, Member States should "*provide clear evidence and analysis to underpin, explain and motivate the investment and reform*" and their interaction. The guidelines also indicate that authorities should propose a methodology for tracking the contribution of their plans and the various indicators and results.

Second, the guidelines underline that an effective implementation of the RRPs needs clear responsibilities. Member States should describe the plan's institutional nature, the role of national/regional parliaments, regional/local authorities and advisory bodies, as well as the decision-making process leading up to the adoption/submission of the RRPs, the list of social partners consulted and the type of contacts. Public administrations are key in the plan's implementation and necessitate an effective use of resources and flexibility to ensure that the reforms/investments proceed. Thus, Member States should ensure adequate administrative capacities for the effective implementation of the plan. This also means that, for a timely absorption of funds, RRPs should describe "*if a mature project pipeline is in place or which steps would be necessary to create such a pipeline and support the maturing of projects*," for the entire plan and for the components. States can "*also request technical support under the Technical Support Instrument, which can take the form of Commission led support or external expertise, to help successfully implement specific reforms and investments*" and to achieve milestones and targets.

Finally, a lead authority should have the overall responsibility for the RRF plans and be "the single point of contact for the Commission ("coordinator").” This would be responsible “for the implementation of the recovery and resilience plans, for ensuring coordination with other relevant authorities in the country (including ensuring coherence regarding the use of other EU funds), for monitoring progress on milestones and targets, for overseeing and assuring implementation of control and audit measures, and for providing all necessary reporting, and requests for payment and the accompanying management declaration.” Furthermore, the RRPs should make sure that the coordinator has the administrative capacity, institutional experience, expertise, and the mandate/authority to exercise all relevant tasks. Lastly, the coordination structure and the reporting responsibilities to the coordinator should be clearly described.

How are Member States going about fulfilling such requirements? Although national plans are still in the making, a number of governance models are emerging. Institutional responsibilities are being attributed in a variable geometry to the Prime Minister (PM), the Finance Minister (FM) or other ministers. In the rest of this article, we will try to understand how and why Member States chose different forms of RRF governance, particularly concerning who “the coordinator” is. We do so by using a veto player theory, which, by looking at the influence of decision-making actors in political systems, can help explain why governance systems differ across various forms of government.

3 The veto player theory: single and multiple veto players

The theory of veto players looks at the impact of single/multiple veto players, namely an individual or collective actor whose agreement is required for a policy decision, within the decision making of a political system (Tsebelis 1995, 2002, 2011). It therefore allows the capacity of political systems to introduce significant policy change/reforms (i.e RRPs) to be assessed. Briefly, veto players are considered to be political parties, parliamentary chambers, and other bodies so long as they can veto a decision. This theory predicts that the policy stability/inertia of a political system increases when the number of veto players increases, when their congruence decreases (dissimilarity of policy positions among veto players) and when their internal cohesion increases (similarity of policy positions among the *constituent units* of a veto player). On the contrary, a political system is more susceptible to change when the number of veto players decreases, their congruence increases and internal cohesion decreases.

Thus, not only the number, but also the similarity of positions and the internal cohesion of veto players influence the capacity for change. Congruence defines the similarity of position *between* parties, whereas cohesion measures the size of the differences on a policy or the variety of positions present *within* a party for facilitating cross-party agreements. Congruence is directly related to policy change (the higher the congruence, the higher the possibilities of change), whereas internal cohesion is inversely related to it (the higher the parties internal cohesion, the lower the chances of change) (Schmidt 2002).

According to this theory, in parliamentary systems following the Westminster model such as the British one (e.g. Greece or Malta), with a majoritarian electoral system, single governing parties and a *de facto* unicameral parliament, there is only one veto player. Consequently, decisions will be taken swiftly and the political system is more inclined to produce change. A similar situation is present in semi-presidential systems with one dominant party, such as in France. The French system has elements of both presidential systems (President as part of the executive) and a dominant, single party parliamentary system, with a Parliament-responsible PM. Moreover, the Parliament is *de facto* unicameral and the President has a limited suspension veto. Yet, this also means that when the PM is of the same party as the President (unified majority), there is a stronger single veto player (governing party). This may change with "cohabitation," namely when the PM and President are from diverse forces, with the potential for friction.

On the contrary, parliamentary systems with different forms of proportional electoral systems typically have coalition governments and therefore a multitude of veto players, especially if there is a bicameral system with both chambers having veto powers. In these cases, in addition to the number of veto players, the congruence and cohesion of such players are relevant. In other words, the closer ideologically the parties in a coalition are, the number of veto players in a coalition will be less problematic. Similarly, the more cohesive the parties are, the fewer chances there will be to find cross party support for a given policy. Here, policy change would be slower than in political systems with only one veto player, as more players would need to agree. Therefore, the veto player theory sees a relationship between policy inertia and government instability. Briefly, when change is impossible, a government's instability may result in it changing to break the deadlock, through a change of ministerial portfolios or parliamentary majority, which often relates to coalition governments in parliamentary systems.

4 Veto players and the governance of the RRF: theory and practice

In light of the considerations above, it may be possible to infer why certain countries chose to adopt a specific form of governance for the RRF. Given the urgency and importance of such matters, swift and coherent decisions would need to be taken to provide a comprehensive and orderly RRP in spring. Following the logic of the veto player theory, countries with heterogeneous coalition governments would tend to give a primary role to the PM, whereas those with semi-presidential systems with a dominant party, parliamentary systems with coalitions with broad/congruent majorities and majoritarian systems (single party governments) would tend to delegate responsibilities to a minister (typically the finance minister).

Given the time constraints and the importance of such decisions, in a broad and heterogeneous coalition with more veto players, the PM is more directly involved in important decisions to ensure greater speed and consistency. Additionally, given the political importance of the RRF, divergences can create instability in the coalition and therefore, contrary to delegating this responsibility to a minister of a party at the expenses of another, entrusting the PM can also ensure the stability of the coalition. The veto player theory would indeed predict that policy inertia, due to strong divergences, may lead to government instability and its replacement to break the deadlock. Thus, as the PM is the keeper of the coalition and its variety of interests, it may prevent such instances of crisis on important issues. Conversely, for the same reasons, when there are fewer veto players or even just one, decisions can be more safely delegated to a minister. As such, and also to ensure effectiveness, the competent minister (Finance/Cohesion minister) will be responsible for the RRF (exclusive jurisdiction model). Indeed, because of ideological congruence and the low possibility of divergences, especially in the case of just one veto player, instability is rare. These considerations are summarised in Table 1.

Table 1 Theoretical considerations, veto players theory predictions for RRF governance

	PM responsible	PM guidance, FM execution	Delegation to FM or other minister
Heterogeneous coalition governments, high cohesion within players	X		
Heterogeneous coalition governments, low cohesion within players	X	X	
Coalition governments, high congruence		X	X
Single party and semi-presidential governments			X
Minority governments			X

Source: Own elaboration.

To what extent are these theoretical predictions matched by the emerging RRF governance in EU countries?

Heterogeneous coalition governments

Political science theories suggest that ministers exercise major influence over individual policy areas that pertains to their portfolio of activities. This would suggest that finance ministers or cohesion ministers (for countries that receive large transfers via EU structural funds) should have the prime responsibility in the design and implementation of the RRF. Yet, following a veto player theory, unlike under exclusive jurisdictions, under coalition governments this power is subject to the constraints imposed by the allies of the coalition (Tsebelis 1995, 2002). Moreover, in coalitions, exclusive jurisdiction may have counterproductive outcomes for the internal coherence RRPs.

For example, in a country subject to temporary political instability potentially leading to a change in portfolios, the exclusive jurisdiction model, where ministers do what is included in their competences, would predict constant policy shifts. However, if we accept that crucial issues are decided collectively by the entire coalition, while less important ones are delegated to individual ministers, different outcomes can be projected. In this case, coherence and potentially slow change at the aggregate level could go hand in hand with continuous change of minor issues (those in the exclusive jurisdiction of the minister) (Tsebelis 1995).

When it comes to the RRF, its systemic importance and time constraints could explain why heterogeneous coalition governments (i.e. Spain, Ireland, Portugal, Slovenia) tend to entrust the PM with the responsibility for the implementation of the RRP (See Table 2). In Bulgaria (slim majority, Parliament fragmented), the Deputy PM and the finance minister co-lead, with the former however having the upper hand with a key strategic role. In addition to this, the PM may also veto projects, as in the case of Latvia. In Italy, given the large, heterogeneous coalition, the FM has been given the role of coordination and monitoring, under the guidance of the PM. The "technical nature" and lack of party affiliation of the FM has favoured the delegation of power.

Importantly, the PM is the keeper of the coalition and can thus represent the variety of interests in the coalition or its "median voter." Regarding the speed of the adoption of such a plan, while it is true that an important issue needs to be agreed by the whole coalition including multiple veto players and can thus require more time, entrusting the PM may facilitate such process given their power of mediation. This could also be the case in federal systems, where in addition to the governing parties, regional/state authorities may have a veto in the process (also through representation in the second parliamentary chamber), thus increasing the number of veto players (Germany, Belgium). In Belgium, while the State Secretary for recovery and strategic investment coordinates, they report to a policy support committee composed of members of the federal government and the regions. Importantly, a concertation committee chaired by the PM and including the minister-presidents adopts the working framework, the various steps and the final plan. In Germany, the Chancellor and the finance minister co-lead.

Single party governments and congruent coalitions

In countries with congruent majorities and/or a single veto player, it is easier to delegate responsibilities to a minister and it is probably more effective given its portfolio (i.e Finance or Cohesion ministers) (See Table 2). For semi-presidential systems like in France (also Cyprus, presidential), where today the President and PM controls a parliamentary majority in a unified government situation, but also in Romania, Poland,

Lithuania, where there are congruent majorities or one prominent party, it is easier to delegate RRF responsibility to the finance minister, given the ideological congruence and thus low risks of divergence. These factors also increase the efficiency of delegating RRF responsibilities to a minister of Finance/Cohesion due to the relationship between the nature of their portfolios, competences and what the RRF plan entails.

Similarly, in single party governments in parliamentary systems as in Malta, Greece and Hungary, decisions can be delegated to a minister(s) as having only one veto player will not lead to problems of disagreement. A similar argument could be made for coalition governments in parliamentary systems with just a few parties and which are also close ideologically or not very internally cohesive. In the first case, ideological congruence reduces the differences, whereas less cohesion within a party may enable cross-party support for a policy. Examples of congruent majorities delegating RRF responsibilities to a minister are found in Estonia, Luxembourg, Slovakia, Finland and Austria. Here, while the minister is the prominent figure, it could also be the case that the PM provides only general political guidance or outreach to stakeholders (Austria, Finland), rather than giving substantial political lead or vetting projects as shown above; or that the final decisions/enforcement are taken by the whole government (Estonia), thus also being consistent with coalitions giving some form of role to the PM. Overall, in addition to the delegation to a minister, it could be expected that they will be quicker in adopting such a plan. France, for example, already had a preliminary version of its *France Relance* this summer.

Lastly, the case of minority governments, such as in Denmark and Sweden, is instructive too. In particular, minority governments are commonly single-party governments, whose dynamics in this instance is not fundamentally different from single-party majority governments. Laver and Schofield (1992) argued that there is a difference between a governmental and a legislative majority, and that the party establishing the minority government is usually located centrally. Therefore, it can fluctuate towards one or another ally to have its policies approved by Parliament. Consequently, from a policy-making point of view, a single-party minority government, as long as it remains in power, resembles a single-party majority government and thus has only one veto player (Tsebelis 2013). For these reasons, RRF responsibilities are more easily delegated to a minister, as in Sweden and Denmark. Lastly, in all these instances, whether with one veto player or congruent majorities in a coalition government, and contrary to the cases

Table 2 From theory to practice, RRF governance in EU Member States

<table>
<tr><th rowspan="2">Type of government*</th><th rowspan="2">PM responsible</th><th colspan="2">Ministers</th></tr>
<tr><th>Finance Minister</th><th>Cohesion or other ministers</th></tr>
<tr><td>Heterogeneous coalition governments (PM prominent or PM and FM on similar level)</td><td>Spain, Portugal, Bulgaria (Deputy PM), Ireland, Slovenia</td><td colspan="2">Germany (Chancellor provides support and political guidance and it is chef de file with FM)
Italy (PM provides guidance, political lead and "technical" FM coordinates in cooperation with other ministries)
Latvia (PM provides political lead and vets projects of line ministries, FM assists drafting the plan)
Croatia (PM and FM co-lead)
Czech Republic (PM oversight and guidance, Industry minister and trade drafting)
Belgium (Final decisions by PM and minister-presidents of the regions, coordination of state secretary which reports to PM)</td></tr>
<tr><td>Coalition governments, high congruence (FM prominent)</td><td>Finland (PM provides guidance)
Austria (Chancellor provides guidance, outreach to social/regional stakeholders)</td><td>Finland (congruent and stable majority)
Austria (congruent and stable majority)
Estonia (conservative-led coalition)
Luxembourg (liberal-led coalition, together since 2013)
Slovakia (broad majority, parties close ideologically, conservatives)
France (LREM is prominent)
Lithuania (3 parties, conservative-liberal)</td><td>Poland (three parties close ideologically, one party very prominent)
Romania (one party prominent, PNL)</td></tr>
<tr><td>Single party governments and minority governments (min. gov. behave like the former)</td><td></td><td>Malta (FM in collaboration with unit of EU funds implementation in PM's office, Ministry for Research, Innovation and the Co-ordination of the Post-COVID-19 Strategy in charge of drafting national post-COVID-19 strategy)
Greece (also PM representative, but FM in the lead)
Cyprus (Presidential, one party)
Denmark, Sweden</td><td>Hungary (initially Ministry of Industry in charge, but the PM's office now leading)</td></tr>
</table>

*Netherlands: final decisions after March 2021 elections and formation of the new government.

Source: Own elaboration.

in the previous section above, the exclusive jurisdiction model more easily applies. Indeed, the RRF responsibilities are predicted to be given to the competent minister, usually the FM or in some cases the cohesion minister.

5 Final remarks

In this paper, we argue that the veto player theory can provide an interpretative framework to explain why certain governments tend to assign the responsibility to or close to the PM, while others delegate this to a minister. Overall, the theory predicts that countries with large and diversified coalition governments tended to give responsibility to the PM, as per the predictions of the veto player theory. Some coalition governments, namely those with more heterogeneous and thus with a bigger variety of possible interests, see the PMs as having the most and final responsibility and the RRF portfolio is usually based in their offices. The finance minister has a role still, but the main decision maker is the PM who has clear prominence. In others, both the PM and the finance minister are responsible and on the same level.

Countries with semi-presidential systems with a dominant party/congruent coalition, parliamentary systems with just a few parties in congruent coalitions, single party governments, and minority governments *tend* to delegate responsibilities to the FM, or in some cases, the Cohesion minister. Here, it could be the case that the PM provides general guidance, but the finance minister is prominent.

Overall, our analysis shows that when there is only one, or just a few similar parties in government and therefore a low risk of divergence and risks to the stability of the government, important issues can more easily be delegated to a minister. Consequently, countries with a low number of congruent veto players are more likely to follow the exclusive jurisdiction model, for which a minister will do what is required by its portfolio and hence the RRP falls mainly in the portfolio of the FM. Instead, when there are multiple veto players final and important decisions tend to be retained by the PM, possibly co-leading with the FM or other ministers. While this may slow down the speed of decisions due to the need for compromises, it may facilitate the latter, avoid deep disagreements among allies and ensure coherence among different interests.

On a final note, a few caveats on the limits of this theory should be flagged. While basic in its assumptions, it may present problems of preference measurement. In fact, in addition to the number of veto players, what they stand for needs to be established. The congruence of parties was theoretically deduced looking at the composition of the governments on a left to right ideological scale and as such, there may be the risk that different conclusions may be drawn for different governments. Clearly, in addition to ideology a more precise measurement of party congruence could comprise other parameters including, for example, party organisation and leadership. Here, the general tendency of the personalization of leadership and the centrality of the leaders/PMs may also influence the RRF governance, especially where majorities are narrow, where administrative and political procedures are less defined, or where leadership has been defined through complex processes after the elections.

Similarly, given the novelty of the RRF and that we are at preliminary stages, this makes the determination of specific party preferences for the RRF, for internal and cross-party comparison, difficult and at best approximate. For example, while party manifestos are useful in that regard, RRF preferences cannot be deduced from those. Similarly, understanding the effectiveness and degree of party discipline may also help to measure the likelihood that veto players will move away from the direction of their party and thus enabling cross-party agreement. Overall, therefore, we limited the governments' classification to a theoretical understanding based on an ideological spectrum and internal analysis.

In this paper, we have used the veto player theory to explain the different choices of Member States concerning the governance of RRPs. We put particular emphasis on the issue of congruence of governments in determining the decisions on where to "anchor" the responsibilities for the implementation of the national plans. Clearly, this is only one factor and as such, it does not fully capture the complexities of national institutional arrangements. Even within the realm of the theory of veto players, other factors are likely to play a role. Amongst these particular relevance would be played by the amount of RRF resources (hence its systemic importance), the time until the next elections (hence the role of the PM as guarantor of the whole coalition), and whether, in coalition governments, the PM and the FM belong to the same party (in which case, delegation is easier). A consequence of veto players and these other factors could also be that RRF governance may in some cases be executed through a clear division of roles and responsibilities and others in more flexible and unwritten ways.

Lastly, it will be fruitful to analyse the final RRPs to see the impact of veto players on the coherence, specificity and requirements of such plans. Here, the impact of veto player on the final RRPs may be only one factor. For example, the fact that the veto player theory takes policies as fixed does not take into account that policy-makers may have other interests at heart and may not be only policy-seekers. They may also seek outcome objectives and may be willing to take credit for the implementation of the RRF given its importance for a country's recovery. Obtaining "positional gains from getting things done" may lead to the acceptance of policy losses (Ganghof 2003). This may be especially true for coalition countries, with some being those most hit by the pandemic, and as such, the coalition may actually not be a problem in introducing significant policy changes,as the theory would predict. Similarly, as Ganghof (2003) argues, it may be the case that big exogenous shocks (i.e pandemic) change actors' "policy preferences by changing their beliefs about the mapping of policies onto outcomes" thus again rendering difficult the measurement of preferences. This also calls for a further differentiation of various actors with veto power according to whether their veto is effective.

These are some of the questions that this theory may raise and, if answered with care, could help further discussions on the impact of veto players on the RRF responsibilities, but also the impact on the final RRPs and make useful cross-country comparisons.

Notes

1 Impossible or inconsistent trinities abound in economics. For a review of those most relevant to European integration and EMU, see chapters 20 and 22.

2 (a) Green transition; (b) Digital transformation; (c) Smart, sustainable and inclusive growth, including economic cohesion, jobs, productivity, competitiveness, research, development and innovation, and a well-functioning single market with strong SMEs; (d) Social and territorial cohesion; (e) Health, and economic, social and institutional resilience, including with a view to increasing crisis reaction capacity and crisis preparedness; and (f) Policies for the next generation, children and youth, including education and skills.

3 These Guidelines are based on the December 2020 compromise on the RRF Regulation between the European Parliament and the Council. The numbering and the wording of the provisions changed during the legal revision. In particular, the numbering of the articles is different between the compromise version and the final Regulation which entered into force in February 2020.

4 Power up, Renovate, Recharge and Refuel, Connect, Modernize, Scale-up.

41 The Legacy of the Pandemic: How COVID-19 Is Reshaping Economic Policy in the EU*

April 2021

1 The EU: a history of resilience

The EU is navigating its third crisis in the space of a single decade, following the Eurozone financial crisis and the migration crisis. Jean Monnet famously stated that "Europe will be forged in crises and it will be the sum of solutions adopted for those crises." Indeed, as in previous crisis, the policy solutions are to be found at the intersection between what economic policy suggests and the political reality, and institutions allow, and reflect a combination of principles, flexibility and pragmatism. But every crisis has its own characteristics, and prompts its own response. This crisis is different, and the policy response, with the Next Generation EU initiative at its heart, is breaking new ground.

Successful crisis response needs to pass what could be called the "Monnet Compatibility Test" (see Graph 1). It needs to be economically coherent, marshalling the policy tools and mechanisms that provide for an effective crisis response, addressing root causes, and allowing European economies to recover while minimising damage. In the complex EU institutional framework, it also needs to have institutional coherence, leveraging common governance mechanisms while respecting both subsidiarity and the EU Treaties. Finally, it needs to be politically coherent, maintaining citizens' support in what tend to be traumatic and divisive periods. Unfortunately, combining all three proves to be a very difficult task.

---

* Co-Author: George Papaconstantinou (European University Institute), CEPR Policy Insights, 23 April 2021.

Graph 1 The Monnet Compatibility Test

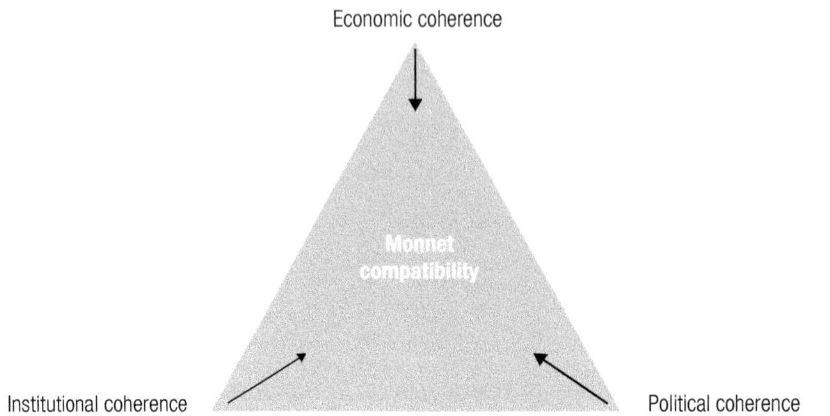

Source: Own elaboration.

In this chapter, we (loosely) apply the Monnet Compatibility Test to the economic policy response to the pandemic. Section 2 reviews policy decisions taken at EU and national level to tackle the economic fallout of COVID-19. The following three sections sketch out the reasons why the current response is different and more ambitious than the policy response to the financial crisis: the evolution of our understanding of macroeconomics (section 3), the nature of the current crisis (section 4), and the policy learning from the financial crisis (section 5). We then review the changes in EU governance and the conditions for success of the national Recovery and Resilience Plans under Next-Generation EU (sections 6 and 7, respectively). In the final section, we examine the factors that will shape the legacy of the pandemic for European integration.

2 The COVID economic policy response

Faced with what amounted to a "sudden stop" of economic activity because of the lockdowns and the simultaneous supply and demand shock in economic systems, the economic policy response at the level of EU Member States was generally swift and decisive. It was aimed at maintaining liquidity through cash, debt and guarantees, ensuring households can delay payments, and workers receive pay-checks even in quarantine or if temporarily laid off; at the same time preventing mass insolvencies, ensuring firms have cash flows to pay workers and suppliers, especially among small and young businesses. The logic was to focus on disaster relief first, followed by policies to facilitate the recovery.

EU Member States differed both in generosity and in their mix of policy instruments, reflecting in part diverse underlying fiscal conditions. Such differences however were significantly less prominent than in the Eurozone crisis, so that taken together, the overall fiscal effort as well as the liquidity provisions added in 2020 to a substantial 2.5 trillion euro response (see Table 1), with a significant part of the effort carried over into 2021.

Table 1 National and EU responses to the COVID crisis

		Fiscal	Liquidity
NATIONAL, EU-27	2020 measures	500bn	2500bn
EU	SUR, ESM, EIB		540bn
	NG – EU	390+bn	360bn
ECB	PEPP		1850bn

Source: European Commission.

While the economic response first came at the national level, it was decisions by the EU institutions (ECB, Commission, Council) that set the stage for recovery and altered the discourse on economic policy and governance moving forwards. In a benign environment of low interest rates, the ECB quickly adopted a key role in ensuring the crisis did not spill over into financial markets, and moved to stabilise markets for sovereign debt. It expanded its targeted and non-targeted refinancing operations, amended its collateral policy (expanding accepted collateral and eligibility, reducing haircuts) and crucially both renewed and expanded its asset purchases programme, while inaugurating the large mission-specific Pandemic Emergency Purchase Programme (PEPP), which included flexibility in the capital key and issuance share.

At the level of the European Commission, the early activation of the general escape clause in the Stability and Growth Pact (SGP) rules allowed Member States to proceed with large scale fiscal relaxation. This was supplemented by measures for liquidity provision aimed at protecting firms (the relaxation of state aid rules allowing the activation of national guarantees, coupled by increased overall lending capacity by the EIB), safeguarding jobs (Commission borrowing and lending to governments to finance expenditures related to short time work – SURE) and assisting sovereigns (for the Eurozone, the decisions on European Stability Mechanism (ESM) pandemic crisis support).

In terms of EU decision-making however, the seminal moment was the July 2020 EU Council decision (European Council 2020), which put in place a new fiscal and governance framework. This built on a Franco-German proposal that for the first time allowed for direct transfers to countries, in addition to loans, and on proposals by the Commission to finance such combined grants and loans by borrowing in markets and temporarily lifting the own resources EU ceiling. The resulting EU Recovery Plan has two pillars (European Commission 2021d): a new recovery instrument of €750 billion which involves funding raised on financial markets for 2021-2024 (Next Generation EU); and a reinforced long-term EU budget for 2021-2027 (€ 1,100 billion). Together, these are aimed at assisting Member States to recover and "build back better," by aligning public and private investment with broader EU goals – notably its green and digital agenda.

These decisions represent a clear break with precedent. This is true in terms of instruments (the use of grants, the push for new "own resources," the issuance of common debt on the part of the Commission); institutional mechanics (the return of the Community method); as well as in terms of the sheer magnitude of the underlying fiscal effort and liquidity provision.

In terms of the magnitude of the effort and its adequacy to the task at hand, we would be amiss if we did not make reference to the ongoing debate comparing the EU response with that of the US. There are a number of elements to this debate: first, whether the US policy response is economically appropriate (discussion focusing on the output gap vs. the war-like crisis response) and conversely whether in comparison, the EU effort is too timid; second, what secondary impact the heating of the US economy will have on the EU economy (Andersson et al. 2021, ECB 2021). On the first issue, whilst the jury is still out, given its composition, the $1.9tr stimulus is likely not to display a huge multiplier, so the impact on inflation may turn out less than feared.

Moreover, the infrastructure plan announced by President Biden at the end of March will be spread over 10 years and will be partly financed by higher taxes, which will limit its stimulative impact. While there is no doubt that in headline numbers the fiscal expansion in the EU will remain lower than that in the United States, in terms of composition its quality will be higher and should give rise to stronger fiscal multipliers. Still, given the sheer size of the US fiscal and monetary stimulus, consolidated growth over the next two years will likely be higher in the United States than in the EU. Because of this, on the second issue, Europe is likely to benefit from positive demand spillovers, whilst the negative spillovers arising from higher interest rates and a stronger Dollar, are more likely to affect emerging market economies, especially those holding a large share of Dollar denominated debt.

However one judges the EU economic policy stance vis-a-vis that of the United States, the decisions taken do represent a significant "stepping up" and a break with past EU policy. What has underpinned this shift? We contend that three broad factors have driven what we are observing. The first is the evolution in our understanding of macroeconomic policy beyond the EU – the new macro paradigm. The second is the different nature of the current crisis. And the third is policy learning from the Eurozone financial crisis. Together, these explain why decisions taken to date differ in scope and nature from those in the financial crisis and potentially set the stage for closer European economic and political integration post-crisis.

3 How macroeconomics has changed

Keynes famously quipped about the power of the ideas of economists and their influence in policy-making that "madmen in authority, who hear voices in the air, are distilling their frenzy from some academic scribbler of a few years back." While this description may not be particularly flattering to politicians, it nevertheless retains an element of truth. Economic policy-making often follows the evolution of academic understanding in the field – with a lag. And over the course of the last two decades, the paradigm of macroeconomic policy in open economies has shifted.

There is nothing new here of course. Over the long-term, the consensus in macroeconomics has constantly evolved, chiefly in response to crises or to an apparent disconnect between theory and reality. In this vein, the global financial crisis led to a change of the thinking in macroeconomics around a number of issues. Chief among these is the insufficient focus on the complex role of banks and of financial institutions in general in the economy, and the associated risks related to liquidity and eventually solvency for economic stability. The nature of macro financial linkages have become more important in economic discourse.

A related set of issues centres on the possibility of secular stagnation in economies (Summers 2013, Teulings and Baldwin 2014), an old concept that has seen some resurgence, suggesting that a number of factors (ranging from demographics to globalisation and the debt overhang) are dragging down the equilibrium real interest rate as well as long-term growth, despite advances in technology and productivity. In an environment characterised by persistently deficient aggregate demand, economies would be operating at the "effective lower bound" (ELB), which is, however, higher than the equilibrium real interest rate: this is captured in Graph 2 by r_0^* being lower than r_L, the rate at the ELB.

The policy implications of this shift in macroeconomic thinking are stark and are already having an impact on policy-making consensus, including in Europe. They relate to a number of policy issues and tools: the overall macro policy stance, our understanding of debt sustainability, the mix of fiscal and monetary policy, and the role of central banks.

In a situation of persistent excess savings, with economies operating at or close to the ELB and little or no inflation, there are strong arguments for a macroeconomic policy stance that attempts to counteract chronically deficient aggregate demand and reach full-employment output with a more expansionary stance of fiscal policy (bringing the economy from point B to point E in Graph 2). This would seem to reverse the overarching emphasis on "prudent" fiscal policies that dominated over a long period.

A corollary relates to the size of fiscal deficits and debt sustainability. In an environment of persistently low interest rates, there is increasing support from academic writing for higher "upper bounds" of fiscal positions as well as a discussion on the quality of fiscal expenditures that enter into their measurement. Equally, with debt to GDP levels historically high, the emphasis on establishing debt sustainability has complemented the focus on headline debt to GDP ratios with a more complex analysis reflecting for example the capacity to service debt.

Graph 2 Policy mix at the effective lower bound

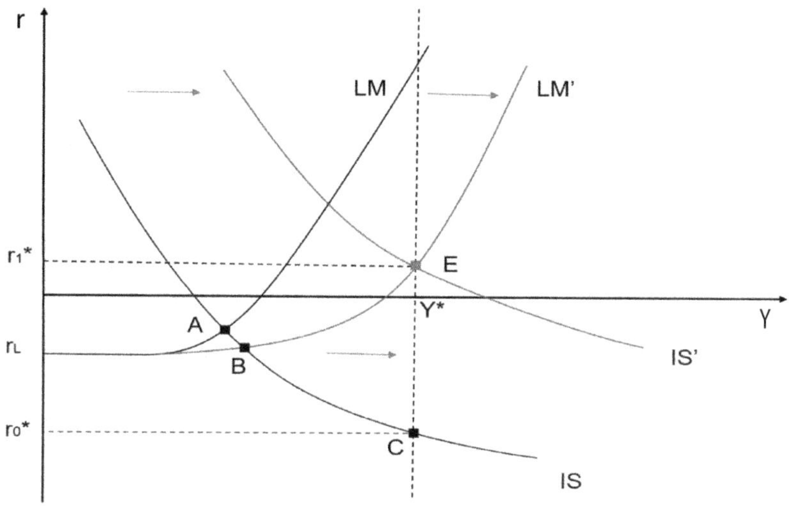

Source: Own elaboration.

Central to this new policy discussion is the fiscal-monetary policy mix and the role of central banks. Operating at or near the ELB, central banks including the ECB have increasingly resorted to unconventional measures, with an emphasis on asset purchases. This has raised a number of issues. The first is the delimitation between fiscal and monetary policy: the expansion of their portfolio with government securities effectively blurs the lines between classic monetary policy and government finance. The second – and related – is their call to governments (repeatedly by the ECB) to step up fiscal policy so as to avoid central banks bearing the brunt of policy adjustment: this is based on the awareness that, in the presence of a very large demand shortfall, the Keynesian spillovers dominate the spillovers via public debt sustainability.[1] And the third is their increasingly important role in acting as a safety valve in avoiding disruption emanating from the financial sector.

The need to ensure a "congruent" policy mix (Bartsch et al. 2021) underpins an evolution in the relations between monetary and fiscal authorities in Europe. The ongoing monetary strategy review undertaken by the ECB and the review of the macroeconomic surveillance framework launched by the Commission, whilst institutionally independent, will need to result *ex post* into a coherent framework in both the short-run and in the medium to long-run.

4 The different features of the COVID-19 crisis

The second broad reason explaining the different policy response at EU level is the features of the COVID-19 crisis compared to the Eurozone crisis. In Table 2, we attempt to capture this difference along several dimensions. As argued in chapter 39, a key difference relates to the exogenous nature of the pandemic shock. Whilst a number of policy circles viewed the Eurozone crisis as self-inflicted because of reckless behaviour, such arguments did not gain traction in the case of the pandemic. The way in which the Eurozone crisis unfolded also tainted the narrative on its nature: the discovery of massive cheating in Greece's budgetary accounts implied that the financial crisis was "read" through fiscal lenses. This didn't happen during the pandemic. The risk of fragmentation between countries, regions or sectors as a result of the COVID-19 shock – which some have characterised as a K-shape recovery – have also justified such help to be delivered via multi-year investment and reform programmes.

These differences in the nature and incidence of the crisis allowed for a completely different political narrative to develop which eventually culminated into a very different policy response. In the Eurozone crisis, the prevailing narrative was one of moral hazard; avoiding it implied the design of policies that could demonstrate policy mistakes had consequences. Creditors dictated the rescue conditions. The leading role of the European Council within an intergovernmental setting was the way to impose those conditions. At a second stage, the rationale for a collective response was the preservation of the euro.

In contrast, the narrative during the current crisis is almost completely devoid of moral hazard elements. The focus is on a common threat that requires a common response. Countries who were hit hardest could benefit from EU solidarity. This also allowed policymakers to avoid operating under the so-called "ultima ratio" doctrine, where the EU help would come only at the very end, after all domestic actions by vulnerable countries had been exhausted and was actually conditional on such actions been undertaken.

The devastating and sudden impact of the pandemic triggered what is commonly considered a very fast response by EU standards: in addition to the prompt action by the ECB, the Commission made sweeping proposals in May 2020 and by the end of the year an agreement at EU level had been achieved. Additionally, the parliamentary ratification of the increased ceiling of the Own Resources part of the EU budget (necessary to allow the Commission to borrow in markets) is planned to be completed in Spring 2021; under normal circumstances, that process would take between two to three years. It is important that delays do not occur in the present phase of the ratification process and the roll out of the RRPs (see below).

Table 2 Comparing crises

	Eurozone crisis	COVID crisis
Source	Fiscal shock and/or financial sector imbalances	Combined supply and demand shock
Nature	Endogenous and asymmetric in origin	Exogenous and common in origin
Impact	Severe; asymmetrical on countries	Severe; asymmetrical on countries (and sectors)
Timing	Full economic shock felt over 1-2 years	Immediate economic shock over 1-2 quarters
Recovery	Slow, but durable	Fast(er), but fragmented

Source: Own elaboration.

5 Policy learning from the financial crisis

The Eurozone financial crisis put EU governance rules and institutions in a stress test, as the very existence of the common currency area was called into question. As a result old rules had to be reinterpreted, new policy tools were devised, new institutions were created, and an overhaul of the EU economic governance started in earnest. However, to justify rescue plans in creditor countries, there was an urge to return to normality, withdraw the fiscal support and start implementing the rules again as quickly as possible. Whilst the institutional and political conditions at the time make *ex post* rationalisation a treacherous exercise, it is fair to conclude that the response to the Eurozone crisis was sub-optimal.

In our view, the main lessons from the Eurozone crisis which are relevant for devising the response to the COVID crisis are the following (see also chapter 39):

First, monetary policy has to be very forceful to stop self-fulfilling dynamics, or the realization of negative equilibria. Whilst the ECB reacted very quickly in the summer of 2007, with liquidity provisions at the first signs of market dislocations, it was more hesitant compared to other central banks in relaxing the monetary stance and embarking on asset purchases. It was only in summer 2015, in the aftermath of the "whatever it takes" statement by Mario Draghi that the ECB came to be perceived by the markets as standing fully behind the integrity of the Eurozone. A certain amount of risk-sharing is needed in EMU, either openly via national budgets, or indirectly via the ECB balance sheet, yet for a time this was in short supply.

Second, after a very severe shock, early withdrawal of fiscal stimulus is very costly. Analyses pioneered by Olivier Blanchard (see Blanchard and Leigh 2013, 2014) showed that fiscal multipliers are much higher under large negative output gaps, especially if monetary policy approaches the effective lower bound. Again, in retrospect, after a strong fiscal expansion in 2009 which helped stem the negative shock, EU countries were too quick to "declare victory" and embark in sharp fiscal retrenchment.

Third, achieving an appropriate Eurozone fiscal stance only via horizontal coordination of national policies is exceedingly difficult. During the Eurozone crisis, countries with fiscal space focused on their domestic situation and refused to use it, whilst countries with fragile fiscal conditions frantically searched for a fiscal space they objectively did not have. As a consequence, when the appropriate fiscal stance at the aggregate level was attained, this was usually via the wrong country distribution, which also meant lower effectiveness due to lower multipliers. The intergovernmental *forma mentis,* at the time led to the ruling out of a central fiscal response, either at EU or Eurozone level, which meant a failure of subsidiarity.

The response to the pandemic benefitted from learning the lessons of the Eurozone crisis. As recalled above, both the ECB and national fiscal policies reacted swiftly and massively. In addition, the commitment to keep a supportive fiscal stance in 2021 and 2022, helped by extending the General Escape Clause of the SGP to 2022 (European Commission 2021c), showed the awareness of maintaining support for the economy for as long as it takes. This was clearly communicated by monetary and policy authorities on both sides of the Atlantic who stressed that the risk of doing too little largely outweighed that of doing too much. Finally, the Next Generation EU (NG-EU) initiative ensured a degree of vertical policy coordination and complemented the national fiscal expansions.

In sum, through the prism of the Monnet Compatibility Test, the policy response during the Eurozone crisis did not fully meet the economic and institutional criteria. Judging by the large support to NG-EU also in so-called Frugal countries (see European Parliament 2021, European Commission and European Parliament 2021), one can conclude that the political compatibility is also more likely to be met this time round, compared to the political divisiveness which marred public opinion during the Eurozone crisis.

6 Getting the EU governance right

Over the past several years, a growing debate has emphasised the importance of institution building relative to a purely rules-based system. Mario Draghi has made this point forcefully in comparing the effectiveness of monetary policy to fiscal policy coordination and response (Draghi 2019a).

To be sure, during the financial crisis there was a strengthening of rules-based coordination and institution building. However, as illustrated in Table 3, this took a very specific complexion: both the main new institution – the ESM – and the most important strengthening of fiscal rules – the Fiscal Compact – were not only intergovernmental in nature, but the adoption of the latter was a condition for the adoption of the former. The first pillar of the Banking Union – the Single Supervisory Mechanism (SSM) – was instead supranational, but the second pillar – the Single Resolution Board (SRB) – was mixed; at the same time, the necessary third pillar – the single deposit guarantee system or EDIS – is still under discussion.

On the contrary, the main innovations during the response to the pandemic had a very clear supranational status: this is the case for the Recovery and Resilience Facility within NG-EU. The support for short time work, SURE, has an intergovernmental component since borrowing by the Commission takes place on the back of guarantees provided by national budgets. However, it is clearly identified in the markets and the

Table 3 Coordination processes in the EU: institution-building vs. rules-based coordination

Coordination mode	Financial crisis	COVID-19 crisis
Institution building	• European Financial Stability (EFSF)/European Stability Mechanism (ESM) * Single Supervisory Mechanism (SSM) ▲Single Resolution Board (SRB) * European Fiscal Board (EFB)/ National Fiscal Councils (NFCs)	* Recovery and Resilience Facility (RRF) ▲Support to mitigate unemployment risks in an emergency (SURE) • ESM Pandemic Crisis Support (PCS)
Rules-based	• Fiscal Compact * Strengthened SGP * Macroeconomic Imbalances Procedure	* SGP General Escape Clause * [Review of the Six-Pack and Two-Pack]

• Intergovernmental   * Supranational   ▲ Mixed

Source: Own elaboration.

public as a Community instrument and indeed this is one of the reasons for the market success and large access by Member States compared to the ESM pandemic facility.

In sum, the response to the COVID-19 crisis is proving very different than that prevailing during the Eurozone crisis. What is emerging is a more balanced institutional landscape with a more robust combination between rules-based and institutional features, which has the potential to lead to more effective vertical coordination. Once again, the Monnet Compatibility Test, most notably institutional coherence, appears to be better satisfied in the current situation. This evolving institutional landscape should also be reflected in the outcome of the ongoing review of the EU macroeconomic policy framework.

7 Making sure the COVID response works – looking at Member States

For the politics to be conducive to more EU integration, there is one essential precondition: that the novel mechanisms and tools currently put into place to address the economic fallout of the COVID pandemic are indeed successful in helping European economies "built back better," and are widely seen as doing so. This implies that the degree of success of national efforts based on EU funding go beyond the positive impact on Member State economies; they will provide a narrative for the evolution of overall EU governance as well.

The timeline for the Recovery Plan process is now fully set out, but the effective use of the large sums involved in the time horizon prescribed represents a huge challenge, as "Next Generation EU" funds require committing the resources by the end of 2023 and completing the payments by the end of 2026 (European Council 2020). To this end, Member States are currently finalising their national Recovery and Resilience Plans (RRPs) with the Commission, setting out a detailed reform and investment agenda based on specific guidelines (European Commission 2021a) and offering a narrative consistent with overall EU objectives (Table 4).

Table 4 Recovery and Resilience Plans content and processes

Narration	Internal consistency of NRRPs		
General objectives	From objectives to projects	Cost estimation	Monitoring
• Addressing the challenges and priorities of the European Semester • Strengthening growth, resilience and job creation • Contributing to economic and social cohesion • Contributing to the green/ digital transition	• Final and intermediate objectives • Individual projects and investment timeframes • Implementation and achievement indicators	• Total costs • Correspondence between costs and impacts on employment and the economy • Possible other EU funding	• Accompanying measures (reforms, investments) • Monitoring procedures

Source: Adapted from Buti and Messori (2020).

As Member States complete their RRPs and move to the implementation phase, a number of issues will be critical for success:

- *Governance structures.* The new funding tools embody new conditionality rules, as well as milestones and targets for the disbursement of funds. As a response, EU Member States have been putting in place new governance arrangements for the design and implementation of what will be in many cases a defining national effort. While one size does not fit all and arrangements will vary, they will need to embody a "whole of government" approach under a strong central direction, with the required flexibility of different administrative structures. Interestingly, this transition seems to be proving easier for countries with experience from support programmes during the Eurozone crisis.

- *Investments plus reforms.* A crucial element of the new Recovery Plan is the "twinning" of investments with reforms in national interventions. It will be important for this complementarity of reform elements and investments to be present in substance in both the design of RRPs as well as in their implementation, going beyond simple "box-ticking" and a formal adherence to rules, and to ground these within an overarching growth strategy in each country based on green/digital transitions.
- *Conditionality and ownership.* During the Eurozone crisis, the heavy conditionality imposed on programme countries meant that in many cases lack of "ownership" in individual countries undermined the reform effort. A new balance needs to be found under the Recovery Plan, where conditionality is lighter and linked to adequately addressing all or a significant subset of country-specific recommendations made in the context of the European Semester that are relevant for recovery and resilience. While respecting this new setup, the review process will need to reflect this conditionality in a substantive and rigorous way, as it relates to both the efficiency of the use of funds in individual cases as well as the future of EU governance more broadly.
- *Digital and climate.* In order to "recover and transform," the twin digital and green transitions have been put at the heart of RRPs. Ensuring the national plans (and their methodology/metrics) attain the digital and climate targets and guaranteeing the "do-no-significant-harm" principle will be important in this respect, as will ensuring additional EU funding in these areas, leveraging and not simply displacing private investment projects. In addition, as a number of green and digital projects will be similar across countries, a process of peer-exchange and learning from best practices in implementation should prove useful.

- *Transnational spillovers.* By design, the Recovery Plan prioritises national investments, and their "ownership" will be national, not EU-wide. In the digital and climate areas however (and even beyond those), there are strong externalities and network spillovers. Neglecting these in the appraisal of projects at national level will result in the loss of an important opportunity to push forward European value-added and European public goods aspects.
- *Fiscal sustainability.* Once the pandemic is over and support is gradually and carefully withdrawn, member states will be left with higher levels of national debt and will have to reverse current fiscal positions. This is why it is important for RRPs to include measures that improve the quality of taxes and of public expenditure and thereby support fiscal sustainability over the medium-term, and clearly distinguishing one-off from recurrent expenditures.
- *Granularity.* For many EU countries, the funding linked to their RRPs will represent a one-off opportunity to reset their national economies. Experience shows that implementing such large investment efforts rests on a host of factors: having clear milestones, setting well-defined targets, adopting proper audits and controls, a robust economic impact assessment and cost estimates, and being complementarity with other EU funds. It is this type of granularity that links the design of RRPs to a successful implementation phase.
- *Stakeholders.* Despite their technical elements, and especially as the RRPs will combine reforms and investments towards transformation, their success will hinge on being embedded in societal acceptance. The timing and quality of the involvement of national stakeholders will therefore be important, in accompanying the process, and operating at different levels (from central to local) of national administrations and government.

8 Conclusions – post-COVID shaping factors

In addition to its human, economic and social toll, COVID-19 is forcing us to rethink attitudes and policies across a number of areas that go beyond the critical success factors of the economic policy response. Some of the issues that stand out could be grouped under four distinct headings: the new emerging boundaries between state and market; revisiting the notion of subsidiarity in the new environment; reconnecting the EU/domestic with the international/global agenda; and the need for EU economies and policy-making to deal with longer-term structural shifts taking place.

1. *Defining the new boundaries between state and market.* As the pandemic ripped through European societies, it brought with it a new realisation of the importance of well-functioning health systems, as well as the ability of national governments and the EU to protect Europeans. This simple realisation is concretely translated in a number of policy shifts, or ongoing discussions, which may break new ground: from an emerging paradigm for fiscal balances and policy mix, to a new social compact (with higher minimum wages, a universal basic income, more progressive tax systems) or to the debate on strategic autonomy in key sectors/products that would increase resilience at national and EU level (encapsulated in the shifts from "just in time" to "just in case"). In all these areas, what is underlying is a rethink of the balance between what is provided by states and what is determined mainly by market forces. This policy shift is evident across most EU nations, as well as in the United Kingdom and the United States. In a medium-term perspective, it will be crucial that the renewed emphasis on strong social protection does not hamper – but actually enhances – the reallocation of factors of production. Shifting from on-the-job protection to in-the-market protection will be a key challenge.
2. *Revisiting subsidiarity.* A related issue concerns the balance of what belongs to the domain of national policy in Member States and what is a matter for the EU collective. This gives a new twist to the discussion on subsidiarity, as can already be seen by the decisions around the EU Recovery Plan or the proposals on a European health union. The pandemic revealed the need for coordination at EU level and forced cooperation in a number of areas, from travel rules to vaccine procurement. Post-crisis, there will be a review of what has worked and what has not: on certain issues, coordination of national policies will suffice; on others, direct supply at EU level will be needed. As health is a global public good, there will be a need to "elevate" a number of issues surrounding the prevention and management of future pandemics to the EU level. At the same

time, the pandemic has highlighted the importance of rebuilding a more "dense society," achieving solidarity through a sense of belonging, and not just from the services delivered by the national welfare state. This would suggest moving policy delivery in the opposite direction, to the local level, closer to citizens. In Einaudi's tradition of marrying economic freedom and social cohesion, in the post-COVID world, the role of communities and intermediate bodies will be enhanced (Einaudi 1949, Gigliobianco 2010).[2]

3. *Reconnecting the EU domestic with the global agenda.* COVID-19 is also pushing the EU to reconnect the domestic with the global agenda. This is where the other dimension of strategic autonomy belongs – the one dealing not with global supply chains but instead with new geo-economic relations. In a situation of geopolitical re-ordering, with difficult trade relations and blocs in flux, upgrading the global role of the EU will be essential in order to be able to influence the discussion on European and global public goods (not just health and pandemics, but also climate and digital governance), as well as to avoid beggar-thy-neighbour policies in areas such as trade or finance. The domestic ramifications of a more assertive global role of the Union are substantial: the Single Market will need to provide a more "indigenous" source of growth and enhance the robustness of Europe's value chains; macroeconomic policies will have to reduce the dependency from external demand, acknowledging that persistent current account surpluses are a source of vulnerability. It is also in this context that one should reflect on the need to complete the EMU; while bringing to a conclusion the reforms that started with the Eurozone crisis is important in terms of better functioning of the EU and increasing its resilience to shocks, it is also essential for bolstering the international role of the euro and thereby increasing the weight of the European Union in the global economy. The issuance of common EU debt under Next Generation EU will also help to increase the attractiveness of the euro.[3]
4. *Responding to longer term shifts.* The final COVID policy take-away concerns the need to respond to longer term structural shifts. In the pandemic, everything digital thrived. At a first level, this clearly requires a European push to digital – and indeed the EU Recovery Plan is supposed to help the EU "recover and transform" with the twin digital and green transitions. At the same time, the dominance

of digital raises new policy issues regarding regulation and competition in digital platforms, as well as issues such as the protection of workers in a new online environment. The changes brought by COVID will also force a broader rethink of the role and nature of work, the role and rights of remote workers and even the new meaning of "essential workers."

The policy response to the current crisis has broken new ground. At the same time, the difficulties over vaccines delivery and uncertainties on the follow up at national level on Next Generation EU have shown that the latest advances will need to be consolidated. Whether the response to the pandemic marks a fundamental shift in the paradigm of European integration – and hence ultimately meets the Monnet Compatibility Test – or it remains an "exceptional one-off" under extreme duress will depend on addressing the four shaping factors highlighted above.

Notes

[1] When Keynesian spillovers prevail and monetary policy is pushed against the ELB, fiscal dominance is actually achieved via excessive fiscal prudence, thereby turning on its head Sargent and Wallace "unpleasant monetarist arithmetic" (Sargent and Wallace 1981). See chapter 38.

[2] The role of communities in breaking the rural-urban divide and the "third pillar" in finding a new balance between the market and the state are explored by Collier (2018) and Rajan (2019).

[3] The huge success of EU debt issuance under the programme SURE shows the large appetite in financial markets for common euro-denominated bonds.

42 A Curiosum: When Dunning-Kruger Meets Carlo M. Cipolla at the Time of COVID-19

Many of you have heard of the Dunning-Kruger effect (Dunning and Kruger 1999) and the basic laws of human stupidity by Carlo M. Cipolla (Cipolla 2021). The first shows empirically that stupid people often overestimate their intelligence and are much more self-confident than intelligent people who tend to doubt their convictions. Graph 1 illustrates such an effect.

Graph 1 Dunning-Kruger effect

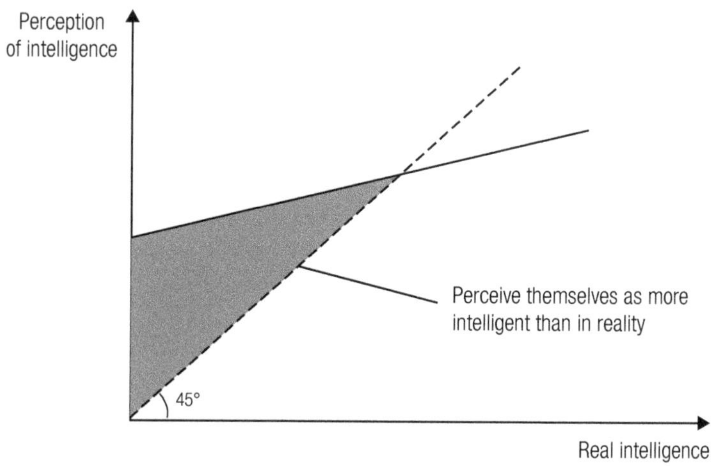

Source: Own elaboration.

The second posits that the population can be divided in four categories: Intelligent, Bandits, Helpless and Stupid according to the benefit/damage they cause to themselves and the society. Intelligent people behave in a way to benefit themselves as well as the society. Bandits profit themselves by harming the rest of us. The helpless benefit others, but in that process harm themselves. Finally, the stupid are the most pernicious of all as the harm both themselves and the others. This is captured in Graph 2.

Graph 2 Carlo M. Cipolla's categories

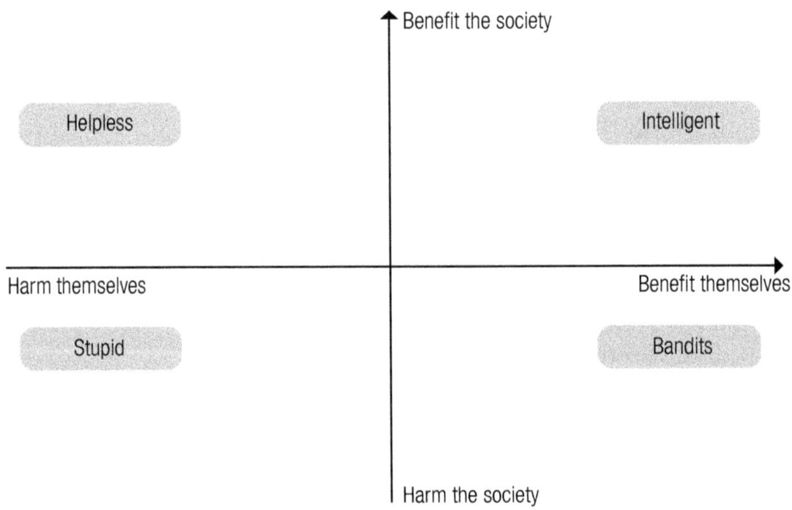

Source: Own elaboration.

What happens when the two theories meet at the time of the COVID-19 crisis? This is depicted in Graph 3. Basically, in the perceived world of the Stupid, the axes are shifted South-West (dotted lines).

Hence we can identify five areas where reality and perception collide:

A. here are people who perceive themselves as intelligent whilst in reality they are helpless. These are people who are tempted to follow Trump and inject themselves with disinfectant.
B. here are those who are perceived as helpless whilst they are stupid, so they cause damage not only to themselves, but to the society.

These are people who go around wearing protective masks on their chin.

C. people who perceive themselves as intelligent whilst in reality are stupid. These are the people who joined the movida at the Navigli in Milan the first day of partial reopening.
D. people perceived as intelligent whilst in reality they are bandits. People who sell miraculous remedies against the virus over the internet.
E. finally, you have people perceived as bandits, whilst in reality they are stupid. Here belong the "sovranists" as portrayed by most mainstream media.

Graph 3 When Dunning-Kruger Meets Carlo M. Cipolla

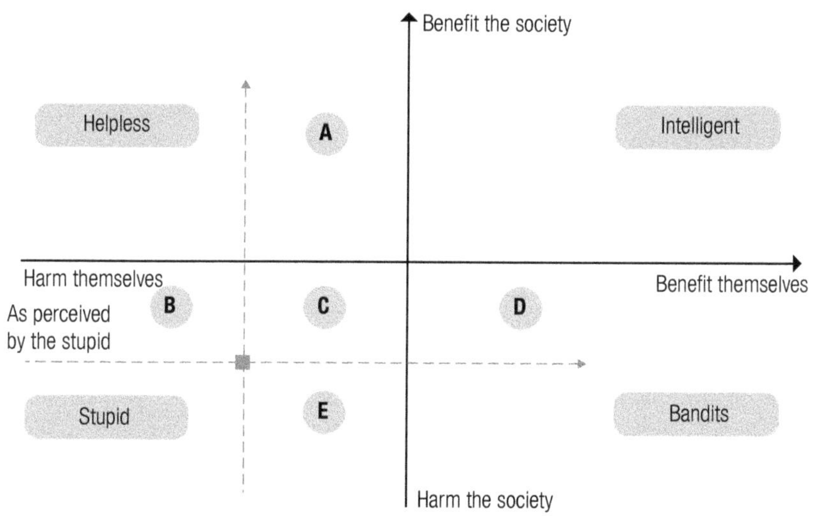

Source: Own elaboration.

Postscript: The Value of "Just in Case" Policymaking

by *Martin Sandbu*

In the summer of 2017, I received an email from Marco Buti. Some of my recent Financial Times commentary had "attracted quite a bit of attention here at the Commission," he wrote. That was putting it politely; I had been fairly critical of Brussels thinking. So it was a pleasant surprise that Buti went on to ask if I could give a seminar at the Directorate-General for Economic and Financial Affairs to share my contrarian analysis with the staff there. It turned out to be a combative but friendly event, in which I presented some sacrilegious theses on Europe's monetary union.

I recount this anecdote as an illustration of something the Commission does not often get credit for. Behind the façade of technocratic rigidity – arguably inevitable and even proper for an unelected civil service, though there can be too much of a good thing – a lot of deeply committed effort goes on to get things right, both analytically and in terms of serving the citizens of Europe.

The volume to which this postscript is a bookend is a rare demonstration of a willingness by a working official to go beyond unresponsive dogmatism. To take just one example, in chapter 17 Buti gamely takes on a line of criticism levelled by a number of academics and financial analysts (I have taken their side myself): the self-avowed Campaign Against Nonsense Output gaps. In brief, the charge is that the commission's technical methodology for calculating output gaps is too "austerian," engineered to make the gaps unreasonably small and hence to unjustifiably weaken arguments for fiscal stimulus. Buti fully engages with the question, accepting its deep political importance, while bringing arguments to bear for his and the commission's analysis. By accepting the need to justify the commission's policy analytically, he subjects the policies he must ultimately defend to contestability on which a democracy depends.

There are many paradoxes in this tension between being, of necessity, a programmatic defender of the bloc's policy and a tentative policy entrepreneur engaging in the public and expert debate. In the former guise, the commission and its officials are saddled with policies that EU politics often reduce to the lowest common denominator, such as the *ultima ratio* financial rescue packages Buti describes. In the latter, this book shows that the Commission has also tried to be part of more ambitious solutions, giving a hearing and sometimes outright support to what would be the best policy solutions were it not for the political constraints.

Admittedly there are not many Commission officials whose pen has been as unreserved as Buti's. What is lacking in frequency is made up for in importance. His public engagement is that of the top official in the policy area – economic and financial affairs – where the Commission arguably has the most influence apart from trade policy. And here lies another paradox: despite all the accusations of democratic deficit, the Commission is more, and more freely, engaged in public policy debate than the civil service of many nation states.

I cannot think of many equivalents to the contributions in this book from career civil servants in finance departments around the world, such as the UK or the US Treasury departments. Central banks – including the European Central Bank – certainly play their part in an intellectually driven policy debate, but the bureaucracies of national executives are usually on a very short leash. The closest may be the White House's Council of Economic Advisors – but its members are of course politically appointed economists serving only at the pleasure of sitting president. (Interestingly, Germany's federal finance ministry has on Olaf Scholz's watch been showing signs of outreach to participate the broader expert debate.)

The Commission, in contrast, uniquely combines the role of an executive of pooled political sovereignty with one more akin to international organisations such as the International Monetary Fund. That, perhaps, is why an at times rigid policy stance – enforced by member states – has co-existed with a greater open-mindedness over which policies would be better.

Reading across Buti's many papers, for example, it is striking to note his demonstration that Eurozone fiscal policy, enforced or at least backed by the Commission, was strongly procyclical in the years 2011 to 2015, meaning it aggravated the recession and slowed the recovery in those years. A robust defence of the bloc's fiscal policy in the Barroso years as "responsible" then gives way to the policy recommendation of robust fiscal stimulus in the Juncker years. This book reveals that thinking was evolving faster than what could have gleaned from statements. Indeed we can even find in Buti's work views that might not long ago have been thought unmentionable, such as the idea greater deficit spending can *reduce* public debt burdens (see the discussion in chapter 16).

No doubt the political leadership of the Commission (and of the European Council) matters for how this contradiction between the mind and the flesh, so to speak, is reduced. In the meantime, political constraints on letting analytical arguments evolve prompted Buti's inquisitiveness to explore how institutional reform could help narrow the distance between the best and the politically possible.

But more consequential, I think, is that what must at times have been an intellectually uncomfortable predicament, bought opportunities for the Commission to move with the big changes taking place in leading economic policy thinking (again, much like the IMF). Recognising that one may have made mistakes – even if implicitly – is a prerequisite for learning. And as time passes, this learning is made more and more explicit, as shown by Buti's deep syntheses of the past 13 years in chapters 38 and 41.

Where in some jurisdictions – the US and the UK are obvious example – one may have to wait for a pivotal election to change ways of thinking in government institutions, in the EU, things tend to work the other way round. Simply put, by sticking its neck out in the sometimes bruising public and expert debates on the best economic policy, the Commission has broached the analytical groundwork needed to adapt to changing political circumstances. Frequently derided as inflexible and sluggish, this sort of preparation in fact improves the commission' ability to jump when the politics are unblocked.

Think of it as "just in case" policymaking – like the pandemic has forced businesses to shift from a "just in time" to a more resilient "just in case" management of their supply chains. "Just in case" policymaking can put the Commission in a place to act quickly once the political winds change. A good example is collective unemployment insurance, which turns up in Buti's chapter 5 as a way to smooth shocks across the Eurozone, responding to academic and think-tank debate at the time. Jump to 2020, and just such a scheme (known as SURE) was put in place in a matter of months, once the pandemic had galvanised political leaders into backing schemes to combat divergence between member states.

How can we project Buti's "just in case" policy analysis into the future? Given how deeply the pandemic has disrupted the politics of economic policymaking, there are a number of areas where the intellectual developments charted in this book are rapidly coming into their own.

One is, of course, fiscal policy – in fact three dimensions of EU fiscal policy, all of which are at or reaching a pivotal moment. First, the evolving thinking on the fiscal stance I have already mentioned – and which chapter 41 describes so clearly – put the Commission in a good place to be a strong advocate for fiscal support in March 2020, when it suspended the fiscal rules. That remains the case at the time of writing, in April 2021, when member states must soon weigh how fast to withdraw emergency fiscal support, and are at the same time watching the US experiment of President Joe Biden's enormous fiscal push. If it turns out that deficit-funded stimulus can permanently raise economic output – positive hysteresis, in the jargon – then there is further intellectual work to do for Buti and his colleagues along these lines.

The second dimension is fiscal union, of which the unprecedented "Next Generation EU" package is a – for the time being temporary – incarnation. Here, too, the hard thinking around fiscal risk-sharing mechanisms on display in these pages has come in handy for the commission's readiness to manage a common budget roughly double the usual size. The imminent test is how it will manage the recipient governments' plans for spending the money. A decade's worth of thinking about the ideal combination of fiscal support and structural reforms will, as the concluding chapter suggests, be brought to bear on this task.

The third dimension is the reform of the fiscal rules, which cannot be postponed very much longer. Everyone agrees they are not fit for purpose, but the politics have proved intractable. Here the Commission's work as illustrated by Buti in this book, together with that of the European Fiscal Board, have arguably sketched out the landing zone: an expenditure growth rule and a debt anchor, differentiated across member states. It may be – one hopes it is – another case of being ready to jump once the politicians give the go-ahead.

Something quite similar can be said about the banking union, a recurrent focus of Buti's writing. Here, too, it is arguable that the technical landing zone has been found – at least one emerges from these pages – comprising a combination of common deposit insurance, a common safe asset, and a reduced exposure of banks to their own sovereigns, all on top of the progress that has already been made in making it easier to restructure failing banks. (On that latter score, note the long and commendable intellectual journey the commission travelled from its refusal to countenance writing down senior bank bonds early in the global financial crisis and Eurozone debt crisis.) While the associated work on capital markets union has not come as far, the direction of travel, and the (for now mostly intellectual) forces driving it, are similar.

Again, the question is when politicians will be ready to make the jump. When they do, they will find the preparations have been made to turn a vision into reality. And one ingredient has been inadvertently put in place: the safe common asset in the form of eurobonds that will finance the recovery package. It is a reasonable bet that the analytical work done by Buti and others will in time impress on political leaders that these eurobonds serve too useful a financial function to be withdrawn as they mature.

These examples should leave us with two notes of caution.

One is that conceivable economic disruptions in the years ahead could also touch on issues where the "just in time" thinking is not yet sufficiently developed.

A renewed public debt crisis, for example, is unlikely but possible even if the prudent thing today is to spend as much as possible. Not enough has been done, and no sufficient technical solution has been developed, to future-proof eurozone countries' debt. Their governments have not, for example, sufficiently heeded Buti's recommendation (chapter 15) to extend debt maturities to lock in low rates.

A greater possibility is the return of starkly asymmetric current accounts within the eurozone. Originally part of the point of monetary union – to let capital flow to where it could do the most good – the lesson drawn in the eurozone debt crisis was to avoid them. Once the monetary union found itself delivered from that existential threat, the thinking on internal current account asymmetries stopped evolving. More Buti-like exploration would come in useful for when they return.

The other caveat is the one topic in this book that has not played the role one might have imagined: reform of the EU's governing institutions. The surprising lesson of the pandemic has been that policy improvements (such as better fiscal stances, Eurobonds, and fiscal risk-sharing) that were thought unachievable without changing political institutions have rapidly emerged without them. It is important to be clear about the semantics here: I would not count innovations in policy instruments such as the Recovery and Resilience Facility or SURE as *institutional* reforms, because they do not formally reconfigure political authority to any significant degree. There are no new bodies and no treaty changes. Of course it is possible that as these instruments are deployed, especially if they are successful, they change the relative influence of power within the many layers of authority in the EU. Yet it will not be by design, but as the result of a process launched by the existing institutional setup.

So perhaps Buti's various politico-institutional trilemmas are not as binding as they may seem. If so, there are two ways of taking this. One – glass half empty –is that in the end, politicians will rule, and if it takes something as enormous as a pandemic to make them act, there is little hope for progress. The alternative, which I prefer, is that a quiet analytical chipping away at the problem –the "puzzling" of policymaking that Adam Tooze refers to in the foreword –matters more than we may think. Indeed when the Commission has been at its boldest –think of the 2015 "flexibility communication" allowing it to encourage more investment-friendly budgeting – it has found that its analytical work reveals that some power is there for the taking.

As Buti recalls, John Maynard Keynes famously wrote that politicians – "madmen in authority" –drew their "frenzy from some academic scribbler of a few years back." It is all the more productive –and better for democratic legitimacy –for that frenzy to be drawn from thinking informed by *in medias res* policymaking experience, and from the much-more-than-scribbling of the sort collected in this book.

Bibliography

Aikman, D., M. Galesic, G. Gigerenzer, S. Kapadia, K. Katsikopoulos, A. Kothiyal, E. Murphy, and T. Neumann (2014), "Taking Uncertainty Seriously: Simplicity versus Complexity in Financial Regulation," Bank of England Financial Stability Paper No. 28, May, London: Bank of England.

Alcidi, C., G. D' Imperio, and G. Thirion (2017), "Risk-sharing and Consumption-smoothing Patterns in the US and the Euro Area: A Comprehensive Comparison," CEPS Working Document No. 2017/4, May, Brussels: Centre for European Policy Studies (CEPS).

Alfaro, L., and M. X. Chen (2012), "Surviving the Global Financial Crisis: Foreign Ownership and Establishment Performance," *American Economic Journal: Economic Policy,* 4(3), pp. 30-55.

Allsopp, C., and M. Artis (2003), "The Assessment: EMU, Four Years on," *Oxford Review of Economic Policy,* 19(1), pp. 1-26.

Andersson, M., C. Checherita-Westphal, R. Gomez-Salvador, L. Henkel, and M. Mohr (2021), "Economic Developments in the Euro Area and the United States in 2020," ECB Economic Bulletin Issue 2/2021, Frankfurt: European Central Bank.

Andor, L. (2015), "Fair Mobility in Europe," FES Social Europe, Occasional Paper, Friedrich-Ebert-Stiftung, January.

Andor, L. (2019), "EU Enlargement: The Social Dimension. Human Capital and East-West Imbalances," pp. 9-15 in I. P. Székely (ed.), *Faces of Convergence*, Vienna: The Vienna Institute for International Economic Studies.

Andor, L., and P. Pasimeni (2016), "An Unemployment Benefit Scheme for the Eurozone," *VoxEU.org*, 13 December. Available at: https://voxeu.org/article/unemployment-benefit-scheme-eurozone.

Andrews, D., and C. Criscuolo (2013), "Knowledge-based Capital, Innovation and Resource Allocation," OECD Economics Department Working Papers No. 1046, May, Paris: OECD Publishing.

Antràs, P., and A. De Gortari (2017), "On the Geography of Global Value Chains," NBER Working Paper No. 23456, May, Cambridge Massachusetts: National Bureau of Economic Research, Inc. (NBER).

Anzoategui, D., D. Comin, M. Gertler, and J. Martinez (2019), "Endogenous Technology Adoption and R&D as Sources of Business Cycle Persistence," *American Economic Journal: Macroeconomics,* 11(3), pp. 67-110.

Arendt, H. (1958), *The Human Condition,* Chicago: The University of Chicago Press.

Arnold, N., B. Barkbu, E. Ture, H. Wang, and J. Yao (2018), "A Central Fiscal Stabilisation Capacity for the Euro Area," IMF Staff Discussion Notes No. 18/03, March, Washington D.C.: International Monetary Fund.

Asdrubali, F., B. Sorensen, and O. Yosha (1996), "Channels of Interstate Risk Sharing: United States 1963-1990," *The Quarterly Journal of Economics,* 111(4), pp. 1081-1110.

Bach, S., G. Baldi, K. Bernoth, B. Bremer, B. Farkas, F. Fichtner, M. Fratzscher, and M. Gornig (2013), "More Growth through Higher Investment," *DIW Economic Bulletin*, 3(8), pp. 5-16.

Bache, I., S. Bulmer, S. George, and O. Parker (2015), *Politics in the European Union*, Oxford: Oxford University Press.

Baker, S. R., N. Bloom, and S. J. Davis (2021), "Economic Policy Uncertainty," *Policyuncertainty.com.* Available at: http://www.policyuncertainty.com/.

Baldwin, R. (2012), "Global Value Chains: Why They Emerged, Why They Matter, and Where They Are Going," CEPR Discussion Paper No. 9103, August, London: Centre for Economic Policy Research (CEPR) Press.

Baldwin, R., and F. Giavazzi (2015), *The Eurozone Crisis: A Consensus View of the Causes and a Few Possible Solutions*, a VoxEU.org eBook, London: Centre for Economic Policy Research (CEPR) Press.

Baldwin, R., and T. Okubo (2019), "GVC Journeys: Industrialisation and Deindustrialisation in the Age of the Second Unbundling," *Journal of the Japanese and International Economies,* 52(C), pp. 53-67.

Barkbu, B., S. P. Berkmen, P. Lukyantsau, S. Saksonovs, and H. Schoelermann (2014), "Investment in the Eurozone: Why Has It Been Weak?," *Eurozone policies*, Selected issues, 26 July.

Barro, R. (1979), "On the Determination of the Public Debt," *Political Economy,* 87(5), pp. 940-947.

Barro, R., and D. Gordon (1983), "A Positive Theory of Monetary Policy in a Natural Rate Model," *Journal of Political Economy,* 91(4), pp. 589-610.

Bartsch, E., A. Bénassy-Quéré, G. Corsetti, and X. Debrun (2021), "It's All in the Mix: How Monetary and Fiscal Policies Can Work or Fail Together," Geneva Report on the World Economy No. 23, December, London, Geneva: Centre for Economic Policy Research (CEPR), International Center for Monetary and Banking Studies (ICBM).

Baumann, Z. (1999), *Liquid Modernity,* Cambridge: Polity Press.

Bean, C. (2015), "Causes and Consequences of Persistently Low Interest Rates", *VoxEU.org*, 23 October. Available at: https://voxeu.org/article/causes-and-consequences-persistently-low-interest-rates.

Beblavy, M., and K. Lenaerts (2017), "Feasibility and Added Value of a European Unemployment Benefits Scheme. Main Findings from a Comprehensive Research Project," January, Brussels: Centre for European Policy Studies (CEPS) and Directorate-General for Employment, Social Affairs and Inclusion, European Commission.

Bénassy-Quéré, A., and F. Giavazzi (eds.) (2017), *Europe's Political Spring: Fixing the Eurozone and beyond*, a VoxEU.org eBook, London: Centre for Economic Policy Research (CEPR) Press.

Bénassy-Quéré, A., B. Mojon, and A. D. Schor (1998), "The International Role of the Euro," CEPII Working Papers No. 1998-03, July, Paris: Centre D'études Prospectives et D'Informations Internationales (CEPII) Research Center.

Bénassy-Quéré, A., M. Brunnermeier, H. Enderlein, E. Farhi, M. Fratzscher, C. Fuest, P. O. Gourinchas, P. Martin, J. Pisani-Ferry, H. Rey, I. Schnabel, N. Veron, B. Weder di Mauro, and J. Zettelmeyer (2018), "Reconciling Risk Sharing with Market Discipline: A Constructive Approach to Euro Area Reform," CEPR Policy Insight No. 91, January, London: Centre for Economic Policy Research (CEPR).

Beyer, A., V. Gaspar, C. Geberding, and O. Issing (2008), "Opting Out of the Great Inflation: German Monetary Policy after the Break Down of Bretton Woods," NBER Working Paper No. 14596, December, Cambridge Massachusetts: National Bureau of Economic Research, Inc. (NBER).

Berglof, E., S. Guriev, and A. Plekhanov (2019), "The Convergence Miracle in Eastern Europe: Will It Continue?," pp. 19-27 in I. P. Székely (ed.), *Faces of Convergence*, Vienna: The Vienna Institute for International Economic Studies.

Bernanke, B. (1983), "Irreversibility, Uncertainty, and Cyclical Investment," *The Quarterly Journal of Economics*, MIT Press, 98(1), pp. 85-106.

Bertelsmann Stiftung (2016), "Fear Not Values. Public Opinion and the Populist Vote in Europe," *eupinions* #3. Available at: https://www.bertelsmann-stiftung.de/fileadmin/files/user_upload/EZ_eupinions_Fear_Study_2016_ENG.pdf.

Bertola, G. (2007), "Finance and Welfare States in Globalizing Markets," in C. Kent, and J. Lawson (eds.), *The Structure and Resilience of the Financial System*, Sydney: Reserve Bank of Australia.

Bertoldi, M., H. Scherrer, and G. Stanoeva (2013), "The G20@5: Is It Still Delivering?," ECFIN Economic Brief, Issue 27, November, Brussels: Directorate-General for Economic and Financial Affairs (ECFIN), European Commission.

Bertoldi, M., H. Scherrer, and G. Stanoeva (2016), "The G20 and the EU: A Win-Win Game," European Economy, Economic Brief No. 009, April, Brussels: Directorate-General for Economic and Financial Affairs (ECFIN), European Commission.

Bhattacharya, A., and H. Kharas (2018), "Time to Reform the Multilateral Development Bank System," *Brookings*, 20 February. Available at: https://www.brookings.edu/blog/future-development/2018/02/20/time-to-reform-the-multilateral-development-bank-system/.

Bickerton C., H. Dermot, and U. Puetter (2015), "The New Intergovernmentalism: European Integration in the Post-Maastricht Era," *JCMS: Journal of Common Market Studies*, 53(4), pp. 703-722.

Bishop, G. (2013), "Bolstering the Still-Fragile Euro: A Plan for a Temporary Eurobill Fund," *GrahamBishop.com*. Available at: https://www.grahambishop.com/StaticPage.aspx?SAID=412.

Blanchard, O. (1984), "Current and Anticipated Deficits, Interest Rates and Economic Activity," *European Economic Review*, 25(1), pp. 7-27.

Blanchard, O. (2007), "Adjustment within the Euro. The Difficult Case of Portugal," *Portuguese Economic Journal*, 6(1), pp. 1-21.

Blanchard, O., and D. Leigh (2013), "Growth Forecast Errors and Fiscal Multipliers," IMF Working Paper 13/1, January, Washington D.C.: International Monetary Fund.

Blanchard, O., and D. Leigh (2014), "Learning about Fiscal Multipliers from Growth Forecast Errors," *IMF Economic Review*, 62(2), pp. 179-212.

Blanchard, O., E. Cerutti, and L. H. Summers (2015), "Inflation and Activity – Two Explorations and their Monetary Policy Implications," IMF Working Paper No. 15/230, November, Washington D.C.: International Monetary Fund.

Blanchard, O., C. Erceg, and J. Lindé (2016), "Jump Starting the Euro Area Recovery: Would a Rise in Core Fiscal Spending Help the Periphery?," in M. Eichenbaum, and J. A. Parker (eds.), *NBER Macroeconomics Annual 2016*, Vol. 31, April 15-26 2016, Chicago: University of Chicago Press.

Blanchard, O., M. Griffiths, and B. Gruss (2013), "Boom, Bust, Recovery: Forensics of the Latvia Crisis," *Brookings Papers on Economic Activity*, 2013(2), pp. 325-388.

Blanchard, O., F. Jaumotte, and P. Loungani (2013), "Labor Market Policies and IMF Advice in Advanced Economies During the Great Recession," IMF Staff Discussion Notes No. 13/02, March, Washington D.C.: International Monetary Fund.

Blinder, A. (2016), "Fiscal Policy Reconsidered," The Hamilton Project, Policy Proposal 2016-05, May, Brookings.

Bofinger, P. (2015), "German Wage Moderation and the EZ Crisis," *VoxEU.org*, 30 November. Available at: https://voxeu.org/article/german-wage-moderation-and-ez-crisis.

Bordo, M., and R. N. McCauley (2017), "Triffin: Dilemma or Myth?," BIS Working Papers No. 684, December, Basel: Bank for International Settlements (BIS).

Borg, A. (2014), "Fiscal Policy in the Shadow of Debt: Surplus Keynesianism Still Works," in G. Akerlof, O. Blanchard, D. Romer, and J. Stiglitz (eds.), *What Have We Learned? Macroeconomic Policy after the Crisis*, Cambridge Massachusetts: MIT Press.

Borio, C., M. Drehmann, and K. Tsatasaronis (2011), "Characterising the Financial Cycle: Don't Lose Sight of the Medium-term!," paper prepared for the Reserve Bank of Chicago-ECB 14th Annual International Banking Conference, *The Role of Central Banks in Financial Stability: How Has It Changed?*, Chicago 10-11 November.

Bourlès, R., G. Cette, J. Lopez, J. Mairesse, and G. Nicoletti (2010), "Do Product Market Regulations in Upstream Sectors Curb Productivity Growth: Panel Data Evidence for OECD Countries," OECD Economics Department Working Papers No. 791, July, Paris: OECD Publishing.

Brainard, W. C. (1967), "Uncertainty and the Effectiveness of Policy," *American Economic Review*, 57(3), pp. 411-25.

Brender, A., and A. Drazen (2008), "How Do Budget Deficits and Economic Growth Affect Re-election Prospects? Evidence from a Large Cross-section of Countries," mimeo, previously appeared as NBER Working Paper No. 11862.

Brunnermeier, M., H. James, and J. P. Landau (2016), *The Euro and the Battle of Ideas*, Princeton: Princeton University Press.

Brunnermeier, M., S. Langfield, M. Pagano, R. Reis, S. Van Nieuwerburgh, and D. Vayanos (2016), "ESBies: Safety in the Tranches," ESRB Working Paper No. 21, September, Frankfurt: European Systemic Risk Board (ESRB).

Buiter, W., and D. Lubin (2019), "Did EU Membership Bring Economic Benefits for CESEE Member States?," pp. 33-37 in I. P. Székely (ed.), *Faces of Convergence*, Vienna: The Vienna Institute for International Economic Studies.

Buti, M. (2016), "Europe in the New Global Economic Governance: Can We Still Make a Difference?," *Economia Politica*, 33(2), pp. 119-127.

Buti, M. (2017), "The New Global Economic Governance: Can Europe Help

Win the Peace?" in *Reform of the International Monetary System and New Global Economic Governance: How the EU May Contribute*, International Monetary Issues No. 3, Robert Triffin International Association – RTI, Brussels: Versant Sud.

Buti, M. (2019), "Renewing the (Damaged) Social Contract," Dahrendorf Forum, Hertie School of Governance, 9 May. Available at: https://ec.europa.eu/info/sites/info/files/economy-finance/mb-dahrendorf_forum_v3.pdf.

Buti, M. (2020), "Riding through the Storm: Lessons and Policy Implications for Policymaking in EMU," *VoxEU.org*, 12 January. Available at: https://voxeu.org/article/lessons-and-policy-implications-policymaking-emu.

Buti, M., and N. Carnot (2013), "The Debate on Fiscal Policy in Europe: Beyond the Austerity Myth," ECFIN Economic Brief No. 20, March, Brussels: Directorate-General for Economic and Financial Affairs (ECFIN), European Commission.

Buti, M., and M. Messori (2020), "Next Generation EU: An Interpretative Guide," LUISS Policy Brief, June, Rome.

Buti, M., and M. Nava (2003), "Towards a European Budgetary System," EUI RSC Working Papers No. 2003/08, Florence: European University Institute (EUI).

Buti, M., and P. C. Padoan (2012), "From Vicious to Virtuous: A Five-point Plan for Euro-zone Restoration," CEPR Policy Insight No. 61, London: Centre for Economic Policy Research (CEPR).

Buti, M., and A. Sapir (1998), *Economic Policy in EMU: A Study by European Commission Services*, Oxford: Clarendon Press.

Buti, M., and A. Turrini (2012), "Slow but Steady? Achievements and Challenges in Competition Disinflation within the Euro Area," ECFIN Economic Brief No. 16, November, Brussels: Directorate-General for Economic and Financial Affairs (ECFIN), European Commission.

Buti, M., S. Deroose, V. Gaspar, and J. N. Martins (2010), *The Euro: the First Decade*, Commission of the European Communities, Cambridge: Cambridge University Press.

Buti, M., D. Franco, and L. R. Pench (1999), *The Welfare State in Europe – Challenges and Reforms*, Cheltenham: Edward Elgar.

Buti M., M. Jollès, and M. Salto (2019), "The Euro – A Tale of 20 Years: What Are the Priorities Going Forward?," *Intereconomics*, 54(2), pp. 65-72.

Buti, M., C. Martinez-Mongay, K. Sekkat, and P. van den Noord (2002), "Automatic Stabilisers and Market Flexibility in EZ: Is There a Trade-off?," OECD Economics Department Working Papers No. 335, Paris: OECD Publishing.

Buti, M., W. Röger, and A. Turrini (2009), "Is Lisbon Far from Maastricht?

Trade-offs and Complementarities between Fiscal Discipline and Structural Reforms," *CESifo Economic Studies*, 55(1), pp. 165-196.

Buti, M., A. Turrini, P. van den Noord, and P. Biroli (2009), "Defying the 'Juncker Curse': Can Reformist Governments Be Re-elected?," *Empirica*, Springer, 36(1), pp. 65-100.

Buti, M., A. Turrini, P. van den Noord, and P. Biroli (2010), "Reforms and Re-elections in OECD Countries," *Economic Policy*, 25(61), pp. 63-116.

Caldera Sánchez, A., A. de Serres, and N. Yashiro (2016), "Reforming in a Difficult Macroeconomic Context: A Review of the Issues and Recent Literature," OECD Economics Department Working Paper No. 1297, May, Paris: OECD Publishing.

Calligaris, S., M. Del Gatto, F. Hassan, G. I. P. Ottaviano, and P. Schivardi (2016), "Italy's Productivity Conundrum: A Study on Resource Misallocation in Italy," European Economy, Discussion Paper No. 030, May, Brussels: Directorate-General for Economic and Financial Affairs (ECFIN), European Commission.

Calmfors, L. (2001), "Wages and Wage-bargaining Institutions in the EMU: A Survey of the Issues," CESifo Working Paper No. 520, Oxdord: CESifo

Carnot, N. (2014), "Evaluating Fiscal Policy: A Rule of Thumb," European Economy, Economic Papers No. 526, August, Brussels: Directorate-General for Economic and Financial Affairs (ECFIN), European Commission.

Carnot, N., M. Kizior, and G. Mourre (2017), "Fiscal Stabilisation in the Euro Area: A Simulation Exercise," CEB Working Paper No. 17-025, October, Brussels: Université Libre de Bruxelles.

Cecchini, P., M. Catinat, and A. Jacquemin (1988), *The European Challenge 1992: The Benefits of a Single Market*, Aldershot: Wildwood House.

Cheung, C., D. Furceri, and E. Rusticelli (2013), "Structural and Cyclical Factors behind Current Account Balances," *Review of International Economics*, 21(5), pp. 923-944.

Chirinko, R. (1993), "Business Fixed Investment Spending: Modelling Strategies, Empirical Results, and Policy Implications," *Journal of Economic Literature*, 31(4), pp. 1875–1911.

Cipolla, C. M. (2021), *The Basic Laws of Human Stupidity*, London: Penguin. Originally published in 1976.

Claeys, G., A. Sapir, and G. Wolff (2014a), "Measuring Europe's Investment Problem," *Bruegel.org*, 24 November. Available at: https://www.bruegel.org/2014/11/measuring-europes-investment-problem/.

Claeys, G., A. Sapir, and G. Wolff (2014b), "Juncker's Investment Plan: No Risk – No Return," *Bruegel.org*, 28 November. Available at: https://www.bruegel.org/2014/11/junckers-investment-plan-no-risk-no-return/.

Cockx, B. (2016), "Do Youths Graduating in a Recession Incur Permanent Losses?," *IZA World of Labor*, Institute of Labor Economics, August.

Cœuré, B. (2013), "Adjustment and Growth in the Eurozone Economies," Speech at the Nova School of Business and Economics and the Banco de Portugal, 22 February. Available at: https://news.europawire.eu/adjustment-and-growth-in-the-euro-area-economies-speech-by-benoit-coeure-0912834566/eu-press-release/2013/02/22/22/50/32/9024/.

Cœuré, B. (2016), "Sovereign Debt in the Euro Area: Too Safe or Too Risky?," Keynote Address at Harvard University's Minda de Gunzburg Center for European Studies in Cambridge Massachusetts, 3 November. Available at: https://www.ecb.europa.eu/press/key/date/2016/html/sp161103.en.html.

Cœuré, B. (2018a), "Scars That Never Were? Potential Output and Slack after the Crisis," Speech at the CEPII 40th Anniversary Conference, Paris, 12 April. Available at: https://www.ecb.europa.eu/press/key/date/2018/html/ecb.sp180412.en.html.

Cœuré, B. (2018b), "Asserting Europe's Leadership," Panel Remarks, Les Rencontres Economiques d'Aix-en-Provence, 8 July. Available at https://www.ecb.europa.eu/press/key/date/2018/html/ecb.sp180708.en.html.

Collier, P. (2018), *The Future of Capitalism: Facing the New Anxieties*, New York: HaperCollins.

Conway P., D. de Rosa, G. Nicoletti, and F. Steiner (2006), "Regulation, Competition and Productivity Convergence," OECD Economics Department Working Papers No. 509, September, Paris: OECD Publishing.

Corsetti, G. (2012), "Has Austerity Gone Too Far?," *VoxEU.org*, 2 April. Available at: https://voxeu.org/article/has-austerity-gone-too-far-new-vox-debate.

Corsetti, G., L. P. Feld, R. Koijen, L. Reichlin, R. Reis, H. Rey, and B. Weder di Mauro (2016), "Reinforcing the Eurozone and Protecting an Open Society," *VoxEU.org*, 27 May. Available at: https://voxeu.org/article/reinforcing-eurozone-and-protecting-open-society.

Corsetti, G., L. P. Feld, P. R. Lane, L. Reichlin, H. Rey, D. Vayanos, and B. Weder di Mauro (2015), "A New Start for the Eurozone: Dealing with Debt," *Monitoring the Eurozone*, 1, London: Centre for Economic Policy Research (CEPR) Press.

Cuerpo, C., I. Drumond, J. Lendvai, P. Pontuch, and R. Raciborski (2013), "Indebtedness, Deleveraging Dynamics and Macroeconomic Adjustment," European Economy, Economic Papers No. 477, April, Brussels: Directorate-General for Economic and Financial Affairs (ECFIN), European Commission.

D'Auria, F., C. Denis, K. Havik, K. Mc Morrow, C. Planas, R. Raciborski, W. Röger, and A. Ross (2010), "The Production Function Methodology for

Calculating Potential Growth Rates and Output Gaps," European Economy, Economic Papers No. 420, July, Brussels: Directorate-General for Economic and Financial Affairs (ECFIN), European Commission.

Dahrendorf, R. (1995), "Economic Opportunity, Civil Society and Political Liberty," UNRISD Discussion Paper No. 58, March, Geneva: United Nations Research Institute for Social Development (UNRISD).

Darvas, Z. (2012), "The Limits of a Purely Intra-euro Rebalancing Strategy," *VoxEU.org*, 5 September. Available at: https://voxeu.org/article/rebalancing-eurozone-internal-adjustments-won-t-be-enough.

Davies, G. (2014), "Draghi Steals the Shows at Jackson Hole," *Financial Times*, 25 August. Available at: https://www.ft.com/content/8e0d2126-f156-3d0a-9d97-0a47ac1124a9.

De Grauwe, P. (2010), "Why a Tougher Stability and Growth Pact Is a Bad Idea," *VoxEU.org*, 4 October. Available at: https://voxeu.org/article/why-tougher-stability-and-growth-pact-bad-idea.

De Grauwe, P. (2013), "Design Failures in the Eurozone: Can They Be Fixed?," European Economy, Economic Papers No. 491, April, Brussels: Directorate-General for Economic and Financial Affairs (ECFIN), European Commission.

De Grauwe, P., and Y. Ji (2013), "Panic-driven Austerity in the Eurozone and its Implications," *VoxEU.org*, 21 February. Available at: https://voxeu.org/article/panic-driven-austerity-eurozone-and-its-implications.

De Grauwe, P., and Y. Ji (2018), "How Safe Is a Safe Asset?," CEPS Policy Insight No. 2018-08, Brussels: Centre for European Policy Studies (CEPS).

De Grauwe, P., and G. Schnabl (2005), "Nominal vs. Real Convergence. EMU Entry Scenarios for the New Member States," *Kyklos*, 4, pp. 537-555.

de Vries, C., and I. Hoffmann (2016), "Fear Not Values. Public Opinion and the Populist Vote in Europe," eupinions #2016/3, November, Gütersloh: Bertelsmann Stiftung. Available at: https://eupinions.eu/de/text/fear-not-values.

Debrun X., L. Eyraud, A. Hodge, V. Ledo, and C. Patillo (2018), "Second-Generation Fiscal Rules: From Stupid to Too Smart," *VoxEU.org*, 22 May. Available at: https://voxeu.org/article/second-generation-fiscal-rules-stupid-too-smart.

Debrun, X., J. Pisani-Ferry, and A. Sapir (2008), "Government Size and Output Volatility: Should We Forsake Automatic Stabilization?," European Economy, Economic Papers No. 316, April, Brussels: Directorate-General for Economic and Financial Affairs (ECFIN), European Commission.

Dehousse, R. (2016), "Why Has EU Macroeconomic Governance Become More Supranational," *Journal of European Integration*, 38(5), pp. 617-631.

Delatte, A-L. (2018), "Fixing the Euro Needs to Go beyond Economics,"

VoxEU.org, 23 October. Available at: https://voxeu.org/article/fixing-euro-needs-go-beyond-economics.

Delors, J. (1989), "Report on Economic and Monetary Union in the European Community," Committee for the Study of Economic and Monetary Union.

Delpla, J., and J. von Weizsäcker (2010), "The Blue Bond Proposal," Bruegel Policy Brief, Issue 2010/03, May, Brussels.

Deltuvaitė, V. (2017), "Consequences of External Macroeconomic Shocks Transmission through International Trade Channel: The Case of the Central and Eastern European Countries," Springer Proceedings in Business and Economics, pp. 631-655 in N. Tsounis, and A. Vlachvei (eds.), *Advances in Panel Data Analysis in Applied Economic Research*, Springer.

Demertzis, M. (2018), "Trust in the EU? The Key Obstacle to Reform," *Bruegel.org*, 9 February. Available at: https://www.bruegel.org/2018/02/trust-in-the-eu-the-key-obstacle-to-reform/.

Demertzis M., J. Pisani-Ferry, A. Sapir, T. Wieser, and G. B. Wolff (2018), "One Size Does Not Fit All: European Integration by Differentiation," Bruegel Policy Brief, Issue 3, September, Brussels.

Demyanyk, Y., C. Ostergaard, and B. Sorensen (2008), "Risk Sharing and Portfolio Allocation in EMU," European Economy, Economic Papers No. 334, July, Brussels: Directorate-General for Economic and Financial Affairs (ECFIN), European Commission.

Derviş, K. (2016), "What Role for Global Governance?," *Brookings*, 22 August. Available at: https://www.brookings.edu/opinions/what-role-for-global-governance/.

Dixit, A., and R. S. Pindyck (1994), *Investment under Uncertainty*, Princeton: Princeton University Press.

Draghi, M. (2014), "Unemployment in the Eurozone," Speech at the *Annual Central Bank Symposium in Jackson Hole*, 22 August. Available at: https://www.ecb.europa.eu/press/key/date/2014/html/sp140822.en.html.

Draghi, M. (2015), "Speech at SZ Finance Day 2015," Frankfurt am Main, 16 March. Available at: https://www.ecb.europa.eu/press/key/date/2015/html/sp150316.en.html.

Draghi, M. (2018), Hearing of the Committee on Economic and Monetary Affairs of the European Parliament, 26 November.

Draghi, M. (2019a), "Twenty Years of the ECB's Monetary Policy," Speech by Mario Draghi, President of the ECB, *ECB Forum on Central Banking*, Sintra, 18 June 2019. Available at: https://www.ecb.europa.eu/press/key/date/2019/html/ecb.sp190618~ec4cd2443b.en.html.

Draghi, M. (2019b), Hearing at the Committee on Economic and Monetary Affairs of the European Parliament, Brussels, 23 September.

Duval, R., and J. Elmeskov (2005), "The Effects of EMU on Structural Reforms in Labour and Product Markets," OECD Economics Department Working Papers No. 438, July, Paris: OECD Publishing.

European Bank for Reconstruction and Development (EBRD) (2018), *Transition Report 2018-2019*, London: EBRD.

European Bank for Reconstruction and Development (EBRD) (2019), *Eight Things You Should Know about Middle-Income Transition*, London: EBRD.

Eggertsson, G. B., and N. R. Mehrotra (2014), "A Model of Secular Stagnation," NBER Working Paper No. 20574, October, Cambridge Massachusetts: National Bureau of Economic Research, Inc. (NBER).

Eggertsson G. B., A. Ferrero, and A. Raffo (2014), "Can Structural Reforms Help Europe?," *Journal of Monetary Economics*, 61(C), pp. 2-22.

Eichengreen, B., A. Mehl, and L. Chitu (2017), *How Global Currencies Work: Past, Present and Future*, Princeton: Princeton University Press.

Einaudi, L. (1949), *Lezioni di Politica Sociale*, Torino: Einaudi, 1977.

Emmanouilidis, J. (2012), "Which Lesson to Draw from the Past and Current Use of Differentiated Integration?," paper presented at the Workshop *Challenges for Multi-tier Governance in the EU*, European Parliament, 4 October.

Enderlein H., E. Letta, J. Asmussen, L. Boone, A. Geus, P. Lamy, P. Maystadt, M. J. Rodrigues, G. Tumpel-Gugerell, and A. Vitorino (2016), *Repair and Prepare: Growth and the Euro after Brexit*, Gütersloh, Berlin, Paris: Bertelsmann Stiftung, Jacques Delors Institut – Berlin and Jacques Delors Institute in Paris.

Escolano, J., and V. Gaspar (2016), "Optimal Debt Policy under Asymmetric Risk," IMF Working Paper, WP/16/178, August, Washington D.C: International Monetary Fund.

Euro Summit (2018), "Statement of the Euro Summit", 29 June. Available at: https://www.consilium.europa.eu/en/press/press-releases/2018/06/29/20180629-euro-summit-statement/.

European Central Bank (ECB) (2016), "Financial Integration and Risk-sharing in a Monetary Union," in *Financial Integration in Europe, April, Frankfurt: European Central Bank.*

European Central Bank (ECB) (2017a), *Monthly Bulletin*, May, Frankfurt: European Central Bank.

European Central Bank (ECB) (2017b), "The International Role of the Euro," Interim Report, July, Frankfurt: European Central Bank.

European Central Bank (ECB) (2021), "ECB Staff Macroeconomic Projections for the Euro Area," March, Frankfurt: European Central Bank. Available at: https://www.ecb.europa.eu/pub/pdf/other/ecb.projections202103_ecbstaff~3f6efd7e8f.en.pdf.

European Commission (1988), "Europe 1992: The Overall Challenge," SEC (88)524 final, 13 April 1988, Brussels.
European Commission (1990), "One Market, One Money, an Evaluation of the Potential Benefits and Costs of Forming an Economic and Monetary Union," European Economy No. 44/1990, October, Brussels: Directorate-General for Economic and Financial Affairs (ECFIN), European Commission.
European Commission (2006), "The EU Economy Review," European Economy No. 6/2006, January, Brussels: Directorate-General for Economic and Financial Affairs (ECFIN), European Commission.
European Commission (2007), "Cross-border Risk Sharing: Has It Increased in the Euro Area?," *Quarterly Report on the Euro Area*, 6(3), pp. 3-47.
European Commission (2008), "EMU@10. Successes and Challenges after 10 years of Economic and Monetary Union," European Economy No. 2/2008, June, Brussels: Directorate-General for Economic and Financial Affairs (ECFIN), European Commission.
European Commission (2009), "Five Years of an Enlarged EU: Economic Achievements and Challenges," European Economy No. 1/2009, Brussels: Directorate-General for Economic and Financial Affairs (ECFIN), European Commission.
European Commission (2010a), "Communication – Reinforcing Economic Policy Coordination," COM(2010) 250 final, 12 May 2010, Brussels.
European Commission (2010b), "Public Finances in EMU – 2010," European Economy No. 4/2010, June, Brussels: Directorate-General for Economic and Financial Affairs (ECFIN), European Commission.
European Commission (2010c), "Communication – Enhancing Economic Policy Coordination for Stability, Growth and Jobs – Tools for Stronger EU Economic Governance," COM(2010) 367/2, 30 June 2010, Brussels.
European Commission (2010d), "A New EU Economic Governance – A Comprehensive Commission Package of Proposals," *ec.europa.eu*, 29 September 2010. Available at: https://ec.europa.eu/economy_finance/articles/eu_economic_situation/2010-09-eu_economic_governance_proposals_en.htm.
European Commission (2010e), "European Economic Forecast – Autumn 2010," European Economy No. 7/2010, November, Brussels: Directorate-General for Economic and Financial Affairs (ECFIN), European Commission.
European Commission (2011a), "Public Finances in EMU – 2011," European Economy No. 3/2011, September, Brussels: Directorate-General for Economic and Financial Affairs (ECFIN), European Commission.
European Commission (2011b), "Communication – A Roadmap to Stabil-

ity and Growth," COM(2011) 669 final, 12 October 2011, Brussels.
European Commission (2011c), "Green Paper on the Feasibility of Introducing Stability Bonds," COM(2011) 818 final, 23 November 2011, Brussels.
European Commission (2012a), "Public Finances in EMU – 2012," European Economy No. 4/2012, July, Brussels: Directorate-General for Economic and Financial Affairs (ECFIN), European Commission.
European Commission (2012b), "Labour Market Developments in Europe," European Economy No. 5/2012, September, Brussels: Directorate-General for Economic and Financial Affairs (ECFIN), European Commission.
European Commission (2012c), "European Economic Forecast – Autumn 2012," European Economy No. 7/2012, November, Brussels: Directorate-General for Economic and Financial Affairs (ECFIN), European Commission.
European Commission (2012d), "Communication – A Blueprint for a Deep and Genuine EMU – Launching a European Debate," COM 2012(777) final, 28 November 2012, Brussels.
European Commission (2012e), "Fiscal Sustainability Report 2012," European Economy No. 8/2012, December, Brussels: Directorate-General for Economic and Financial Affairs (ECFIN), European Commission.
European Commission (2013a), "European Economic Forecast – Spring 2013," European Economy No. 2/2013, May, Brussels: Directorate-General for Economic and Financial Affairs (ECFIN), European Commission.
European Commission (2013b), *Quarterly Report on the Euro Area*, 12(2), pp. 1-45.
European Commission (2013c), "Assessing the Impact of Uncertainty on Consumption and Investment," *Quarterly Report on the Euro Area*, 12(2), pp. 7-16.
European Commission (2013d), "European Economic Forecast – Autumn 2013," European Economy No. 7/2013, November, Brussels: Directorate-General for Economic and Financial Affairs (ECFIN), European Commission.
European Commission (2013e), "The Growth Impact of Structural Reforms," *Quarterly Report on the Euro Area*, 12(4), pp. 17-28.
European Commission (2014a), "IDR Macroeconomic Imbalances, 2014," European Economy – Occasional Papers No.172-188, 5 March, Brussels: Directorate-General for Economic and Financial Affairs (ECFIN), European Commission.
European Commission (2014b), "Recommendation on a New Approach to Business Failure and Insolvency," C(2014) 1500 final, 12 March 2014, Brussels.
European Commission (2014c), "Communication – Long-term Financing of the European Economy," COM(2014) 168 final, 27 March 2014, Brussels.

European Commission (2014d), "European Economic Forecast – Spring 2014," European Economy No. 3/2014, May, Brussels: Directorate-General for Economic and Financial Affairs (ECFIN), European Commission.
European Commission (2014e), "European Economic Forecast – Autumn 2014," European Economy No. 7/2014, November, Brussels: Directorate-General for Economic and Financial Affairs (ECFIN), European Commission.
European Commission (2014f), "Communication – An Investment Plan for Europe," COM(2014) 903 final, 26 November 2014, Brussels.
European Commission (2014g), "Communication – Annual Growth Survey 2015," COM(2014) 902 final, 28 November 2014, Brussels.
European Commission (2014h), "Communication – 2015 Draft Budgetary Plans: Overall Assessment," COM(2014) 907 final, 28 November 2014, Brussels.
European Commission (2015a), "European Economic Forecast – Winter 2015," European Economy No. 1/2015, February, Brussels: Directorate-General for Economic and Financial Affairs (ECFIN), European Commission.
European Commission (2015b), "Communication – A Roadmap for Moving Towards a More Consistent External Representation of the Euro Area in International Fora," COM(2015) 602 final, 21 October 2015, Brussels.
European Commission (2015c), "Drivers and Benchmarks of Current Account Balances, Update," 4 November 2015.
European Commission (2016a), "Fiscal Sustainability Report 2015," European Economy, Institutional Paper No. 018, January, Brussels: Directorate-General for Economic and Financial Affairs (ECFIN), European Commission.
European Commission (2016b), "Staff Working Document – Country Report Germany 2016, Including an In-depth Review on the Prevention and Correction of Macroeconomic Imbalances," SWD(2016) 75 final, 26 February 2016, Brussels.
European Commission (2016c), "Cross-border Risk Sharing after Asymmetric Shocks: Evidence from the Euro Area and the United States," *Quarterly Report on the Euro Area,* 15(2), pp. 7-18.
European Commission (2016d), "Labour Market and Wage Developments in Europe," *Annual Review 2016*, Brussels: Directorate-General for Economic and Financial Affairs (ECFIN), European Commission.
European Commission (2016e), "European Economic Forecast – Autumn 2016, Box 1.4 'How Is the Recovery Proceeding in the Euro Area?'," European Economy, Institutional Paper No. 038, 9 November 2016, Brussels.
European Commission (2016f), "Communication – Towards a Positive Fiscal Stance for the Euro Area," COM(2016) 727 final, 16 November 2016, Brussels.
European Commission (2016g), "Report – Alert Mechanism Report 2017," COM(2016) 728 final, 16 November 2016, Brussels.

European Commission (2016h), "Staff Working Document – Statistical Annex Accompanying the Report Alert Mechanism Report 2017," SWD(2016) 354 final, 16 November 2016, Brussels.
European Commission (2016i), "Reforms to Further Strengthen the Resilience of EU Banks," *ec.europa.eu*, 23 November 2016.
European Commission (2016l), "Standard Eurobarometer – 86," Public Opinion in the European Union, December 2016, Brussels: European Commission.
European Commission (2017a), "White Paper on the Future of Europe. Reflections and Scenarios for the EU27 by 2025," COM 2017(2025) final, 1 March 2017, Brussels.
European Commission (2017b), "Reflection Paper on Harnessing the Benefits of Globalization," COM(2017) 240 final, 10 May 2017, Brussels.
European Commission (2017c), "Reflection Paper on the Deepening of the Economic and Monetary Union," COM(2017) 291 final, 31 May 2017, Brussels.
European Commission (2017d), "Communication – Completing the Banking Union," COM(2017) 592 final, 11 October 2017, Brussels.
European Commission (2017e), "Communication – Further Steps Towards Completing Europe's Economic and Monetary Union: A Roadmap," COM(2017) 821 final, 6 December 2017, Brussels.
European Commission (2018a), "Commission Measures to Address the Risks Related to NPLs," IP/18/1802, *ec.europa.eu*, 14 March 2018, Brussels. Available at: https://ec.europa.eu/commission/presscorner/detail/en/IP_18_1802.
European Commission (2018b), "Communication – A Modern Budget for a Union that Protects, Empowers and Defends – The Multiannual Financial Framework for 2021-2027," COM(2018) 321 final, 2 May 2018, Brussels.
European Commission (2018c), "Communication – European Semester, Country-specific Recommendations," COM(2018) 400 final, 23 May 2018, Brussels.
European Commission (2018d), "Staff Working Document Accompanying the Communication on the Review of the Flexibility under the Stability and Growth Pact," SWD(2018) 270 final, 23 May 2018, Brussels.
European Commission (2018e), "Proposal for a Regulation of the European Parliament and of the Council on the Establishment of a European Investment Stabilisation Function," COM(2018) 387 final, 31 May 2018, Brussels.
European Commission (2018f), "Staff Working Document – Impact Assessment Accompanying the Proposal on the Establishment of a European Investment Stabilisation Function," SWD(2018) 297, 31 May 2018, Brussels.
European Commission (2018g), "European Economic Forecast – Summer 2018," European Economy, Institutional Paper No. 077, 12 July 2018,

Brussels: Directorate-General for Economic and Financial Affairs (ECFIN), European Commission.

European Commission (2018h), "Flash Eurobarometer 473 – The Euro Area Report," October, Brussels: European Commission.

European Commission (2018i), "Communication – Towards a Stronger International Role of the Euro," COM(2018) 796/4 final, 5 December 2018, Brussels.

European Commission (2019), "Vade Mecum on the Stability and Growth Pact," European Economy, Institutional Paper No. 101, April, Brussels: Directorate-General for Economic and Financial Affairs (ECFIN), European Commission.

European Commission (2020a), "Staff Working Document – Identifying Europe's Recovery Needs Accompanying the Communication Europe's Moment: Repair and Prepare for the Next Generation," SWD (2020) 98, May, Brussels.

European Commission (2020b), "European Economic Forecast – Summer 2020," Interim, European Economy, Institutional Paper No. 132, July, Brussels: Directorate-General for Economic and Financial Affairs (ECFIN), European Commission.

European Commission (2020c) "Standard Eurobarometer – 93," Public Opinion in the European Union, Summer 2020, July, Brussels: European Commission.

European Commission (2021a), "Staff Working Document – Guidance to Member States Recovery and Resilience Plans – Part 1," SWD(2021) 12 final, 22 January, Brussels.

European Commission (2021b), "European Economic Forecasts – Winter 2021," Interim, European Economy, Institutional Paper No. 144, February, Brussels: Directorate-General for Economic and Financial Affairs (ECFIN), European Commission.

European Commission (2021c), "Communication – One Year since the Outbreak of COVID-19: Fiscal Policy Response," COM(2021) 105 final, 3 March 2021, Brussels.

European Commission (2021d), "Recovery Plan for Europe," *ec.europa.eu*. Available at: https://ec.europa.eu/info/strategy/recovery-plan-europe_en.

European Commission and European Parliament (2021), "Future of Europe," Special Eurobarometer 500 – First Results, March, Brussels: European Commission's and European Parliament's Directorates-General for Communication.

European Commission and the Economic Policy Committee (2008), "The 2009 Ageing Report: Underlying Assumptions and Projection Methodologies for the EU-27 Member States (2007-2060)," European Economy No. 7/2008, December, Brussels: Directorate-General for Economic and

Financial affairs (ECFIN) and Economic Policy Committee (AWG), European Commission.

European Commission and International Monetary Fund (IMF) (2009a), "The European Commission and the International Monetary Fund Welcome the Reaffirmed Commitments of the Largest Foreign Banks in Romania," *ec.europa.eu*, 20 May 2009. Available at: https://ec.europa.eu/commission/presscorner/detail/en/IP_09_821,

European Commission and International Monetary Fund (IMF) (2009b), "The European Commission and the International Monetary Fund Welcome the Commitment of the Six Largest Foreign Banks in Hungary," 20 May 2009, *ec.europa.eu*. Available at: https://ec.europa.eu/commission/presscorner/detail/en/IP_09_822.

European Council (2011), "Euro Summit Statement," *consilium.europa.eu*, 26 October 2011. Available at: https://www.consilium.europa.eu/uedocs/cms_data/docs/pressdata/en/ec/125644.pdf.

European Council (2017), "The Rome Declaration," *consilium.europa.eu,* 27 March 2017. Available at: https://www.consilium.europa.eu/en/press/press-releases/2017/03/25/rome-declaration/.

European Council (2018), "European Council Conclusions," *consilium.europa.eu,* 28 June 2018. Available at: https://www.consilium.europa.eu/en/press/press-releases/2018/06/29/20180628-euco-conclusions-final/.

European Council (2020), "Special Meeting of the European Council (17, 18, 19, 20 and 21 July 2020) – Conclusions," EUCO 10/20, *consilium.europa.eu*. Available at: https://data.consilium.europa.eu/doc/document/ST-10-2020-INIT/en/pdf.

European Fiscal Board (2018), *Annual Report 2018*, Brussels: EFB.

European Investment Bank (2018), "EIB Investment Survey", EIB Group Survey on Investment and Investment Finance Country Overview – European Union, Luxemburg: EIB.

European Parliament (2021), "Parlemeter 2020: A Glimpse of Certainty in Uncertain Times," Eurobarometer Survey 94.2 of the European Parliament – A Public Opinion Monitoring Study, December, Brussels: Directorate-General for Communication, European Parliament.

European Parliament and Council of the EU (2020), "Proposal for a Regulation of the European Parliament and of the Council Establishing a Recovery and Resilience Facility – Confirmation of the Final Compromise Text with a View to Agreement," 21 December 2020. Available at: https://data.consilium.europa.eu/doc/document/ST-14310-2020-INIT/en/pdf.

European Parliament and Council of the EU (2021), Regulation (EU) 2021/241 of the European Parliament and the Council of 12 February 2021 Establishing the Recovery and Resilience Facility. Available at: https://eur-lex.europa.eu/legal-content/EN/TXT/PDF/?uri=CELEX:32021R0241&from=EN.

European Stability Mechanism (ESM) (2019), *Annual Report 2018*, Luxemburg: Publications Office of the European Union.

European Systemic Risk Board (ESRB) (2015), "ESRB Report on the Regulatory Treatment of Sovereign Exposures," March, Frankfurt: ESRB.

European Systemic Risk Board (ESRB) (2018), "*Sovereign Bond-backed Securities: A Feasibility Study*," Report of the High-Level Task Force on Safe Assets, Frankfurt: ESRB.

Fabbrini, F. (2015), "States' Equality v States' Power: the Euro-crisis, Inter-state Relations and the Paradox of Domination," *Cambridge Yearbook of European Legal Studies*, 17, pp. 3-35.

Fabbrini, S. (2014), "After the Euro Crisis: A New Paradigm on the Integration of Europe," ARENA Working Paper No. 5, 18 March, Oslo: ARENA Centre for European Studies.

Farhi, E., and M. Maggiori (2016), "A Model of the International Monetary System," Harvard University OpenScholar Working Paper No. 395921, March, Cambridge Massachusetts: Harvard University.

Fahri, E., and I. Werning (2017), "Fiscal Unions," *American Economic Review*, 107(12), pp. 3788-3834.

Fall, F., D. Bloch, J. M. Fournier, and P. Hoeller (2015), "Prudent Debt Targets and Fiscal Frameworks," OECD Economic Policy Papers No. 15, July, Paris: OECD Publishing.

Fatás, A. (2013), "The Only Uncertainty Is Why Some Cannot See Facts," *Antonio Fatás on the Global Economy*, 15 September 2013. Available at: http://antoniofatas.blogspot.com/2013/09/the-only-uncertainty-is-why-some-cannot.html.

Fatás, A. (2018), "Self-fulfilling Pessimism: The Fiscal Policy Doom Loop," *VoxEU.org*, 28 September. Available at: https://voxeu.org/article/europes-fiscal-policy-doom-loop.

Fatás, A., and I. Mihov (2003), "The Case for Restricting Fiscal Policy Discretion," *Quarterly Journal of Economics*, 118(4), pp. 1419-47.

Federal Reserve Bank of Kansas City (2014), "Re-Evaluating Labor Market Dynamics," *Jackson Hole Economic Policy Symposium, kansascityfed.org.*, August 2014. Available at: https://www.kansascityfed.org/research/jackson-hole-economic-symposium/re-evaluating-labor-market-dynamics/.

Feld, L. (2018), "Whither a Fiscal Capacity in EMU," *VoxEU.org*, 31 July. Available at: https://voxeu.org/article/whither-fiscal-capacity-emu.

Fisher, S. (2016), "Low Interest Rates," Remarks at the *40th Annual Central Banking Seminar* Sponsored by the Federal Reserve Bank of New York, *federalreserve.org.*, 5 October. Available at: https://www.federalreserve.gov/newsevents/speech/fischer20161005a.htm.

Forbes, K. J. (2019), "Inflation Dynamics: Dead, Dormant, or Determined Abroad?," NBER Working Papers No. 26496, November, Cambridge Massachusetts: National Bureau of Economic Research, Inc. (NBER).

Frankel, J., and A. K. Rose (1998), "The Endogeneity of the Optimum Currency Area Criteria," *Economic Journal*, 108(449), pp. 1009-25.

Fuest, C., and F. Heinemann (2015), "Accountability Bonds: Das Ausmaß der Gemeinsamen Haftung Eindämmen," *Euractive*, 5 March. Available at: https://www.euractiv.de/section/finanzen-und-wirtschaft/opinion/accountability-bonds-das-ausmass-der-gemeinsamen-haftung-eindammen/.

Furceri, D., and A. Zdzienicka (2015), "The Euro area Crisis: Need for a Supranational Fiscal Risk Sharing Mechanism?," *Open Economies Review,* 26(4), pp. 683-710.

Furman, J. (2016), "The New View of Fiscal Policy and its Application," *VoxEU.org*, 2 November. Available at: https://voxeu.org/article/new-view-fiscal-policy-and-its-application.

Furman, J., and L. H. Summers (2019), "Who's Afraid of Budget Deficits?," *LarrySummers.com*, 28 January. Available at: http://larrysummers.com/2019/01/28/whos-afraid-of-budget-deficits/.

G20 Framework Working Group (FWG) (2016), "G20 Enhanced Structural Reform Agenda," Prepared by the G20 Framework Working Group, September.

Ganghof, S. (2003), "Promises and Pitfalls of Veto Player Analysis," *Swiss Political Science Review*, 9(2), pp. 1-25.

Gaspar, V., M. Obstfeld, and R. Sahay (2016), "Macroeconomic Management When Policy Space Is Constrained: A Comprehensive, Consistent, and Coordinated Approach to Economic Policy," IMF Staff Discussion Note, SDN/16/09, September, Washington D.C.: International Monetary Fund.

Geithner, T. F. (2015), *Stress Test: Reflections on Financial Crises*, New York: Broadway Books.

Giavazzi, F., and L. Spaventa (2010), "The European Commission's Proposals: Empty and Useless," *VoxEU.org*, 14 October. Available at: https://voxeu.org/article/european-commission-s-proposals-empty-and-useless.

Gigliobianco, A. (2010), *Luigi Einaudi: Economic Freedom and Social Cohesion*, Serie Saggi e Ricerche Volume VI, Bari: Editori Laterza.

Gilchrist, S., J. Sim, and E. Zakrajsek (2010), "Uncertainty, Financial Friction and Investment Dynamics," 2010 Meeting Papers No. 1285, Society for Economic Dynamics.

Gill, I., and M. Raiser (2012), *Golden Growth: Restoring the Lustre of the European Economic Model,* Washington D.C.: World Bank.
Goldberg, L. S., and C. Tille (2016), "Micro, Macro and Strategic Forces in International Trade Invoicing: Synthesis and Novel Patterns," *Journal of International Economics*, 102(C), pp. 173-187.
Gopinath, G., and J. Stein (2018), "Banking, Trade, and the Making of a Dominant Currency," NBER Working Paper No. 24485, April, Cambridge Massachusetts: National Bureau of Economic Research, Inc. (NBER).
Gopinath, G., S. Kalemli-Özcan, L. Karabarbounis, and C. Villegas-Sanchez (2017), "Capital Allocation and Productivity in Southern Europe," *Quarterly Journal of Economics,* 132(4), pp. 1915–1967.
Gordon, R. J. (2014), "The Turtle's Progress: Secular Stagnation Meets the Headwinds," in C. Teulings, and R. Baldwin (eds.), *Secular Stagnation: Facts, Causes and Cures*, a VoxEU.org eBook, London: Centre for Economic Policy Research (CEPR) Press.
Gourinchas, P. O., and H. Rey (2007), "International Financial Adjustment," *Journal of Political Economy,* 115(41), pp. 665-703.
Gourinchas, P. O., and H. Rey (2013), "External Adjustment, Global Imbalances, Valuation Effects," NBER Working Paper No. 19240, July, Cambridge Massachusetts: National Bureau of Economic Research, Inc. (NBER).
Gourinchas, P. O., N. Govillot, and H. Rey (2010), "Exorbitant Privilege and Exorbitant Duty," Institute for Monetary and Economic Studies (IMES), Bank of Japan Discussion Paper No. 2010-E-20, August, Tokyo: Bank of Japan.
Gros, D. (2011), "Can Austerity Be Self-defeating?," *VoxEU.org*, 11 November. Available at: https://voxeu.org/article/can-austerity-be-self-defeating.
Gros, D. (2013), "Learning from Small Countries? Contemporary Nordic Sagas," CEPS Commentaries, *CEPS.eu*, February. Available at: https://www.ceps.eu/ceps-publications/learning-small-countries-contemporary-nordic-sagas/.
Gros, D. (2014), "The Juncker Plan: From €21 to €315 billion, through Smoke and Mirrors," CEPS Commentaries, *CEPS.eu*, 27 November, Available: http://aei.pitt.edu/57876/1/CEPS_Commentary_The_Juncker_Plan_D_Gros.pdf.
Gros, D. (2016), "Ultra-low or Negative Yields on Euro Area Long-term Bonds: Causes and Implications for Monetary Policy," CEPS Working Documents No. 426, September, Brussels: Centre for European Policy Studies (CEPS).
Gros, D., and A. Belke (2015), "Banking Union as a Shock Absorber – Lessons for the Eurozone from the US," CEPS Paperback, Brussels: Centre for European Policy Studies (CEPS).
Gros, D., and T. Mayer (2010), "How to Deal with Sovereign Default in Eu-

rope: Create the European Monetary Fund Now!," CEPS Policy Brief No. 202, May, Brussels.

Gurría, A. (2015), "Fair Play – The Rule of the Game in International Taxation," Remarks at the *Antalya G20 Summit Session on Enhancing Resilience*, *OECD.org.*, November. Available at: http://www.oecd.org/fr/fiscalite/fair-play-the-rule-of-the-game-in-international-taxation.htm.

Habermas, J. (2008), "European Union: Are We Still Good European?," Interview in *die Welt*, 6 July.

Hagemejer, J., and J. Muck (2019), "Export-led Growth and its Determinants: Evidence from CEEC Countries," *The World Economy*, 42(7), pp. 1994-2025.

Harding, T., and B. Smarzynska Javorcik (2011), "FDI and Export Upgrading," University of Oxford Department of Economics Discussion Paper No. 526, January, Oxford: Oxford University Press.

Heclo, H. (1974), *Modern Social Politics in Britain and Sweden: From Relief to Income Maintenance*, New Heaven Connecticut: Yale University Press.

Heijdra M., T. Aarden, J. Hanson, and T. van Dijk (2018), "A More Stable EMU Does Not Require a Central Fiscal Capacity," *VoxEU.org*, 30 November. Available at: https://voxeu.org/article/more-stable-emu-does-not-require-central-fiscal-capacity.

Hepp, R., and J. von Hagen (2013), "Interstate Risk Sharing in Germany: 1970-2006," *Oxford Economic Papers,* 65(1), pp. 1-24.

Holland, D., and J. Portes (2012), "Self-defeating Austerity?," *VoxEU.org*, 1 November. Available at: https://voxeu.org/article/self-defeating-austerity.

Hristov A., V. Vandermeulen, and R. Raciborski (2017), "Assessment of the Plausibility of the Output Gap Estimates," European Economy, Economic Brief No. 023, April, Brussels: Directorate-General for Economic and Financial Affairs (ECFIN), European Commission.

Institut Français d'Opinion Publique (IFOP) (2016), "Les Européens et le Brexit," 15 July, *ifop.com*. Available at: https://www.ifop.com/publication/les-europeens-et-le-brexit/.

International Monetary Fund (IMF) (2012a), "Toward Lasting Stability and Growth," Umbrella Report for G-20 Mutual Assessment Process, June, Washington D.C.: International Monetary Fund.

International Monetary Fund (IMF) (2012b), "Nurturing Credibility while Managing Risks to Growth," in *Fiscal Monitor Update*, July, Washington D.C.: International Monetary Fund.

International Monetary Fund (IMF) (2013a), "Global Prospects and Policy Challenges," Note for the Group of Twenty, February, Washington D.C.: International Monetary Fund.

International Monetary Fund (IMF) (2013b), "Toward a Fiscal Union for the Euro Area," IMF Staff Discussion Note, SDN/13/09, September, Washington D.C: International Monetary Fund.

International Monetary Fund (IMF) (2015a), "Can Fiscal Policy Stabilise Output?," in *Fiscal Monitor, April 2015: Now is the Time: Fiscal Policies for Sustainable Growth,* Washington D.C.: International Monetary Fund.

International Monetary Fund (IMF) (2015b), "Germany – Selected Issues," IMF Country Report No. 15/188, June, Washington D.C.: International Monetary Fund.

International Monetary Fund (IMF) (2016a), "Strengthening the International Monetary System – A Stocktaking," Policy Papers Series, March, Washington D.C.: International Monetary Fund.

International Monetary Fund (IMF) (2016b), "A Guiding Framework for Structural Reforms," IMF Staff Note, Policy Papers Series, April, Washington D.C.: International Monetary Fund.

International Monetary Fund (IMF) (2016c), "Taking Stocks of Monetary and Exchange Rate Regimes in Emerging Europe," Departmental Paper No. 16/12, November, Washington D.C.: IMF European Department.

International Monetary Fund (IMF) (2017a), *World Economic Outlook: Gaining Momentum?*, April, Washington D.C.: International Monetary Fund.

International Monetary Fund (IMF) (2017b), "Germany Article 4 – Staff Report," IMF Country Report No. 17/192, 7 July, Washington D.C.: International Monetary Fund.

International Monetary Fund (IMF) (2017c), "2017 External Sector Report," IMF Policy Paper, 28 July, Washington D.C.: International Monetary Fund.

International Monetary Fund (IMF) (2018), *World Economic Outlook Update: Less Even Expansion, Rising Trade Tensions*, July, Washington D.C.: International Monetary Fund.

International Monetary Fund (IMF) (2019), *World Economic Outlook 2019: Global Manufacturing Downturn, Rising Trade Barriers*, October, Washington D.C.: International Monetary Fund.

In't Veld, J. (2016), "Public Investment Stimulus in Surplus Countries and their Euro Area Spillovers," European Economy, Economic Brief No. 16, August, Brussels: Directorate-General for Economic and Financial Affairs (ECFIN), European Commission.

In't Veld, J. (2019), "Productive Spending and Public Debt in a Low Interest Rate Environment," mimeo, Brussels: Directorate-General for Economic and Financial Affairs (ECFIN), European Commission.

Intergovernmental Panel on Climate Change (IPCC) (2018), "Global Warming of 1.5°C," An IPCC Special Report, Geneva: IPCC.
Issing, O. (1999), "Monetary Policy of the ECB in a World of Uncertainty," Contribution to the Policy Panel at the ECB, CFS Conference *Monetary Policy Making under Uncertainty*, Frankfurt am Main, December 3-4 1999.
Issing, O. (2008), *The Birth of the Euro*, Cambridge: Cambridge University Press.
Johansson, Å., Y. Guillemette, F. Murtin, D. Turner, G. Nicoletti, C. Maisonneuve, P. Bagnoli, G. Bousquet and, F. Spinelli (2013), "Long-Term Growth Scenarios," OECD Economics Department Working Papers No. 1000, January, Paris: OECD Publishing.
Jones E., R. D. Keleman, and S. Meunier (2016), "Failing Forward? The Euro Crisis and the Incomplete Nature of European Integration," *Comparative Political Studies*, 49(7), pp. 1010-1034.
Juncker, J-C. (in cooperation with D. Tusk, J. Dijsselbloem, M. Draghi, and M. Schulz) (2015), *Completing Europe's Economic and Monetary Union. Five Presidents' Report,* Brussels: European Commission.
Juncker, J-C. and G. Tremonti (2010), "E-bonds Would End the Crisis," *Financial Times*, 6 December. Available at: http://www.astrid-online.it/static/upload/protected/Junc/Juncker-Tremonti.pdf.
Kalemli-Ozcan, S., E. Luttini, and B. Sorensen (2014), "Debt Crises and Risk Sharing: The Role of Markets and Sovereigns," *Scandinavian Journal of Economics,* 116(1). pp. 253-276.
Keynes, J. M. (1933), "An Open Letter to President Roosevelt," *New York Times*, 31 December. Available at: https://www.nytimes.com/1933/12/31/archives/from-keynes-to-roosevelt-our-recovery-plan-assayed-the-british.html?searchResultPosition=1.
Kiel Institute (2019), "Estimating Potential Output and the Output Gap – An Analysis of Revisions and Cyclicality," Policy Article No. 19 February, Kiel: Kiel Institute.
Klasing, M. J., and P. Milionis (2014), "Quantifying the Evolution of World Trade, 1870-1949," *Journal of International Economics*, 92(1), pp. 185-197.
Kollmann, R., W. Röger, and J. in't Veld (2012), "Fiscal Policy in Financial Crisis: Standard Policy versus Bank Rescue Measures," *American Economic Review: Papers and Proceedings*, 102, pp. 1-7.
Koo, R. (2008), *The Holy Grail of Macroeconomics: Lessons from Japan's Great Recession*, New Jersey: Wiley.
Kruger, J., and D. Dunning (1999), "Unskilled and Unaware of It: How Difficulties in Recognizing One's Own Incompetence Lead to Inflated Self-assessments," *Journal of Personality and Social Psychology*, 77(6), pp. 1121–1134.

Krugman, P. (1984), "The International Role of the Dollar: Theory and Prospect," pp. 261-278 in J. Bilson, and R. Marston (eds.), *Exchange Rate Theory and Practice,* Chicago Illinois: University of Chicago Press.
Krugman, P. (2011), "Can Europe Be Saved?," *The New York Times*, 12 January. Available at: https://www.nytimes.com/2011/01/16/magazine/16Europe-t.html.
Krugman, P. (2013), "Uncertain at the OECD," *The New York Times*, 12 September. Available at: https://krugman.blogs.nytimes.com/2013/09/12/uncertain-at-the-oecd/.
Kuhmar, M. S., and J. Woo (2012), "Public Debt and Growth," paper presented at the Bank of Italy's 14th Public Finances Workshop *Fiscal Policy and Growth*, Perugia (S.A.Di.Ba), 29-31 March.
Lagarde, C. (2018), "A Compass to Prosperity: The Next Steps of Euro Area Economic Integration," Speech at the German Institute for Economic Research, Berlin, *IMF.org.*, 26 March. Available at: https://www.imf.org/en/News/Articles/2018/03/26/sp032618-a-compass-to-prosperity-the-next-steps-of-euro-area-economic-integration.
Laver, M. J., and N. Schofield (1992), *Multiparty Government: The Politics of Coalition in Europe*, Oxford: Oxford University Press.
Leandro, A., and J. Zettelmeyer (2018), "The Search for a Euro Area Safe Asset," PIIE Working Paper No. 18-3, March, Washington D.C: Peterson Institute for International Economics (PIIE).
Lenarcic, A., and K. Korhonen (2018), "A Case for a European Rainy Day Fund," European Stability Mechanism Discussion Paper No. 5, November, Luxemburg: European Stability Mechanism.
Lowe, D., and M. Luckman (2019), Global Protectionism, Gowling WLG Report.
Manasse, P. (2010), "Stability and Growth Pact: Counterproductive Proposals," *VoxEU.org*, 7 October. Available at: https://voxeu.org/article/stability-and-growth-pact-counterproductive-proposals.
Marelli, E., and M. Signorelli (2005), "Institutional, Nominal, and Real Convergence in Europe," *Banks and Bank Systems,* 5(2), pp. 140-155.
Mayer, T., and K. Head (2019), "Brands in Motion: How Frictions Shape Multinational Production," *American Economic Review*, 109(9), pp. 3073-3124.
Maystadt, P. (2014), "Jump-starting Investment," Foundation Robert Schuman Policy Paper No. 337, December.
Mazzucato, M., and P. Caetano (2014), "Juncker's Investment Plan: How to Radically Transform It," *The Guardian,* 27 November. Available at: https://www.theguardian.com/science/political-science/2014/nov/27/junckers-investment-plan-how-to-radically-transform-it.

Mckinsey (2020), "Safeguarding Europe's Livelihoods: Mitigating the Employment Impact of COVID-19," *mkinsey.com*, April. Available at: https://www.mckinsey.com/industries/public-and-social-sector/our-insights/safeguarding-europes-livelihoods-mitigating-the-employment-impact-of-covid-19.

Merkel, A. (2010), "Speech by Federal Chancellor Angela Merkel at the Opening Ceremony of the 61st Academic Year of the College of Europe in Bruges," *coleeurope.eu.*, 2 November 2010. Available at: https://www.coleurope.eu/events/mrs-angela-merkel-delivered-opening-address-opening-ceremony.

Merler, S., and J. Pisani-Ferry (2012), "The Simple Macroeconomics of North and South in EMU," Bruegel Working Paper No. 740, July, Brussels: Bruegel.

Merlevede, B., and V. Purice (2019), "Border Regimes and Indirect Productivity Effects from Foreign Direct Investment," Ghent University Department of Economics Working Paper No. 965, March, Ghent: Ghent University.

Milanović, B. (2016), *Global Inequality – A New Approach for the Age of Globalization*, Harvard: Harvard University Press.

Mody, A. (2018), *EuroTragedy: A Drama in Nine Acts*, Oxford: Oxford University Press.

Mongelli, F. P. (2008), "European Economic and Monetary Integration and the Optimum Currency Area Theory," European Economy, Economic Papers No. 302, February, Brussels: Directorate-General for Economic and Financial Affairs (ECFIN), European Commission.

Monti, M. (2010), "A New Strategy for the Single Market," Report to the President of the European Commission José Manuel Barroso, pp. 61- 65.

Moscovici, P. (2017), "Towards Enhanced Cohesion, Integration and Prosperity," Keynote Speech at the *Brussels Economic Forum 2017*, *ec.europa.eu.*, 1 June. Available at: https://ec.europa.eu/commission/presscorner/detail/en/SPEECH_17_1509.

Mourre G., C. Astarita, and S. Princen (2014), "Adjusting the Budget Balance for the Business Cycle: The EU Methodology," European Economy, Economic Papers No. 536, November, Brussels: Directorate-General for Economic and Financial Affairs (ECFIN), European Commission.

Müller, J. W. (2016), "Capitalism in One Family," *London Review of Books,* 38(23), pp. 10-14.

Münchau, W. (2014), "The Juncker Fund Will Not Revive the Eurozone," *Financial Times*, 30 November. Available at: https://www.ft.com/content/dc41888c-76f2-11e4-8273-00144feabdc0.

Munkhammar, J. (2007), *The Guide to Reform; How Policymakers Can Pursue Real Change, Achieve Great Results and Win Re-Election*, Stockholm: Timbro/IEA.

Musgrave, R. A. (1959), *The Theory of Public Finance: A Study in Public Economy,* New York: McGraw-Hill.

O'Rourke, K. (2016), "Brexit: This Backlash Has Been a Long Time Coming," *VoxEU.org*, 7 August. Available at: https://voxeu.org/article/brexit-backlash-has-been-long-time-coming.

Obstfeld, M. (2013), "Finance at Center Stage: Some Lessons of the Euro Crisis," European Economy, Economic Papers No. 493, April, Brussels: Directorate-General for Economic and Financial Affairs (ECFIN), European Commission.

Organisation for Economic Co-operation and Development (OECD) (2012), *Economic Policy Reforms: Going for Growth 2012*, Paris: OECD Publishing.

Organisation for Economic Co-operation and Development (OECD) (2013a), *Economic Policy Reforms: Going for Growth 2013*, February, Paris: OECD Publishing.

Organisation for Economic Co-operation and Development (OECD) (2013b), *Economic Outlook*, No. 93, May, Paris: OECD Publishing.

Organisation for Economic Co-operation and Development (OECD) (2013c), *OECD Employment Outlook 2013*, July, Paris: OECD Publishing.

Organisation for Economic Co-operation and Development (OECD) (2015), *Aligning Policies for a Low-carbon Economy*, Paris: OECD Publishing.

Organisation for Economic Co-operation and Development (OECD) (2017), *OECD Economic Surveys: Italy 2017*, February, Paris: OECD Publishing.

Organisation for Economic Co-operation and Development (OECD) (2018), *OECD Economic Surveys: Euro Area 2017*, June, Paris: OECD Publishing.

Organisation for Economic Co-operation and Development (OECD) (2019a), *Under Pressure: The Squeezed Middle Class,* May, Paris: OECD Publishing.

Organisation for Economic Co-operation and Development (OECD) (2019b), *OECD Economic Outlook*, 2019(1), May Paris: OECD Publishing.

Organisation for Economic Co-operation and Development (OECD) (2019c), *Economic Policy Reforms: Going for Growth 2019*, July, Paris: OECD Publishing.

Organisation for Economic Co-operation and Development (OECD) (2019d), *OECD Economic Outlook*, Interim Report, September, Paris: OECD Publishing.

Orphanides, A., and S. Van Norden (2002), "The Unreliability of Output Gap Estimates in Real Time," *Review of Economics and Statistics*, 84(4), pp. 569-583.

Ossa, R. (2019), "A Quantitative Analysis of Subsidy Competition in the U.S.," Zurich, London: University of Zurich and Centre for Economic Policy Research (CEPR).

Ostry J., A. Ghosh, and R. Espinoza (2015), "When Should Public Debt Be

Reduced?," IMF Staff Discussion Notes No. 15/10, June, Washington D.C.: International Monetary Fund.

Padoan, P. C., U. Sila, and P. van den Noord (2012), *A Dual Equilibrium Model for Public Debt and Growth.*

Padoa-Schioppa, T. (1987), *Efficiency, Stability, and Equity: A Strategy for the Evolution of the Economic System of the European Community. A Report*, Oxford: Oxford University Press.

Pettis, P. (2018), "Protectionism Can't Fix Trade Imbalances," *Carnegie Institute*, 25 January. Available at: https://carnegieendowment.org/2018/01/25/protectionism-can-t-fix-trade-imbalances-pub-75363.

Philippon, T. (2015), "The State of the Monetary Union," *VoxEU.org*, 1 August. Available at: https://voxeu.org/article/state-monetary-union.

Philippon, T., and C. Hellwig (2011), "Eurobills, Not Eurobonds," *VoxEU.org*, 2 December. Available at: https://voxeu.org/article/eurobills-not-euro-bonds.

Piattoni, S. (2017), "The European Union between Intergovernmentalism and 'Shared and Responsible Sovereignty': The Haptic Potential of EMU's Institutional Architecture (The Government and Opposition/Leonard Schapiro Lecture, 2016)," *Government and Opposition*, 25(3), pp. 385-411.

Pisani-Ferry, J. (2012), "The Euro Crisis and the New Impossible Trinity," *Moneda y Credito*, 234/2012, pp. 7-36.

Pisani-Ferry, J. (2015), "Rebalancing the Governance of the Euro Area," France Stratégie, Document de Travail No. 1, May, Paris: France Stratégie.

Pisani-Ferry, J. (2016), "The Eurozone's Zeno Paradox – and How to Solve It," *VoxEU.org*, 10 April. Available at: https://voxeu.org/article/eurozone-s-zeno-paradox-and-how-solve-it.

Powell, G., and G. Whitten (1993), "A Cross-national Analysis of Economic Voting: Taking Account of the Political Context," *American Journal of Political Science*, 37(2), pp. 391-414.

Puetter, U. (2012), "Europe's Deliberative Intergovernmentalism: The Role of the Council and European Council in EU Economic Governance," *Journal of European Public Policy*, 19(2), pp. 161-178.

Rajan, R. (2019), *The Third Pillar: How Markets and the State Leave the Community behind,* London: Penguin Press.

Ramey, G., and V. Ramey (1995), "Cross-Country Evidence on the Link between Volatility and Growth," *American Economic Review*, 85(5), pp. 1138-51.

Rawls, J. (1999), *The Law of Peoples*, Harvard: Harvard University Press.

Reinhart, C. M., and K. S. Rogoff (2009a), "The Aftermath of Financial Crises," *American Economic Review*, 99(2), pp. 466–72.

Reinhart, C. M., and K. S. Rogoff (2009b), *This Time Is Different: Eight Centuries of Financial Folly*, Princeton: Princeton University Press.

Reinhart, C. M., and K. S. Rogoff (2012), "This Time Is Different, Again? The US Five Years after the Onset of Subprime," *VoxEU.org*, October 22. Available at: https://voxeu.org/article/time-different-again-us-five-years-after-onset-subprime-0.

Rodríguez-Pose, A. (2018), "The Revenge of the Places that Don't Matter (and What to Do about It)," *Cambridge Journal of Regions, Economy and Society*, 11(1), pp. 189-209.

Rodrik, D. (2000), "How Far Will International Economic Integration Go?," *Journal of Economic Perspectives*, 14 (1), 177-186.

Rodrik, D. (2018), "How to Avoid a Trade War," *Project Syndicate*, 10 July. Available at: https://www.project-syndicate.org/commentary/china-europe-reaction-trump-trade-tariffs-by-dani-rodrik-2018-07?barrier=accesspaylog.

Röger, W., and J. in't Veld (2010), "Fiscal Stimulus and Exit Strategies in the EU: A Model Based Analysis," European Economy, Economic Papers No. 426, September, Brussels: Directorate-General for Economic and Financial Affairs (ECFIN), European Commission.

Röger, W., and J. in't Veld (2012), "On the Appropriate Fiscal Stance in the Current Crisis," mimeo, Brussels: Directorate-General for Economic and Financial Affairs (ECFIN), European Commission.

Röger, W., K. Mc Morrow, A. Hristov, and V. Vandermeulen (2019), "The Current Debate on Output Gaps and Cyclical Indicators," European Economy, Discussion Paper No. 104, July, Brussels: Directorate-General for Economic and Financial Affairs (ECFIN), European Commission.

Rogoff, K. (1985), "The Optimal Degree of Commitment to an Intermediate Monetary Target," *Quarterly Journal of Economics*, 100(4), pp. 1169-1189.

Ruscher, E., and G. Wolff (2012), "Corporate Balance Sheet Adjustment: Stylised Facts, Causes and Consequences," European Economy, Economic Papers No. 449, February, Brussels: Directorate-General for Economic and Financial Affairs (ECFIN), European Commission.

Sackmann, H. (2012), "IG Metall Gets Highest Pay Rise in 20 Years," *Reuters*, 19 May. Available at: https://www.reuters.com/article/us-germany-wages/german-ig-metall-get-highest-pay-rise-in-20-years-idUKBRE84I05K20120519?edition-redirect=uk.

Salto, M., and A. Turrini (2010), "Comparing Alternative Methodologies for Real Exchange Rate Assessment," European Economy, Economic Papers No. 427, September, Brussels: Directorate-General for Economic and Financial Affairs (ECFIN), European Commission.

Sapir, A. (2020), "Why Has COVID-19 Hit Different European Union Economies So Differently?," Policy Contribution No. 2020/18, Brussels: Bruegel.
Sapir, A., and G. Wolff (2015), "Euro-area Governance: What to Reform and How to Do It," Bruegel Policy Brief, February, Brussels.
Sapir, A., P. Aghion, G. Bertola, M. Hellwig, J. Pisani-Ferry, D. Rosati, J. Viñals, and H. Wallace (2003), *An Agenda for a Growing Europe. Making the EU Economic System Deliver,* Report of an Independent High-Level Study Group Established on the Initiative of the President of the European Commission.
Sargent, T., and N. Wallace (1981), "Some Unpleasant Monetarist Arithmetic," *Federal Reserve Bank of Minneapolis Quarterly Review*, 5(3), pp. 1-17.
Scharpf, F. (1999), *Governing in Europe: Effective and Democratic?,* Oxford: Oxford University Press.
Schimmelfennig, F. (2015), "Liberal Intergovernmentalism and the Euro Area Crisis," *Journal of European Public Policy*, 22(2), pp. 177-195.
Schmidt, M. (2002), "Political Performance and Types of Democracy: Findings from Comparative Studies," *European Journal of Political Research*, 41(1), pp.147-163.
Schmidt, V. (2013), "Democracy and Legitimacy in the European Union Revisited: Input, Output and Throughput," *Political Studies,* 61(1), pp. 2-22.
Schmidt, V. (2015a), "Forgotten Democratic Legitimacy: 'Governing by the Rules' and 'Ruling by the Numbers'," in M. Matthijs, and M. Blyth (eds.), *The Future of the Euro*, New York: Oxford University Press.
Schmidt, V. (2015b), "The Eurozone's Crisis of Democratic Legitimacy. Can the EU Rebuild Public Trust and Support for European Economic Integration?," European Economy, Discussion Paper No. 015, September, Brussels: Directorate-General for Economic and Financial Affairs (ECFIN), European Commission.
Schmidt, V. (2016), "The New EU Governance: New Intergovernmentalism, New Supranationalism, and New Parliamentarianism," IAI working papers No.16/08, May, Rome: Istituto Affari Internazionali (IAI).
Schmidt, V. (2019a), "The Future of Differentiated Integration: A 'Soft-core,' Multi Clustered Europe of Overlapping Policy Communities," *Comparative European Politics*, 17(2), pp 294-315.
Schmidt, V. (2019b), "Politicization in the EU: Between National Politics and EU Political Dynamics," *Journal of European Public Policy*, 26(3), pp. 1-19.
Schoenmaker, D. (2011), "The Financial Trilemma," *Economics Letters,* 111(1), pp. 57-59.
Seater, J. J. (1993), "Ricardian Equivalence," *Journal of Economic Literature*, 31(1), pp. 142-190.
Sorensen, B., and O. Yosha (1998), "International Risk Sharing and European

Monetary Unification," *Journal of International Economics,* 45(2), pp. 211-238.

Summers, L. H. (2008), "Why America Must Have a Fiscal Stimulus," *Financial Times*, 5 January. Available at: https://www.ft.com/content/3b3bd570-bc76-11dc-bcf9-0000779fd2ac.

Summers, L. H. (2013), "IMF Economic Forum: Policy Responses to Crises," Speech at the IMF Fourteenth Annual Research Conference, Washington D.C., *larrysummers.com.*, 9 November. Available at: http://larrysummers.com/imf-fourteenth-annual-research-conference-in-honor-of-stanley-fischer/.

Summers, L. H. (2014), "Reflections on the New 'Secular Stagnation' Hypothesis," *VoxEU.org*, 30 October 2014. Available at: https://voxeu.org/article/larry-summers-secular-stagnation.

Summers, L. H., and M. Schoenfeld (2012), "The G20 in Retrospect and Prospect," Working Paper, June.

Szabo, S. (2019), "Foreign Direct Investment in the Czech Republic: A Visegrád Comparison," European Economy, Economic Brief No. 042, February, Brussels: Directorate-General for Economic and Financial Affairs (ECFIN), European Commission.

Székely, I. P. (2019), "What Difference Has the EU Made to the Convergence Process? Facets of the Faces of Convergence," pp. 1-4 in I. P. Székely (ed.), *Faces of Convergence, Vienna:* The Vienna Institute for International Economic Studies.

Székely, I. P., and M. Ward-Warmedinger (2018), "Reform Reversals: Areas, Circumstances and Motivations," *Comparative Economic Studies,* 60(4), pp. 559-582.

Tabellini, G. (2010), "Reforming the Stability Pact: Focus on Financial Supervision," *VoxEU.org*, 5 October. Available at: https://voxeu.org/article/reforming-stability-pact-focus-financial-supervision.

Teulings, C. and R. Baldwin (eds.) (2014), *Secular Stagnation: Facts, Causes, and Cures,* a VoxEU.org eBook, London: CEPR Press.

The Economist (2007), "The Quest for Prosperity," Special Report, March. Available at: https://www.economist.com/special-report/2007/03/17/the-quest-for-prosperity.

Thirion, G. (2017), "European Fiscal Union: Economic Rationale and Design Challenges," CEPS Working Document No. 2017-01, Brussels: Centre for European Policy Studies (CEPS).

Tooze, A. (2018), *Crashed: How a Decade of Financial Crises Changed the World*, London: Penguin.

Tooze, A. (2019), "Output Gap Nonsense," *Social Europe*, 30 April. Available at: https://www.socialeurope.eu/output-gap-nonsense.

Tsebelis, G. (1995) "Decision Making in Political Systems: Veto Players in Presidentialism, Parliamentarism, Multicameralism and Multipartyism," *British Journal of Political Science*, 25(03), pp. 289–325. doi: 10.1017/s0007123400007225.

Tsebelis, G. (2002), *Veto Players*, Princeton: Princeton University Press.

Tsebelis, G. (2011), "Veto Player Theory and Policy Change: An Introduction," pp. 3-18 in T. König, M. Debus, and G. Tsebelis (eds.), *Reform Processes and Policy Change*, Studies in Public Choice, 16, New York, NY: Springer. Available at: https://doi.org/10.1007/978-1-4419-5809-9_1.

Tsebelis, G., and E. Ha (2013) "Coalition Theory: A Veto Players' Approach," *European Political Science Review*, 6(3), pp. 331-357, Available on CJO, doi: 10.1017/S1755773913000106

Tuori K., and K. Tuori (2014), *The Eurozone Crisis: A Constitutional Analysis*, Cambridge: Cambridge University Press.

Valiante, D. (2016), *Europe's Untapped Capital Market: Rethinking Integration after the Great Financial Crisis*, Brussels: CEPS Paperback.

van Riet, A. (2017), "Addressing the Safety Trilemma: A Safe Sovereign Asset for the Eurozone," ESRB Working Paper Series No. 35, February, Frankfurt: European Systemic Risk Board (ESRB).

Van Rompuy, H. (2012), *Towards a Genuine Economic and Monetary Union,* Four Presidents' Report, June, Brussels: European Commission.

Vandenbussche, H., W. Connell, and W. Simons (2017), "Global Value Chains, Trade Shocks and Jobs: An Application to Brexit," CEPR Discussion Paper No. 12303, London: Centre for Economic Policy Research (CEPR).

Varga, J., and J. in't Veld (2014) "The Potential Growth Impact of Structural Reforms in the EU: A Benchmarking Exercise," European Economy, Economic Papers No. 541, December, Brussels: Directorate-General for Economic and Financial Affairs (ECFIN), European Commission.

Verwey, M., S. Langedijk, and R. Kuenzel (2020), "Next Generation EU: A Recovery Plan for Europe," *VoxEU.org*, 9 June. Available at: https://voxeu.org/article/next-generation-eu-recovery-plan-europe.

Veugelers, R. (2014), "The Achilles' Heel of Juncker's Investment Plan – How Will the Right Investment Projects Be Selected?," 8 December, *Bruegel.org*. Available at: https://www.bruegel.org/2014/12/the-achilles-heel-of-junckers-investment-plan/.

Von der Leyen, U. (2019), *A Union that Strive for More, My Agenda for Europe: Political Guidelines for the Next European Commission 2019-2024*, Luxemburg: Publication office of the European Union.

Wach, K., and L. Wojciechowski (2016), "Determinants of Inward FDI into Visegrad Countries: Empirical Evidence Based on Panel Data for the Years 2000–2012," *Economics and Business Review*, 2(1), pp. 34-52.

Walters, A. (1986), *Britain's Economic Renaissance*, Oxford: Oxford University Press.

Watt, M. (2013), *Social Europe Journal*, 24 September.

Wolf, M. (2012), "The Pain in Spain Will Test the Euro," *Financial Times*, 6 March. Available at: https://www.ft.com/content/f54332d2-66dc-11e1-9e53-00144feabdc0.

Wolf, M. (2013), "The Sad Record of Fiscal Austerity," *Financial Times*, 27 February. Available at: https://www.ft.com/content/73219452-7f49-11e2-89ed-00144feabdc0.

Wolff, G. (2013), "Austerity Needed to Start, Now We Need a Fiscal Union," *Bruegel.org*, 25 February. Available at: https://www.bruegel.org/2013/02/austerity-needed-to-start-now-we-need-a-fiscal-union/.

World Economic Forum (2015), "Executive Opinion Survey of the Global Competitiveness Index," in *The Global Competitiveness Report 2015–2016*, World Economic Forum.

Wyplosz, C. (2010), "Eurozone Reform: Not Yet Fiscal Discipline, but a Good Start," *VoxEU.org*, 4 October. Available at: https://voxeu.org/article/eurozone-reform-not-yet-fiscal-discipline-good-start.

Zlate, A. (2016), "Offshore Production and Business Cycle Dynamics with Heterogeneous Firms," *Journal of International Economics*, 100(C), pp. 34-49.

Zuleeg, F. (2014), "Juncker's Investment Plan: a New Deal for the EU?," European Policy Centre (EPC), *epc.eu.*, 17 December. Available at: https://www.files.ethz.ch/isn/186770/pub_5112_juncker_s_investment_plan_-_a_new_deal_for_the_eu.pdf.

Index of names

www.ingramcontent.com/pod-product-compliance
Ingram Content Group UK Ltd.
Pitfield, Milton Keynes, MK11 3LW, UK
UKHW020128290926
15471UKWH00003B/353

9 788831 322355